Special Educational Provision in the Context of Inclusion

Professional Development for Special Educational Needs Co-ordinators

This reader is part of a course: Professional Development for Special Educational Needs Co-ordinators, that is itself part of the Open University MA programme.

The Open University MA in Education
The Open University MA in Education is now firmly established as the most popular postgraduate degree for education professionals in Europe, with over 3,000 students registering each year. The MA in Education is designed particularly for those with experience of teaching, the advisory service, educational administration or allied fields.

Structure of the MA
The MA is a modular degree, and students are therefore free to select from a range of options the programme which best fits with their interests and professional goals. Specialist lines in management, applied linguistics and lifelong learning are also available. Study in the Open University's Advanced Diploma can also be counted towards the MA, and successful study in the MA Programme entitles students to apply for entry into The Open University Doctorate in Education programme.

OU Supported Open Learning
The MA in Education programme provides great flexibility. Students study at their own pace, in their own time, anywhere in the European Union. They receive specially prepared study materials, supported by tutorials, thus offering the chance to work with other students.

The Doctorate in Education
The Doctorate in Education is a part-time doctoral degree, combining taught courses, research methods and a dissertation designed to meet the needs of professionals in education and related areas who are seeking to extend and deepen their knowledge and understanding of contemporary educational issues. The Doctorate in Education builds upon successful study within the Open University MA in Education programme.

How to apply
If you would like to register for this programme, or simply find out more information about available courses, please write for the *Professional Development in Education* prospectus to the Course Reservation Centre, PO Box 724, The Open University, Walton Hall, Milton Keynes MK7 6ZW, UK (Telephone +44 (0) 1908 653231). Details can also be viewed on our web page http://www.open.ac.uk

Special Educational Provision in the Context of Inclusion

Policy and practice in schools

Edited by
Janice Wearmouth

David Fulton Publishers
London

in association with

David Fulton Publishers Ltd
Ormond House, 26–27 Boswell Street, London WC1N 3JZ

www.fultonpublishers.co.uk

British Library Cataloguing in Publication Data
A catalogue record for this book is available from the British Library

ISBN 1-85346-791-X

The publishers would like to thank John Cox for copy-editing and Sheila Harding for proofreading this book.

Typeset by Textype Typesetters, Cambridge
Printed in Great Britain by The Cromwell Press Ltd, Trowbridge, Wilts

Contents

Acknowledgements

I would like to thank all those who have contributed chapters to this Reader or have approved their reprinting from other publications, and Liz Freeman, Liz Santucci and Sue Glover for their endless support and encouragement.

Grateful acknowledgement is made to the following sources for permission to reproduce material in this book:

Chapter 1: DES (1978) *Report of the Committee of Enquiry into the Education of Handicapped Children and Young People* (The Warnock Report). Crown copyright is reproduced with the permission of the Controller of Her Majesty's Stationery Office.

Chapter 2: Mittler, P. (1999) 'Equal opportunities – for whom?', *Support for Learning: British Journal of Special Education,* **26**(1) (1999) 30–6, © NASEN.

Chapter 5: Clark, C., Dyson, A., Millward, A. J. and Skidmore, D. (1997) 'The case of Downland', *New Directions in Special Needs: Innovations in Mainstream Schools,* Cassell, reprinted by permission of The Continuum International Publishing Group Ltd.

Chapter 8: Norwich, B. and Daniels, H. (1997) 'Teacher support teams for special educational needs in primary schools' *Educational Studies,* **23** (1997) pp. 5–24, Carfax Publishing Ltd, reprinted by permission of Taylor & Francis Ltd, PO Box 25, Abingdon, Oxfordshire, OX14 3UE.

Chapter 10: Mercer, N. (1988) 'Talking and working together', *The Guided Construction of Knowledge: Talk amongst Teachers and Learners,* Multilingual Matters Ltd.

Chapter 11: Merrett, F. (1998) 'Helping readers who have fallen behind', *Support for Learning: British Journal of Learning Support,* **13**(2) (1998) 59–64, © NASEN.

Chapter 13: Coulby, J. and Coulby, D. (1995) 'Pupil participation in the social and educational processes of a primary school', *Advocacy, Self-Advocacy and Special Needs*, Garner, P. and Sandow, S. (eds), David Fulton Publishers.

Chapter 14: Harris-Cooksley, R. and Catt, R. (1995) 'Classroom strategies for teacher and pupil support', *Advocacy, Self-Advocacy and Special Needs*, Garner, P. and Sandow, S. (eds), David Fulton Publishers.

Chapter 15: Wearmouth J. (1997) 'Pygmalion lives on', *Support for Learning: British Journal of Learning Support*, **12**(3) (1997) 122–5, © NASEN.

Chapter 17: Garner, P., Hinchcliffe, V. and Sandow, S. (1995) 'Teachers and differentiation', *What Teachers Do: Developments in Special Education*, Copyright © 1995, Philip Garner, Viv Hinchcliffe and Sarah Sandow, Sage Publications Ltd, reprinted by permission of Paul Chapman Publishing.

While the publishers have made every effort to contact copyright holders of previously published material in this volume, they would be grateful to hear from any they were unable to contact.

Introduction

The chapters in this book outline the historical context for the development of 'special' educational provision in the UK and the moves towards including pupils in mainstream schools. They discuss some of the complexity of meaning underlying this term, and offer examples of practical ways in which schools have attempted to address principles of individuality, diversity, inclusion and equal opportunities.

There are numerous ways in which a nation's education system might be designed to address the learning needs of its children. The way in which educational provision is currently organised is a product both of its own history and of the values, beliefs and political ideology of our society. In the UK, the Elementary Education Act of 1870 (Education (Scotland) Act of 1872) marked the beginning of compulsory state education. For the next hundred years subsequent Acts improved and expanded the system of state education, increasing access to it for the nation's children. The continually evolving and expanded notion of who was entitled to schooling put pressure on schools also to evolve as institutions capable of including all pupils.

After the 1870 Act (1872 Act in Scotland) made attendance at school compulsory, the question of what to do with children who made little or no progress and whose presence in the classroom was felt to be holding others back now became important. Historically local education authorities responded to this challenge by creating and maintaining a dual system of mainstream and special schooling built upon the pre-existing structure which had developed out of voluntary enterprise.

Categorisation of pupils was a major element of developing legislation. The labels used to describe particular groups of pupils reflected the way in which they were generally viewed. The use of particular labels offers an interesting insight into social perspectives on pupils with particular difficulties. The changing social and historical context of provision has meant that many labels once attached to pupils ('imbeciles'; 'feeble-minded') have become unacceptable. Pupils may well have been damaged by their awareness of the attribution to themselves of descriptors with negative connotations. For example, the 'maladjusted' label which was in use for many years during the twentieth century was one 'which has a powerful history of stigma, being associated with undesirable personal and social characteristics' (Galloway, Armstrong and Tomlinson 1994).

Once the old school boards were abolished and the two-tier system of local education authorities for elementary and secondary education was established in 1902, the statutory foundation of special provision continued broadly in Great Britain until the 1944 Act. In seeking to develop a common national framework for the education of (nearly) all children, the creators of the 1944 Act were faced with the dilemma of how to construct an educational framework that would support the learning of a diverse pupil population. The legislators addressed it by formalising a system of selection and segregation based on the results of assessment techniques that, they believed, could differentiate different 'types' of learners. Different curricula could then be designed for different learning 'types' to be educated in separate sectors of the system. Segregation operated between mainstream and special schools, and selection between types of secondary school in mainstream: grammar, technical and secondary modern. The educational hierarchy that developed was seen by many as both equitable, because pupils appeared to be able to rise to a level which reflected their ability, and stable because it was based on psychometric testing considered at that time to be largely reliable and valid.

In the area of special education, the 1944 Education Act in Great Britain, Sections 33 and 34, set out the legal basis for subsequent provision. It adopted the 'medical model', i.e. the difficulties in learning experienced by pupils were conceptualised as disabilities of body and mind and intrinsic to the pupils themselves. The Handicapped Pupils and School Health Service Regulations 1945 developed a new framework of eleven categories of pupils, including that of 'maladjusted' for the first time. Local education authorities were required to ascertain the needs of children in their areas for special educational treatment. Blind, deaf, epileptic, physically handicapped and aphasic children were deemed educable only in special schools; those children thought to have a severe mental handicap were perceived as ineducable and dealt with by health authorities.

However, a number of factors militated against the stability of the selective system established in the 1944 Act and many commentators in education came to view this system as divisive and functioning to sustain the position of some already advantaged groups over others, rather than as a rational and equitable response to scientifically-measured differences between pupils. Considerable doubt was increasingly thrown on the reliability and validity of the psychometric tests being used and it became clear that there was obvious overlap between the learning needs of pupils in mainstream and special schools. Even so, movement between school types was very difficult indeed, regardless of the amount of progress made by individual pupils. Differing proportions of pupils were selected for each type of school in different local education authority areas. There was a growing concern for equality of opportunity and social cohesion in society at large. The net outcome of all this was the establishment of comprehensive schools in mainstream, the importation of special school methods and curricula into mainstream through the introduction of special classes and 'remedial' provision, and the integration of some children from special to mainstream schools.

The concept of education for all was finally established in law in Great Britain by the 1970 Handicapped Children Education Act which transferred responsibility for children with severe handicaps from health to education authorities. Children perceived to have severe cognitive disabilities were entitled to a school-based education for the first time.

By the time of the Warnock Report (DES 1978) the boundaries between special and mainstream had become permeable and pragmatic solutions to coping with the diversity of the pupil population had been adopted by many schools. In mainstream schools, some large secondary schools developed a proliferation of alternative forms of curricula, for example academic courses leading to externally-accredited qualifications, non-examination vocational and/or life skills courses and 'remedial' tuition in withdrawal groups.

The Warnock Report reviewed educational provision in Great Britain for children and young people who, up to that time, were considered 'handicapped by disabilities of body or mind'. Until then around 2 per cent of children had been legally classified as 'handicapped'. This report recommended that it should replace categorisation of handicap with the concept of 'special educational needs' and suggested that up to 20 per cent of pupils might have such a need at some time in their school career.

The 1981 Education Act in Great Britain attempted to translate Warnock's recommendations into legislation. The old categories of handicap were replaced with the idea that difficulties occur on a continuum, and that a 'special educational need' existed if a child had 'significantly greater difficulty in learning' than peers, or a disability that hindered him or her from using educational facilities normally available in the local school. Local authorities were given responsibilities to identify needs which called for special provision, that is, provision in addition to that normally available in the school. This Act also affirmed the principle of integration. All children should be educated in mainstream schools but with certain provisos: that their needs could be met there, and that it was compatible with the education of other children and with the 'efficient use of resources'.

The principle of universal access to education and, within that, the inclusion of all pupils in mainstream schools wherever possible, is now enshrined in public policy. Policy makers are faced with the fundamental dilemma of how to make educational provision for all pupils, which takes full account of 'sameness' and, at the same time, pays due regard to 'difference' and 'diversity' amongst individuals.

Whilst in recent years UK government policy has moved towards an inclusive approach to providing for all pupils' learning needs there has also been a shift in focus towards the raising of standards through competition. The new National Curriculum framework introduced by the 1988 Education Reform Act in England and Wales was intended to raise the standards of all schools in England. In a sense the introduction of a National Curriculum for all was the first time that functional, rather than simply 'locational', integration was realised for pupils (Bines 1986). In that this Act intervened in the area of the curriculum with its introduction of the National Curriculum it had far-reaching consequences for pupils who experience difficulties. It was compulsory and subject-based. However, a number of features of the Act encouraged a new 'market' approach, competition, consumer choice and pressure on resources: the national system of assessment based on norms and focused on results which could be used to evaluate the 'effectiveness' of schools, local management of schools, Grant Maintained Status and open enrolment in schools. Many feel that the pressures on individual schools to meet the demands of this market approach to education often conspire to make mainstream schools less hospitable places for those pupils who experience difficulties in learning and may function to squeeze those pupils out of the mainstream system.

In our current system, most pupils are expected to be able to cope with the curriculum offered in mainstream schools. Why some pupils fail can be explained in a range of ways. There are examples of central government simultaneously acknowledging a number of different explanations at different levels in the social system by promoting interventions at societal level and at the level of the whole-school, as well as supporting the notion of 'special' provision for individual pupils. The dilemmas created in schools by what often appear to be somewhat fragmented and contradictory government policies may be insoluble. The problem might be interpreted as rooted in social factors, for example, family poverty and unemployment or in cultural differences in understanding and expectations between family and school. Some of these social factors are addressed in Circulars 10/99 and 11/99 on 'social inclusion'. These Circulars outline the role of schools and LEAs in supporting pupils 'at particular risk', for example children 'with special educational needs', those who are looked after, travellers, those from families under stress and teenage mothers.

Alternatively, the child's difficulties might be seen as arising out of the immediate learning environment, for example inappropriate teaching methods or texts, or inadequate school resources. The way in which the school context may create barriers to pupils' learning is addressed in the new statutory statement on inclusion in the revised National Curriculum for 2000 (QCA 2000). This statement sets out three principles for inclusion which relate to 'setting suitable learning challenges', responding to 'diverse learning needs' and 'overcoming potential barriers to learning'. Schools are urged to 'take action at all levels of curriculum planning' to meet the learning needs of individuals and to offer 'relevant opportunities' to all pupils. However, the encouragement of competition between schools, league tables and an ever-increasing focus on academic league tables is at odds with the principle of inclusion of pupils experiencing difficulties in learning.

Another view might be to see the problem as located at the level of the learner themselves and an individualised approach taken to identifying and assessing their 'special' learning needs. In the British education system all students of school age have a legal entitlement to access to the National Curriculum. There is a duty for local education authorities to make special provision at the level of the school for those students identified as needing it because students have the statutory right to having their 'special educational needs' assessed and met. The 1993 Education Act empowered the Secretary of State to issue regulations and a Code of Practice concerning the education of children with special educational needs. The 1994 *Code of Practice for the Identification and Assessment of Special Educational Needs*, which, for the most part, carries the force of guidance only, accepts that schools can make a difference in reducing or exacerbating difficulties experienced by pupils. Nevertheless, the model of meeting pupils' needs is seen in terms of identifying, assessing and resourcing the perceived needs of individual pupils rather than the adoption of a whole-school approach. Under the terms of Part III of the 1993 Act, now subsumed into Part IV of the 1996 Education Act in England and Wales (Part II of the Education Order 1996 in Northern Ireland) a child 'has *special educational needs* if he or she has a *learning difficulty* which calls for special educational provision to be made for him or her'. That is, a child only has 'special educational needs' when special provision is required to meet them: learning difficulties do not in themselves constitute such a need. Learning difficulty and 'special educational need' are, in law at least, not synonymous.

How far the effect of imposing additional pressure on schools to improve their overall academic standards will result in raising the level of 'achievement' among all pupils, or in squeezing out of the system pupils perceived as 'lower-achieving' remains to be seen. What is clear from these apparently conflicting signals is that considerable thought will have to be given to the changes which individual schools will have to make at the level of whole-school policy if they are to raise mean achievement levels and include all pupils. Given the current focus on inclusion within a context of 'Standards' (TTA 1998) for the co-ordination of special educational provision, all schools need to be aware of the challenges facing them in facilitating the learning of pupils who experience difficulties.

The chapters in Part 1 of this book outline the history of special education in Great Britain prior to the 1981 Education Act, and debate some of the issues associated with national and local policy in the area of special educational needs. Topics addressed by the chapters in Part 2 discuss some of the implications of policy into practice in schools, and describe practical initiatives to bring about inclusion at school and classroom level.

REFERENCES

Bines, H. (1986) *Redefining Remedial Education.* London: Croom Helm.

Department of Education and Science (DES) (1978) *Report of the Committee of Enquiry into the Education of Handicapped Children and Young People* (The Warnock Report). London: HMSO.

Galloway, D. M., Armstrong, D. and Tomlinson, S. (1994) *The Assessment of Special Educational Needs: Whose problem?* Harlow: Longman.

Qualifications and Curriculum Authority (QCA) (2000) *Curriculum 2000.* London: QCA.

Teacher training Agency (TTA) (1998) *National Standards for Special Educational Needs Co-ordinators.* London: TTA.

Part I

Policy at national and local levels

INTRODUCTION TO PART I

Part 1 addresses the historical context within which current special educational provision can be understood, outlines some of the current debates in the area of special educational needs and inclusive education, discusses policy at national and local levels including the focus on inspection, and describes policy into practice in one inclusive education authority in England.

Chapter 1 traces the historical development of special education in Great Britain to 1978. Warnock comments on the relatively recent origin of special education for those pupils deemed to have difficulties of various sorts. She notes how the first special schools were solely vocational as befitted the societal context where child labour was the norm. She also notes the time lag between provision for various groups: the first 'special' group for whom schools were founded were the blind and the deaf, then came schools for pupils with a physical disability, then schools for 'mentally handicapped' pupils and, finally, special provision for the 'maladjusted' and for those having speech impairments.

The Warnock Report recommended that the concept of 'special educational needs' should replace categorisation of handicap. The 1981 Education Act followed on from Warnock's recommendations. Since Warnock there has been a move away from 'remedial' education to a 'whole-school approach' that Clark *et al.* argue constituted the first attempt at a coherent structural merger of special and mainstream education. Recent government initiatives have given mixed messages to schools about provision for all pupils. For example, documents associated with what is often termed the 'special needs' area of education, for example the Green Paper, *Excellence for All Children* (DfEE 1997), together with the Meeting Special Educational Needs: A programme for action (DfEE 1998) which was drawn up following consultation on the Green Paper, and the 'Inclusion Statement' in *Curriculum 2000* promote an inclusive approach to children's education. Simultaneously, however, the government reiterates that 20 per cent of the school population is not expected to achieve the same academic level as other pupils.

Additionally, the encouragement of competition between schools and a market-oriented approach to education may help to raise the standard of achievement of some pupils but may militate against the achievement of those who experience difficulties in learning. Where a democratically-elected government has the power to determine the structure of the national system of education and the content of a national curriculum, education itself is bound to be highly politicised. In Chapter 2 Mittler argues that we take for granted the relationship between low achievement and social and economic deprivation and notes that policy makers have conceptualised special educational needs in terms of disability rather than disadvantage. He proposes that special educational needs should be 'reconceptualised' so that poverty, marginalisation and social exclusion are seen as 'the major obstacles to children's learning'.

One way in which the government has attempted to raise the standard of achievement of all children is through nationally-organised inspection procedures. Any framework for inspection of special educational provision in schools will necessarily have to be based on a view of what constitutes effective provision for both the sum total of pupils as well as the diversity of individual pupils' needs. There is clearly a dilemma here of whether a national inspection framework should be the same for all schools and the quality of teaching and learning within them, or should be different, depending on the context of the individual school and the diversity of its pupil population. Chapter 3 critiques the OFSTED inspection framework operating in England and Wales which assumes that the extent of all pupils' achievement can and should be judged on common criteria. It offers pragmatic advice to those working in the area of special educational provision in schools on how to prepare for an inspection.

Policy at any level within the education system should be compatible with the policies operating at any other level in the same domain as well as with general overarching policies in education. Sometimes local education authorities, or Library Boards in Northern Ireland, promote particular initiatives in their own areas which have a strong impact on schools, teachers and individual students. In Chapter 4 Wearmouth describes how the inclusive policies of one local education authority in England were reflected in teachers' research projects during the course of a postgraduate teachers' professional development course designed to promote an inclusive approach to curriculum design and planning. It outlines ways in which the teachers felt local authority policy could be developed and its implementation could be improved.

REFERENCES

Clark, C., Dyson, A., Millward, A. J. and Skidmore, D. (1997) *New Directions in Special Needs: Innovations in Mainstream Schools.* London: Cassell.

Department for Education and Employment (DfEE) (1997) *Excellence for All Children: Meeting Special Educational Needs.* Sudbury: DfEE.

Department for Education and Employment (DfEE) (1998) *Meeting Special Educational Needs: A programme for action.* Sudbury: DfEE.

Qualifications and Curriculum Authority (QCA) (2000) *Curriculum 2000.* London: QCA.

The Warnock Report: 'The Historical Background'

INTRODUCTION

2.1 Special education for the handicapped in Great Britain is of relatively recent origin. The very first schools for the blind and deaf were founded in the life-time of Mozart; those for the physically handicapped awaited the Great Exhibition; day schools for the mentally handicapped and epileptic arrived with the motor-car; whilst special provision for delicate, maladjusted and speech impaired children is younger than living memory. Even so, the early institutions were nothing like the schools we know today and they were available only to the few. As with ordinary education, education for the handicapped began with individual and charitable enterprise. There followed in time the intervention of government, first to support voluntary effort and make good deficiencies through state provision, and finally to create a national framework in which public and voluntary agencies could act in partnership to see that all children, whatever their disability, received a suitable education. The framework reached its present form only in this decade.

I EARLY DEVELOPMENTS TO 1870

2.2 The first school for the BLIND in Great Britain was established by Henry Dannett in Liverpool in 1791. Named the School of Instruction for the Indigent Blind, it offered training in music and manual crafts for blind children and adults of both sexes. No education as such was given: child labour was the rule and pupils were taught to earn a living. The Liverpool foundation was quickly followed by other private ventures: the Asylum for the Industrious Blind at Edinburgh (1793), the Asylum for the Blind at Bristol (1793), the School for the Indigent Blind in London (1800) and the Asylum and School for the Indigent Blind at Norwich (1805). As at Liverpool, these institutions were solely concerned to provide vocational training for future employment, and relied upon the profits from their workshops.

2.3 The next schools, which came thirty years later, saw the beginnings of a genuinely educational element in the instruction. Thus the Yorkshire School for the Blind (1835) set out to teach arithmetic, reading and writing as part of vocational training; whilst the school established by the London Society for Teaching the Blind to Read (1838) regarded general education as the foundation for subsequent training in manual skills. The Society later opened branches in Exeter and Nottingham. The General Institution for the Blind at Birmingham (1847) combined industrial training with a broad curriculum in general subjects: and, following early concentration on training, Henshaw's Blind Asylum at Manchester (1838) eventually developed a thriving school with educational objectives. Nevertheless by 1870 there were only a dozen or so institutions for the blind, most of them in the nature of training centres; and only a small proportion of the blind benefited from their provision. However the first senior school for the blind had been founded in 1866 at Worcester and named "College for the Blind Sons of Gentlemen".

2.4 The first school for the DEAF in Great Britain was started by Thomas Braidwood in Edinburgh in the early 1760s. Mr Braidwood's Academy for the Deaf and Dumb, as it was called, took a handful of selected paying pupils to be taught to speak and read. In 1783 the Academy moved to London, where in 1792 the first English school for the deaf opened with six children under the direction of Braidwood's nephew. This Asylum for the Support and Education of the Deaf and Dumb Children of the Poor flourished: in 1809 it moved to larger buildings and later opened a branch at Margate. In 1812 another Braidwood School opened in Birmingham. Other schools for the deaf followed in the 1820s at Liverpool, Manchester, Exeter and Doncaster. By 1870 a further six schools had been founded, including the first in Wales at Aberystwyth (1847) and Donaldson's Hospital (now Donaldson's School) in Edinburgh. These early institutions for the deaf, no less than those for the blind, were protective places, with little or no contact with the outside world. The education that they provided was limited and subordinated to training. Many of their inmates failed to find employment on leaving and had recourse to begging.

2.5 The first separate educational provision for PHYSICALLY HANDICAPPED children was made in 1851, when the Cripples Home and Industrial School for Girls was founded at Marylebone. A training Home for Crippled Boys followed at Kensington in 1865. Both institutions set out to teach a trade, and education as such was rudimentary. The children came mainly from poor homes and contributed to their own support by making goods for sale. Little further was done for the physically handicapped until 1890.

2.6 Before the middle of the nineteenth century so-called MENTALLY DEFECTIVE children who required custodial care were placed in workhouses and infirmaries. The first specific provision made for them was the Asylum for Idiots established at Highgate in 1847. Like the institutions for the blind and deaf, the Asylum took people of all ages. By 1870 there were five asylums, only three of which purported to provide education. Admission was generally by election or payment. In the same year the newly created Metropolitan Asylum Board established all-age asylums at Caterham, Leavesden and Hampstead. The children were later separated from the adults, and those who were considered to be educable followed a programme of simple manual work and formal teaching. The staff were untrained and classes were very large. In Scotland, the first establishment for the education of "imbeciles" was set up at Baldovan in Dundee in 1852 and later became Strathmartine Hospital. An institution for "defectives" was founded later in Edinburgh: it transferred to a site in Larbert in 1863 and is today the Royal Scottish National Hospital. The Lunacy (Scotland) Act of 1862 recognised the needs of the mentally handicapped and authorised the granting of licences to charitable institutions established for the care and training of imbecile children.

II 1870–1902

2.7 The Forster Education Act of 1870 (and the corresponding Education (Scotland) Act of 1872) established school boards to provide elementary education in those areas where there were insufficient places in voluntary schools. The Acts did not specifically include disabled children among those for whom provision was to be made, but in 1874 the London School Board established a class for the DEAF at a public elementary school and later began the training of teachers. By 1888 there were 14 centres attached to ordinary schools, with 373 children.[1] A number of other boards followed suit over the same period, but they were a small minority. Boards generally made no specific provision for the deaf; some had genuine doubts about their legal powers to do so, while others either did not have the money or believed that it was not in any case a proper charge upon the rates. Moreover school districts varied enormously in their size and resources and many of them had no school board.

2.8 It was equally so with the BLIND. Two years after the Scottish Act 50

---

1 Royal Commission on the Blind, the Deaf and Others of the United Kingdom, Vol 2, Appendix 26. Cited in D. G. Pritchard, *Education and the Handicapped 1760–1960 (1963)*. The early part of this chapter draws extensively on Pritchard's history.

blind children were being taught in ordinary classes in Scottish schools, and in 1875 the London Board first arranged for the teaching of blind children in its elementary schools. By 1888 there were 23 centres attached to ordinary schools, where 133 children were taught part-time by teachers who were themselves blind. The children received the rest of their education in ordinary classes, where they mixed freely with the other children. These developments were matched by a handful of other boards, including the Cardiff Board, which appointed a blind teacher to visit the ordinary schools attended by blind children.

2.9 Special educational provision for PHYSICALLY AND MENTALLY HANDICAPPED children was even slower off the mark. Those who attended elementary schools profited as best they could from the ordinary teaching. The more severely handicapped received care and sometimes education in institutions. However, in 1892 the Leicester School Board established a special class for selected "feeble-minded" pupils, and in the same year the London Board opened a school for the special instruction of physically and mentally defective children who could not be suitably educated by ordinary methods. The emphasis was upon occupational activity rather than formal education. By 1896 there were 24 special schools in London attended by 900 pupils and before the end of the century schools for defective children had been established by six other boards.

2.10 These first, hesitant efforts by a few school boards to cater for some handicapped children owed nothing to educational legislation. The middle of the nineteenth century had seen a stirring of social conscience over the plight of the disabled, especially of the blind, but it was primarily concerned to relieve their distress, not to educate them. Yet as the principle of universal elementary education took root, it could be only a matter of time before the educational needs of handicapped children began to be recognised. Six years after the Forster Act the Charity Organisation Society was pressing the right of blind children to receive education and the duty of school boards to provide it, and later applying the same arguments to the education of the deaf. The Society for the Training of the Deaf made approaches to government. Other bodies added their voices and through meetings, publications and propaganda created the climate of reform.

2.11 The time had come for an inquiry, and the Royal Commission on the Blind and Deaf was constituted in 1886. The Commission had started work the year before with a remit confined to the blind, but now extended to include the deaf. The amended terms of reference were to report on the provision for the education of the blind and deaf in the

United Kingdom, the opportunities for their employment and the educational changes needed to increase their qualifications for employment. The Commission was also required to consider "such other cases as from special circumstances would seem to require exceptional methods of education". [. . .]

2.12 The Commission reported in 1889. It recommended the introduction of compulsory education for the blind from five to 16 and proposed that it should be provided by school boards either in their own schools or in institutions run by others if certified by the Education Department as being suitable. A two-stage arrangement was envisaged whereby pupils would receive elementary education to the age of 12 and thereafter follow a technical or an academic course. Boards should have the power to continue to pay grants beyond the age of 16 to assist pupils to establish themselves in a trade. At the elementary stage it was envisaged that the children would be taught in ordinary classes by ordinary teachers, although in town schools special instruction in reading might be given by visiting teachers or by attendance at a centre on certain days. There would be a need for special boarding schools for pupils who were delicate, neglected or lived too far from the nearest day school to be able to attend it without difficulty.

2.13 The Commission also recommended compulsory education for the deaf, to be provided by school boards, but with important differences. Since deaf children were generally less forward than hearing children they would not be ready to start school until the age of seven. Moreover, they would need to be taught not in ordinary classes but in separate schools or classes. There should be one teacher for every eight children where oral methods were used and one teacher for every 14 children for instruction by the manual system. The sexes should be educated separately. Teachers of the deaf should be paid higher salaries than ordinary teachers, their training should be under government supervision, and they should have qualified as ordinary teachers before beginning their special training.

2.14 The Commission's report was well received. Legislation quickly followed for Scotland in the Education of Blind and Deaf Mute Children (Scotland) Act of 1890, but three years elapsed before England and Wales were similarly covered by the Elementary Education (Blind and Deaf Children) Act of 1893. The Act required school authorities* to make provision, in their own or other schools, for the education of blind and

---

* The term "school authority" includes school boards, and, for areas not under a school board, the district council where such existed, or otherwise the body responsible for appointing a school attendance committee for the area.

deaf children resident in their area who were not otherwise receiving suitable elementary education. As the Commission had recommended, blind children were to receive education between the ages of five and 16 and deaf children between seven and 16. (The higher age of 16 was far ahead of contemporary provision for normal children, who, from the age of 11, might be given total or partial exemption from attending school.) Certified institutions were entitled to receive a per capita Parliamentary grant for each child received but had to be open to inspection.

2.15 The new Act meant that all blind or deaf children would in future be sent to school as of right. The uncertainties of the 1870 Act which had affected the special provision made in board schools were thus finally removed, and monetary support assured. In most cases the extra places were provided by the extension of existing schools. The larger school boards generally made real efforts to maintain good standards in their own schools, but many boards, particularly those of small towns and country districts, were less efficient. Moreover there were some 20,000 voluntary schools, over which the school boards had no control, and these difficulties persisted until the creation of local education authorities in 1902.

2.16 Before the Forster Education Act the needs of MENTALLY HANDICAPPED children were little recognised. Mental disability was for many children no substantial handicap in coping with the simple demands of everyday life in a largely uneducated and relatively uncomplicated world, and institutional provision was available for those who needed looking after. Their needs first became apparent after 1870 when large numbers of children of below average or poor intellectual ability entered public elementary schools. Many of them made scarcely any progress and their presence hindered normal teaching. There were no systematic means of assessing their individual capabilities and requirements. The range of disability was very wide and there were unresolved questions of definition. Instruction was based upon the official Code for normal children; classes were large and there was no opportunity, even if teachers had the skills, to shape a special curriculum for them. Unlike the blind and deaf they had no organised opinion to plead their cause. Apart from isolated examples of private provision in London and elsewhere very little had been achieved when the Royal Commission on the Blind and Deaf reported in 1889.

2.17 The Commission had distinguished between the feeble-minded, imbeciles and idiots. The last group, having the greater degree of intellectual deficiency, were not generally considered to be educable. The

Commission argued that imbeciles, having a lesser degree of deficiency, should not remain in asylums or workhouses, but school authorities should be responsible for ensuring their admission to institutions where they should wherever possible receive an education which concentrated upon sensory and physical development and the improvement of speech. This would be given by ordinary teachers. As to the feeble-minded, these should receive special education separately from ordinary children in "auxiliary" schools. The nature of the education to be given was not specified.

2.18 Following the Commission's report the Charity Organisation Society campaigned for the imposition of a duty on school boards to provide for the mentally handicapped and, to this end, sponsored in 1896 the National Association for Promoting the Welfare of the Feeble-Minded. The campaign drew support from the findings of Dr Francis Warner, who investigated 100,000 children in district poor law schools and the London Board Schools in the early 1890s and concluded that about 1% of the children required special care and training in separate schools on the grounds of their mental and physical condition. The Report of the Metropolitan Poor Law Schools Committee in 1896 also called for separate provision to be made for feeble-minded children. It recommended that they should be boarded out or placed in special training homes.

2.19 In 1896 the Education Department established a Committee on Defective and Epileptic Children, under its Chief Inspector of Schools. The Committee was asked to enquire first into the need for any changes in the system of education of feeble-minded and defective children not in the charge of guardians and not idiots or imbeciles; secondly into the means of discriminating between educable and non-educable children and between those who could be taught in an ordinary school and those who should attend special classes; and thirdly into the provision of elementary education for children suffering from epilepsy.

2.20 Like the Royal Commission seven years earlier the Committee had to grapple with definitions. It decided that imbecile children were those who by reason of mental defect could not be educated to be self-supporting; and that feeble-minded children were those who, not being imbeciles, could not be taught in ordinary elementary schools by ordinary methods. Logically this distinction meant that all imbeciles would attend asylums and the feeble-minded would attend special schools or classes: but admission to asylums was only on the basis of certification, and many imbeciles were not certified. Thus some imbeciles would be presented for admission to special schools or classes. The Committee therefore concluded that the schools would need to exercise their own judgement on whether an individual child was capable of receiving proper benefit from special instruction. Dr Warner's study of London children had suggested that the children could be assessed by physical examination, and on this footing the Committee envisaged that a medical officer appointed by the school board would decide whether a particular child should be educated in an ordinary school, in a special school or not at all.

2.21 The Committee proposed that school authorities should have the duty to make special provision for all defective children in their area, and be given the power to compel attendance. Admission should be at age seven, and all children should remain until 14, unless the authority decided that they should stay until 16. Classes in special schools should be small, generally not greater than 20 or 30 in the case of senior classes. All headteachers should be qualified. The majority of assistant teachers should also be qualified and should moreover have additional training. None should be under 21. There would be not more than 4½ hours of teaching each day, and lessons should be short. There should be a varied programme of activities with emphasis on manual and vocational training for senior pupils.

2.22 The Committee had classed the feeble-minded with PHYSICALLY HANDICAPPED children under the general description of "defective". It recommended that defective children of normal intelligence should attend ordinary schools, and be provided with transport, guides or boarding accommodation to enable them to do so. Even where a separate school was provided for them they should receive an ordinary education.

2.23 With regard to EPILEPTIC children the Committee proposed that where attacks occurred at intervals of a month or longer attendance at an ordinary class was possible: otherwise school authorities should be required to provide for them in residential special schools or to pay for their education and maintenance in a voluntary institution. Attendance should be compulsory.

2.24 The Committee reported in 1898. Its proposals were far ahead of contemporary ideas, made heavy organisational demands upon the boards and were, moreover, costly. Not surprisingly therefore the Elementary Education (Defective and Epileptic Children) Act of 1899 merely permitted school boards to provide for the education of mentally and physically defective and epileptic children. The Act applied to children who "not being imbecile, and not being merely dull or backward, are defective, that is to say . . . by reason of mental or physical defect are incapable of receiving benefit from the instruction in ordinary elementary schools but are not incapable by reason of such defect of receiving benefit from instruction in special classes or schools". Although an enhanced rate of grant was payable for this special provision, ten years later only 133 out of 327 local education authorities were using their powers under the Act.[2]

III 1902–1944

2.25 The Education Act 1902 abolished the school boards and established a two-tier system of local education authorities for elementary and secondary education respectively. The functions formerly exercised by school boards, including those relating to special education, were transferred to the new authorities for elementary education, whilst the higher education powers conferred upon county and county borough councils included the power to provide secondary education for blind, deaf, defective and epileptic children. With these changes the statutory foundation of special educational provision which had been laid in the last decade of the nineteenth century, though consolidated in the Education Act 1921, continued in broadly the same form until 1944. However, the Elementary Education (Defective and Epileptic) Act 1914 converted into a duty the earlier powers conferred on authorities by the 1899 Act to provide for the education of mentally defective children; and the Education Act 1918 did the same in respect of physically defective and epileptic children. Thus the intentions of the Committee on Defective and Epileptic Children were belatedly fulfilled and compulsory provision extended to all the categories of handicapped children which had so far been recognised.

2.26 New provision continued to be made, much of it by voluntary effort and of a pioneering nature. Open air schools, day and boarding schools for physically handicapped children, schools in hospitals and convalescent homes and trade schools all contributed to more varied facilities available to local education authorities and parents. Examples were the Heritage Craft Schools and Hospital at Chailey, Sussex (1903), the Swinton House School of Recovery at Manchester (1905), the London County Council's Open Air School at Plumstead (1907) and the Lord Mayor Treloar Cripples' Hospital and College at Alton (1908). The Manchester Local Education Authority had opened a residential school for

---

2 Annual Report for 1909 of the Chief Medical Officer of the Board of Education (HMSO 1910), p 152.

epileptics in 1910: by 1918 there were six such schools throughout the country.

2.27 The education of MENTALLY HANDICAPPED children however faced a period of uncertainty following the report in 1908 of the Royal Commission on the Care and Control of the Feeble-Minded. After four years' investigation the Commission concluded that institutional provision for mentally defective children on occupational lines was to be preferred to provision in special schools; it consequently recommended that the Elementary Education (Defective and Epileptic Children) Act of 1899 should be amended to exclude these children and that responsibility for their training should lie with local mental deficiency committees. In the event this proposal was not accepted and the 1899 Act remained intact. Instead the Mental Deficiency Act of 1913 required local education authorities to ascertain and certify which children aged seven to 16 in their area were defective. Only those who were judged by the authority to be incapable of being taught in special schools were to pass to the care of local mental deficiency committees. The duty to provide for the educable children which naturally followed was enacted a year later. In fact by 1913 175 out of 318 authorities had used their powers under the 1899 Act, about a third of them having established their own special schools: there were altogether 177 schools catering for some 12,500 mentally defective children.[3] By 1939 the number of children had risen to about 17,000.[4]

2.28 In Scotland, the Education of Defective Children (Scotland) Act of 1906 empowered school boards to make provision in special schools or classes for the education of defective children between the ages of five and 16, whilst the Mental Deficiency (Scotland) Act of 1913 required school boards to ascertain children in their area who were defective, and those who were considered incapable of benefiting from instruction in special schools became the responsibility of parish councils for placement in an institution. By 1939 the number of mentally defective children on the roll of special schools and classes had reached 4,871.

2.29 The education of mentally defective children again came under scrutiny with the appointment in 1924 of the Mental Deficiency Committee (the Wood Committee). This had been set up informally by Sir George Newman, Chief Medical Officer to the Board of Education, in association with the Board of Control. It set itself to inquire into the incidence of

---

3 Annual Report for 1912 of the Chief Medical Officer of the Board of Education (HMSO 1913), p.239.
4 D. G. Pritchard, *op cit.*, p.188.

feeble-mindedness and to suggest what changes were necessary in the arrangements for the education of feeble-minded children. Reporting in 1929 the Committee concluded that some 105,000 schoolchildren were mentally defective in terms of the Elementary Education (Defective and Epileptic) Act 1914 and accepted evidence that only a third of them had been ascertained and that moreover only a half of these were actually attending special schools. The Committee also estimated that a further 10% of all children, though not mentally deficient, were retarded and failing to make progress in the ordinary school. (This broader concept of need found expression after 1944 in the category of educationally sub-normal pupils.)

2.30 The Committee's suggestions were very different from those of the Royal Commission twenty years before. Far from proposing the separation of mentally deficient children from the mainstream of education the Committee pressed for their much closer association with it. It proposed that the system of certification, which inhibited proper ascertainment of children's needs, should be abolished and that there should be a single system for dealing with the feeble-minded and the backward which allowed greater flexibility in the development of special schools and classes and the placement of pupils. It used these prophetic words: "We do not however contemplate that these [special] schools would exist with a different legal sanction, under a different system of nomenclature and under different administrative provisions. If the majority of children for whom these schools . . . are intended are, *ex hypothesi*, to lead the lives of ordinary citizens, with no shadow of a 'certificate' and all that that implies to handicap their careers, the schools must be brought into closer relation with the Public Elementary School System and presented to parents not as something both distinct and humiliating, but as a helpful variation of the ordinary school".

2.31 This view of special education as a variant of ordinary education had been expressed in relation to the feeble-minded only. But the Committee had, consciously or not, advanced a principle extending to all forms of disability; and also to all degrees of disability, because if no clear distinction could be drawn between feeble-mindedness and back-wardness the same must also be true of feeble-mindedness and imbecility. However, forty years were to pass before the right of mentally handicapped children to education was recognised without qualification.

2.32 In contrast to the education of the physically and mentally handicapped that of BLIND and DEAF children had made substantial advances by the turn of the century. Provision for their education had been a statutory duty of the school authorities since 1893 and by 1902 most of the children were receiving education, either in maintained schools or in voluntary schools or institutions, and education was free to those children whose parents could not afford to contribute towards the cost. There were however three areas of deficiency. Their education was entirely neglected before they became of school age; moreover the statutory education of deaf children did not begin until the age of seven and even the blind were not in practice always able to gain admission to voluntary schools at five. Secondly, children with partial sight or partial hearing were at a disadvantage in ordinary schools, and even in special schools their usable sensory faculties were insufficiently exploited. Thirdly, whilst Worcester College provided an academic education for boys, there was no comparable provision for girls.

[. . .]

2.34 . . . They were not brought into line with the blind until 1938 (under the Education (Deaf Children) Act 1937). Although the need for a grammar school for the deaf was recognised before the Second World War no public provision was made until 1946, when the Mary Hare Grammar School for the Deaf was founded to take boys and girls sent there by local education authorities. The only earlier provision had been in private schools.

[. . .]

2.36 . . . This period also saw the very beginnings of provision for the MALADJUSTED. Before the turn of the century a psychological laboratory began to study difficult children at University College, London, and the British Child Study Association was founded in 1893. In 1913 the London County Council appointed a psychologist (Cyril Burt) to examine, among other things, individual cases referred by teachers, school doctors, care workers, magistrates and parents. Largely influenced by developments in America the concept of child guidance on multi-professional lines began to emerge, and in 1927 the Child Guidance Council, which later merged into the National Association for Mental Health, was formed. It aimed "to encourage the provision of skilled treatment of children showing behavioural disturbances". A number of clinics was subsequently started by voluntary bodies and hospitals. Provision by local education authorities came later, but by 1939 22 clinics, officially recognised as part of the school medical service, were wholly or partly maintained by authorities. However, since maladjustment was not officially recognised as a form of handicap calling for special education, practically no provision was made by authorities for these pupils before 1944, although some authorities paid for children to attend voluntary homes. In Scotland in the late 1920s an "educational" clinic was opened by Dr William Boyd of the Education Department of the University of Glasgow and a "psychological" clinic was established by Professor James Drever in the Psychology Department at Edinburgh University. The term "child guidance clinic" was first used in 1931 when the Notre Dame clinic was opened in Glasgow. Glasgow was the first education authority to establish a child guidance clinic on a full-time basis, in 1937. Seven education authorities had child guidance clinics prior to the Education (Scotland) Act 1945.

[. . .]

IV 1944–1955

The Education Act 1944

2.41 The provisions of Part V of the Education Act 1921 which (like earlier enactments) had treated the education of handicapped children as an entirely separate category of provision, were replaced by a requirement that local education authorities must meet the needs of these children, in the form of special educational treatment, within their general duty to provide a sufficiency of primary and secondary schools. Special educational provision was to be included in authorities' development plans for primary and secondary education. The 1921 Act had provided for handicapped children to be educated only in special schools or special classes. Now, the less seriously handicapped children might be catered for in ordinary schools (not necessarily in special classes), although those with serious disabilities would, wherever practicable, continue to be educated in special schools. The options were later extended by the Education (Miscellaneous Provisions) Act 1953 to include independent schools, subject to the Minister's power of veto in a particular case.

2.42 Other major changes were introduced. The duty of local education authorities to ascertain which children required special educational treatment, hitherto confined to defective and epileptic children, was extended to children with all types of disability. They were generally described in the Act as "pupils who suffer from any disability of mind or body" and definition of the types or categories was flexibly delegated to the Minister, acting under statutory regulations, instead of being written into the Act. Certification of defective children within the education system was abolished: any child considered to be educable would in future have access to schooling as of right. But children not considered to be capable of being educated in school were to be reported to the local authority for the purposes of the Mental Deficiency Act 1913. The lower age of compulsory school attendance at special schools was uniformly reduced to five years and the right to remain beyond the age of 16 was established.

2.43 For the purposes of ascertainment, authorities were empowered to require parents to submit their children for medical examination, subject to a lower age limit of two years: and they could not unreasonably refuse the parents' request that their child should be so examined. No specific provision was made for parental appeal against an authority's decision that their child required special educational treatment, but parents could appeal to the Minister against an authority's refusal to consent to their child being withdrawn from a special school. Moreover, the normal procedures for the enforcement of school attendance applied, so that in the event of disagreement between the parents and the authority as to the school to be named in a School Attendance Order, the question could be referred to the Minister for his determination.

2.44 In Scotland, the Education (Scotland) Act 1945 repeated much of the content of the Education Act 1944, but with certain important differences. The duty of education authorities to ascertain which children required special educational treatment applied to children from the age of five. Education authorities were specifically empowered to provide a child guidance service in a child guidance clinic or elsewhere, its functions being to study handicapped, backward and difficult children, to advise teachers and parents as to the appropriate methods of education and training for these children and in suitable cases to provide special educational treatment in child guidance clinics. The creation of this service did a great deal to establish the importance in ascertainment procedures of the assessment of children by educational psychologists. In addition, the 1945 Act specifically recognised the educational importance of the early discovery and treatment of any disability of mind or body by placing upon education authorities the duty to make this known.

Planning the new structure

2.45 The intention of the 1944 Act, fulfilled by regulations made by the Minister in the following year, was to extend greatly the range of children's special needs for which authorities would be obliged to make specific provision, either in special schools or in ordinary schools. The Handicapped Pupils and School Health Service Regulations 1945 defined 11 categories of pupils: blind, partially sighted, deaf, partially deaf, delicate, diabetic, educationally sub-normal, epileptic, maladjusted, physically handicapped and those with speech defects. Maladjustment and speech defects were entirely new categories. Partial blindness and partial deafness were extensions of existing categories, whilst delicate and diabetic children had previously been treated as physically handicapped. The categories (though not the detailed definitions) have remained unchanged since 1944 except that in 1953 diabetic children ceased to form a separate category and have since then been included with the delicate. The regulations prescribed that blind, deaf, epileptic, physically handicapped and aphasic children were seriously disabled and must be educated in special schools. Children with other disabilities might attend ordinary schools if adequate provision for them was available.

2.46 The new framework of categories entailed the development of existing and new forms of special educational provision. Detailed guidance on the provision to be made for each category by local education authorities in their development plans was issued by the Ministry of Education.[6] The small number of blind children (estimated to be about 1,200) would need to be educated in special boarding schools. Deaf children, though somewhat more numerous than the blind, might also require residential special schooling, except in the larger urban authorities, where special day school provision might be feasible. The more seriously affected partially sighted children should attend special schools (either day or boarding), but others could, with special help, be educated in regular classes in ordinary schools or in open-air schools. About half of partially deaf children might with suitable support be capable of attending an ordinary day school: others would require the more sophisticated services of a day or boarding special school. Provision for delicate children not in hospital schools should be in open-air day schools or in boarding schools for the delicate. The great majority of children would expect to return to ordinary schools within two years. Diabetic children should normally attend ordinary day schools, and be accommodated in special hostels if they could not receive adequate treatment and care whilst living at home. Epileptic children requiring regular medication should be sent to a boarding special school for epileptic children. The special educational needs of a maladjusted child should be assessed by an educational psychologist or a child guidance team and, depending on the assessment, might be met by his own teacher, with appropriate specialist advice; by periods of specialist teaching (often in a separate setting); by attendance at another day school (ordinary or special); or by transfer to a boarding special school. Local

---

6 *Special Educational Treatment.* Ministry of Education Pamphlet No 5 (UMSO W6).

education authorities were reminded that effective assessment and placement called for proper arrangements for child guidance.

2.47 The guidance indicated that all children assessed as needing special educational treatment on account of physical handicap should be sent to an appropriate special school. Those with physical disabilities not requiring medical or surgical treatment or interfering with their progress in ordinary schools should not be regarded as physically handicapped. Aphasic children whose disability was not merely a defect of articulation should, given imperfect knowledge of the best methods of treatment, be admitted to a school for the deaf. Children with other speech defects should receive treatment at clinics whilst continuing to attend their own schools. A very large proportion of them could be expected to be cured by regular treatment.

2.48 The category of educationally sub-normal children was seen as consisting of children of limited ability and children retarded by "other conditions" such as irregular attendance, ill-health, lack of continuity in their education or unsatisfactory school conditions. These children would be those who for any reason were retarded by more than 20% for their age and who were not so low-graded as to be ineducable or to be detrimental to the education of other children. They would amount to approximately 10% of the school population. Detailed suggestions were made for provision. In large urban areas about 1–2% of the school population would need to be educated in special schools (including 0.2% in boarding schools); the remaining 8–9% of the school population would be provided for in ordinary schools. They should be taught in small groups, in attractive accommodation and by sympathetic teachers. They should not however be isolated, but should be regarded as full members of the ordinary school and should share in general activities. In the absence of well-tried methods there would be need for experimentation to discover the most effective ways of helping them. In small urban areas rather more provision (for 0.4% of the school population) might be required in boarding special schools: and where numbers were insufficient to support a day special school or a special class the remaining children would need to be educated in regular classes in ordinary schools.

The first ten years

2.49 The official guidance of 1946 had provided estimates for each category of handicap of the number of children who might be expected to require special educational treatment, not necessarily in special schools. In sum these amounted to a range between 14% and 17% of the school population. These were however planning objectives to be achieved in the fullness of time. The first task was to make good a shortage of places inherited from the war, through the interruption of school building and the effect of enemy bombing. In 1946 the number of children in special schools had for a variety of reasons fallen to 38,499 compared with 51,152 in 1939. Scarcity of building resources and the heavy demand for places to match the rapidly increasing post-war birth rate dictated the use of country mansions and other large buildings which were coming on to the market. Largely by these means the number of special schools increased between 1945 and 1955 from 528 to 743 (41%) and the numbers of pupils in them from 38,499 to 58,034 (51%). During the same period the number of full-time teachers in special schools rose from 2,434 to 4,381 (80%). Of 16,159 places provided between 1945 and the end of 1955, 68% were for ESN pupils, 14% for the physically handicapped and 7% for the maladjusted. Three out of five places were for boarders. In the same period 68 new boarding homes were provided, mainly for maladjusted pupils. The planning of these developments had been assisted by a series of regional conferences of local education authorities in 1946 and 1947 and again in 1954 and 1955.

[. . .]

2.52 The first local education authority to employ speech therapists was the Manchester Local Education Authority in 1906. By 1945 70 authorities were employing them. But the development of provision for children with SPEECH DEFECTS had been delayed by lack of qualified staff. Before 1945 there was no single recognised qualification, no agreed syllabus of study and some professional rivalry. In 1945 the College of Speech Therapists was formed and became the sole organising and examining body and mode of entry for speech therapists to the National Register of Medical Auxiliaries. The College's syllabus and final examinations were thereafter adopted by all training schools in England and Scotland. On this foundation, the number of speech therapists employed full or part-time by local education authorities increased from 205 to 341 in the five years 1949–1954 (an increase of nearly 90% on a full-time basis), whilst the number of children treated each year rose from 25,098 to 44,800. In 1969 the Quirk Committee,[7] reporting to the Secretaries of State for Education and Science, Social Services, Scotland and Wales, recommended unification of the speech therapy service, further expansion of professional staff, a broader based training at degree level and the

---

7 *Speech Therapy Services.* Report of the Committee appointed by the Secretaries of State for Education and Science, for the Social Services, for Scotland and for Wales in July 1969 (HMSO 1972).

establishment of a professional organisation. As a result the speech therapy services were reorganised in 1974 under area health authorities in England and Wales and under health boards in Scotland. But the government concluded that a fully graduate profession would need to be regarded as an aspiration for the future.

[. . .]

2.54 But if special provision for most categories of handicap appeared to be nearing sufficiency in amount (as distinct from quality) the needs of EDUCATIONALLY SUB-NORMAL pupils remained obstinately unsatisfied in spite of continuous expansion since 1945. By the end of 1955 nearly 11,000 new places had been provided and a further 8,000 places were in hand. The number of children in ESN special schools had nearly doubled between 1947 and 1955 (from 12,060 to 22,639) yet the number of children awaiting placement remained high at over 12,000. It was clear that the rate of ascertainment of these pupils was constrained by the number of special school places available. Indeed a special enquiry of authorities conducted in 1956 showed that although 12,437 had been shown in the official returns as awaiting places in special schools, as many as 27,000 were considered to need such placement. These were children who were not being satisfactorily helped in ordinary schools.

2.55 Provision for MALADJUSTED pupils was also characterised by expansion in the decade 1945–55. Little had been done for them before the war. In 1945 the only facilities for examining maladjusted children were in 79 child guidance clinics (22 in 1939), some war-time hostels, a few independent boarding schools and two day special schools. Ten years later there were some 300 child guidance clinics, about two-thirds of them provided by local education authorities, 45 boarding homes or hostels, 32 boarding special schools, three day special schools and a number of special classes. Further, local education authorities had placed over 1,000 maladjusted children in 158 independent boarding schools and were providing education for seriously disturbed children in six children's departments of mental hospitals. This expanded provision had been accompanied by greater discrimination in the referral, assessment, placement and education of children. The importance of early referral and of prevention as well as cure was increasingly recognised, and maladjustment was seen as having manifestations in passive introverted behaviour as well as in disruptive or anti-social forms of conduct. Moreover the staff of clinics had expanded, though not in step with need. Whereas in 1945 clinics were generally run single-handed by a psychologist, in 1955 most of them were served by a team consisting of a child psychiatrist, an educational psychologist and a psychiatric social worker, and the teams worked more closely with the staff of special schools and hostels. A start had been made on providing courses of training for teachers and house-staff concerned with maladjusted children. Even so this branch of special education was recognised as being relatively undeveloped. With this in mind the Minister of Education had in 1950 appointed a Committee to enquire into and report upon the medical, educational and social problems relating to maladjusted children, with reference to their treatment within the education system. The Underwood Committee, as it was called, reported in November 1955.[8]

[. . .]

2.57 In Scotland an attempt was made to bring together expert opinion on all forms of handicap. In 1947 the Secretary of State remitted to the Advisory Council in Scotland the task of reviewing the provision made for the primary and secondary education of pupils suffering from disability of mind or body or from maladjustment due to social handicaps. The Council produced between 1950 and 1952 seven reports which were valuable guides to education authorities on the provision for different handicaps, although their predictions of future need have not all stood the test of time. For example, it was thought that special provision should be made for 20,000 physically handicapped pupils, whereas the number of these children in special schools in 1976 was only 1,076: conversely the Council's estimate that four residential child guidance clinics would suffice to meet the needs of all children maladjusted because of social handicap has proved to be hopelessly inadequate. The Scottish Education Department Circular No 300[9] in presenting these reports placed special education within the mainstream of primary and secondary education. "Special educational treatment should not be thought of mainly in terms of the provision on a large scale of separate schools for handicapped children. . . . It is recognised that there must continue to be situations where it is essential in the children's interest that those who are handicapped must be separated from those who are not. Nevertheless as

8 Report of the Committee on Maladjusted Children (HMSO 1955).
9 The Education of Handicapped Pupils: The Reports of the Advisory Council (21 March 1955). The titles of the Reports were as follows:

Pupils who are Defective in Hearing	(Cmd 7866)
Pupils who are Defective in Vision	(Cmd 7885)
Visual and Aural Aids	(Cmd 8102)
Pupils with Physical Disabilities	(Cmd 8211)
Pupils with Mental or Educational Disabilities	(Cmd 8401)
Pupils handicapped by Speech Disorders	(Cmd 8426)
Pupils who are Maladjusted because of Social Handicap	(Cmd 8428)

medical knowledge increases and as general school conditions improve it should be possible for an increasing proportion of pupils who require special educational treatment to be educated along with their contemporaries in ordinary schools. Special educational treatment should, indeed, be regarded simply as a well-defined arrangement within the ordinary educational system to provide for the handicapped child the individual attention that he particularly needs."

2.58 In the year prior to the issue of Circular No 300 Scottish regulations were made laying down definitions of the nine statutory categories of handicap. Delicate and diabetic children were not included as they were in England and Wales. These Regulations, together with the 1956 Schools Code, which prescribed maximum class sizes for the various categories of handicap, ensured for handicapped children in Scotland the benefit of favourable pupil-teacher ratios.

V 1955–1977

2.59 This section sketches the main events in special education from 1955 to the present day [i.e. 1977, ed.] and looks at particular areas where significant developments have taken place with which we are especially concerned in this report.

Developments in child guidance

2.60 The important recommendations of the Underwood Committee on child guidance were brought to the attention of local education authorities in Circular 347.[10] The Circular accepted the Committee's report as the basis for the organisation and future development of child guidance. The Committee had urged that there should be a comprehensive child guidance service available for the area of every local education authority, involving a school psychological service, the school health service and child guidance clinics, all of which should work in close co-operation. Authorities and regional hospital boards should plan their provision in consultation. The Circular asked local education authorities, in consultation with hospital authorities, to give effect to these recommendations and to submit progress reports by June 1960. At the same time hospital and local authorities were asked by the Ministry of Health to co-operate with local education authorities. In their subsequent reports most local education authorities accepted the pattern of child

---

10 Ministry of Education Circular 347, Child Guidance (10 March 1959).

guidance clinics suggested in Circular 347, whereby the authority would provide the premises and employ the psychologists and psychiatric social workers, whilst the hospital service would provide psychiatrists.

2.61 The major bar to progress was a continuing shortage of professional staff, demand for which was increased by the recommendation of the Underwood Committee (endorsed by the Ministry of Education in Circular 348[11]) that a maladjusted child should, wherever possible, continue to live at home during treatment and attend an ordinary school or special school or class. This had led the Department to ask authorities to consider the need for more day schools or special classes, and, through their regional machinery, to review the need for boarding provision in schools or homes. The number of child guidance clinics increased modestly each year from 162 in 1950 to 367 twenty years later, but that of professional staff continued to lag behind. The duties, training and supply of educational psychologists were considered by the Summerfield Working Party which reported in 1968.[12] The Working Party recommended new and expanded arrangements for training and a doubling of numbers. By 1977 the position had substantially improved. . . .

2.62 In 1974, on transfer of responsibility for the school health service to area health authorities, the provision and organisation of child guidance was the subject of further advice,[15] jointly from the Departments of Education and Science and Health and Social Security. This recommended that the child guidance service should be based on a multi-professional team, providing assessment, diagnosis, consultation, treatment and other help as needed by the child, his parents or other people in regular contact with him. Local and health authorities were asked to extend the available help to children with behavioural, emotional and learning difficulties, and to the families of these children through more flexible use of distinct but collaborating services, and to report their new arrangements. The Court Committee on Child Health Services[16] which reported to the Secretaries of State for Social Services, Education and Science and Wales in 1976 recommended "that the child guidance clinics and psychiatric hospital

---

11 Ministry of Education Circular 348, Special Educational Treatment for Maladjusted Children (10 March 1959).

12 *Psychologists in Education Services.* The Report of a Working Party appointed by the Secretary of State for Education and Science: the Summerfield Report (HMSO 1968).

15 DES Circular 3/74, DHSS Circular HSC(IS)9, Welsh Office Circular WHSC(IS)5, Child Guidance (14 March 1974).

16 *Fit for the future.* The Report of the Committee on Child Health Services. Cmnd 6684 (HMSO 1976).

services should be recognised as part of an integrated child and adolescent psychiatry service". In its Circular advising health authorities of the government's conclusions on the Committee's recommendations, the Department of Health and Social Security accepted the need for further progress in the integration of services, in the sense of co-ordinated planning and working as distinct from fusion of the existing services into a new one.[17] The Circular also indicated that a document illustrating some aspects of good practice in the integrated services would be issued jointly with the Department of Education and Science during 1978.

2.63 In Scotland the child guidance service developed much more rapidly than in England and Wales. By 1966, 25 of the 35 education authorities had a child guidance service. The Education (Scotland) Act of 1969 made the provision of such a service a duty and the functions referred to in paragraph 2.62 were extended to include advice to social work departments, which had been established by the Social Work (Scotland) Act 1968. (The Scottish child guidance service has no direct medical component as in England and Wales and is organisationally similar to the school psychological service south of the border. The agreed ratio of educational psychologists to children in Scotland is 1:3,000, which it is hoped to attain by 1980.)

[. . .]

Mentally handicapped children

2.66 Increasing unease about the principle and practice of excluding large numbers of mentally handicapped children from school found expression in the Mental Health Act 1959. The Act replaced Section 57 of the Education Act 1944 (as amended) by less rigid provisions. Parents were allowed extra time in which to appeal to the Minister against a local education authority's decision that their child was incapable of being educated in school; and given the right to call for a review after one year, with like opportunity to appeal. Parents were to be given more detailed information about the functions of the local authority in relation to treatment, care and training, and, wherever possible, a statement of the arrangements proposed to be made for their child by the local authority in discharge of those functions. Thus co-operation between local education and health authorities was enforced by statute.

---

17 DHSS Health Circular HC(78)5 Local Authority Circular LAC(78)2, Welsh Office Circular WHC(78)4, Health Services Development (January 1978).

2.67 But whilst the 1959 Act was a response to unhappiness, particularly amongst parents, about the labelling of some children as not being entitled to education, it had merely tempered the procedures leading to segregation. Criticism of the system continued to grow, and moreover, the concept of special education was broadening to encompass needs hitherto regarded as beyond its reach These tensions were finally resolved in April 1971 when local education authorities assumed responsibility for the education of mentally handicapped children, following the Education (Handicapped Children) Act 1970, which removed the power of health authorities to provide training for these children and required the staff and buildings of junior training centres to be transferred to the education service. In this way some 24,000 children in junior training centres and special care units, 8,000 in about 100 hospitals, and an uncertain number at home or in private institutions ceased to be treated as being mentally deficient and became entitled to special education. For this purpose they were to be regarded as severely educationally sub-normal (ESN(S)), as distinct from the moderately educationally sub-normal (ESN(M)) who had previously made up the ESN category. Many of the children had other difficulties.

2.68 Detailed advice to local education authorities on the operation of the new arrangements was given in Circular 15/70.[20] Junior training centres would normally be approved by the Secretary of State as special schools. Provision in hospitals might take the form of hospital special schools or arrangements for teaching under the terms of Section 56 of the Education Act 1944. In the event about 400 new special schools were so formed. The training of teachers of mentally handicapped children would be integrated as soon as possible into the ordinary three-year initial teacher training, but to assist the transition special one-year courses would be provided at selected colleges for those teachers who held the Diploma of the Training Council for Teachers of the Mentally Handicapped and who could satisfy the minimum entrance qualifications. . . .

2.69 In Scotland education authorities became responsible in 1947 for the education of children who were described as "ineducable but trainable". Those children were placed in junior occupational centres and trained by instructors, but following the Report of the Melville Committee[21] and subsequent provisions in the Education (Mentally Handicapped Children)

---

20 DES Circular 15/70, Responsibility for the Education of Mentally Handicapped Children (22 September 1970).

21 *The Training of Staff for Centres for the Mentally Handicapped.* Report of the Committee appointed by the Secretary of State for Scotland (HMSO 1973).

(Scotland) Act 1974 the centres were renamed schools, and teachers were appointed in addition to the instructors. The 1974 Act also gave education authorities responsibility for the education of children who had previously been described as "ineducable and untrainable".

Community homes and List D schools

2.70 Under the Children and Young Persons Act 1969 a new system of community homes was established in England and Wales which called for new forms of collaboration between local education authorities and social services departments. The new system brought together establishments for the accommodation of children in the care of local authorities and the former remand homes and approved schools. Approved schools, which had been established in 1933, were residential institutions approved by the Home Secretary for the education and training of boys and girls who, with few exceptions, were ordered to be sent to them by the courts. They provided a general education, with considerable attention to craft training for the older children, but their primary objective was the social readjustment of the boys and girls in preparation for their return to the community. In Scotland all the functions of the former approved schools, including the provision of education, were transferred in 1971 to local authority social work departments under the terms of the Social Work (Scotland) Act 1968, and these institutions are now known as List D schools.

The school health service

2.71 The school health service originated in the Education (Administrative Provisions) Act 1907, which gave local education authorities the duty to provide for the medical inspection of children in public elementary schools and the power (which became a duty in 1918) to make arrangements, with the sanction of the Board of Education, for attending to their health and physical condition. The Education (Provision of Meals) Act 1906 similarly enabled authorities to provide or assist the provision of meals for children attending public elementary schools. In 1918 local education authorities were given the duty to provide for the medical inspection of children in secondary schools and the power to arrange for their medical treatment. The powers and duties of the Board of Education relating to the medical inspection and treatment of children and young persons were formally transferred under the Ministry of Health Act 1919 to the newly created Ministry of Health, but continued to be exercised, as permitted under the Act, by the Board on behalf of the Health Minister. The Chief Medical Officer of the Ministry of Health became also Chief

Medical Officer of the Board, and subsequently of its successors, the Ministry of Education (1945) and the Department of Education and Science (1964). The Education Act 1944 and Education (Scotland) Act 1945 gave education authorities the duty to provide meals and milk for pupils at maintained schools; the duty to provide medical and dental inspection in all maintained schools; and the duty to provide or to secure for children attending maintained schools all forms of medical and dental treatment other than domiciliary treatment, without cost to parents. The National Health Service Act 1946 and the equivalent Act of 1947 in Scotland enabled education authorities by arrangement to use the services of regional hospital boards and teaching hospitals.

2.72 In April 1974 the school health service in England and Wales became absorbed into the National Health Service under the National Health Service Reorganisation Act 1973. A similar change took place at the same time in Scotland. The Act transferred responsibility for providing for the health of schoolchildren from education authorities to the Secretary of State for Social Services. From its inception, the school health service pioneered development in preventive medicine at a time when the importance of prevention was not generally recognised, and achieved much success in competition with therapeutic medicine, despite recurrent economic crises. Throughout its life the Service has been particularly concerned with the needs of handicapped children; and the importance of continuing co-operation between the health, education and social services was stressed by the government in the White Paper that preceded the 1974 Act. Machinery was provided in Section 10 of the Act, which required health and local authorities to establish Joint Consultative Committees to promote the co-operative development of services.

Assessment

2.73 The construction of educational programmes for individual children with special needs depends for its success upon the accurate assessment of their needs. This was the theme of a joint departmental Circular issued in 1975.[22] It examined the composite process of discovery, diagnosis and assessment, emphasised its multi-professional character and stressed the value of informality and the importance of parental participation. It also introduced an improved set of forms for recording the educational, medical, psychological and other data required for deciding the nature of

---

22 DES Circular 2/75, Welsh Office Circular 21/7S, The Discovery of Children Requiring Special Education and the Assessment of their Needs (17 March 1975).

a child's special educational needs, and a summary sheet for use during the process of assessment, placement and review. Comments received in 1977 from local education authorities indicated their general satisfaction with the new procedures and their wish to develop them further.

2.74 In Scotland the 1960s had seen some confusion over the procedures for the assessment of handicapped children. Working parties examined the assessment of four groups of handicapped children: mentally handicapped, visually handicapped, maladjusted and hearing impaired. As a result major procedural changes were included in the Education (Scotland) Act 1969. The Act redefined special education in terms which excluded the concept of a fixed disability of mind or of body. It recognised the importance of early discovery by abolishing the minimum age at which a child could be ascertained by an education authority and established that the decision to ascertain a child was not exclusively a medical one. It required that in every case reports of psychological as well as medical examinations should be considered, with, wherever possible, the views of the child's parents and those of his teacher. It also recognised the widely held view that assessment is a continuing process.

Special qualifications of teachers

2.75 The enactment of compulsory education for blind and deaf children in 1893 was unaccompanied by any requirement relating to the training or qualifications of teachers. In 1886, when the Royal Commission on the Blind and Deaf was constituted, there existed three rival voluntary colleges which acted as examining bodies and issued certificates in the teaching of the deaf, but they were not recognised by the Education Department. The Commission recommended that training colleges for teachers of the deaf should operate under government supervision and that entrants to them should already be certificated teachers: but it made no proposals for compulsory further training or additional qualifications. In 1907, however, the three voluntary examining colleges were brought together to form a single joint examining body, and two years later the Board of Education approved its examination and recognised the diploma that it awarded. The Commission had offered no positive views about the training of teachers of the blind, but in 1907 the College of Teachers of the Blind was established as a voluntary examining and awarding body, and was also accepted by the Board. Thereafter the Board's regulations laid down that teachers in schools for the blind and deaf must obtain within two years of their appointment an approved qualification. The 1908 regulations have broadly continued to the present day [ie. 1977, ed.].

2.76 The McNair Committee (1944)[23] did not consider in detail the training of teachers of the handicapped, but the Fourth Report of the National Advisory Council on the Training and Supply of Teachers (NACTST) (1954) was devoted wholly to it. The Report recommended that with certain exceptions all intending teachers of handicapped children should, after experience in ordinary schools and some preliminary experience with handicapped children, take a full-time course of additional training. The Ministry of Education's Circular 324[24] accepted the recommendation in principle but declared it to be impracticable for the present. Teachers in special schools for blind, deaf and partially deaf pupils were already required to obtain a prescribed additional qualification within three years of taking up their appointment: whilst teachers in special schools taking classes of pupils who were both deaf (or partially deaf) and blind were required to hold a prescribed additional qualification for teachers of deaf and partially deaf children. The Circular urged that they should be encouraged to obtain also the qualification required of teachers of the blind. The requirement of an additional qualification was now extended to teachers of partially deaf pupils in special classes or units in ordinary schools.

2.77 The question of whether teachers of pupils with other kinds of disability should be required to have an additional qualification was considered again by the NACTST in 1962, but the Council concluded that the time was still inopportune. Ten years later the Vernon Committee[25] recommended that teachers of partially sighted children should (like those of the partially hearing) be required to have an additional qualification. This was also accepted in principle but not implemented. However a range of courses of in-service training continued to be available to teachers of handicapped pupils.

2.78 In Scotland following the first World War the National Committee for the Training of Teachers established a Central Executive Committee to make arrangements for the training of teachers of mentally defective children. In 1923 Kennedy Fraser was appointed to Jordanhill College of Education to be responsible for the endorsement course in special

---

23 *Teachers and Youth Leaders*. Report of the Committee appointed by the President of the Board of Education to consider the Supply, Recruitment and Training of Teachers and Youth Leaders (HMSO 1944).

24 Ministry of Education Circular 324, The Training and Supply of Teachers of Handicapped Pupils (29 May 1957).

25 *The Education of the Visually Handicapped*. Report of the Committee of Enquiry appointed by the Secretary of State for Education and Science in October, 1968 (HMSO 1972).

education. This was initially a one-year course but it had to be shortened to a term because of lack of numbers. For the next 30 years this course was the sole source of training of teachers in special education in Scotland. In 1956 a course was established at Moray House College of Education and by 1974 five such courses were available in Scotland. Until 1972 teachers of the deaf in Scotland were trained at Manchester. From that date, however, training was provided at Moray House College of Education and in 1972 the Scottish Centre for the Education of the Deaf was established in that College.

Integration

2.79 In 1928 the Wood Committee had stressed the unity of ordinary and special education. The philosophy of the Education Act 1944 had been explained during the Debate on the Education Bill by the Parliamentary Secretary (Mr Chuter Ede) in these words: "May I say that I do not want to insert in the Bill any words which make it appear that the normal way to deal with a child who suffers from any of these disabilities is to be put into a special school where he will be segregated. Whilst we desire to see adequate provision of special schools we also desire to see as many children as possible retained in the normal stream of school life."[26] Accordingly, Section 33(2) of the Act provided for the less severely handicapped (the great majority of all handicapped) to be catered for in ordinary schools, and the ensuing departmental guidance to local education authorities contained detailed suggestions as to how this might be achieved. The post-war planning of special educational treatment thus proceeded on two main assumptions: first, that special educational treatment would be required for up to 17% of the school population; and secondly, that ordinary schools would have the major share in providing it.

2.80 These intentions were not in the event fulfilled: special educational treatment came to acquire a much narrower connotation than the official guidance had indicated; and its provision in ordinary schools failed to develop on the scale envisaged. With the benefit of hindsight it is possible to discern a number of interacting reasons why this happened. In the first place the statutory framework was not conducive to a broad conception of special educational treatment or to its positive development in ordinary schools. The children for whom special educational treatment was to be provided were defined in Section 8(2)(c) of the Education Act 1944 in a way which apparently excluded those whose needs did not spring from

---

26 Parliamentary Debates: Hansard Vol 398 Col 703 (21 March 1944).

physical or mental disability. Further, Section 33(2) imposed a dichotomy between serious and less serious disabilities and, though stipulating that children with severe disabilities were to be educated in special schools wherever possible, merely permitted those with less serious disabilities to be educated in ordinary schools. The fact that ascertainment might entail resort to the compulsory procedure of medical examination and invariably meant formally assigning a child to one of the statutory categories of handicap, none of which might, in fact, fit his condition, was a disincentive to action. Inevitably ascertainment tended to be directed to children with more severe disabilities whom the law required to be educated in special schools. The widespread use of intelligence testing in determining the need for special education so far as mentally handicapped children were concerned also tended to perpetuate the notion of the separateness of such children.

2.81 Practical factors, too, impeded the development of special educational provision in ordinary schools. In the decade after the war local education authorities were hard pressed simply to maintain the fabric of the education service. Much school accommodation had been destroyed and many surviving buildings were in bad condition. Scarcity of building materials restricted work to essential needs including provision for raising the school leaving age, for the rapidly rising school population and for new housing estates, and the Building Regulations for schools allowed new building only on the basis of classes of 30 pupils in secondary schools and 40 in primary schools. Such classes were too large to enable effective special educational provision in ordinary schools to be developed. Nor was it a question of building alone. There were other shortages, for example of suitably trained teachers and other professionals required for effective assessment and treatment, and the quota of teachers then in operation did not allow for any appreciable reduction in the size of classes. For these reasons ordinary schools were badly placed to provide special education. The expansion of provision in special schools, in contrast, was greatly facilitated by the opportunities which existed for local authorities to purchase large town houses or country mansions relatively cheaply. In this way a large though not entirely adequate number of new special schools was provided, though at the price of their isolation. Since local authorities anxious to develop their special education could do so only in special schools, special educational treatment came to be associated with provision in special schools.

2.82 However, once the post-war difficulties had been overcome, developments followed which encouraged revival of the idea of special educational provision in ordinary schools. In particular, completion of the reorganisation of all-age schools in the 1960s and the progressive ending of selection for secondary education which followed the issue of Circular 10/65[27] enabled ordinary primary and secondary schools to broaden their educational programmes and to take greater account of children's individual needs. Special classes and units were established for children who had been ascertained as needing special educational treatment and a variety of forms of "remedial" education was developed for other children. Local education authorities were encouraged to minimise the formalities of ascertainment, to widen the basis of assessment and to diversify the provision. Integration became a topical subject of discussion.

2.83 Support for integration found Parliamentary expression in the Chronically Sick and Disabled Persons Act 1970, a private member's measure, which in Sections 25–27 required local education authorities, so far as was practicable, to provide for the education of deaf-blind, autistic and acutely dyslexic children in maintained or assisted schools. Although the legal description of the schools in which provision was to be made included special schools the intention was clearly that provision should, except for good reason, be made in ordinary schools. In Scotland, the same theme lay behind the report of the McCann Committee[28] on the secondary education of physically handicapped children. The Committee's report, whilst recognising that some physically handicapped children would require education in special schools, envisaged an ever-increasing number of them being educated in ordinary schools.

2.84 This partial modification of the 1944 provisions was overtaken by the Education Act 1976, which in Section 10 required local education authorities to arrange for the special education of all handicapped pupils to be given in county and voluntary schools, except where this was impracticable, incompatible with the efficient instruction in the schools or involved unreasonable public expenditure, in which case it could be given in special schools or, with the Secretary of State's approval, in independent schools. The provision, which took the form of an amendment of Section 33(2) of the Education Act 1944, would come into force on a day to be appointed by the Secretary of State. In January 1977 the Secretary of State announced that before deciding to introduce the new provision she proposed to consult widely with the educational and other interests and also to await our findings. At the same time she made clear that the new legislation had not introduced a new principle, but had

---

27 DES Circular 10/65, The Organisation of Secondary Education (12 July 1965).

28 *The Secondary Education of Physically Handicapped Children in Scotland.* Report of the Committee appointed by the Secretary of State for Scotland (HMSO 1975).

rather given a new impetus towards integrated provision, in which special schools would continue to have an important place.

CONCLUSION

2.85 Since the implementation of the Education (Handicapped Children) Act 1970 and the Education (Mentally Handicapped Children) (Scotland) Act 1974 all handicapped children, however serious their disability, have been included in the framework of special education.* Section 10 of the Education Act 1976, when implemented, will shift the emphasis of special educational provision within the framework in England and Wales significantly in the direction of greater integration and improved provision in ordinary schools. The quality of special education, however, cannot be guaranteed merely by legislation and structural change. The framework provides the setting within which people work together in the interests of children, and the quality of education depends essentially upon their skill and insight, backed by adequate resources – not solely educational resources – efficiently deployed.

---

* Also in 1970 The Transfer of Functions (Wales) Order provided for the Secretary of State for Wales to assume responsibility for a range of functions previously exercised by the Secretary of State for Education and Science, including special education.

2

Equal opportunities – for whom?

Peter Mittler

INTRODUCTION

> Children of below average ability and attainments are badly served by our educational system. The less academically able continue to suffer disproportionately from whatever chronic or acute problems affect the education service.
>
> (Department of Education and Science 1991, p.2)

The above extract from the annual report of HM Chief Inspector of Schools is based on HMI reports for 1989 and 1990. Despite the avalanche of reforms since then, his assessment still has the ring of truth. This article suggests that educational reforms have been too narrowly conceived in terms of raising standards and have not come to grips with the effects of poverty and disadvantage on children's learning and development.

ADDRESSING POVERTY

Children who fail to benefit from schooling tend to come from families and communities characterised by poverty, high rates of unemployment, poor health, sub-standard housing and family breakdown. Because schools inevitably reflect the values and priorities of society, school reform can only succeed if it is part of an integrated social policy aimed at creating a more inclusive society. Unfortunately, social and economic inequalities have widened rather than narrowed in the last 25 years and are greater in Britain than in any other country in Europe.

Although the Warnock Committee (DES 1978) broadened its remit at least tenfold from 'handicapped children' to 'children with special educational needs', it was explicitly instructed not to consider poverty or social disadvantage as a handicap. Nevertheless, it was already apparent that the majority of children embraced by the new concept of special educational needs were living in some degree of poverty. This certainly included almost all children then attending special schools for children with 'moderate learning difficulties' and many of those labelled as having emotional and behavioural difficulties. In addition, large numbers of families of children with learning and behavioural difficulties already attending mainstream schools came from the more socially and economically disadvantaged sectors of society.

The strong relationship between educational achievement and social background is taken for granted but is little understood and rarely discussed. For the last 25 years, we have conceptualised special educational needs in terms of a dynamic interaction between the individual child and the various environments in which the child is living and learning. But we still understand very little about the nature of that interaction, far less how the quality of the interaction could be enhanced to benefit children. Just as we have traditionally sought the origins of learning difficulties in the child, we now look for ways in which schools can create or complicate learning difficulties and, as a corollary, how schools might prevent such difficulties occurring in the first place. As a result, we have become sucked into a whirlwind of reform of the school, its curriculum and its organisation without considering the wider social and economic context within which schools must operate (Dyson 1997).

Our preoccupation with school and curriculum reform is at least in part responsible for our failure to develop new ideas and practices which would lead to the development of more effective partnerships between home and school. All too often, parents living in poverty have been blamed for not providing home environments conducive to learning, not being interested in their children's education and not co-operating with the school. Many people took the view that 'education cannot compensate for society' and that there was little that schools or the educational system could do to counteract the adverse effects of home and social conditions.

This stereotype of parents is refuted by studies both from the American *Head Start* programmes and from the UK. These provide many examples of schools and individual teachers finding ways of winning the support and active co-operation of parents living in very poor circumstances. Long-term follow-up of children from poor backgrounds who had been exposed to high-quality early intervention programmes in the USA showed that these had a major impact on later development in terms of educational achievement, employment and social adjustment. *Head Start* programmes were broadly based and included attention to nutrition, direct support to families and help in securing employment. Although it is difficult to disentangle which aspects of the intervention were more effective than others, it was clear that the active involvement and collaboration of parents with schools was highly beneficial to their children (Bronfenbrenner 1974; Consortium of Longitudinal Studies 1983).

In the UK, there is also plentiful evidence that the development of partnerships between home and school in inner city areas makes a significant difference to children's learning and development (Ball 1994; Osborn and Millbank 1987; Rennie 1996).

Nevertheless, the 'discourse' concerning special needs has been dominated by the interests of a minority of children whose families cover the whole social spectrum. Powerful and highly articulate parent and professional groups have lobbied successfully for children with a range of sensory and movement disorders, severe learning difficulties, autism, dyslexia, attention deficit disorders and many others. No such parent lobby has defended the rights and interests of children with moderate learning difficulties (by far the most numerous group in special schools) or those with emotional and behavioural difficulties. No comparably effective parents' organisation has been developed to represent children with special needs in mainstream schools.

It is not surprising, therefore, that both the general public and not a few legislators, decision makers and professionals still conceptualise special needs in terms of disability rather than disadvantage. Nor should it be surprising that a disproportionate share of LEA (local education authority) expenditure is tunnelled to independent special schools in this country and overseas. This is inevitably at the expense of other children who lack powerful advocates with the time and resources to take their case to the LEA, the Tribunal, the High Court and the House of Lords.

Poverty: some facts

Each year, NCH (National Children's Homes) Action for Children publishes summaries of official statistics on poverty in Britain. Here are some examples, taken from recent reports (NCH Action for Children 1998).

> The proportion of children living in households whose income was below half the average income increased from eight per cent in 1979 to 32 per cent in 1993 – an increase from 1.4 to 4.2 million children. Children and young people have now overtaken the elderly as the largest age group in poverty.

> Over three quarters of children living in lone parent families are living in poverty, compared with 18 per cent of two parent families.

> Homes where there is a disabled child have about 25 per cent fewer resources than other families with children.

> Two in three families on benefits sometimes miss meals and half have to borrow for basic necessities.

A family of four living on income support only receives between 67 and 90 per cent of the minimum for an adequate standard of living.

Health inequalities

Children from families living in poverty are highly vulnerable to ill health as well as to educational failure. We now have detailed studies of ill health in relation to social background but few attempts have been made to integrate health and educational data, although the two are complementary and interactive. The most recent information comes from an independent report commissioned by the Department of Health from its former Chief Medical Officer, Sir Donald Acheson (1998). This documents in considerable detail the huge socio-economic disparities in health and morbidity within the UK. The Preface to the Report applies as much to the field of education as to health:

> This Report addresses an issue which is fundamentally a matter of social justice: namely that although the last 20 years have brought marked increases in prosperity and substantial reductions in mortality to the people of the country as a whole, the gap in health between those at the bottom and those at the top of the social scale has widened. Yet there is convincing evidence that provided an appropriate agenda of policies can be defined and given priority, many of these inequalities are remediable. The same is true for those that exist between various ethnic groups and between the sexes.
>
> (Acheson 1998, p.v)

The following are extracts from the Report:

> Marked social class and gender differences in health and morbidity are found for major disorders, including lung cancer, coronary heart disease, stroke, accidents, poisoning and violence, suicide and undetermined injury.

> The nutritional status of poor expectant and young mothers is a matter of grave concern and should receive priority attention.

> Out of every 10,000 babies born into social class five, 99 were still born or died within the first week of life, compared with 67 for social class one. Comparable figures for death in the first year were 83 and 46 respectively. There are also marked differences in birth weight.

> Suicide rates in young men are three times more frequent in poorer than in affluent areas.

Over half of households accepted by local authorities as homeless had dependent children and a further tenth had a pregnant household member.

People from Pakistani and Bangladeshi communities were 50 per cent more likely to suffer ill health than the rest of the population. The corresponding figure for the Afro-Caribbean community was 30 per cent. These figures are mainly a direct outcome of poverty.

Children with low levels of educational attainment have poor health as adults.

POVERTY AND EDUCATIONAL ATTAINMENT

Evidence concerning the association between social background and educational attainment has been available for a long time (see Kumar 1993, for a wide-ranging review of research into childhood poverty). For example, the National Child Development Study of all children born in one week in 1958 documented the educational and social development of cohorts of children from different backgrounds over a period of many years (Davie, Butler and Goldstein 1972, Wedge and Prosser 1973, Fogelman 1983). More recently, similar results have been obtained from analyses of Standard Attainment Tasks (SATs) in relation to social background, as assessed by postal code (e.g. Sharrocks 1993).

A few results from the *National Child Development Study* provide clear illustrations of the strength of the links between social background and educational outcomes:

At age seven, five times as many children from social class five had reading difficulties as compared with those from social class one.

At the age of 11, children with fathers in non-manual occupations were three years ahead in maths and reading compared with children in social class five.

At 16, 75 per cent of pupils from social class five had below average reading and maths scores and more showed behaviour problems.

8.8 per cent of boys and 6.5 per cent of girls still leave school without any GCSE or equivalent qualifications.
    (Davie *et al.* 1972)

Half the pupils on free school meals had GCSE scores below 15 points, compared with on sixth of those not on free school meals.
    (Acheson 1998)

Similarly, there are major social class differences in the proportion of students who continue at school beyond 16 or proceed to higher education. Only around 2 per cent of undergraduate students currently come from homes where the parents' occupation is semi-skilled or unskilled, compared with 29 per cent from professional families and 17 per cent for the population as a whole. The fact that innumerable individual children who have grown up in conditions of severe hardship and adversity have nevertheless been successful both at school and in later life (Pilling 1990) should not obscure the high risk of educational failure of children living in poverty.

An OFSTED study of schools, support services and further and adult education provision in seven urban areas characterised by 'high levels of social and economic disadvantage' concluded that 'residents of disadvantaged urban areas were poorly served by the education system' (OFSTED 1993, p.6). The report highlighted a number of key findings which indicated that particularly disadvantaged children came from economically deprived communities.

Curricular planning does not address the needs of children from disadvantaged backgrounds and does not focus sufficiently on raising achievement.

Underachievement is apparent at an early stage. Many pupils never recover from early failure in basic skills.

Arrangements for learning support are poor. Schools lack expertise in initial assessment.

Much teaching is superficial and lacks pace. Atmosphere in many classrooms is good natured but neither challenges the pupils nor secures their participation.

The report concluded that while the quality and standards of work revealed by the survey are inadequate and disturbing, there is enough work of good quality in each sector to mean that the situation is not irremediable. The report recommended that 'long-term planning, improved dissemination of effective practice, carefully focused interventions and concerted efforts are required to bring about improvement'.

Ministers have tended to dismiss the association between social background and educational attainment as 'excuses', pointing to evidence that some schools in very poor areas are able to achieve better results than others. This is confirmed by an important study by Smith and Tomlinson (1989) which showed that some schools in inner city areas were able 'against the odds' to narrow the gap between children from different social backgrounds. The distinguishing characteristics of such schools included effective leadership, good staff morale and low staff turnover, teaching of consistently high quality and good teaching resources. Reviews of the school effectiveness literature in general also consistently identify high expectations and good leadership as a key feature of such schools. Unfortunately, research is still needed to identify the characteristics of those schools which are particularly effective in meeting the needs of underachieving pupils (Sammons, Hillman and Mortimore 1995).

Low expectations are a major handicap as they result in self-fulfilling prophecies. If children are not expected to achieve above a certain level, it is only a few who 'beat prediction'. Early research on streaming (Douglas 1964) indicated that teachers were greatly influenced by the social background of the child in making streaming decisions even for children with comparable levels of general ability. Once allocated to streams, children tended to live up to teachers' expectations (see Rogers 1990, for a brief review of teacher expectancy effects). In one notorious and probably unethical study, children's attainments improved dramatically after teachers were informed (wrongly) that special tests had revealed evidence of high innate ability in certain pupils (Rosenthal and Jacobson 1968).

MEETING THE CHALLENGE

As failure at school is only one reflection of a dynamic interaction of complex social problems, any government drive for 'higher educational standards' or 'school effectiveness' cannot hope to succeed if it only addresses one facet of the challenge in isolation. Schooling has to be set in a wider family, social and community context. A government that wants to tackle educational low achievement must do so as part of a wider strategy which addresses gross social inequalities and aims to reduce poverty and all that goes with it. This will not in itself have a dramatic or immediate impact on educational standards but it will lay firm foundations for such a change.

The present (Labour) government has launched some major new initiatives to combat poverty and social exclusion but these do not seem, so far, to have been effectively integrated with educational reforms which specifically aim to prevent or reduce the deep-seated educational inequalities which affect millions of our children. For example, the work of the Social Exclusion Unit has up to now been concerned with exclusion from school. There is not yet enough evidence of the 'joined up thinking' needed to develop an integrated approach to the alleviation of poverty and disadvantage in such communities and to link this to plans to address gross educational inequalities. Such an approach to community development would, for example, fund the development of links between schools and parents in order to give parents a sense of partnership in the work of the school and to help teachers to work more closely with families and community agencies.

The present (Labour) government is committed to the principle of 'zero tolerance' for underachievement but seems to have taken the view that an insistence on raising standards will automatically benefit all children, including those from the poorest backgrounds with the lowest levels of educational attainment. For example, although schools in the new *Education Action Zones* (EAZ) will be 'under new management' and will be exempted from strict adherence to the National Curriculum and from national pay scales for their staff; it remains to be seen whether they can succeed in raising the educational achievements of their pupils, particularly those who are seriously under-functioning.

If 'class size under 30' is accepted as essential to all children at Key Stage 1, why not extend the policy to all EAZ primary schools and to the end of Key Stage 2? Priority could also be given to the recruitment and training of classroom support assistants in all schools in areas of disadvantage and to the development of more effective links between schools, parents and community social work teams.

Sure Start is a more promising initiative which aims to prevent learning difficulties occurring in the first place by focusing on young children from birth to three years in areas of greatest need:

> supporting parents in promoting the physical, intellectual and social development of their children by means . . . of integrated health care, child care and play facilities, including support for children with learning difficulties and emotional and behavioural difficulties.
> (DfEE 1998, p.4)

It is not yet clear how this programme will work or how it will reach those families most in need. Earlier initiatives along these lines failed because parents resented the stigmatisation of whole communities as being unable to bring up their children without armies of support workers (Rennie 1996). We need to learn from past experience; in this connection, we can take heart from the plans for the next stage in the work of the Social Exclusion Unit which will consider:

> the current multiplicity of statutory plans with a view to developing a local planning framework for all children's services, including services for children with SEN.
> (DfEE 1998, p.34)

CONCLUSIONS

In the past, we have too easily accepted as inevitable that children from economically deprived backgrounds will not succeed as well in school as those from more advantaged sections of society. It is now time to reconceptualise special needs education within a wider social and community context in which poverty, marginalisation and social exclusion are seen as the major obstacles to children's learning. We need to transcend current preoccupations with raising standards in favour of a wider programme of social reform in which schools are working with other agencies to address the deep-seated social and educational inequalities in our society.

REFERENCES

Acheson, D. (Chair) (1998) *An Independent Inquiry into Inequalities in Health: Report.* London: Stationery Office.

Ball. C. (1994) *Start Right.* London: Royal Society of Arts.

Bronfenbrenner, U. (1974) *Is Earth, Intervention Effective?* Washington, DC: US Department of Health and Welfare.

Consortium of Longitudinal Studies (1983) *As the Twig is Bent: Lasting Effects of Preschool Programmes.* New Jersey: Lawrence Erlbaum.

Davie, R., Butler, N. and Goldstein, H. (1972) *From Birth to Seven: A Report of the National Child Development Study 1958 Cohort.* London: National Children's Bureau.

Department of Education and Science (DES) (1978) *Special Educational Needs: Report of the Committee of Enquiry into the Education of Handicapped Children and Young People* (The Warnock Report). London: HMSO.

Department of Education and Science (DES) (1991) *Standards in Education: Annual Report of HM Chief Inspector of Schools 1989–1990.* London: HMSO.

Department for Education and Employment (DfEE) (1998) *Meeting Special Educational Needs: A Programme of Action.* London: DfEE.

Douglas, J. W. B. (1964) *The Home and the School.* London: McGibbon and Kee.

Dyson, A. (1997) 'Social and educational disadvantage: reconnecting special needs education', *British Journal of Special Education* **24**(4), 152–7.

Fogelman, K. (ed.) (1983) *Britain's Sixteen Year Olds.* London: National Children's Bureau.

Halsey, A. H. (1992) *Opening Wide the Doors of Higher Education.* Briefing No. 6. London: National Commission for Education.

Kumar, V. (1993) *Poverty and Inequality in the UK: The effects on Children.* London: National Children's Bureau.

National Children's Homes Action for Children (1998) *'98 Fact File*. London: National Children's Homes.

Office for Standards in Education (OFSTED) (1993) *Access and Achievement in Urban Education*. London: HMSO.

Osborn, F. and Millbank, J. (1987) *The Effects of Early Education: A Report from the Child Health and Education Study*. Oxford: Oxford University Press.

Pilling, D. (1990) *Escape from Disadvantage*. London: Falmer Press.

Rennie, D. (1996) 'Working with parents', in Pugh, G. (ed.) *Contemporary Issues in the Early Years*. London: Paul Chapman and National Children's Bureau.

Rogers, C. (1990) 'Teachers' expectations and pupil achievements', in Entwistle, N. (ed.) *Handbook of Educational Ideas and Practices*. London: Routledge.

Rosenthal, R. and Jacobson, L. (1968) *Pygmalion in the Classroom*. New York: Holt, Rhinehart and Winston.

Sammons, P. Hillman, J. and Mortimore, P. (1995) *Key Characteristics of Effective Schools*. London: Institute of Education and Office for Standards in Education.

Sharrocks, D. (1993) *Implementing National Curriculum Assessment in the Primary School*. London: Hodder and Stoughton.

Smith, D. and Tomlinson, S. (1989) *The School Effect: A Study of Multi-Racial Comprehensives*. London: Policy Studies Institute.

Wedge, D. and Prosser, H. (1973) *Born to Fail?* London: Arrow Books and National Children's Bureau.

3

Inclusive schools, the quality of education and OFSTED school inspection

Robin C. Richmond

INTRODUCTION

The framework and schedule for the inspection of schools in England and Wales establishes a fixed set of relationships between specified outcomes of schooling and specified contributory factors. The central measure of the success of a school in the Office for Standards in Education inspection model is the comparative attainment of pupils in a school as measured by standard assessment tasks and the results of external examinations particularly GCSE grades. This chapter argues that the effect of this is to promote exclusive schooling. The progress children make is perhaps a fairer measure of the success of schools and has the potential for promoting inclusive schools. However a broader, inclusive view of the desirable outcomes of education is necessary. The inspection has to seek causes for the comparative level of attainment results from within the school: what a school does do or does not do in a specified number of its activities. The perceived central contributory cause is the quality of teaching in lessons observed in a school. However, good teachers work co-operatively to respond effectively to the full diversity of pupils' educational needs. The OFSTED inspection model does not fit easily alongside the individual needs of children and the quality of a school's response to those needs.

THE OFSTED INSPECTION FRAMEWORK AS A FIXED SET OF RELATIONSHIPS

The framework for the inspection of schools (OFSTED 1999a) is a statutory framework and applies equally to nursery, primary, middle, secondary and special schools. It is inclusive of all schools. Whatever the population of the school the same test of the quality of education provided by a school is applied. However, three separate but almost identical OFSTED handbooks of guidance on the inspection of schools in each of three phases are published: primary and nursery schools (OFSTED 1999b), secondary schools (OFSTED 1999c), and special schools and pupil referral units (OFSTED 1999d), but these allow for little diversity.

In the year 2000 short inspections were introduced, which, in contrast to full inspections, do not report fully on each subject. Short inspections are:

> for the most effective schools ... and reflect(s) the Government's commitment to less intervention in schools which are more successful.
> (OFSTED 1999b, p.2)

Any fall in standards, in national test or General Certificate of Secondary Education (GCSE) results, is likely to prompt a full inspection.

The OFSTED inspection process is in effect organisational research (Shaw 1979). It uses a planning model, a statutory framework for the inspection of schools. Planning models can be useful for researching organisations but they also have serious weaknesses in that a fixed set of relationships are suggested. The model adopted for the framework for the inspection of schools (OFSTED 1999a) has three components:

- the context of the school (What sort of school is it?);
- the outcomes of the school (How high are the standards?);
- the contributory factors to those outcomes (How well are the pupils or students taught? How well is the school led and managed?).

The framework and schedule establishes an exclusive set of fixed relationships between outcomes and contributory factors or causes of those outcomes. Figure 3.1 outlines the structure of the inspection schedule and the specified relationships which in early guidance were described as:

> the key to producing a report which evaluates the school accurately and informatively.
> (OFSTED 1995c, p.42)

In the statutory framework and schedule (see Figure 3.1) the specified outcomes are the:

- school's results and pupil's or student's achievement;
- pupils' attitudes, values and personal development.

CONTEXT AND OVERVIEW	(What sort of school is it?)
OUTCOMES	**(How high are the standards?)**
	The school's results and achievements
	Pupil's attitudes, behaviour and personal development

CONTRIBUTORY FACTORS

Quality of provision	(Teaching: **How well are pupils or students taught?**)
	(Curriculum including provision for pupils' spiritual, moral, social and cultural development: **How good are the curricular and other opportunities offered to pupils or students?**)
	(Assessment, support and guidance arrangements: **How well does the school care for its pupils or students?**)
	(Parental involvement in and links with the school: **How well does the school work in partnership with parents?**)

Efficiency and effectiveness of management

	(How well is the school led and managed?)
	Approaches to enhancing performance of staff and pupils
	Role of Governors
	Staffing, accommodation and resources
ISSUES FOR THE SCHOOL (What should the school do to improve	

Figure 3.1 The structure of the evaluation schedule (OFSTED 1999a)

In practice the central and dominant outcome specified by the framework and guidance is the standards achieved:

> the educational attainment of pupils in relation to some clear (national) benchmark.
>   (OFSTED 1999b, p.23)

Although implicit in current guidance (OFSTED 1999b, c and d), the priorities of inspection are made explicit in previous guidance (OFSTED 1995c, d and e):

> to assess what pupils know, understand and can do (that is to say, their attainment) and evaluate progress.
>   (OFSTED 1995c, d and e, p.55)

As OFSTED (1998a) reminded Registered Inspectors:

> In all that you (inspectors) do when inspecting schools, you should be evaluating:
>
> what is achieved and in particular: attainment – educational standards and whether they are high enough; and progress – whether pupils are learning well enough;
>
> how well the school promotes pupils' achievements, particularly through the quality of teaching.
>
> (OFSTED 1998a, p.9)

The standards are attainments of pupils in the subjects of the National Curriculum, particularly in the core subjects of English, mathematics and science. The standards of any particular school are judged against Key Indicators: the expected attainments of children at a given age as identified by level statements in the National Curriculum Programmes of Study and particularly comparative attainment data (OFSTED 1999b, c and d). In practice the quality of the education provided by a school has to be judged against the actual average attainments of children of the same age as measured by the national Standard Assessment Tasks (SATs) at the end of the year in which children are 9, 11 and 14 years of age and the actual attainments of children in the year in which they are 16 in the General Certificate of Secondary Education (OFSTED 1998a and 1999b). The key statistic for secondary schools is the proportion of children attaining five A* to C grades. Some Registered Inspectors will refer to the comparative proportion of pupils attaining A* to G grades as a measure of the success of the school which includes pupils with learning difficulties.

History has taken a broader view of school outcomes. The Central Advisory Council for Education (DES 1963) expressing concern at the half of all young people 'of average or less than average ability' who left school with no record of their achievements, recommended a certificate of achievement which included subject achievements but in which:

> Other qualities might also count high . . . patience and persistence in seeing a job through, for example where care matters rather than speed; general attitudes to learning, rather than performance in a single test; honesty, cheerfulness, pleasant manners and an ability to get on with people.
>
> (DES 1963, para. 258)

The recording of achievement movement (DES 1989) also recognised a broad view of curricular experience in addition to the subjects of the curriculum:

- communication skills: written, spoken and graphic;
- working with others: in and beyond school;
- organising work: preparing, planning and carrying out tasks to time;
- information handling: finding, analysing, presenting information and forming and testing hypotheses;
- personal qualities: reliability, enthusiasm.

The Warnock Committee (DES 1978) expressed a view of the outcomes of education:

> first to enlarge a child's knowledge, experience and imaginative understanding, and thus his awareness of moral values and capacity for enjoyment; and secondly, to enable him to enter the world after formal education is over as an active participant in society and as a responsible contributor to it, capable of achieving as much independence as possible.
> (DES 1978, p.5)

Attainment in the subjects of the National Curriculum and religious education is a relevant but limited view of the outcomes of schooling on which to judge the effectiveness of schools. Attainment data in the subjects of the curriculum is easily obtained in the form of test and examination scores. Consequently comparative attainment has assumed a central position for judgements about the standards achieved by schools. Test results are a limited measure of what children know, understand and can do. Additionally, the quality of the information gathered still depends on a variety of factors: not least the quality of the tests and the way they are applied. The data is made available in comparative form about individual schools in the Pre-inspection and Contextual School Indicator Reports (PICSI) received by schools and Registered Inspectors before an inspection. OFSTED claims that this data provides:

> an increasingly secure picture of the past standards achieved by the school.
> (OFSTED 1998a, p.9)

However, the use of comparative attainment data is an unfair measure of the effectiveness of a given school. For example the existing arrangements for comparison do not account for the difficulties experienced by different schools serving very different populations. Like is not compared with like. The practice implies that all schools, with more effort on the part of teachers, are equally capable of achieving as well as the highest attaining schools.

PROGRESS AS A MEASURE OF THE QUALITY OF EDUCATION

Registered Inspectors are also required to make judgements about the achievements of pupils. An achievement is defined by OFSTED as:

> the accomplishments of pupils in relation to what you (the Registered Inspector) would expect of those particular pupils.
> (OFSTED 1999b, p.23)

The judgement must take account of the progress, defined by OFSTED as the rate of learning, pupils have made as a measure of the quality of the education they receive: that is, if pupils are learning 'well enough' in the subjects of the curriculum. The OFSTED guidance on assessing progress requires inspectors to judge if:

> pupils with special needs, those with English as an additional language or who are gifted or talented make good progress.
> (OFSTED 1999b, p.33)

The judgement about the progress of pupils with SEN:

> should be summative judgements based on how well pupils are doing in relation to specific targets or goals.
> (OFSTED 1999b, p.33)

The progress made by pupils has potential as a fairer test of one measure of the effectiveness of the education provided by a school but there are difficulties. Data does not exist about the progress, or rate of learning, 'expected' of individual or groups of children. It has not been established what learning 'as well as expected' or 'well enough' actually means. The expectations of the National Curriculum Programmes of Study for any given age for example are merely expectations and have no foundation in the actual progress that any children make over a given period of time or over a Key Stage.

To obtain data on the actual progress made by pupils, information would be required about pupils' attainments on entry to a school: their knowledge, understanding and skills. Profiles of pupils' skills on entry to infant school are being recorded (Education Act 1997 Sections 15 to 18). OFSTED is paying more attention to the proportion of pupils receiving free school meals (OFSTED 2000b), a statistic which is known to have a significant association with the attainment of pupils in school and which is made available in PICSI reports. OFSTED is also exploring how prior attainment might be used as the basis for evaluating achievement. The availability of data on the incidence of free school meals allows some comparison of the attainment of schools with similar intakes (Sammons *et al.* 1994 and OFSTED 2000c). This information is now available in PICSI reports. Registered Inspectors are now required to evaluate and report on:

> how well pupils achieve taking account of the progress they have made.
>   (OFSTED 1999b, p.22)

and recognise that:

> broader indicators such as measures which compare standards with those in similar schools and value added measures are helpful in indicating the relative progress of pupils and providing a clue to how they are achieving.
>   (OFSTED 1999b, p.23)

A change of emphasis to judging the quality of education provided by a school based on the progress made by pupils would radically challenge existing OFSTED judgements about the quality of education provided by schools. However, two exemplars (OFSTED 1999b, p.26) of where Registered Inspectors are to 'pitch' their judgements for given characteristics of results and achievements suggest judgements are clearly dominated by comparative attainment.

Inspectors are directed to particular first hand sources of evidence (OFSTED 1999d) about the progress of pupils for example:

- responses in lessons;
- what pupils say about their learning;
- their written work.

The detailed curriculum planning and monitoring of the learning of children on the school register of special needs can provide good evidence on which to judge the progress of individual children (OFSTED 1999d). Responding to statements, individual educational planning and reviews of progress is the process by which teachers themselves assess what children know, understand and can do and plan future learning. However, learning targets can be concerned only with literacy and numeracy, rarely specify subjects and are often imprecise (OFSTED 1999f).

The OFSTED guidance directs inspectors to:

> find out how the school uses its entry assessment data, test and other assessment data and target setting procedures in Individual Educational

> Plans (IEPs) or in statements to set appropriately challenging targets. . . . This will help judge whether the progress made is good enough

and

> obtain different types of evidence, for example progress from records, pupils' responses to questions in class and their performance across the full range of subjects, as well as how they are learning in small groups as well as one to one teaching.
>   (OFSTED 1999b, p.34)

The framework guidance appears to recognise the value of the learner's perspective of the experience of learning: that is 'what they say about their learning' (OFSTED 1999b, c and d). The DFE Code of Practice (1994) and proposed revised Code of Practice (DfEE 2000) recognises that children with special needs should be consulted about the planning for their needs which is further but briefly developed in a SENCO guide (DfEE 1997). The learner's perspective as a means of understanding and explaining events is receiving increased attention, for example Cooper (1993) and Potts *et al.* (1995). However, in honestly gathering, representing and understanding the learner's perspective, if that is the purpose of consulting pupils during school inspections, inspectors receive little guidance.

PROGRESS AND PUPILS WITH SPECIAL EDUCATIONAL NEEDS

For pupils with special educational needs, the inspection requirements have an important difference from those for other pupils. Exceptionally, there is no requirement to report the standard of the 'attainments' to some clear benchmark (OFSTED 1999d) of children with special needs although comparison with similar schools is suggested (OFSTED 1999b, p.23). Emphasis is placed on 'achievements' and particularly 'progress' in relation to prior or earlier attainment (OFSTED 1999d). To paraphrase the earlier quotation (OFSTED 1998a), in all that inspectors do in inspecting provision for special educational needs they are evaluating:

- the progress made by pupils identified as having special educational needs;
- how well the school promotes the progress made by pupils with special educational needs.

A special school inspection report might contain wording to the effect that:

It is inappropriate to judge the attainment of pupils for whom this school provides against age related national expectations or averages. The report does, however, give examples of what pupils know, understand and can do. Judgements about progress, and references to attainment, take account of information contained in pupils' statements (of special educational needs) and annual reviews.
(OFSTED 1996, p.21)

All children are part of a continuum of educational need (DES 1978). The point at which an educational need is identified as a special educational need is arbitrary. Children perceived to have special educational needs might be defined as those children whose educational needs a school fails to meet. If it is inappropriate to assess the attainments of children with special needs against the average attainments of children of the same age as a measure of the quality of the education they receive then it must be inappropriate to do this for all children. But OFSTED does not recognise that what sensibly applies to children with special needs applies equally to all children. Consequently, unlike special schools, mainstream schools serving disadvantaged populations continue to be judged for the quality of the education they provide against schools serving advantaged populations (OFSTED 2000c). OFSTED appears to think that in these schools it is a merely a matter of the pupils 'catching up':

Many pupils will have underachieved in the past and they need to learn how to make up the lost ground.
(OFSTED 1999f, p.12)

and this is identified as a strategy to promote educational inclusion.

OTHER OUTCOMES

The Warnock Committee (DES 1978) clearly were of the opinion also that educational outcomes or goals apply to all children:

The purpose of education for all children is the same; the goals are the same. But the help that individual children need in progressing towards them will be different. Whereas for some the road they have to travel towards the goals is smooth and easy, for others it is fraught with obstacles. For some the obstacles are so daunting that, even with the greatest possible help, they will not get very far. Nevertheless for them to progress will be possible, and their educational needs will be fulfilled, as they gradually overcome one obstacle after another on the way.
(DES 1978, p.5)

Learning as overcoming obstacles is perhaps not helpful but the important issue here is fulfilling educational needs. Thomas *et al.* (1998) argue that inclusive schools are essential to an inclusive, and by definition, a fairer and just society. They state that an inclusive school is accepting of all children. The inclusive school adapts and responds to diversity by accepting, for example, any children that are at a disadvantage for any reason. O'Brien asserts that:

> The school curriculum should emphasise individuality whilst recognising and valuing communality. The affirmation of diversity and difference is an important feature of an inclusive society.
> (O'Brien 1998, p.147)

He argues that provision should be based on learning needs not learning difficulties, and claims that learning difficulties emphasise deficits which can appear intractable and imply teaching will be difficult. Three areas for understanding and analysing learning needs are postulated which provide a framework for inclusive curriculum planning. One of these is 'communal learning needs', for example 'feeling a sense of belonging; being recognised as a communicator; being respected as a person; being challenged as a learner and being afforded learning with dignity' (p.148). The reality of sub-group membership determined by gender, race, culture, disability and family identifies another, which he calls 'distinct learning needs'. Finally 'individual learning needs' are needs which other pupils do not have. Such an approach would require a broader view of the outcomes of education than that contained in the Framework for the Inspection of Schools.

The extent to which a mainstream school includes children with special needs in the educational, social and community life of the school ought to be an important outcome of the quality of education for all the children who attend the school. An important statutory responsibility of governors is to ensure that pupils with SEN join in the activities of the school along with all the other pupils who attend the school (Education Act 1996 Section 313) but there are conditions: the inclusion has to be reasonably practical, the special needs must be able to be met, arrangements must not interfere with the education of the other children in the school and resources must be used efficiently. OFSTED guidance (OFSTED 1999b) includes evaluation for example that:

> planning takes into account the differing needs of pupils such as those with specific difficulties (p.58)

the school is socially inclusive by ensuring equality of access and opportunity for all pupils (p.64)

the curricular arrangements promote inclusion of all pupils with SEN (p.69).

However, further guidance (OFSTED 2000b) tries to reconcile the criteria of an effective school as measured by national comparative attainment with the notion of an effective school as one which is inclusive of all pupils:

Effective schools are educationally inclusive schools. This shows not only in their performance, but also in their ethos and their willingness to offer new opportunities to pupils who may have experienced previous difficulties.
(OFSTED 2000b, p.4)

The extent to which entitlement and access to the full curriculum, including the National Curriculum, exists for children with special needs is a contributory factor to the progress they make. Clearly if pupils do not have access to the subjects taught then they are unlikely to make progress in those subjects. That the National Curriculum applies to all the nation's children including those with special educational needs, was clearly established in the then 1988 Education Reform Act. Inspectors are required to judge:

that, overall, pupils (with statements of SEN) have their entitlement to a broad and balanced curriculum . . . pupils have full access to the whole of the school's curriculum.
(OFSTED 1999b, p.65)

The extent to which a school is inclusive: accepting of all children, adaptive and responsive to diversity, requires a different view of the curriculum. The framework and inspection schedule, defines the curriculum as:

all the planned activities within and beyond the time tabled day.
(OFSTED 1999c, p.59)

Others have defined the curriculum in much broader terms. For example, Her Majesty's Inspectors of schools defined the curriculum as:

all those activities designed or encouraged within a school's organisational framework to promote the intellectual, personal, social and physical development of its pupils. It includes not only the formal programme of lessons but also all those activities designed or encouraged within a school's

organisational framework to promote the personal, social and physical development of its formal programme of so called extra curricular activities as well as those features which produce the school's ethos such as the quality of relationships, the concern for the equality of opportunity, the values exemplified in the way the school sets about its task and the way in which it is organised and managed.
(DES 1985b, p.7)

Booth *et al.* (1987), claiming that what pupils are offered in school cannot be 'written down on bits of paper and handed out in classrooms', refers to the importance of community:

for us curriculum encompasses the experience of pupils, teachers and others in school and the interactions between school and community, rather than merely the written intentions of departmental heads. The kind of community a school provides is as important a feature of the curriculum as the words transmitted in formal lessons. (p.xi)

Clearly the OFSTED guidance touches upon the provision for the inclusion of children with special needs preparing them and enabling them to access the life of the school and the curriculum as it is and as the law requires. There is some implicit reference to curriculum diversity in the schedule; for example, under curriculum and assessment inspectors must consider to what extent a school:

provides a broad range of worthwhile opportunities which meet the interests, aptitudes and particular needs of pupils, including those having special educational needs.
(OFSTED 1999b, p.64)

Further guidance (OFSTED 2000b) prompted by Circular 10/99 (DfEE 1999a), places greater emphasis on educational inclusion, and by implication diversity, within the existing set of fixed relationships between outcomes and contributory factors in the inspection framework (OFSTED 1999a). However, the full implications for a different view of curriculum, a broader view of the outcomes of a quality education are not possible within the existing framework, schedule and guidance.

The notion, implied by concepts of inclusion (O'Brien 1998), that the school might demonstrate a process of adaptation and change to respond to a wider range of needs, is limited to a few references in the framework guidance to differentiated teaching and differentiated learning tasks. The development of inclusive schooling is expressed government policy (DfEE 1997). However, government thinking appears to be, even after consultation (DfEE 1998a), a little confused about the implications for schools and the communities they serve, of a move from integration – associated with matching the child to the curriculum on offer, to inclusion – associated with changing the curriculum to meet the needs of the child.

A central difficulty is the nature of the National Curriculum. A national curriculum by definition is for all the nation's children. That Regulations made in 1999 under Section 363 of the Education Act 1996 allow schools to disapply aspects of the National Curriculum for 14 to 16 year olds, in order for them to participate in wider work-related learning (Qualifications and Curriculum Authority (QCA) 1999) suggests some inadequacy of the existing National Curriculum as a curriculum for all the nation's children. The Chief Inspector of Schools describes work-related learning in his annual report for 1998/99 as:

> for children who are unlikely to make a great deal of progress if they continue to study an exclusively academic curriculum.
> (OFSTED 2000c, p.2)

Clearly he perceives the National Curriculum as an academic curriculum. These developments along with such simplistic advice that:

> Teaching pupils with similar learning needs together as a group, rather than individually can be the most efficient and effective way of ensuring they reach their targets.
> (OFSTED 1999f, p.17)

are not helpful to educational inclusion. If the current National Curriculum does not include the needs of all children then it should be re-created starting with some agreement about the desirable aims of education. The law does not help in that the inclusion of children with different needs in mainstream schools must not interfere with the efficient education of other children in the school.

CONTRIBUTORY FACTORS TO THE QUALITY OF EDUCATION

Contributory factors specified by the framework and schedule which promote or inhibit attainment or progress in a school are perceived under two main headings:

- provision made by the school;
- management of the school.

The sub components of these two factors are further specified (see Figure 3.1). The central and dominant contributory factor determined by the Framework is the teaching of lessons.

In the structure of the Framework and guidance, not only are the contributory factors specified but, in addition, the model relentlessly contains within it a subtle process of definition. The process of inspection, the gathering of acceptable and available evidence as outlined in the handbooks of guidance (OFSTED 1999b, c and d) for example, defines the meaning of the factors in more detail. In addition a regular bulletin to all inspectors called 'Update', and meetings for Registered Inspectors, control and define the factors even more closely.

In the original *Framework for the Inspection of Schools* (OFSTED 1993) provision for special needs was a specified separate aspect, a contributory factor in itself, reported separately. The revised Framework (OFSTED 1995a) and the current Framework (OFSTED 1999a) sensibly integrated the features of special needs provision under other aspects of the work of the school thus emphasising that provision for special needs was a responsibility of the whole school and similarly a responsibility of the whole of the inspection team. For example, under the contributory factor of leadership and management in the previous inspection framework and guidance inspectors were advised to judge the extent to which:

> provision for SEN permeates the school's organisational and curricular structures and the practice in the school and that all staff work closely with the SEN co-ordinator.
> (OFSTED 1995d, p.107)

In the revised framework and guidance this has been replaced with a reference to:

> good schools being led and managed for all their pupils.
> (OFSTED 1999b, p.93)

Previous inspection frameworks required inspectors to report specifically on the performance of pupils with special educational needs. In the current Framework (OFSTED 1999a) there is a more general requirement to:

> Identify whether any children are excluded from making full use of the available opportunities provided by the school and evaluate reasons for this. They must judge how effective are the efforts made by schools to overcome barriers to pupils' full participation in learning.
> (OFSTED 2000d, p.17)

However, the extent to which a school provides for all educational needs, i.e. is inclusive of all the children who attend the school, is not, in the inspection framework, a measure of the success of the school in itself. The achievements and progress of the children will be the basis of the judgement. If the progress is judged to be below expectations the nature of the inspection framework implies that the children are excluded from making full use of the available opportunities at the school. Reasons for unacceptable progress are to be found in the contributory factors of the framework.

IDENTIFYING THE FIXED LINKS: THE CONTRIBUTORY FACTORS

The second priority of school inspection (OFSTED 1998b) is to evaluate:

• how well the school promotes pupils' achievements, particularly through the quality of teaching (p.9)

or paraphrased, in the case of children with special educational needs:

• how well the school promotes the progress made by pupils with special educational needs.

In the specified fixed set of relationships in the OFSTED model all the provision and actions of the staff on behalf of pupils with special educational needs however thorough, conscientious and imaginative, are only important in that they impact on the achievements of and progress made by pupils. Therefore, the extent to which a school: includes children with special needs and increases their participation in the educational, social and community life of the school; as a whole takes responsibility for the education of all the children who attend including those with special educational needs; provides entitlement and access to the full curriculum; involves parents in the educational decision making for pupils and so on, are not, in theory, of merit in themselves but only in so far as they are perceived to promote or contribute to or impact on the progress the children do or do not make.

   Clearly a school has to meet the statutory obligations, for example: provide a school special needs policy, report on the success of that policy in the parents' annual meeting, appoint a special needs co-ordinator and describe the provision for special needs in the school prospectus. The logic of the fixed set of relationships specified in the framework guidance of which the statutory requirements are identified as contributory factors, is that the statutory requirements are essential to pupils' successful progress. All those Code of Practice (DFE 1994) guidance things: a register of children with special needs, keeping meticulous records, individual education plans, parental contacts and so on, or a show piece learning support base, are similarly only of value in that they also are perceived to have an impact on the progress made by the children.

If children are judged by inspectors not to be making expected progress and some of the above provision does not exist then that will be identified as the cause of the unsatisfactory progress. If the provision does not exist and the progress made by pupils is judged to be unsatisfactory then the quality of the provision will be culpable.

Registered Inspectors report on specific SEN issues under particular aspects of the school. In addition to attainment and progress, reporting is specifically on the contributory factors of teaching: the curriculum and assessment; support and guidance, and the management sections of the inspection report. For example, the contribution of the quality of assessment, support and guidance to the educational achievements of pupils with special educational needs will include the effectiveness of the identification, assessment and meeting of individual needs; assessment of pupils' attainments and progress; provision of medical supervision and therapy, and the effectiveness of liaison with support agencies. The contribution of the efficiency and effectiveness of the management of a school will include the use of new technologies, specific grants and staff working with pupils with SEN. However, in a scrutiny of inspection reports for the reporting of special needs issues, the National Association for Special Educational Needs (NASEN 1997) found that only in one of the sections did all reports meet the reporting requirements.

A school does have an influential effect on the promotion of pupils' attainments and progress (Mortimore *et al.* 1988). A mismatch between any pupil's learning needs and the curriculum can result in difficulties in learning. If what a pupil is expected to know, understand and do is not based on the pupil's existing knowledge, understanding and skills then progress will be negligible. The Audit Commission (Audit Commission/ HMI 1992) provides a telling example of the reading attainments of pupils over four years of age in similar primary schools. Some features which lifted performance in the more successful schools were:

- the provision of extra support at Key Stage 1;
- a system of recording progress which included records of the teaching approaches;
- the use of reading tests to monitor school performance;
- a significant level of parental involvement;
- opportunity to practise reading silently every day.

In contrast, characteristics depressing performance in other schools were:

- the inadequacy of passing information about pupils with reading difficulties from teacher to teacher;
- low expectations of what pupils could achieve;
- no teacher with a school oversight of reading policy;
- the use of library and books was unsupervised;
- school to home reading initiatives were not pursued;
- pupils with serious learning difficulties were not identified;
- insufficient money for support assistance for weak readers.

TEACHING IN LESSONS AS A CAUSE OF COMPARATIVE ATTAINMENT

The major contributory factor which the Registered Inspector must identify as a cause of comparative attainment and 'expected' progress, is the quality of teaching in observed lessons:

> The quality of teaching and impact of teaching is central to inspection.
>   (OFSTED 1998c, p.45)

The National Union of Teachers, in evidence to the parliamentary enquiry into the work of OFSTED, claimed that:

> at the core of the inspection process are high stakes judgements about teaching quality which are based on snap shots of evidence . . . which take no account of the composition and attitude of classes at any one time . . . lessons observed by inspectors are atypical, the quality of which are influenced by whether teachers can rise to the occasion to give demonstration lessons . . . (consequently) inspectors are in no position to evaluate the quality of teaching taking place in normal circumstances.
>   (NUT 1998, para. 21)

Observing lessons and grading teaching has only the appearance of objectivity and therefore is accorded a status in the evidence to explain pupils' attainments and progress which is not merited. For a start, the inspectors know what the comparative attainment of the school is and what they are guided to say about it. It is in the PICSI report for the school. OFSTED criticises Registered Inspectors if grades for progress are at odds with the teaching grade on the basis that if for example progress is poor, teaching cannot be satisfactory.

The criteria provided by OFSTED (1999c) against which teaching is to be judged is vague:

- subject knowledge of teachers;
- technical competence in teaching basic skills;
- planning of lessons;
- ability to 'challenge' and 'inspire' pupils;
- effective teaching methods;
- management and discipline of pupils;
- use of time and resources;
- assessment of pupils' work;
- the use of homework.

There is no guidance on what constitutes very good, good, satisfactory, less than satisfactory or poor performance in any of these areas. No grade descriptors are given. The brief OFSTED criteria on which teaching is to be judged are not informed by any of the research into effective lessons, let alone the features associated with effective teachers. Neither does the wide experience of assessment and grade descriptors for school experience in initial teacher training inform the criteria in the OFSTED framework guidance.

For pupils with special needs (OFSTED 1999d) inspectors are directed to look for evidence in lessons that:

- work is well matched to pupils' needs;
- pupils' work is assessed against any individual learning targets;
- teachers plan and manage the work of support assistants in the lesson.

A survey (OFSTED 1996a) evaluating the effects of recent legislation and which coincided with the implementation by schools of the Code of Practice (DFE 1994) identified the features of lessons in which high-quality provision was made using in-class support for pupils with SEN. The key features were:

- good team working between support staff and class teacher (joint planning);
- support staff supplied with information about the work to be attempted;
- support staff introducing additional materials and strategies (often of use to a wider group of pupils) to enable pupils with SEN to take part;
- support staff working with a more able group to enable class teacher to focus on those who need more help;
- ensuring that pupils of all abilities are adequately challenged to solve problems, reflect, formulate strategies and act independently: it is not

helpful to a pupil if the support staff do the work for the child;
- ensuring the integration of pupils into the whole class.

In 1995 the Annual Report of the Chief Inspector of Schools (OFSTED 1995b) reported broad features of good and poor lessons frequently identified by inspectors in lessons observed in special schools. The features of good lessons were:

- careful lesson planning that took account of individual needs;
- skilful questioning;
- a balance of individual and group work;
- pupils challenged by the activities;
- pupils working co-operatively and assuming some personal responsibility for their own learning.

The features of poor lessons were:

- failure to ensure effective deployment of support staff in lessons;
- little consideration to matching tasks to pupils' abilities and learning needs; insufficient opportunity for pupils to take a degree of responsibility for their own learning;
- pupils required to listen for unduly long periods and offered too few opportunities to demonstrate their knowledge and understanding.

A preoccupation with the presence or otherwise of a limited set of observed events in lessons can be a distraction from what it is to be an effective teacher responding to the diversity of educational needs. Powell (1985b), after observing many teachers at work in Scottish primary school classrooms, claimed that

> good teaching practices cannot be had 'off the shelf': they arise from analysis of needs, from the monitoring of effects, and from imaginative and insightful attempts to meet ever changing and complex requirements. (p.36)

Commenting on how misleading appearances could be, Powell (1985a) claimed that:

> there were at least some grounds for thinking that what the teacher does may be less important than the way he does it. (p.6)

In an conclusion consistent with O'Brien's (1998) notion of 'communal learning needs', DES (1985a) in a study of good teachers, concluded that the educational development of pupils is dependent on:

the respect which (teachers) show for their pupils, their genuine interests and curiosity about what pupils say and think and the quality of their professional concern for individuals.

(DES 1985a, p.3)

Powell (1985b) demonstrated that 'there are many ways of being a good teacher and that rigidity of mind was the enemy of good teaching' (p.35). Educational change in schools is dependant as, Fullan (1992) states, on what teachers think. Collaborative working with colleagues provides opportunities for improvement and change. Good teaching involves a process of professional development involving collaborative learning close to the job. The capacity of schools to improve the quality of education for all the pupils who attend, that is become more inclusive, is as Hopkins and Harris (1997) argue dependent on a school's capacity for continuous change and development. It would seem that good teachers, and hence good schools, do see professional development and hence school improvement as an attitude and a way of working (Hewton and Jolly 1991). If it were, inspection or rather evaluation would then be something done in partnership with schools rather than to them (Boothroyd *et al.* 1996). Unfortunately, what teachers think or say receives little recognition in the OFSTED guidance.

MATTERS OF OPINION

Like all planning models, the OFSTED inspection framework, guidance and process has 'a superficial appearance of rationality and often of spurious neutrality' (Bastiani and Tolley 1982). On the surface it all appears eminently plausible that the teaching; quality of the curriculum; assessment, support and guidance arrangements; the degree of parental involvement and the efficiency and effectiveness of the management of a school, and so on, affects the quality of examination and test results.

However, the central concern is not of the limitations of planning models as means of researching or in this case inspecting organisations but that the OFSTED model contains one view of what the outcomes of education should be and then one view of the contributory causes of those outcomes. Planning models and the ways in which they are applied are value laden: as Allen points out in the Foreword to Barrs (1990), any assessment system

> is always saying something about the assessors and the assessed and the world that the assessor is seeking to bring about. It has behind it a view of learning, of the place of the child in the larger world and of what counts as worthwhile.

Desirable outcomes of education are a matter of opinion. The OFSTED view of what is worthwhile, average or above national attainment in formal tests, cannot apply equally to all the nation's children. The framework and schedule for the inspection of schools values an exclusive model of schooling in which the educational needs of many children and school responses to these are ignored. The extent to which individual schools might be developing inclusive curricular to respond to the diversity of children in the school, thereby increasing equality in the education system as a whole is devalued. However, current government education policies, for example on social inclusion (DfEE 1999a), disadvantage (DfEE 1999b) and SEN (DFE 1994, DfEE 1998a, DfEE 2000) are beginning to impact upon the issue of school inspection (for example, OFSTED 1999e, 1999f, 2000b and 2000c).

POSTSCRIPT: RESPONDING TO CURRENT INSPECTION REQUIREMENTS

With inspection a practical reality, the sensible school will recognise that education reform legislation clearly states the requirements of schools. The OFSTED framework is a test of the effectiveness of the school in implementing those requirements. Personal views about what is important for the education of children with special needs or for that matter what school inspections ought to be are irrelevant to the reality of an inspection under the current regulations. The requirements for an effective education for children with special needs are those requirements established by the government and it is those requirements on which the quality of education provided for pupils with special needs will be judged. It is probably in the interests of children with special needs that the school responds well to those requirements.

The special needs co-ordinator who manages the process of the inspection effectively and confidently will be anticipatory and proactive, rather than reactive. However, the rewriting of policy documents smacks of panic, while the maintenance of clear and consistent records of pupils' progress and teachers' practice is more considered. In any test situation, knowledge about the test; the nature, the scope of the test, the rules of the test and the criteria to be applied is essential for a successful response. The wise SENCO will keep notes during the process of the inspection as evidence of events, what is said and what is done.

Under the present arrangements for the inspection of schools, as has been discussed, the central outcome on which provision for special educational needs will be judged is the progress made by pupils identified as having special educational needs. Effective provision will include monitoring the progress of the pupils across the curriculum. The prepared SENCO, along with class or subject teachers, will therefore:

- have some good reliable and clear evidence of pupils' progress recorded;
- will ensure inspectors see this;
- will produce examples for inspectors.

The evidence about that progress will be drawn from:

- responses of pupils in subject lessons;
- written work in subject lessons and any special teaching arrangements;
- what pupils and their parents say about their learning across the curriculum.

The evidence will be recorded in writing and might include:

- contents of Statements of Special Educational Needs;
- detailed curriculum planning in Individual Education Plans;
- reviews of progress meetings;
- informed test results;
- relevant samples of work, including work from subject lessons.

(The records will include parents' and pupils' views.)

The quality of the provision for pupils with special needs and the management of that provision is not of importance in itself, only in that the quality is associated with the judgements made about the progress of the pupils. Governors are required to inform parents about the success of the special educational needs policy in their annual report. The effective school will be regularly monitoring the effectiveness of the special needs provision as it impacts on pupils' progress. Inspectors will seek causes of the progress or lack of progress made by pupils in the quality of the provision for:

- the curriculum: e.g. access, entitlement, teaching/timetable arrangements, provision for specific needs, the use of assessment;
- teaching (*the major factor to be associated with the progress made by pupils*): e.g. planning for differentiation, use of support staff, use of resources and special equipment, assessment against learning targets;
- support and guidance: e.g. pastoral support, including that for pupils with emotional and behavioural difficulties, medical supervision, therapy, liaison with support agencies;
- partnership with parents: e.g. that parents are properly informed and involved in the educational planning for their children.

and the quality of the management of arrangements for:

- leadership and management: e.g. of statutory responsibilities and the Code of Practice, policy, provision, funding, staffing, identification and assessment, reviews of progress, that school staff work closely with the SENCO and are aware of procedures, parents know the point of contact and outside support is well managed;
- staffing, accommodation and resources: e.g. additional support for Statements, the level of any designated unit staffing, that support staff work with teachers planning and recording progress, the appropriateness of staff training and experience, adaptions to accommodation for physical and sensory needs, ensuring the adequacy of technological communication aids;
- efficiency of provision: e.g. use of funds made available for SEN, any LEA devolved funding, specific grants and the deployment of support staff.

Verbal feedback is very likely to be offered to the special needs co-ordinator at the end of the inspection. This might take the form of a report under each of the relevant aspects of the framework. The effective special needs co-ordinator, during the course of the inspection, will have developed a professional dialogue with the inspectors and particularly the lead inspector for special educational needs. If this dialogue and the provision of additional supporting evidence has been successful there should be no serious surprises in the verbal report. However, the verbal report does not have to be a passive activity. Asking for further explanation of unclear points is acceptable. All the judgements by inspectors must be based on reliable evidence and if points made are not genuinely considered a fair reflection of the school then the alert SENCO will ask for the evidence on which particular judgements are based, perhaps even challenge that evidence if appropriate. In the written inspection report the quality of education for pupils with special needs and the contributory factors will not be in a separate section but be under the appropriate headings in the inspection report.

REFERENCES

Audit Commission/Her Majesty's Inspectorate (HMI) (1992) *Getting in on the Act. Provision for Pupils with Special Educational Needs: the National Picture.* London: HMSO.

Barrs, R (1990) *Words not numbers: assessment in English.* Exeter: Short Run Press.

Bastiani, J. and Tolley, H. (1982) *Rediguide 16. Research into the curriculum.* Oxford: TRC Rediguides.

Booth, T., Potts, P. and Swann, W. (1987) *Preventing Difficulties in Learning. Curricular for All.* Oxford: Blackwell.

Boothroyd, C., Fitz-Gibbon, C., McNicholas, J., Stern, E., Thompson, M. and Wragg, T. (1996) *A better system of inspection?* London: OFSTED.

Cooper, P. (1993) 'Learning from the pupils' perspectives', *British Journal of Special Education* **20**(4), 129–33.

Department For Education (DFE) (1994) *Code of Practice on the Identification and Assessment of Special Educational Needs.* London: DFE.

Department for Education and Employment (DfEE) (1996) *Guidance on School Prospectuses and Governors' Annual Reports in Primary/Secondary Schools.* London: DfEE.

Department for Education and Employment (DfEE) (1997) *Excellence for All Children. Meeting Special Educational Needs.* London: Stationery Office.

Department for Education and Employment (DfEE) (1998a) *Meeting Special Educational Needs. A programme for action.* London: Stationery Office.

Department for Education and Employment (DfEE) (1998b) *The SENCO Guide.* London: Stationery Office.

Department for Education and Employment (DfEE) (1999a) Circular 10/99 Social Inclusion: Pupil Support. London: DfEE.

Department for Education and Employment (DfEE) (1999b) *Education Action Zones: Meet the Challenge.* London: DfEE.

Department for Education and Employment (DfEE) (2000) *Consultation: Pupil Support and Access. SEN Code of Practice on the Identification and Assessment of Pupils with Special Educational Needs and SEN Thresholds: Good Practice Guidance on Identification and Provision for Pupils with Special Educational Needs.* London: DfEE.

Department of Education and Science (DES) (1963) *Half Our Future. A Report of the Central Advisory Council for Education (England).* London: HMSO.

Department of Education and Science (DES) (1978) *Special Educational Needs. Report of the Committee of Enquiry into the Education of Handicapped Children and Young People* (The Warnock Report). London: HMSO.

Department of Education and Science (DES) (1985a) Education observed 3. Good teachers. Paper by H.M. Inspectorate. London: DES.

Department for Education and Science (DES) (1985b) The Curriculum from 5 to 16. Curriculum Matters 2. An HMI Series. London: HMSO.

Department of Education and Science (DES) (1989) *Records of Achievement. Report of the Records of Achievement National Steering Committee January 1989.* London: DES/Welsh Office.

Fullan, M. G. (1992) *The new meaning of educational change.* London: Cassell.

Hewton, E. and Jolly, M. (1991) *Making time for staff development. A report for the DES.* Sussex: Institute of Continuing Development, University of Sussex.

Hopkins, D. and Harris, A. (1997) 'Improving the quality of education for all', *Support for Learning* **12**(4), 162–5.

Mortimore, P., Sammons, P., Stoll, L., Lewis, D. and Ecob, R. (1988) *School Matters. The Junior Years*. Wells: Open Books.

NASEN (1997) *OFSTED Inspection Reports and Special Educational Needs: a report from the National Association for Special Educational Needs*. Tamworth: NASEN.

National Union of Teachers (NUT) (1998) The submission of the NUT to the House of Commons Education and Employment Sub-committee inquiry into the work of OFSTED. London: NUT.

O'Brien, T. (1998) 'The millennium curriculum: confronting the issues and proposing the solutions', *Support for Learning* **13**(4), 147–52.

Office for Standards in Education (OFSTED) (1993) *Framework for the Inspection of Schools*. London: HMSO.

Office for Standards in Education (OFSTED) (1995a) *Framework for the Inspection of Schools*. London: HMSO.

Office for Standards in Education (OFSTED) (1995b) *The Annual Report of HMCI of Schools*. London: HMSO.

Office for Standards in Education (OFSTED) (1995c) *The OFSTED Handbook. Guidance on the inspection of Nursery and Primary Schools*. London: HMSO.

Office for Standards in Education (OFSTED) (1995d) *The OFSTED Handbook. Guidance on the inspection of Middle and Secondary Schools*. London: HMSO.

Office for Standards in Education (OFSTED) (1995e) *The OFSTED Handbook. Guidance on the inspection of Special Schools*. London: HMSO.

Office for Standards in Education (OFSTED) (1996a) *Promoting High Achievement for Pupils with Special Educational Needs in Mainstream Schools. A Report of the Office of Her Majesty's Chief Inspector of Schools*. London: HMSO.

Office for Standards in Education (OFSTED) (1996b) *Update*, Nineteenth issue, Summer.

Office for Standards in Education (OFSTED) (1996c) *Update*, Twentieth issue, Winter.

Office for Standards in Education (OFSTED) (1998a) *Inspection '98. Supplement to the inspection handbooks: continuing, new requirements and guidance*. London: OFSTED.

Office for Standards in Education (OFSTED) (1998b) 'Judging attainment'. An occasional paper on the relationship between inspectors' judgements and school results. London: OFSTED.

Office for Standards in Education (OFSTED) (1999a) *Inspecting schools. The Framework*. London: OFSTED.

Office for Standards in Education (OFSTED) (1999b) *Handbook for inspecting primary and nursery schools with guidance on self evaluation*. London: Stationery Office.

Office for Standards in Education (OFSTED) (1999c) *Handbook for inspecting secondary schools with guidance on self evaluation*. London: Stationery Office.

Office for Standards in Education (OFSTED) (1999d) *Handbook for inspecting special schools and pupils referral units with guidance on self evaluation.* London: Stationery Office.

Office for Standards in Education (OFSTED) (1999e) *Lessons Learned from Special Measures. A report from the Office of Her Majesty's Chief Inspector of Schools.* London: OFSTED.

Office for Standards in Education (OFSTED) (1999f) *Raising the attainment of ethnic minority pupils: School and LEA responses. A report from the Office of Her Majesty's Chief Inspector of Schools.* London: OFSTED.

Office for Standards in Education (OFSTED) (1999g) *The SEN Code of Practice: three years on. The contribution of individual education plans to the raising of standards for pupils with special educational needs. A report from the Office of Her Majesty's Chief Inspector of Schools.* London: OFSTED.

Office for Standards in Education (OFSTED) (2000a) *Annual Report of Her Majesty's Chief Inspector of Schools. Standards and Quality in Education 1998/1999.* London: Stationery Office.

Office for Standards in Education (OFSTED) (2000b) *Evaluating educational inclusion. Guidance for inspectors and schools.* London: OFSTED.

Office for Standards in Education (OFSTED) (2000c) *Strategies to promote inclusion. Improving City Schools. A report from the Office of Her Majesty's Chief Inspector of Schools.* London: OFSTED.

Office for Standards in Education (OFSTED) (2000d) *Update*, Thirty-second issue.

Powell, J. L. (1985a) *The teacher's craft.* Edinburgh: Scottish Council for Research in Education.

Powell, J. L. (1985b) *Ways of teaching.* Edinburgh: Scottish Council for Research in Education.

Potts, P., Armstrong, F. and Masterton, M. (eds) (1995) *Equality and Diversity in Education 1. Learning, Teaching and Managing in Schools.* London: Routledge.

Qualifications and Curriculum Authority (QCA) (1999) *Wider Opportunities for Work-Related Learning at Key Stage 4.* Sudbury: QCA Publications.

Sammons, P., Thomas, S., Mortimore, P., Owen, C., Pennell, H. and Hillman, J. (1994) *Assessing school effectiveness: Developing measures to put school performance in context.* London: OFSTED/Institute of Education University of London.

Shaw, K. E. (1979) *Researching an organisation.* Nottingham: University of Nottingham.

Thomas, G., Walker, D. and Webb, J. (1998) *The making of the inclusive school.* London: Routledge.

—————— 4 ——————

Investigating inclusion: an evaluation of a teachers' professional development course

Janice Wearmouth

INTRODUCTION

Recent United Kingdom government documents promote an inclusive approach to children's education, for example the statutory guidance offered in 'Inclusion: providing effective learning opportunities for all pupils' in *Curriculum 2000* (QCA 2000). Professional development for teachers has also featured strongly both in government policy documents, for example the SEN Action Programme (DfEE 1998a), and in press releases from the Secretary of State for Education. However, there appears to be a lack of discussion about the kind of teacher professional development that supports the change in school organisation and practices that is necessary to implement inclusive practices. At the same time, the Standards and Framework Act 1998 has clarified the role and function of local education authorities (LEAs) in relation to the way in which they support schools to improve pupils' learning. Section 127 of the School Standards and Framework Act 1998 required the Secretary of State to publish a Code of Practice on LEA-School Relations to which LEAs and schools must, by law, pay regard. In this Code the role assigned to LEAs is that they are:

> the main means through which external support and intervention can be applied . . . through the provision of services, advice and challenge to help schools raise standards.

Offering schools 'advice and challenge . . . to raise standards' of learning may include, at LEA level, guidance on, and support for, particular kinds of teacher professional development designed to promote inclusion in schools.

In 1997 Birmingham City Council, as part of its initiative on city-wide inclusion, sponsored a group of its teachers in a distance-learning professional development course which focused on developing inclusive curricula through reflective practitioner research. An evaluation of the work of the teachers on this course offers evidence that a course of this kind can support the development of inclusive practices which reflect the principles in the statutory guidance of 'Inclusion: providing effective learning opportunities for all pupils' in *Curriculum 2000* (QCA 2000). It also indicates how LEA inclusion policy can be embedded in teachers' practices and school organisation. Additionally, it points to other, broader factors not addressed in statutory guidance given in the 'Inclusion' statement which nevertheless are prerequisites to adopting inclusive approaches in schools.

MOVES TOWARDS INCLUSION

Since the 1981 Education Act reaffirmed the principle of integration, the law has made provision for all pupils to be educated in mainstream schools with three provisos: that their needs can be met there, it is compatible with the education of peers and with the 'efficient use of resources'. However, many writers have noted how the integration of pupils who experience difficulties in learning has often been accompanied by 'bolt-on' provision which has not affected the structure and organisation of the school system. Dyson (1997), for example, has argued that an 'army' of special educators has 'colonised' rather than transformed mainstream schools. OFSTED (1996) noted that planning programmes for individual pupils has tended to remain peripheral to the planning of the whole-school curriculum rather than becoming an integral part of it. The development of 'more inclusive' approaches to meeting pupils' special learning needs is one of the topics on which it is proposed to offer 'expanded guidance' in the new Code proposed for 2001.

Fullan's (1992) explanation for the failure to incorporate changes such as development towards inclusion is that insufficient note has been taken of the current practices and needs of those teachers who are expected to put the consequences of change into effect. Fullan and Hargreaves (1996) have identified a number of problems in what they see as the struggle between reform stemming from teachers themselves and reform that is centrally imposed. One major problem is that teachers are 'dangerously overloaded' as a result of innovation in the curriculum, the implications of the changing profile of class groups for more complex planning and preparation, the emphasis on greater accountability, and the explosion of knowledge with which teachers are expected to keep pace. They identify a number of factors that cause concern to teachers. Among these are: 'the effects of special education legislation and the mainstreaming of special education students into regular classes' (p.3).

There is a further explanation for this failure to include pupils. The most recent attempt to bring about reform in education has created tension by imposing incompatible demands on teachers and schools. The creation of a competitive climate in education predisposes to an individualisation of pupils' difficulties in learning which can attract additional resources. This does not sit comfortably with policy initiatives on 'inclusion'. The dominant perspective on the difficulty in learning faced by a pupil in school is that these problems exist within the pupil themselves – the so-called 'medical', 'deficit' or 'within child' view of difficulty. Any 'special educational need' identified on a pupil's Statement of Special Educational Need must be matched to provision in a quantifiable, prescription-like way. It is not easy to conceptualise individual learning plans which are designed to address 'deficits' in the child alone and which can be embedded into the whole-school curriculum.

The statement on inclusion in *Curriculum 2000* has been statutory since September 2000. It sets out three principles for developing a 'more inclusive curriculum':

A   Setting suitable learning challenges . . . teachers should aim to give every pupil the opportunity to experience success in learning . . . and . . . should teach the knowledge, skills and understanding in ways that suit their pupils' abilities.

B   Responding to pupils' diverse learning needs . . . by:
(a) creating effective learning environments
(b) securing their motivation and concentration
(c) providing equality of opportunity through teaching approaches
(d) using appropriate assessment approaches
(e) setting targets for learning.

C   Overcoming potential barriers to learning and assessment for individuals and groups of pupils. Curriculum planning and assessment for pupils with special educational needs must take account of the type and extent of the difficulty experienced by the pupil . . . . Teachers should, where appropriate, work closely with representatives of other agencies . . .

A brief scrutiny of this statement shows that it appears to incorporate two different perspectives on the root of pupils' difficulties in learning. On the one hand the principles espoused for providing 'effective learning opportunities' for all children include a recognition of the way in which the context may influence a child's education, and thereby contribute to the reduction to, or increase in, learning. The references to 'creating effective learning environments' and 'providing equality of opportunity through teaching approaches' imply a source of barriers to learning outside the pupil. On the other hand, Section C of this document which refers to 'pupils with special educational needs' adopts the within-child, 'deficit' model: 'A minority of pupils will have particular learning and assessment requirements which . . . are likely to arise as a consequence of a pupil having a special educational need or disability . . .'.

What is clear from these discrepant models is that considerable thought will have to be given to professional development for teachers if they are to conceptualise how to raise mean achievement levels and include all pupils. One way to reconcile the contextual source of barriers to learning with that of the characteristics of the individual child is through the 'interactive' model of difficulties in learning. In this 'interactive' model a child's difficulties are seen to arise as a result of the interaction between what the child brings to their learning and what is offered to them through the method of teaching, the content of the particular activity, the supporting resources, and so on (Wedell 2000).

IMPLICATIONS OF THE MOVE TOWARDS INCLUSION FOR TEACHERS' CONTINUING PROFESSIONAL DEVELOPMENT

The move towards a focus on inclusion in government policy implies that schools as institutions will need to change (Clark, Dyson and Millward 1997). Appropriate continuing professional development for teachers which is intended to promote change in schools needs to take account of both teachers' beliefs and attitudes (Fullan 1992) and of the interactive model of difficulties in learning which embraces both the environment and the characteristics of the individual child. Issues raised by McNiff (1993) in her discussion of two different approaches to teacher professional development are particularly relevant to a consideration of how change in the direction of inclusion might be embedded in practice. She outlines the assumptions underlying a traditional 'line-management' approach to teacher professional development and contrasts these with an alternative, teacher-centred 'shifting centres model'. The underlying assumptions of the traditional approach she identifies as:

- the existence of a theoretical or procedural 'standard model' which teachers are invited to adopt for themselves;
- the duty of the teacher educator to advise on the best course of action;
- the institutional focus of teachers' activities with the aim of improving institutionalised procedures and pedagogy;
- an objectives approach where research is predetermined as working towards specific outcomes within institutionalised procedures;
- research operationalised in terms of skills, offering checklists of expertise.

This traditional model is clearly compatible with central government's competency approach to meeting acceptable 'standards' in schools. However, this traditional approach will not necessarily do anything either to reduce the gulf between external agencies imposing 'standards' on schools and practitioners who may feel marginalised by the procedures, or to embed any significant change towards inclusive practices.

The second model noted by McNiff is much more clearly compatible with bringing about embedded change in schools of the sort that is conducive to moving towards inclusion. This model is teacher-centred and rests on an underlying assumption that pedagogical practice is able to metamorphose. Some of the assumptions underlying this approach are that:

- teachers should be accorded the status of 'experts' in their own institutions, and, as such, should be encouraged actively to draw out theories from their own practice, and to develop these personal theories through their reports of their work. Those eligible to 'validate' their work should be peers and 'clients';
- everybody in the school community is involved in the process of the development of their own, and each other's learning;
- the focus of the research is the understanding of oneself with the aim of improving the process of education within a particular institution;
- learning is a process, not a product. There is no 'end-product' other than new questions and the beginning of new learning;
- research is to be seen as a form of pedagogy which explores new approaches with the potential to benefit the school community.

One example of practitioner research is that of action research. Action research stresses the contribution of the learning context to the difficulties experienced by the learner. Nothing improves simply as a result of assessment, but only if it leads to some action. As a method of enquiry action research is driven by a focus on the process of teaching and learning, aiming, as it does, on bringing about change to practice.

PROMOTING INCLUSION AT LEA LEVEL

Policy at any level within the education system should be influenced by the policies operating at any other level in the same domain as well as general overarching policies in education. For example, policy within a specific department in a secondary school should reflect and be compatible with general school policy through the School Development

Plan. This plan should also reflect and be compatible both with LEA and national policy. Some LEAs have promoted particular initiatives to support inclusion which have had a strong impact on schools, teachers and individual students. An example of such an LEA is Birmingham City Council.

The approach of Birmingham LEA has been to develop an inclusive policy intended to achieve the aim of offering as many pupils as possible the opportunity for education in a mainstream school alongside peers from their local community. 'Inclusion' is seen as vital to the well-being of the city and its inhabitants:

> inclusion – the economic prosperity of the City and its social and moral climate depend on the reality of social inclusion in a multi-ethnic, multi-faith community. Educational inclusion is clearly a central pillar of our commitment to equality of opportunity.
> (Birmingham City Council Education Department 1988)

A number of strategies were designed both to meet schools' concerns about including all pupils and to put into operation the Council's inclusive principles. Two examples feature strongly in this chapter: the 'Supported Places Initiative' and 'New Outlooks, Framework for Intervention', a behaviour support strategy. Under the 'Supported Places Initiative', the additional support required to support pupils identified as experiencing serious barriers to their learning was calculated on set criteria for specific types of perceived needs, converted into a cash amount and transferred to the school. The school then made its own arrangements for the required provision. In 'New Outlooks, Framework for Intervention', the interactive model of pupils' difficulties in the area of behaviour is clear. Principles for action in schools where pupil behaviour was perceived to be a cause for concern were underpinned by three assumptions:

> Children's behaviour is central to the learning process and is an intrinsic element of education

> Problems in behaviour in educational settings are usually a product of a complex interaction between the individual, school, family, community and wider society

> Social interaction based on mutual respect is a fundamental basis of an optimal educational environment

and six 'practical principles':

- Equal opportunity and maximum inclusion
- Respect for all
- Positive approaches to behaviour
- Organisational consistency and improvement
- Working with children and parents
- Provision from appropriate and effective agencies.

'New Outlooks, Framework for Intervention' adopted the view that the most appropriate response to concerns about pupil behaviour is to look to the learning environment for an explanation and solution:

Schools can exercise control of the environment at whole-school level by reviewing a series of issues that present themselves in the following areas:

- Curricular organisation
- Curricular content
- Physical Environment
- Pastoral Structure
- Staff Support
- Development and Training
- Recruitment
- Listening to Children
- Working with Parents.

Three levels of intervention were to be adopted. Level 1 'followed an expression of concern' and was marked by an audit of the behavioural environment and a plan of action to meet identified difficulties (Behavioural Environment Plan). Level 2 followed a continued audit and BEP together with an Individual Behavioural Plan. Parents were involved at this stage. At Level 3 outside agencies were also involved.

PROMOTING INCLUSION THROUGH TEACHERS' CONTINUING PROFESSIONAL DEVELOPMENT

One of the ways in which Birmingham City Council has promoted its inclusive strategies in schools is by sponsoring teachers on continuing professional development courses. In 1997, the LEA sponsored ten teachers on a distance-learning course the aim of which was to promote inclusive practices through practitioner research of the kind outlined in McNiff's second model above (p.76). During the year teachers were to research issues within their own work situation.

A letter was sent by Birmingham LEA to all schools inviting teachers to apply to study the course. More teachers applied than the number for which there were places. The criteria applied by the Council for selection of students were:

- personal potential to reach the required academic level of a Masters module;
- representation from a cross section of sectors: nursery, infant, junior, secondary, mainstream and special;
- experience of working with pupils who experienced difficulties that warranted additional provision;
- evidence that participation in the course would promote inclusion in the teacher's school;
- a letter of support from the head.

Of the ten teachers registered for study on the course, nine were female, one male. One was a teacher of nursery-aged children, three of infants, four of juniors, one of pupils of all ages in a special school, and one of secondary. They held posts at different levels of responsibility: one head, one deputy head, four Special Needs Co-ordinators, one Behaviour Co-ordinator, one local authority support service teacher, and two classroom teachers.

The course on which the teachers enrolled comprised the experience of planning, carrying out, analysing and writing-up three ten-week projects designed to explore ways of identifying, analysing and reducing barriers to learning. Project One consisted of a close study of the learning of an individual or group of learners, in which the focus was on the representation and understanding of the perspective of the learners themselves.

Project 2 consisted of three parts which together comprised an action research cycle:

(i) the analysis of an existing curriculum (or a section of it) and the identification of barriers to pupils' learning within it;

(ii) based on the earlier analysis, the planning and implementation of a curriculum initiative which is designed to reduce these barriers and increase the participation of a wider group of pupils;

(iii) an evaluation of this development work with suggestions for further improvements.

Project Three consisted of an investigation into an aspect of institutional, community, local or national policy of interest to the student. Given the focus on inclusion in the course, teachers were expected to make the link between policy and individual pupils' experiences of learning and to ask what are the possibilities for change in educational contexts. Students' projects were required to proceed in a systematic manner, exploring and justifying sources and methods of gathering evidence with which to illuminate issues and discuss possible answers to questions investigated. The choice of data-gathering methods in the course tended to be qualitative and favour the questionnaire, interview, use of field notes, diaries and direct observation.

EVALUATION CRITERIA

The criteria employed here to evaluate the impact of the course relate to the principles of inclusive practices outlined in the statement on inclusion in *Curriculum 2000* as well as to staff development in schools. This statement was not statutory in 1997 when the course was undertaken by the students. However, a post hoc comparison of students' conclusions from their own practitioner research against a current policy document is important to establish whether this kind of teacher professional development has generic relevance. It also has the potential for revealing other salient aspects of inclusive practices which are not addressed in the principles of the statement. The evaluation criteria are, therefore:

- the extent to which conclusions drawn from individual teachers' coursework relate to the principles of inclusive practices outlined in the general statement on inclusion in *Curriculum 2000*;
- the significance of generic issues relating to prerequisites of inclusive educational practices which were discussed in the research projects but not addressed in the 'general statement on inclusion' in *Curriculum 2000*;
- the importance of conclusions about staff development in schools.

CONCLUSIONS DRAWN FROM THE INVESTIGATIONS IN RELATION TO THE PRINCIPLES FOR INCLUSION

The statement on inclusion sets out three principles for inclusion: (A) Setting suitable learning challenges, (B) Responding to pupils' diverse learning needs and (C) Overcoming potential barriers to learning and assessment for individuals and groups of pupils. The most significant conclusions regarding these principles were drawn from investigations carried out with two particular groups of pupils:

- those identified as experiencing serious difficulties in verbal communication and supported in schools through Birmingham's Supported Places Initiative. For this group of pupils the most significant conclusions were the result of Project One research: investigations of pupil perspectives;

● those identified as the focus of disruptive behaviour for whom plans were made following the LEAs Framework for Intervention. The most significant conclusions here were those drawn from Project Two work: action research designed to improve an aspect of the curriculum.

Conclusions from projects related to difficulties in communication

The projects that focused on pupil perspectives enabled teachers to reflect on all three principles in the statement on inclusion.

A *Setting suitable learning challenges*

It would be easy to assume that pupils who experience great difficulty in expressing themselves are incapable of being active agents in their own learning and in relationships with others. However, some teachers concluded that it is possible to work through a child's strengths and preferences to develop language skills, rather than focus on weaknesses. One class teacher observed that a particular pupil wanted to be 'one of a crowd' rather than 'singled out' by overly obvious attention from the classroom assistants, and that the activities he was successful at were less closely supervised. Activities that he initiated were sometimes obvious only through close observation. The integration assistants felt he needed support with 'everything at the moment to keep him on task'. This clearly conflicted with the pupil liking to be the same as peers and with the perception of his mother and his class teacher. The latter two felt he was becoming more independent whereas the integration assistants did not.

All time in the learning environment needs to be meaningful for the learner. Trying to understand classroom experiences from the pupils' view showed that classroom tasks often need to be more relevant to the pupils' needs. In the mainstream classroom it seemed that little was done to differentiate the work expected of some pupils. Without an adult to explain things individually they were left with little that they could accomplish alone. Clearly there is a fine balance to be drawn between encouraging independence and setting work at an appropriate level. One teacher observed:

> More could have been done to make the task more relevant to J's needs. For example, alternative problems could have been written on the board, a separate work card could have been given to him or a larger calculator.

> J was not able to start work until the teacher came to direct him. He did occupy himself, but not with an educationally valuable activity.

Another teacher's observations allowed her to recommend the following to encourage further inclusion:

- further differentiation to make some areas of the curriculum more accessible;
- planning and preparation time between the integration assistant and the class teacher;
- more differentiated resources;
- speech development through activities that pupils enjoy;
- encouragement of alternative forms of pupil expression;
- structured activities for the development of fine motor skills;
- more use of the computer to help learning and co-ordination;
- building his esteem through music and physical activities.

B *Responding to pupils' diverse learning needs*

One project investigating pupil perceptions indicated that, in classrooms where pupils experience difficulties in understanding what peers and teachers say to them, and also in expressing themselves verbally, a great deal of attention needs to be given to planning activities and to the teachers' modes of communication. The class teacher of 'Alan', who had been in a language unit prior to starting in a mainstream infant school, developed her approach to his learning through a process of trial and error. She had found that it helped him to understand and hold his attention if instructions given to his peers were repeated or broken down into steps by the support assistants. She had also ensured that all classroom activities were accompanied by a Rebus symbol and word card which were available to the whole class. This was for two reasons: so that Alan could develop an understanding of a symbolic system of communication and also so that this system could be shared by his peers. Additionally she had produced a pictorial grid from which the children might choose different activities. Alan used this successfully to make his choice of favourites. This overt method of enabling choice gave an indication of his strengths and weaknesses. His preference was for the more physical type of activities:

> When using his pictorial grid to choose activities he first chose the beads (in preference to the writing) and then the computer. Near the end of the session when asked to choose between construction and cutting he chose the former. All the activities he chose require less fine motor skills than the ones he rejected. When asked to choose his favourite activity he pointed to the computer symbol.

In recent years it has often been assumed that withdrawal from mainstream lessons is 'anti-inclusive', that it devalues learners and contravenes their right to be included in the mainstream class. However, another teacher concluded that the facility to provide withdrawal groups may be one legitimate way for a school to respond flexibly to diverse learning needs. Being withdrawn from groups does not necessarily socially isolate or stigmatise any particular pupil if this arrangement is part of the usual arrangements to support the learning of all pupils. One of her pupils was withdrawn for four sessions a week for forty minutes with five other children for a structured reading programme, and he was also withdrawn by the integration assistant for phonics, spelling, handwriting, memory games, reading activities and writing. A prime motivating factor in this investigation was to find out how the boy felt about this situation, whether it was hindering social interaction with children who were not in his withdrawal group and what kind of progress he was making. Withdrawing children into a separate quiet working area for particular reasons was a regular feature of the school for everyone: it appeared that although he was withdrawn for the majority of the week, it did not interfere with his social relationships in the playground. His social group was not restricted only to those other children that were withdrawn alongside him:

> J was part of a large group of boys – about eight in total. They all were very vocal debating the game they were to play and the rules they must follow. One child took the lead in organising the rest of the group and J followed his instructions carefully. The children that J played with were of mixed academic ability.

The boy stated that he liked everything about school. However, the teacher concluded that attention must be given to the possibility that a high level of support from adults may lead to a sense of 'learned helplessness' (Garber and Seligman 1980) and a passive approach to learning.

C *Overcoming potential barriers to learning and assessment for individuals and groups of pupils*

Clearly an understanding of the context in which any assessment is made is essential. A medicalised diagnosis of a particular kind of problem should not lead to the presupposition that a pupil will not thrive in a mainstream environment. For several pupils it became apparent that an assessment carried out by a speech therapist which focused on the child's deficits constituted only one aspect of factors which need to be addressed. 'Alan', for example, was being educated in accordance with his personal learning needs and the wishes of his immediate family rather than being grouped together with others who experienced difficulties in communication. For his teacher the course highlighted the importance of classroom-based assessment of individual pupils' needs. It became obvious that Alan was capable of intelligible verbal interaction and that immersion in regular, everyday patterns of language used by peers could support the development of his communication skills.

Conclusions from projects related to behaviour

A *Setting suitable learning challenges*
There is a very fine line between work that is sufficiently challenging to sustain pupils' interest and that shows respect to pupils' feelings of self-worth and dignity but is not so demanding that it is impossible for pupils to tackle. In all three pieces of research on ways to encourage more positive pupil behaviour inappropriate work was provoking pupil frustration and behaviour that disrupted the work of peers. Differentiation consisting only of supplying low-level demeaning tasks was perceived as patronising and devaluing by pupils.

The work for one project was undertaken in a two-form entry inner-city primary school in an area of urban deprivation with a high level of poverty among the local families. Concern had arisen because a few pupils, all boys, were regularly being punished with exclusion from classroom activities, and therefore from access to the curriculum, as a result of behaviour which was seen as disruptive to the work of peers. The framework for action was clear: investigate the learning environment in the first instance to identify barriers to the learning of these pupils. The appropriateness of this response was validated at the stage of interviews with the pupils when one of the boys, 'Damien', remarked that the school could help him best by offering him work he could do. In-class observation revealed that this particular child often was unable to complete work given to the others. Damien's alienation from writing-related activities was given overt expression when he:

> just stopped working altogether after being reprimanded by the teacher for getting crayons to colour the pictures . . . lay his head down on the desk, swung on the chair and played with his watch. He showed no interest until a (practical) activity was introduced into the lesson.

Teacher expectation of Damien was low and the boy's work was so poor that there was no possibility of taking any pride in achievement:

> his books are untidy with spaces left, crossing out, graffiti, etc. which all add to his lack of pride in his work.

Meeting the perceived barriers to Damien's learning involved modifications to the learning environment and to the teaching approach which would also benefit every other child in the class:

- room prepared in advance, resources distributed (ensuring that every child would have a sharp pencil and that there were crayons, an eraser and a glue stick on every table), room arranged, visual aids displayed, work written up on board, worksheets ready;
- revision of previous work and understanding;
- teaching the lesson, children sitting around me (I was careful to get those who were easily distracted close to me where I could prompt their attention back to me), visual aids . . . both purchased and teacher-made . . . at eye level;
- checking understanding of subject;
- answering questions;
- giving out tasks (at different levels of difficulty, both conceptually and textually) to groups X, Y, Z . . . I gave more time to group Z to go through the work, reading it with them to ensure understanding;
- moving around room, checking work, answering queries, offering assistance, encouraging, etc.;
- concluding lesson with a revision of what had been achieved.

B *Responding to pupils' diverse learning needs*

It became clear in some research that disaffected, apparently less able pupils wanted to do well too. Attention to the learning environment meant that two pupils who might otherwise have been categorised as 'deviant' had avoided this descriptor which might have had continued deleterious effects on them. However, any short-term improvement in the behaviour of pupils might not be sustainable without deliberate and consistent attention to that environment. This included improving the organisation of classroom resources.

For all pupils the kind of reward offered was clearly very important. What 'works' for one may be irrelevant to another. Damien in particular was keen and eager to display his knowledge and understanding in lessons where he could respond verbally, but reacted negatively to suggestions of written work:

> With the geography activity I saw him recoil at the sight of the worksheets, due, I believe, to his inability to read the sheets . . . . He appeared to be almost afraid of the written word.

Damien needed to be given work which is differentiated but not obviously so different from that of peers that it is stigmatising and alienating. He also needed additional support to develop his reading and spelling with some one-to-one assistance to work through tasks set, either from the teacher or from supportive peers.

C Overcoming potential barriers to learning and assessment for individuals and groups of pupils

If, from a belief in equality for all pupils, the intention is to treat all children in fundamentally the same way, there is a clear implication of differentiation through encouraging a diversity of means of access to the same task. Differentiating teaching approaches in these projects included taking into account the variety of personal interests among pupils in the group, different presentation of activities for example, offering the use of audiotape facilities to pupils with a visual impairment, and the expectation of responses to activities through different modes, for example the use of information technology with pupils who found it difficult to express themselves in writing. Behavioural programmes were instituted in some cases with targets and rewards adjusted to be meaningful to individual children. Additionally there was scope to increase the active involvement of children in decision making regarding their own learning even when the behaviour of those children was challenging or when communication was very difficult.

Additional issues related to inclusive educational practices

The teachers' conclusions from Project Three which focused on policy issues led them to consider a number of issues outside those addressed by the principles of the statutory statement on inclusion. Some of the features associated with the successful implementation of inclusive policies have implications for considering prerequisites to inclusive approaches.

- The beliefs and positive attitudes of individual people often in influential positions. Inclusive policy was driven by personalities in the local authority and in schools alongside legislation and national guidance. Teachers' research clearly reflected the findings of Fullan and Hargreaves that practitioners' attitudes strongly influence the degree of success with which new initiatives are implemented:
  - The Chief Education Officer had clearly been influential in changing thinking from 'structures to process' as is shown by the fact that policy documents in various areas connected with inclusive education are set out as 'strategies' for action rather than simply sets of principles.
  - The successful inclusion of a pupil with physical disabilities into a secondary school was the product of a happy coincidence of a local authority intent on pursuing inclusion, a governing board and school staff all persuaded that including physically disabled pupils was a positive step towards a direction in which the school should be moving, and, immediately afterwards, a physically disabled pupil

wishing to join the school and parents who supported her wishes.
- In one infant school it was the head teacher who was influential in initiating a particular form of organising provision for pupils with Statements before the Supported Places Initiative was introduced. She established the principle that in-class support provided through Statements should be spread fairly across all classes; there should be two children with Statements in each class with the addition of a support teacher for half the week, thus enabling the Special Needs Co-ordinator to work across the school and with outside agencies.

• Consultation with and commitment of all concerned with the implementation of the policy:
- In one infant school there was a willingness to include pupils who experience difficulties in learning but the staff had a number of serious reservations:
  (i) the school might gain a reputation as one for 'problem children';
  (ii) the large numbers of children whose perceived difficulties were seen to warrant statements might militate against 'quality' teaching appropriate to their needs;
  (iii) other children's progress in learning might be adversely affected by the presence of large numbers of those experiencing difficulties;
  (iv) staff would be placed under undue stress.

• Good information for parents and the use of parents as advisers:
- The open involvement of parents in the 'New Outlooks, Framework for Intervention' behaviour strategy emphasised parents as stakeholders in this initiative in contrast with the previous behaviour policy.
- The teachers raised a number of issues related to the fact that schools' admissions policies gave priority to pupils with statements:
  (i) information is available to parents but not always accessible;
  (ii) parents with means and access do participate and are aware of their rights.

• The need for awareness raising and professional development:
- Transfer of pupils from special school to mainstream was seen to imply a need for further training for mainstream staff.
- All those involved with the local authority's inclusive policy, particularly head teachers, needed to be fully acquainted with all its implications.

• The importance of the stability of resources to ensure pupils receive the support they needed in inclusive settings:
- Strong features of the Supported Places Initiative were the bringing of resources into schools to enable flexible provision for all pupils' learning needs. This initiative allows schools themselves to make

decisions related to the use of resources, enabling provision for all pupils to benefit. The removal of Statements from two pupils was perceived by one school as a measure of the success of this initiative. However, the funding of the SPI was a continuing debate; annual decisions on funding do not allow long-term planning of provision by a school.

- Sound organisation of support within the classroom situation:
  - There was strong potential for further development of the role of integration assistants as a major resource to support inclusion policy.
  - Mainstream staff needed to be much more aware of the challenges faced by support staff if the pupils they support are fully to access the educational and social life of mainstream schools.
- A recognition of the demanding role of the classroom teacher:
  - Criticising teachers for apparent weaknesses in classroom organisation and teaching approach is easy; it is much more difficult to sustain enthusiasm, patience with pupils, some of whom may have arrived in school troubled and aggressive or withdrawn, and time-consuming prior preparation for lessons every day.

CONCLUSIONS ABOUT STAFF DEVELOPMENT IN SCHOOLS

Staff development aimed at promoting inclusive practices is particularly pertinent at the present time. The government Green Paper *Excellence for All Children* (DfEE 1997) which claimed to promote an inclusive approach referred to professional development for teachers and others but was almost wholly preoccupied with the administration of the Code of Practice, the identification and assessment of pupils, meeting needs, the quality of teaching, the raising of standards and so on. The kind of professional development appropriate for encouraging change in schools is distinctly lacking in the following press release from David Blunkett, the Secretary of State for Education:

Professional development is all about making sure that teachers have the finest and most up-to-date tools to do their job. This means, above all, developing the most important elements in teaching – the extraordinary talent and inspiration of so many teachers and, especially, their classroom practice which is central to our shared determination to raise standards.

Professional development can take place in a variety of settings and can take many forms. What matters is that it is of high quality and focused on teaching and learning. I want to help teachers to share their expertise in and out of the classroom, and to become the learning managers of the future.

It may be that individual schools will be left to consider for themselves what kind of teacher professional development will best support inclusion.

In evaluating features of effective professional learning as evidenced by the group of teachers it is useful to examine conclusions drawn from other studies of professional development. From work undertaken in 154 schools in 53 LEAs, Hewton and Jolly, (1991) concluded that:

- effective development becomes an attitude and a way of working rather than a series of specially organised events;
- a notion of the school and classroom as a workshop for staff development (development can and in most circumstances should take place on or close to the job as a normal part of school life);
- LEAs have a major role to play in encouraging and monitoring development in schools;
- five professional training days play only a small part in most schools. The major thrust comes from what teachers, schools and LEAs together contribute.

Development as a way of working

The importance of this kind of research to teacher professional development should not be underestimated. Since the 1981 Education Act and increasingly in recent years there has been a much greater emphasis on integrating pupils identified as 'having special educational needs' into mainstream schools. Despite this, as noted above, in many schools provision to meet their learning needs has been 'bolted-on', rather than conceptualised as an integral part of the whole-school curriculum. Models of research which involve the teacher as researcher in their own school, collecting and analysing data and sharing with a community of learners and enquirers can aid the transformation of educational practices. As Pacino (2000) and Cochran-Smith and Lytle (1993) argue, teacher research can bring about social change and alter classrooms in terms of the knowledge base and pedagogy. Clearly this is important to the area of inclusion. Cochran-Smith and Lytle go on to argue that local knowledge can be generated within a community of learners and shared with the larger public community of educators. In Birmingham, local knowledge was generated and shared about how to include pupils in schools, how to set suitable learning challenges, respond to pupils' diverse learning needs and overcome potential barriers to learning and assessment for individuals and groups. Experiences and transactions among teachers and pupils within the context of schooling shape theory-building:

collective theory is grounded in data from authentic classroom contexts and mediated by the explicit personal theories of all those involved.
   (Patterson *et al.* 1990, p.45, quoted in Pacino 2000)

The kind of practitioner research seen in one of the investigations, Project Two, as appropriate to investigating ways to reduce barriers to individuals' learning is action research. It necessarily constitutes an 'insider' form of research study because it adopts the perspective of the practitioner in a systematic enquiry that is collective, collaborative, critical, and undertaken by the participants of the enquiry. In their role of researchers these teachers used their own site as the focus of their study. Action research often implies development of practice that is oriented in a particular direction (McKernan 1996). Within the course this direction is towards greater inclusion of pupils in the mainstream of education.

The purpose of research at the level of the individual pupil is to give regular feedback about the 'goodness of fit' between teaching approaches, resources and pupils' learning. In recognising the significance of the interaction between the learner, the task and the context action research provides a way of assessing levels of need which does not assume an individual's learning difficulties result solely, or even mainly, from problems within the child.

The classroom as a workshop for staff development

Decontextualised staff training with the aim of producing change in schools has a very poor record of success, as we have seen. The teachers in this study who looked first at the environment for barriers to their pupils' learning before assuming a defect in the children themselves, intervened on the basis of what they identified and then evaluated what they had done, enabled some pupils to remain in the classroom who otherwise might have been excluded.

The investigations demonstrate that some barriers to inclusion in relation to groups of children who are not popular in mainstream schools can be overcome through attention to the learning environment and an emphasis on the interactive model of pupils' difficulties. This is particularly important for pupils identified as the focus of disruptive behaviour.

THE ROLE OF THE LEA

Recent government policy development has aimed to strengthen the links between policy-making at local education authority and school level.

The Code of Practice on LEA – School Relations (DfEE 1998b) is intended to:

> sit alongside Education Development Plans . . . EDPs are focused on the positive role of the LEA in working with schools to set targets and identify priorities for raising standards; the Code is focused on . . . establishing the LEA's functions of leadership, support and intervention without undermining the responsibility of schools for their own performance.
>
> (DfEE 1998b, Preface, para. 12)

Section 6 of the School Standards and Framework Act places the duty on each LEA to prepare an EDP which should set out the LEA's proposals for raising the standards of education for the children in its area and to improve the performance of its schools. LEAs should 'aim to agree their EDPs with schools and other partners in order that all should understand and accept the part they have to play in achieving the plan' (Preface to the Code, para. 36). Regulations made under Section 46 of the School Standards and Framework Act (1998) allow LEAs to retain funds centrally to support their role in relation to schools in four areas, including that of special educational provision. The lead taken by any LEA in negotiating an interpretation of initiatives such as inclusion and in promoting change in schools through particular kinds of teacher professional development is therefore crucial to support the way schools put such initiatives into operation.

The inclusive approach of Birmingham LEA is clearly apparent at every level in these projects. Teachers concluded that the use of 'New Outlooks, Framework for Intervention' had a significant effect on supporting pupils to remain in classrooms. The 'Supported Places Initiative' enabled pupils identified as experiencing difficulties in language and communication to access the curriculum with the help of support assistants whose mode of working can be tailored to fit the needs of the individual pupil and school.

CONCLUSION

In the current competitive climate, pupils who experience difficulties in learning are not popular in some schools. Nevertheless, in all areas of the UK, schools are increasingly being expected to move towards an inclusive approach to providing for all pupils' learning needs.

In sponsoring teachers on a course which focuses on practitioner research, Birmingham LEA recognised the importance of linking the professional development of teachers which aims at embedding change in practice with the development of a local authority inclusive approach to education. This approach is compatible with the School Standards and Framework Act's requirement (1998) that LEA policy development should be compatible with that of schools. It is difficult to see how the necessary changes in practice can take place and be sustained without professional development of this sort.

ACKNOWLEDGEMENTS

I would like to thank the teachers whose work has been cited in this chapter, Birmingham City Council Education Department for their co-operation, and my two colleagues, Robin Richmond and Gwenn Edwards, for their support and valuable contributions to the whole project.

REFERENCES

Birmingham City Council Education Department (1998) *Achieving in Partnership*. Birmingham: Birmingham City Council Education Department.

Birmingham LEA (1993) *Birmingham SEN Handbook*. Birmingham LEA.

Birmingham LEA (1998) 'Report of the Chief Education Officer. Education Committee LEA Inspection Report'. Birmingham City Education Department Minutes of Education Committee, 10 February.

Birmingham LEA Education Department (1998) Inclusion strategy workshop, 17 March. Birmingham LEA Education Department.

Clark, C., Dyson, A. and Millward, A. (1997) *New Directions in Special Needs*. London: Cassell.

Cochran-Smith, M. and Lytle, S. L. (1993) *Inside/Outside: Teacher research and knowledge*. New York: Teachers' College Press.

Department for Education and Employment (DfEE) (1997) *Excellence for All Children*. Sudbury: DfEE.

Department for Education and Employment (DfEE) (1998a) *Meeting Special Educational Needs: A programme for action*. Sudbury: DfEE.

Department for Education and Employment (DfEE) (1998b) *The Code of Practice on LEA – School Relations*. London: DfEE.

Dyson, A. (1997) 'Social and educational disadvantage', *British Journal of Special Education* **24**(4).

Fullan, M. (1992) *The New Meaning of Educational Change*. London: Cassell.

Fullan, M. and Hargreaves, D. (1996) *What's Worth Fighting For in Your School?* New York: Columbia Press.

Garber, J. and Seligman, M. E. P. (1980) *Human Helplessness: theory and applications*. New York: Academic Press.

Hewton, E. and Jolly, M. (1991) *Making time for staff development. A report for the DES*. Sussex: Institute of Continuing Development, University of Sussex.

McKernan, J. (1996) *Curriculum Action Research*. London: Kogan Page.

McNiff, J. (1993) *Teaching as Learning*. London: Routledge.

Office for Standards in Education (OFSTED) (1996) *Implementation of the Code of Practice*. London: HMSO.

Pacino, M. A. (2000) 'Transforming educational practices through action research', Paper presented at Qualitative Evidence-based Practice Conference, Coventry University, 15–17 May.

Patterson, L. *et al.* (1990) *Teacher research: from promise to power*. New York: Richard C. Owen.

Qualifications and Curriculum Authority (QCA) (2000) 'Inclusion: providing effective learning opportunities for all pupils', *Curriculum 2000*. London: QCA.

Wedell, K. (2000) Audiotape Programme 1 in *E831 Professional Development for Special Educational Needs Co-ordinators*. Milton Keynes: Open University.

those who experience difficulties. In Chapter 8, Norwich and Daniels (1997) report on a project aimed at increasing teachers' 'active engagement' with pupils with special learning needs in primary schools through the use of such groups, termed 'Teacher Support Teams for Special Educational Needs'. They note how responding to increasing diversity among the pupil population necessitates open-minded flexibility on the part of individual teachers. This flexibility can be strengthened in discussion with others who may be able to offer a range of possible courses of action in facilitating pupil learning and help to restore a sense of balance in difficult situations.

For schools, knowing when and how to interact with the vast array of outside professionals who may become involved with a particular child and family can be very important to the pupil's welfare and progress. There is a long history of problems in the exchange of information between agencies and of disputes over responsibility for offering particular services. Different agencies operate to different legislative frameworks with different priorities and definitions of what constitutes a need. There is common acknowledgement (Dyson, Lin and Millward 1998) of the need for closer co-operation between agencies which exist to support children in difficulties and their families or carers. In Chapter 9 Roaf outlines ways in which a school special needs co-ordinator might conceptualise ways of working effectively with outside agencies, areas that might be prioritised for action by the three primary care agencies and what might be done to reduce the frustration generated by these.

In many schools there has been debate around appropriate grouping arrangements for delivering the formal curriculum for a number of years now. Collaboration between peers is often recommended as one way in which pupils who experience some kind of difficulty in learning in a mainstream class might be included without risking being stigmatised for being different in some way from other pupils. There is a logic in assuming that a more competent peer might be able to scaffold the learning for another who is experiencing difficulty (Bruner 1985). We might also agree with the view that having to explain ideas to a peer helps to clarify thinking. Recent research has, however, provided mixed support for the assumption that collaborative grouping arrangements between pupils is necessarily valuable. In Chapter 10 Mercer notes the conditions under which pupil learning appears to be the most successful: pupils have to use language to make plans explicit, make decisions and interpret feedback; decision making is shared between partners; learners are paired with friends; the activity is designed to encourage co-operation; pupils are explicitly taught the ground rules for collaborative activity in the classroom. A special kind of grouping that is adopted in some schools is that of peer tutoring in reading. In Chapter 11 Merrett notes that peer tutoring can be seen as enhancing the function of the teacher as facilitator and developer of the whole initiative, rather than detracting from the teacher's role. He describes a strategy which must be carried out on a regular daily basis which is intended for those students who have acquired some skill in reading, not for those who have not yet begun.

The notion of pupil self-advocacy is supported by international law, and by British legislation. There is conflict between these rights and practice in many schools for a number of reasons. Teachers are professionals in the education industry. It is their role to make informed decisions based on their knowledge and experience. In many school staffrooms, attempting to claim the high moral ground by appealing to colleagues to respect the rights of the individual child is insufficient to justify pupil participation in decision making processes. It is important, therefore, that a greater degree of pupil participation can clearly be seen to be effective. While the Code of Practice encourages the participation of pupils in decision making it does not provide guidance on how this should be achieved. Questions about access to and the validity of pupils' personal viewpoints are left unanswered. An outline of ways in which pupil self-advocacy has been encouraged in schools in one local education authority is offered in Chapter 12 by Gersch. In the following chapter, Chapter 13, Batheaston School offers some interesting ideas about how to encourage children's ownership of a school behaviour policy. Among other factors Coulby and Coulby highlight the importance of the underlying assumption of the model of the child as active agent in their own learning, capable and worthy of making responsible decisions.

Avenues for participation need to be established before proper account can be taken of pupils' views. In Chapter 14 Harris-Cooksley and Catt describe an initiative where an outsider was able to offer support to a classroom teacher to foster the mutual respect between teacher and pupils needed to establish classroom conditions conducive to more effective pupil learning.

Chapter 15 reports on an initiative which illustrates how the pressure to maintain equilibrium in the school system may militate against change which addresses the needs of individual pupils who experience difficulties in learning. Wearmouth describes how a special needs co-ordinator in an upper school introduced laptop computers to assist pupils who experienced difficulty in expressing themselves in writing. When the pupils using the word processing program on the new laptops began to produce written work of a higher standard than some other pupils, this disruption to the anticipated hierarchy of achievement appeared to cause considerable feelings of discomfort.

In the debate around inclusion in mainstream schools a crucial issue is that of whether there is ever any place for a 'special' sector within the education system. A group of pupils about whom teachers often express very serious concerns are those with complex physical disabilities. Some may feel that some students are so vulnerable that the overriding consideration for them is a protective environment where both individual care needs and education can be considered. In Chapter 16 Pickles highlights a number of issues to be taken into account by mainstream schools attempting to include this group of pupils: the need to maintain a clear focus on the individuality of the pupil; the kind of teamwork that it is necessary to orchestrate between the members of a support network; issues relating to withdrawal from the mainstream classroom; long- and short-term target setting; the embedding of individual programmes devised for particular pupils into classroom activities for all pupils; the distinction between learning targets and therapeutic targets.

One perspective on the process of 'differentiation' is that it comprises a straightforward way of enabling access to the broad balanced curriculum in order to meet individual young people's learning needs in school. However, there is a serious dilemma between offering alternative provision to accommodate a diversity of needs and interests and supporting pupils' entitlements to a common programme. In Chapter 17 Garner, Hinchcliffe and Sandow reflect on the differences of opinion among teachers in one school that were generated by the imposition of the National Curriculum on pupils assessed as 'having severe learning difficulties', offer practical suggestions for shaping Programmes of Study to fit the needs of individual pupils, and discuss the view that a focus on the developmental curriculum in schools designated as catering for pupils 'with severe difficulties in learning' is incompatible with a focus on the National Curriculum.

REFERENCES

Bruner, J. (1985) 'Vygotsky: a historical and cultural perspective', in Wersch, J. (ed.) *Culture, Communication and Cognition: Vygotskian Perspectives.* Cambridge: Cambridge University Press.

Department For Education (DFE) (1994) *Code of Practice on the Identification and Assessment of Special Educational Needs.* London: DFE.

Dyson, A., Lin, M. and Millward, A. (1998) *Effective Communication between Schools, LEAs and Health and Social Services in the Field of Special Educational Needs,* Research Report No. 60. London: DfEE.

Teacher Training Agency (TTA) (1998) *National Standards for Special Educational Needs Co-ordinators.* London: TTA.

alternative to traditional approaches to the whole school approach.

The school espoused a particularly strong values position based on a commitment to the participation of all its students in a full entitlement curriculum in which individual and collective achievement were celebrated. Full participation of all pupils was the distinguishing characteristic of the school's policy and was regarded as an essential component of a strategy through which a positive whole school ethos could be created in which all pupils would be able to realise their potential. In this respect the school could be regarded as seeking to realise inclusive values; though it should be noted that, unlike the inclusive schools we shall consider in the next chapter, Downland did not include in its population pupils with marked learning or physical difficulties who might otherwise have been placed in a special school.

Despite these limits, Downland had a number of distinctive features in respect of its attempt to realise its values which we believed made it distinctive at that time. The school had consciously adopted a language within the school which avoided, as far as possible, the traditional terminology of special education. There had been a deliberate attempt to purge the internal language of the school of discriminatory terms and the use of what was regarded as language which conveyed any negative images of groups or individuals. Instead a vocabulary based on potential and achievement was used to encourage a dialogue at all levels within the school which emphasised success, achievement and participation. Thus in place of the traditional notion of 'pupils with special educational needs' the school used instead the term 'children who challenge the curriculum'. In this way the school was concerned to convey the extent to which it regarded difficulties with learning as fundamentally a problem related to the nature of the curriculum rather than as characteristics of individual learners. The school was concerned to establish the principle that resolutions of learning difficulties should be seen in terms of the development of the curriculum and the approaches that were adopted to teaching and learning rather than through the creation of a separate system in which something 'special' was done for individual pupils. In this sense, when pupils were experiencing difficulties in accessing the curriculum they were regarded by the senior management as 'opportunities not threats' in that they acted as key indicators of the effectiveness of the quality of the teaching and learning that was taking place throughout the school, and the extent to which the curriculum had been sufficiently developed to accommodate a range of learning styles. A metaphor of 'energy' was thus encouraged to describe the relationship between teachers and students. Students were to be given headroom: 'they have to find their own levels' (teaching and learning co-ordinator). All pupils were seen as being imbued with an enormous potential which it was the task of the school to release. The head teacher, who had been instrumental in introducing this particular vocabulary, reinforced this view regarding pupils experiencing difficulties as 'not a problem but an opportunity' for the school; he was concerned that the discourse of the school reflected this view and that such pupils were not seen as 'threats' to an existing *status quo* but as the key indicators of the effectiveness of the school in 'unleashing' potential.

To reinforce the adoption of this powerful rhetoric, further attempts were made to challenge traditional conceptualisations of special needs. This was reflected in the way that the school sought to structure its response to those pupils who were 'challenging' the curriculum. The school's teaching and learning policy document for example sought to convey an alternative view of how pupils should be viewed:

> there is not a distinct and identifiable group of pupils who always and exclusively have SEN . . . and . . . SEN only exists in contexts . . . the classroom organisation and delivery of the curriculum will have to be considered.

This view of special educational needs as a dynamic phenomenon which was located within the context of the classroom and the curriculum rather than within individual pupils was central to the way that the school sought to ensure entitlement and participation. Exclusionary forms of provision such as withdrawal were eschewed in favour of a dual approach of in-class support and curriculum development led by a charismatic co-ordinator of teaching and learning. This attempt to avoid any form of segregation was expressed thus: 'The policy of the school is that all educational needs are best met in mainstream classes' (Staff Handbook).

Instead of seeking to identify a group of SEN pupils, and to make them the subject of a distinctive system, all pupils were seen as having individual needs and a potential which was capable of being released within the context of the curriculum offered in the mainstream classroom. The principal vehicle for achieving this, the extensive support system, was not concerned, therefore, with supporting an identified group of pupils but with working with the whole class and the teacher. Class teachers were encouraged to experiment with different ways of working with support teachers, and support teachers, who were also all class teachers, were encouraged to see their role as offering advice, 'not on what is taught but ways in which it can be taught'. A member of staff involved in providing support described this process as one of 'trying to slide in ideas', whilst at the same time asking themselves: 'Does what I am observing help me improve my own teaching?' The process was regarded as one in which all staff were able to review and reflect on their *own* teaching as they observed and participated in the teaching of other staff. The overall goal of the support teachers was, therefore, to ensure that every pupil in the classroom was accessed to a full curriculum and that they achieved their full potential.

Support teachers also fulfilled other vital roles. They were able to attend meetings in departments which they supported, offering feedback on the quality of teaching and the extent of differentiation within lessons. They were also charged with providing the teaching and learning co-ordinator with feedback on the effectiveness of the school's approach to diversity. The teaching and learning co-ordinator was central to this process and his role was clearly different from that of many SENCOs. He had been appointed by the head teacher with whom he clearly shared a common philosophy in respect of how teaching and learning should be conducted. He had an extremely flexible role which enabled him to observe any aspect of the teaching and learning in the school as well as to marshal the support system which the school had established. This gave him a unique insight into the way the school's values were being realised. He became, as he was later described by the head teacher, the 'conscience of the school', having an overview of teaching and learning, able to identify any particular difficulties that were emerging either at the level of individual pupils, staff or departments and to provide feedback into the school's development programme.

Interestingly, the teaching and learning co-ordinator, who was a long-standing member of the staff, was not ingrained in the traditions of special education, having been a subject teacher before taking on this role, a background which perhaps freed him from some of the preconceptions which sustain many traditional conceptualisations of special education. He also had a clear view of his role as relating to the improvement of teaching and learning across the school rather than as being directed at the needs of a select group of pupils. He saw his role as one of development and change which involved the collection and dissemination of information from all areas of the school, reporting on successes and failures in attempting to realise the school's avowed values; this enabled him to design both whole school development activities as well as group or individual staff support. The process of staff development was regarded as integral to the realisation of the values of the school, and an extensive staff development programme with a focus on improving access and achievement had been implemented by the head teacher immediately on his appointment.

It was in this context, therefore, that we identified Downland as the clearest example of a 'new approach' to special educational needs in mainstream schools, one which appeared to extend the standard systems and approaches of the whole school approach. If a new approach was to be successful in reconciling the issues and dilemmas which we believe underpin provision of special needs education in mainstream schools then we hoped that evidence of its success would be found in Downland. As we have suggested, our initial impressions were that there was indeed a reconstruction of provision and practice; that the values of participation and equity were being realised in the radical approach of this school.

Accordingly, we undertook a more detailed analysis of provision and practice to establish whether our initial impression was correct. Further data were collected through a series of interviews, and observations across most aspects of the school's functioning. Policy documentation was analysed and key architects of the policy of the school were tracked, observed and interviewed on a number of occasions. In this way we sought a deeper understanding of the school and the ways that it sought to achieve the realisation of its values.

As our analysis of the data proceeded and our understanding of the school deepened, we became increasingly aware of certain factors which caused us to question the extent to which Downland was successful in its ambitious project. As we developed an understanding of how the school operated we were able to identify a number of trends and developments which suggested to us that the resolution which had apparently been achieved was not as stable as it at first appeared. We came to the conclusion that the apparent stability was temporary and that many of the issues we have referred to were in fact merely in a state of partial equilibrium, ready at any moment to re-emerge within this school. The school's avowed aim of realising a powerfully articulated set of values was also being undermined by other developments within the wider educational field as well as because of certain internal tensions.

In particular it seemed to suggest that the problems experienced in Downland related to a failure to take account of two key factors which make the provision of special needs education in mainstream schools so problematic. Firstly, we suggest there was a failure to develop, in conjunction with the change in language and views about teaching and learning, an actual technology within the school through which both the pedagogic, curricular and organisational problems of responding to diversity could be resolved. Secondly, we believe the school failed to appreciate the extent to which the changing socio-political climate was actually requiring schools to be able to demonstrate precisely the extent to which they were making 'special' provision for statemented and registered pupils. In our continuing analysis of Downland, therefore, we will focus on three main themes: the re-emergence of traditional notions of special education; the reproduction of traditional special needs structures; and the issues of inclusion and exclusion. We will take each of these in turn.

THE RE-EMERGENCE OF TRADITIONAL NOTIONS OF SPECIAL EDUCATION

The values position of this school was one based very firmly in notions of commonality, potential and success. It was, except for a small number of pupils attending special schools, the only comprehensive in a small town and therefore in a limited sense offering something akin to an 'inclusive' education. This view was articulated at every opportunity: within formal staff meetings; at the interface between the staff and the pupils; in discussions with parents; and at governors' meetings. It was used to convey to visitors, such as ourselves, both a view of the school and also the basis on which any dialogue should be conducted when discussing the school. Its emphasis was on the potential which resided in every individual and which could be 'unleashed' given appropriate circumstances. The culture of the school was premised around a positive and achievement-driven ethos which was expressed in all the operations of the school. Discipline problems, for example, were dealt with in terms of the degree to which particular pupil behaviours had failed to match this view of achievement, value and individual self-worth.

The issue for us was to establish the extent to which this rhetoric was not only shared by all the staff but actually realised at the level of the classroom. What became apparent as we considered this feature of the school was the extent to which this rhetoric was actually layered in terms of the rate of its absorption and use and the extent to which it actually impacted on practice. We became increasingly aware that the further one moved from senior and middle management the more obvious it was that this rhetoric lost its power. Initially this was obscured from us as many class teachers made a point of referring to the use of the particular language as a part of an institutional tradition – a tradition which they saw as in part a chore but which they were happy to endorse, as it formed such an important aspect of the way the school worked. As we undertook detailed classroom observation and gradually became more integrated into the school, it became obvious that the rhetoric was severely weakened at classroom level both in its use and much more importantly in the actual practices that were being utilised by the teachers. We found for instance that at a general level some teachers were struggling to implement the new vision. In many classrooms there was not the evidence of a systematic implementation of the principles of differentiation which were central to the realisation of its inclusive values. The curriculum was in many cases still being delivered in a traditional way with those students experiencing most difficulty receiving varying degrees of support from either the class teacher or the support staff when they were present. These pupils, far from opening the window on the effectiveness of existing teaching and learning strategies, were in effect producing a growing resistance on the part of some staff, as was evidenced in a return to practices which were reminiscent of those associated with more traditional notions of special education.

We observed particular resistance at a number of specific levels. Firstly, there was resistance from some long-stay members of staff in particular departments who argued that their subject discipline required the maintenance of a traditional approach. This was evidenced by the pressure exerted on the senior management team (SMT) to reintroduce streaming in one of the core subjects of the National Curriculum, backed up by the claim that exams results would decline if mixed ability grouping was forced on the department. Secondly, there were some members of staff who pre-dated the head teacher, maintained an adherence to the old values of the previous regime and saw no justification in changing their practices. Finally, there was resistance from some members of the girls' school who made no secret of the fact that they felt the provision made in their former school, based on the withdrawal of small groups of pupils, provided a much more appropriate education for those with difficulties than the system on offer in Downland. They regarded the system at Downland as having much to commend it at the level of values and principles but as failing to deliver in practice and therefore being deleterious for a number of 'vulnerable' pupils.

In all of these cases we can see the existence of an alternative values position being argued and voices suggesting a return to a more traditional view of special needs education, suggesting that instead of the consensus which the SMT portrayed there was in fact considerable diversity of view within the staff group. This presented an obvious challenge to the SMT who depended on a consensus among the staff if their vision was to be fully realised. Their response was surprisingly traditional. When we presented our evidence of this resistance their reaction was in terms of the existence of certain 'unreconstituted' elements within the staff who, for a variety of reasons, were beyond redemption. It was suggested to us that this was just the residual resistance of a small minority who were unable to respond to the new challenges of the adoption of an approach based on equity and participation. We noted that those who had expressed resistance, especially those from the former girls' school, had been increasingly marginalised within the new school, occupying few positions of responsibility.

This ability to suppress or sideline resistance within the school was in contrast to the SMT's inability to deal with external challenges. Two examples illustrate this and reveal the extent to which the school's internal values system can be undermined by a hostile external environment and factors in the wider socio-political context. In Downland there were a number of pupils with statements of special educational needs, largely for specific learning difficulties. These statements had included reference to individual non-specialist support. This was at odds with the ethos of inclusion and non-withdrawal from the mainstream classroom. Initially, the response of the school had been to provide non-specialist support in the context of the classroom, but this had been challenged by the parents of the statemented pupils who demanded that the requirements of the statement were fulfilled. The response of the school was to set up an alternative system in which the statemented pupils were to become the responsibility of a former member of the girls' school and to receive the 'entitlement' of their statement through her specialist teaching.

Clearly, the school, forced by the pressure of parents and the existing legislation, had been obliged to modify its overall response. The solution was in effect to 'hive off' a small sub-group of pupils in an effort to retain the liberal values of the school for the overwhelming majority by leaving the existing system intact. This may well have been a genuine attempt by the school to maintain its participatory and inclusive principles whilst at the same time bowing to the inevitable pressure of parents who were supported by a statutory entitlement to something that was 'special'. However, it pointed to an interesting dilemma for the school. The system was based on individual potential and made no provision for needs that could not be met in the context of the ordinary class. When confronted by a need that was apparently demanding of something additional to that on offer in the ordinary class the school reverted to a very traditional 'special' response.

The second example relates to the impact of the Code of Practice on the school. The Code requires schools to demonstrate in a number of formal ways that they are taking steps to identify, assess and respond to the 'special' needs of pupils that cannot be met in the mainstream class. The formality of the assessment and recording procedures of the Code and its requirement for differentiation of pupils with special needs from their peers, was in many ways counter to the principles of Downland and presented a significant dilemma for the school. At Downland the emphasis was on meeting individual needs and releasing potential for all pupils within the context provided by the mainstream classroom. This is an admirable notion but does not, as we have seen, address the issue of what happens when that potential proves difficult to release in a mainstream classroom or when it is challenged by parents. It was clear to us that in some classrooms the system was not meeting the individual 'needs' of many of the pupils, not just those with statements. As a result of the Code, the school would have to demonstrate that it was effectively responding to the 'needs' of these pupils. In subsequent interviews it was not surprising to find the teaching and learning co-ordinator expressing considerable ambivalence about the Code because of the extent to which it required the school to create a distinctive special needs system and structure in place of the embedded approach they had sought to reflect their values of participation and equity. For the teaching and learning co-ordinator this represented the very antithesis of the approach the school was wanting. He saw in the Code a resurrection of a deficit model, a view of special education which was concerned with the failure and inability of a pre-determined population of pupils to access an unreconstructed curriculum. He contrasted this view with the view of the school in which the focus was on individual pupils as learners with potential requiring teachers and schools to rethink concepts of 'ability, difficulty and curriculum'.

There is here, therefore, a clear and understandable dilemma: the attempt to maintain the values position of the school in the face of an external imperative for the adoption of a more traditional view of special education. It is not surprising therefore that the teaching and learning co-ordinator was equally critical about one of the major features of the Code which can be seen as reinforcing the separateness of special educational provision. For him the use of a staged process of assessment and identification was a further retrograde step. He saw stages as being linked with a return to a form of labelling which was contrary to the values of equity and participation that the school wished to develop. He believed that this would reproduce a reductionist view of students rather than reflect the metaphors of 'potential' and 'energy' with which the school wished its students to be viewed.

This again demonstrates the admirable consistency with the formal views of the school but clearly indicates the tensions that faced the school as it was forced to review its provision in the light of the Code. The response of the school is interesting and consistent with that adopted to deal with the problems generated by the statemented pupils. It was based on a dividing of responsibilities. A special educational needs co-ordinator was appointed taking responsibility for those pupils for whom the mainstream curriculum was insufficiently responsive to 'release their potential' whilst the teaching and learning co-ordinator maintained a development role striving to make the curriculum *more* responsive to individual need across the school. As the school was confronted by these various challenges it was increasingly obliged to reintroduce more traditional notions of special educational needs. In the next section we shall see how the attempt to achieve greater equality and participation was further compromised.

THE REPRODUCTION OF TRADITIONAL SPECIAL NEEDS STRUCTURES

When reviewing the way in which Downland actually responded to pupils who 'challenged the curriculum' it is interesting to note the extent to which it continued to rely on a significant support system. A large number of staff were involved in this system, acting as the primary response mechanism of the school to the issue of difference. The teaching and learning co-ordinator may well have acted as the 'conscience' of the school and carried out reviews of practice in departments, identifying particular areas of need and development, but the face-to-face response to difference remained a traditional piece of the armoury from the 'whole school approach'. The existence of pupils who presented as different, regardless of the label ascribed to them, presupposes the existence of mechanisms for their identification and allocation of additional 'special' help or support. The rhetoric may have been that these support teachers were there to act in the general support of the curriculum or for a range of pupils in a class, but our experience was that they were used primarily to ensure that pre-identified children were nursed through a largely unreconstituted curriculum.

The existence of this gap between rhetoric and practice produced in Downland, a reversion to and significant reliance on a traditional model of support teaching as the principal means through which this particular contradiction could be managed. By relying so heavily on supporting pupils who were experiencing difficulties with the curriculum, the school was, in effect, acknowledging in practice what it disavowed in public – the existence of a level of difference within its pupil population which it was unable to accommodate within its standard form of provision. In this way we would argue that in Downland, despite the rhetoric of equity and participation, what was often actually happening was the extensive use of the traditional techniques of the whole school approach and a tacit acknowledgement of special need as the basis of the response to children who 'challenged' the curriculum.

It is also significant to note the high number of children with statements relating to specific learning difficulty. This suggests to us yet a further example of the extent to which the response to diversity through classroom provision was perceived, by some at least, as failing to meet the needs of all the pupils. Even with a reconstituted view of individual difference and a significant level of support provided to class teachers, here was a further group of pupils whose characteristics were seen as requiring them to have access to external resources so that they could be accommodated within the standard curriculum of the school. The case of specific learning difficulties is of course complex. It is interesting to reflect on the extent to which, in this school, the pupils with a specific learning difficulty and those who required classroom support because of more generalised learning difficulties were actually experiencing anything that was innovatory or in any other way significantly different from what they would have received in any other mainstream school. Certainly, they would not have been labelled in the same way and it may well have been that their contributions to the life of the school were in a context in which they were certain to receive a high and sustained level of praise. But in terms of their being able to access a curriculum that was more differentiated or engage in learning activities that were new or novel, the case remains unproven.

ISSUES OF INCLUSION AND EXCLUSION

An issue of growing concern nationally – the exclusion of pupils with behaviour problems – also impacted on the situation at Downland. The school was not unwilling to exclude pupils who did not live up to the high expectations that it set, or who were considered to damage the internal or external image and reputation of the school within the wider community. Indeed, the head teacher made it clear to us that he regarded the exclusion of non-conforming pupils as an appropriate response in order to establish the type of ethos and climate that he was seeking to establish. It would, of course, be unreasonable to assume that a head teacher should not retain the ultimate sanction of exclusion as a part of the repertoire of responses that a school has to deal with difficult pupils. However, it did appear to us that this was a school which was not having to deal with an over representation of pupils who were likely to prove especially problematic. The rate of exclusion did, therefore, appear to us to be high, and not in the overall spirit of inclusion that the school espoused. Recent research on exclusion (Imich 1994, Parfrey 1994) points to the differential rates of exclusion that occurs between areas and individual schools. This suggests that it is within-school factors which may play the most significant part in accounting for this phenomenon. If this is the case, then a school as committed to inclusion as Downland is placed in a somewhat contradictory position in terms of the extent of the match between the rhetoric and the practice. The issue of the rate of exclusion, moreover, was not something that was concealed from us; for the school it was clear that those pupils who could not function successfully represented a threat to the integrity of the overall ethos of the school and had, therefore, to be excluded.

This is just one example of what we might refer to as the dilemma of inclusion and exclusion that characterised at least part of the culture of this school. Exclusion existed at other levels within the school. For example, we have already suggested that there was a tendency to stereotype those staff who were most resistant to the rhetoric of inclusion and most demanding in respect of their call for support in the classroom. It was clear to us that these staff were in effect an excluded minority insofar as they were characterised as the irredeemable and those unable to respond to the challenges of an inclusive approach. Many of these staff were formerly employed at the girls' school which became a part of the newly created Downland during the process of rationalisation of secondary provision in the town. It was made clear to us that this was far from a merger of equals but essentially a takeover whereby the longer established and financially better endowed boys' school effectively subsumed the girls' school.

Any merger which involves the loss of identity of one of the partners is necessarily painful, the more so for those with a very strong sense of identity and attachment to what we can describe as the victim. In a situation which can be conceived as one where there are winners and losers, there may well have been a sense in which opposing camps were established as a means of maintaining some sense of that lost identity. What we found in Downland was that there had been a high rate of attrition of the former members of the girls' school staff, and that most of them had become stereotyped as 'the unreconstituted' members of the new school. As we untangled the process of the merger it became clear to us that not only had members of the girls' school been encouraged to leave but that there had also been a deliberate attempt to undermine the practices and systems which the former school had operated. This was confirmed by the few remaining staff including one who had become a member of the senior management team in the new school. It was suggested to us that the response to diversity as it was practised in the girls' school, although not having the high profile that it was accorded in Downland, and although relying very heavily on withdrawal and the nurturing of the most vulnerable in small groups, did in fact produce better outcomes for both the pupils and staff.

We were not able to check these assertions out in any rigorous sense, but they are interesting indicators yet again of what we might refer to as an exclusionary attitude within Downland. The existence of alternative perspectives was not tolerated and although the school focused on the development of the institution through the development of its staff, it was clear that only certain perspectives were likely to be tolerated as part of the process of that development. The exclusion of staff insofar as they were either encouraged to leave or in terms of their being marginalised within the school was a characteristic of the situation as we found it at Downland. The notion of the existence of dissonance as an adjunct to the process of development at either individual or institutional level was not, therefore, part of the rationale of the senior staff. Pupils were excluded if they could not or would not respond. Staff who were not 'one of us' were encouraged to leave; those that remained found themselves marginalised and often denied a voice within the school.

INNOVATION OR RENOVATION

In seeking to locate the developments in Downland into the wider context of this book we must stress that we are not seeking to undermine the serious effort that this particular school had made in seeking a new resolution of the dilemmas involved in attempting to realise the values of equity and participation. Nor are we suggesting that Downland was the only school taking this particular path or that it was the only site where these issues were emerging. In striving to realise human values through these kinds of radical approaches it would appear that schools do not simply resolve the problem of how to respond to difference. What appears to happen is that they generate a new range of issues and dilemmas which continue to resonate as an agenda for debate. These issues and dilemmas have some common features and it is worth exploring them here.

It is clear that attempting to realise the values of equity and participation does not remove but increases pressures for schools. In particular there are pressures and issues for schools at an organisational level along the lines suggested by Skrtic (1991), and Ainscow (1991, 1994). There are also pressures and issues for those teachers who are asked to take on board new ways of working; this presents a number of problems for those teachers in the way they view themselves as developing professionals. Writers such as Ainscow point to the likelihood that change within an institution is likely to produce casualties amongst the staff. It is certainly likely to produce resistance amongst those expected to realise it in practice, and this is perhaps why in the school effectiveness literature (Ainscow 1994, etc.) there is an emphasis on the need for a clear lead from the senior management team. For those who remain 'unconverted', the senior management team are left with a range of options. Internal exclusion is one of these as we saw at Downland and elsewhere. This does, however, generate mixed messages for those who view exclusion of this nature as a part of a contradictory process within the school as a whole community. Furthermore, teachers charged with implementing change need to have the confidence that a range of support will be available to them as they begin to explore, implement and accept new approaches. In Downland, as elsewhere, the potential danger was that the rush to achieve change in the way that teaching and learning was undertaken exceeded the capability of the school to deliver the new materials, professional development and other support necessary for its implementation. Where this 'technology' is not immediately available there is always the potential for resistance and retrenchment to occur. Similarly, for those experiencing the most difficulty in implementing the new approaches there is the danger that they become the institutional scapegoats for the failure to achieve change.

What appears to happen in the struggle for greater participation and equity is that resistance is generated throughout the system. From within the mainstream itself, subject teachers, for example, faced with a range of competing demands, are understandably faced with a major readjustment of their pedagogy if they are to accommodate the values of equity and participation. Without a 'technology' to support them, they are inevitably confronted with complex pressures which not all will be able to assimilate. Furthermore as that 'technology' emerges it may well be that it demands of these teachers a change in their working practice which they are not willing to make, despite the impact this might have on realising the liberal values to which they apparently subscribe. The effect of this may well be to increase rather than reduce the resistance within schools.

In this situation, it appears that even the most 'radical' schools may be forced to revert to some of the provision associated with more traditional special education values. Schools are increasingly forced to balance competing values and demands. They are required to compete in a market place and will inevitably adjust their systems and structures to the prevailing climate. Many of the changes in the external context have increased the 'voice' of parents, leaving schools and LEAs to attempt to balance what may well be a number of competing and conflicting views as to how schools should respond to the various pressures they face. The extent to which an individual school can reconcile competing parental 'voices' is open to conjecture, and that even LEA planning can be blown off course if there is significant parental opposition. A set of liberal values and its accompanying rhetoric of participation and equity may not be sufficient to counter the demands of well organised pressure groups demanding 'special' treatment for *their* children.

We would reiterate, however, that the processes and systems that we found in the innovatory schools that we identified despite their difficulties in implementation are not to be regarded as simply temporary. In all the schools that we visited, the attempt to reconceptualise special needs education and to develop new systems and structures were often producing a dynamic and self-critical context in which new ideas were subject to constant scrutiny and adaptation. The schools and the majority of the staff were actively trying to work through the implications of viewing special needs as the result of an interactive process rather than simply operating some loose but convenient rhetoric of a 'whole school approach' which would have provided them with a legitimate reason for not attempting the very difficult tasks of breaking new ground in respect of pupils with special educational needs. Where we report in a critical light the implications of some of these attempts at rethinking, or highlight contradictions in rhetoric and practice, or point to contradictions between the degree of assimilation and practice, we do so as part of a process of reflection and analysis. Such an endeavour is intended to support the development of ideas and practice by providing an interpretation of developments in such a way that those charged with their actual implementation have an alternative perspective through which they might seek a further extension of their practice systems and structures.

Tensions and contradictions in these schools are indicative to us of the dilemmas inherent in attempting to resolve the fundamental problem that schools face in attempting to realise an agenda of liberal values. In attempting a response which might be regarded as more 'inclusive', these schools were seeking one particular resolution of this problem. The problems that we identified can be seen in relation to a number of levels. There are clearly those that revolve around the development of an 'effective' school. They relate to the development of an organisational culture and ethos through which the response to diversity is seen in terms of an indicator of individual and institutional effectiveness rather than as a characteristic of aberrant individual pupils. Also, there are problems that relate directly to the application of actual pedagogical practices in individual classrooms and in which individual teachers have to become fluent. This is an issue which, we contend, has not been given sufficient prominence within the inclusive schools movement.

Finally, there are those problems which relate to the broader context of education and to issues such as the appropriateness of a centrally defined curriculum for *all* pupils. In the absence of a fully developed and effective pedagogy through which this can be achieved by all teachers this will remain a fundamental tension and the source of continuing dilemmas for schools and teachers. Striking a balance between the notions of curricular entitlement and full inclusion will require a period of intense reflection before it is both fully understood by all involved and a pedagogy evolved through which it can become a practical reality. It is in this light, therefore, that developments in the innovatory schools should be seen.

ISSUES OF RESISTANCE IN THE DOWNLAND EXPERIENCE

Although this might appear a disappointing way of reporting on developments in this school, we believe it quite clearly demonstrates the inherent instability which exists within attempts to resolve the complex issues which underlay special education in mainstream schools. Resolutions of these issues based on a powerful articulation of a values position premised on the rhetoric of participation and equity may, therefore, be only temporary. We will suggest in the case of Downland we find an attempt to respond to diversity which engages with some of the dimensions of this complexity but ignores others. In particular we will point to the problem of resistance to the adoption of this approach at a number of levels. For example, one explanation of the failure of the rhetoric to be realised in practice could be in terms of the inevitable weakening of messages that takes place as they are transmitted throughout a complex organisation. The evidence from Downland suggests that in attempting to realise this value position the proponents of the 'vision' failed to take account of the extent of the resistance they would meet from subject teachers. The extent to which staff could be 'converted' by a continued assertion of the 'correctness' of the vision was to misunderstand the nature of change within professional groups. In particular the SMT failed to appreciate the extent to which the adoption of a new approach to special educational needs depended on the active participation of subject staff who were expected to carry through this significant innovation. Downland represents an example of how, when there is a mismatch between institutional rhetoric and the availability of a suitable technology through which it can be delivered, resistance is likely to be experienced, frustrating the intended change. In the case of Downland where the rhetoric of participation and equity was articulated so forcefully, it is interesting to compare the extent to which the zeal of the senior management was replicated in those who were required to realise the vision on a practical basis. Those invested with promulgating the rhetoric maintained their enthusiasm and conviction; some of those required to deliver the new approach were clearly losing faith and returning to traditional classroom practices, seeing no benefit to them as class teachers in changing their practices in the absence of a better alternative though the new vision might be realised.

Staff development was central to the overall strategy within Downland, but much of it had focused on the recharging of the rhetoric in the expectation that the practice would follow the rhetoric. Although there had been some interesting work attempted in developing the curriculum, this was not universal throughout the school, and where gaps existed the message from the teaching and learning co-ordinator tended to stress the need for staff to find their own solutions to problems. Although congruent with the general vision of the school, this hardly inspired confidence in those staff who were used to a more 'traditional' teaching role. Calls for 'creative' solutions in the absence of a systematic and sustained commitment to developing the curriculum are unlikely to sustain an initiative. In Downland the understandable reluctance of some staff to replace carefully developed pedagogic repertoires for an only partially developed alternative remained as a major problem for the SMT and the teaching and learning co-ordinator as they attempted to realise their vision. The failure of this alternative to emerge contributed to the resistance of many of the staff.

Other commentators in this field offer a similar analysis. Ainscow (1991, 1994), for example, writing about the creation of effective schools for all, suggests that the question of school improvement and development depends on more than the straightforward espousal of a particular rhetoric from the senior management. He identifies five widely acknowledged key conditions involved in the development of inclusive schools:

- Effective leadership spread through the school.
- Involvement of staff, students and community in school policies and decision making.
- A commitment to collaborative planning.
- Attention to potential benefits of enquiry and reflection.
- A policy of staff development.

For Ainscow the key to the process of creating effective schools is staff development. He is concerned to ensure that the staff of a school see their own professional development as intimately linked to the overall development of the school as a whole. This requires the development of a group of teachers who become skilled in the art of problem solving. Without the capacity to respond to problems as they emerge *in situ*, rhetoric alone is not sufficient. For Ainscow (1995): 'the professional learning of teachers is central to the development of an inclusive policy, and the classroom is an important centre for teacher development as the training workshop' (p.72).

The work of Skrtic (1991) can also be adduced to support this perspective. For Skrtic the failure of schools to develop along inclusive lines is a function of the tendency of many institutions to develop into bureaucratic organisations. Drawing on a number of sources (Mintzberg 1979, 1983), Skrtic argues that there is a likelihood for schools to configure themselves as professional bureaucracies. This results in the emergence of organisational and professional structures which are designed to maintain an institutional homeostasis or inertia in the ways that it responds to client groups. For schools, this results in the establishment of principles and professional practices which are concerned to preserve existing and established notions of what constitutes 'good practice'. These boundaries, once established, become extended into standardized systems which are resistant to change. When confronted by atypical clients who are not easily assimilated into the existing organisational systems and practices, the response is usually one of rejection or exclusion.

For Skrtic this account helps to explain the development of exclusive schools. There is a clear tendency for schools to resist the challenge presented by non-standard clients; to react to such clients by a re-statement and endorsement of existing practices. Such a process can lead to the development of non-innovative approaches on the part of professionals, of a tendency for practices to revert to an acceptable and standardised norm, and the emergence of a culture that is exclusive and resistant to changes in the way it performs its basic routines. According to Skrtic what is needed to develop inclusivity in schools is: 'A fully open ended process – one that seeks a truly creative solution to each unique need – requires a problem-solving orientation premised on innovation rather than standardisation' (Ainscow 1991, p.25).

This search for 'creative effort to find a novel solution . . . and . . . divergent thinking aimed at innovation' (Mintzberg 1979, p.436) was, we suggest, at the heart of the approach that was adopted in Downland. The role of the teaching and learning co-ordinator, someone deliberately chosen from a non-special needs background, was clearly an attempt to challenge from within, the existing notions of how the teaching and learning of these pupils could be approached to meet the inclusive criteria of the school. This represents in Skrtic's terms an attempt to create the basis on which a 'discursive coupling' could take place throughout the school in which novel solutions could emerge and be promulgated by the catalytic effect of a change agent and the ending of traditional structural arrangements for the response to the problems created by diversity. Whether as problem-solvers (Ainscow 1995) or reflective thinkers (Skrtic 1991), those at the 'sharp' end of delivery are seen as central to the development of alternative responses to diversity.

The rhetoric of 'reflection' is deeply enshrined in much of the writing on teacher/school development. It is, however, a problematic concept easier to describe than to establish and, therefore, not immune from criticism (Smyth 1991). In Downland, despite the strong emphasis on professional and institutional development, there remained, at the level of the classroom teacher, a continuing gulf between the espoused institutional rhetoric and the actual practices in relation to pupils with special needs. When we presented our evidence of this gulf to the teaching and learning co-ordinator and the senior management team, it was significant to note how this resistance was interpreted in terms of individual culpability on the part of some teachers to reconstitute their practice rather than a failure on the part of the school to realise its aim through the development of an inadequate pedagogy, or the appropriate organisational structures. Locating the failure of *all* teachers to rise to the challenge of diversity as the result of the inadequacy of a small unreconstituted minority is one way of avoiding the issue of the adequacy of the available pedagogy. It highlights the extent to which, when an emphasis is placed on participation and equity, there is a significant risk of breakdown at the level at which this policy is realised, that is at the level of the classroom teacher. Unless there is an adequate and appropriate technology available to ensure that teachers have the confidence to adjust their methods and procedures to accommodate the new demands, there is the danger of significant resistance.

In much the same way there was resistance on the part of a section of the parents to the attempt to respond to diversity through an approach based on equity and participation. Parents who had struggled to achieve statements of special educational needs which specified individual support and tuition to meet specific difficulties were quick to challenge the situation in Downland when that individualised support was not forthcoming. This particular 'voice' expressed no interest in participation if that meant that their children were not receiving the additional 'special' support which the statement had recommended. The realisation of equity for this group was a tangible system of individualised and specialist support delivered to individual pupils rather than a less tangible realisation of a values position which offered little of concrete value other than placement within the mainstream classroom. Faced with this resistance the school reverted to a more conventional approach.

If resistance from parents constituted a local resistance then the final dimension of resistance that the school faced can be seen in relation to the national context. It is extremely difficult for a school to resist guidance issued at national level. For Downland the introduction of the Code of Practice represented the vehicle through which the resistance inside the school and from within the parent body could be given formal expression. It placed the school in a vulnerable position in respect of parents as it legitimised their demands for a 'special' and 'distinctive' provision for statemented pupils; it also allowed the voice of those staff who were calling for a more 'effective' provision for non-statemented special needs pupils to press for the systems and structures which the school had consciously attempted to eradicate. As much as the absence of the systems and structures was regarded as an expression of the commitment to equity and participation for the SMT, so it represented an omission for external scrutineers such as OFSTED which might have resulted in an adverse report. As we have indicated, the school was thus forced to reinvent vestiges of a traditional approach to the special education system to meet an external imperative which, in requiring schools to demonstrate the distinctiveness of their provision for special needs, actually ran counter to the attempts to achieve a greater equity and participation on the part of this school.

It is of course always easy to focus on aspects of a school's provision, and we could be accused of criticising a school that was in the process of evolving its response to diversity at a time when external factors were requiring a greater uniformity and consistency of practice in respect of special educational needs. In making this analysis we are not concerned with undermining what Downland was trying to achieve; indeed we still regard the developments in this school as an important contribution to the response to special educational needs in mainstream schools. Our concern, however, is to raise questions about the implications implicit in attempting to achieve a certain values position in mainstream schools, and the extent to which the mere espousal of a powerful rhetoric is sufficient in its own right to realise these values. Our choice of Downland is grounded very much in the knowledge that as a school concerned about its own development, this analysis will be viewed as a contribution to the process of self-review and reflection on which it prided itself and on which it based its institutional development.

REFERENCES

Ainscow, M. (ed.) (1991) *Effective Schools for All.* London: David Fulton Publishers.

Ainscow, M. (1994) *Special Needs in the Classroom,* London: Jessica Kingsley/Unesco.

Ainscow, M. (1995) 'Education for all: making it happen', *Support for Learning,* **10**(4), 147–55.

Dyson, A., Millward, A. and Skidmore, D. (1994) 'Beyond the whole school approach', *British Educational Research Journal* **20**(3), 301–7.

Imich, A. J. (1994) 'Exclusions from school', *Educational Research Journal* **36**(1), 3–11.

Mintzberg, H. (1979) *The Structuring of Organisations.* Englewood-Cliffs, NJ: Prentice Hall.

Mintzberg, H. (1983) *Structure in Fives.* Englewood-Cliffs, NJ: Prentice Hall.

Parfrey, V. (1994) 'Exclusions: failed children or systems failure?', *School Organisation* **14**(2), 107–20.

Skrtic, T. M. (1991) *Behind Special Education.* Denver: Love.

Smyth, I. (1991) 'Teachers' work and the politics of refection'. Paper presented to the conference 'Conceptualising Reflection in Teacher Development'.

6

What's the weight of a badger? Teachers' experiences of working with children with learning difficulties

Philip Garner

INTRODUCTION

I was recently involved in a conversation with a colleague from another institution. He talked about an ongoing research interest of his, which sought to understand the nature and meaning of children's questions during science lessons. We were both intrigued, and amused, by the story of one child who asked his science teacher, 'Please, Miss, what's the weight of a badger?' We went on to discuss the possible responses to such a searching question, and agreed that it would depend on a wide variety of factors and conditions. This did not, however, reduce the potency or relevance of the question to a host of science-related topics.

So, too, with the work that teachers do with children who are regarded as having learning difficulties of one kind or another. If one was asked 'What does a SENCO actually *do?*' it would be extremely difficult to venture an unilateral response. Even given the well-refined official protocols laid down in the original Code of Practice (DFE 1994) it is doubtful whether the work patterns and professional experiences of any two SENCOs are the same, notwithstanding the introduction of a set of *National Standards for Special Educational Needs Co-ordinators* (TTA 1998a). Similarly, with regard to the *National Standards for Special Educational Needs (SEN) Specialist Teachers* (TTA 1998b), there is little possibility that, beyond a superficial generality, the work that such teachers engage in can be reduced to what ultimately might become a pious shopping list of knowledge and understanding and skills. And the classroom teacher, who assumed responsibility at stage 1 of the Code for initial identification, assessment and intervention, is required to adopt an increasingly wide range of teaching strategies in order to respond to a variety of pupil needs and school contexts.

Both the Code and the National Standards documents, while being immensely helpful in delineating ideal, standardised practice, fail to accommodate the badger's weight phenomenon – that the work that teachers engage in with pupils categorised as having special educational needs cannot easily be summarised, let alone reduced to a set of bullet points in a policy document or inspection framework. This is surprising, not least because the Code included a premonitional remark that 'the detail of what they decide to do may vary according to the size, organisation, location and pupil population of the school' (DFE 1994, p.ii). The statement is also conceptually commensurate with individualised approaches to meeting the curricular needs of children who have learning difficulties, as evidenced by the proliferation of advice regarding differentiated teaching and learning in mainstream schools.

From the outset, therefore, it is critical to keep in mind the endless variation in the ways that teachers and whole schools choose to work with children who have special educational needs. Thus, for example, rather than talking in terms of 'the role of the SENCO', it is both more accurate and, from a professional development sense, more meaningful, to talk of the *roles* of the SENCO. These will be variously delineated according both to the total number of schools (and SENCOs) in England and Wales and to the characteristics of their children at given points in time. In a similar vein, it can be argued that we should be talking of a set of 'National Standards' which prescribe the work of specialist teachers which incorporate flexibility in their application according to context and individual pupil need.

The material I present in this chapter is illustrative of the possibilities and tensions which particularise work in special educational needs, together with the benefits and challenges which accompany them. In exploring these connections and interfaces I draw on the 'lived experience of three groups of workers – SENCOs, subject teachers in mainstream schools and 'specialist' teachers in special schools – as represented by their own words.

'THE MAIDEN VOYAGE OF THE SS *INCLUSION*': SENCOS' VIEW FROM THE BRIDGE

The new requirements placed on those teachers in mainstream schools who in their previous incarnation as 'head of department' dealt with children with learning difficulties, resulted in numerous evaluatory studies and commentaries throughout the period 1995–2000 (Evans, Docking, Bentley and Evans 1995, Lewis, Neill and Campbell 1996, OFSTED 1996, Derrington, Evans and Lee 1996, Davies, Garner and Lee 1998). This work has done much to highlight the tensions inherent in meeting the guidance requirements of the Code of Practice. On the one hand, many SENCOs reported that they had insufficient time to attend to the complex and time-consuming set of procedures introduced by the Code. On the other, there was a general feeling that, after years on the periphery, SEN work was now officially recognised as central to the teaching and learning function of schools.

Subsequently, however, SENCOs have had to undertake a further shift in their approach, as a result of three official publications; the Green Paper *Excellence for All Children* (DfEE 1997), the *National Standards for Special Educational Needs Co-ordinators* (TTA 1998a) and *Meeting Special Educational Needs: a programme for action* (DfEE 1998). These combined to demonstrate (a) that the effectiveness of the SENCO is, to a very large extent, dependent upon the attitudes, expertise and collaboration of all staff in a school, and (b) that the role had now achieved a degree of maturity. At the same time, however, these official documents were indicative of the high level of scrutiny now being afforded to the work done by SENCOs; further expectations and increased responsibilities followed, particularly in the unwritten understanding that the SENCO would be a figurehead for developing inclusive practices. Finally, the consultation papers relating to *National Standards for Special Educational Needs* (SEN) *Specialist Teachers* (TTA 1998b) also required further consideration from the SENCO, particularly in respect of the likely impact of such 'standards' on managing the SENCO-specialist teacher relationship. In the words of one of the SENCOs in this study, the role was now akin to that of 'the captain of the ship, setting out on a glorious voyage of discovery'.

This first section explores some, but by no means all, aspects of this 'voyage'. It draws upon some current research which utilises data obtained from a series of interviews with a nationally (England and Wales) representative sample of SENCOs. For the purposes of this section the transcripts of interviews with 24 SENCOs were used, 12 from primary schools and 12 from secondary schools. These were selected from schools in three local education authorities (LEAs), each broadly representative of a shire county, a unitary authority and a metropolitan borough. Six schools (three primary, three secondary) were randomly identified from each LEA. Each of the schools was comparable to others selected from the sample in terms of age range, number of pupils on roll, non-grant-maintained status and socio-economic characteristics of its location, though no further attempt was made to standardise the set of schools chosen.

SENCOs' views on collaboration with colleagues in an era of scrutiny and accountability

Research by Lewis (1995) identified at least one notable distinction between the experiences of SENCOs in primary schools compared with their colleagues in the secondary sector. Survey data from the former suggested that SENCOs found it somewhat easier to maintain an effective working partnership with their classroom teacher colleagues. Those working as SENCOs in secondary schools, on the other hand, reported that it was sometimes difficult to obtain the co-operation of subject teachers. This contextual discrepancy has clearly continued up to the present time, with Bearn and Smith (1998) and Digby, Lewis, Taylor and Yates (1999) indicating that some subject teachers in secondary schools perceived some pupils to be 'outside of their teaching range'. Indeed, the latter indicate that teachers in certain curriculum areas (for example, science and technology) can hold a somewhat jaundiced view of the work of the SENCO (Digby *et al.* 1999).

The period following the implementation of the Code of Practice has been characterised as one in which SENCOs have been required to operate 'in the context of zero tolerance' (Davies, Garner and Lee 1998). In this, an increasingly inspection-, evaluation- and performance-led approach to education has led to far greater accountability than ever before in the history of education. These are emphatic features of recent governments' heightened focus on learning failure and children's behaviour – special educational needs became, following the Code of Practice, an overt policy component, with OFSTED releasing dedicated review reports concerning its implementation (OFSTED 1996, 1997).

Considerable emphasis was placed on collaborative work in the original Code of Practice. Indeed, it is worth reminding ourselves that the Code introduced the term 'co-ordinator', which taken literally means a preoccupation with 'adjust[ing] [parts of a whole] so that they will work efficiently together'. In emphasising the specificities of this role the Code states that, of the seven functions envisaged for the SENCO, four of them are directly connected with that process, while the remainder are reliant on effective collaboration to succeed (DFE 1994, pp.9–10, para. 2:14):

- liaising with and advising fellow teachers;
- co-ordinating provision for children with special educational needs;
- liaising with parents of children with special educational needs;
- liaising with external agencies, including the educational psychology service and other support agencies, medical and social services and voluntary bodies.

The *National Standards for Special Educational Needs Co-ordinators* identifies a 'core purpose' for the SENCO as including that of providing professional guidance and ensuring active collaboration with subject leaders, while 'supporting, guiding and motivating colleagues' (TTA 1998a, p.5). It may be a sobering realisation that the parallel set of

Standards for Subject Leaders' makes no specific mention in its 'core purpose' of their role in respect of children who have learning difficulties. In other words, there is an inference that it will be left to the SENCO to develop and sustain collaborative practice.

SENCOs' views on the inclusion debate and its impact on day-to-day school routines

The inclusion debate assumed frenzied activity during the period when SENCOs sought to establish themselves as the pivotal focus of SEN policy and practice in schools. This was a period marked by considerable tension, with competing paradigms, of differences between children (Dyson and Millward 1997). The publication of *Excellence for All Children: meeting special educational needs* (DfEE 1997) provided official recognition that inclusion was a guiding principle for central government policy; 'Because of the nature of their roles and responsibilities SENCOs are caught within the web of this debate' (Davies, Garner and Lee 1998, Garner 2000). The ideological struggle, and its practical implications for classroom teachers, is best exemplified by the differences in opinion concerning children with emotional and behavioural difficulty (EBD). Such children are the least likely to engender that sympathy akin to the charity discourse of special education, and they are, in turn, the least likely to benefit from the support of advocates or pressure groups in securing full inclusion. Moreover, EBD children seem to offer a visible and seemingly intractable threat to class teachers.

The SENCOs in this small sample reflect these tensions and dilemmas. Thus, one respondent indicated that 'Inclusion does not pose any problems for me. I see it as a natural development in terms of SEN provision . . . where we have been moving towards for quite for a few years' (SE4). Conversely, there was a body of opinion which believed that it is 'ludicrous to place such a responsibility on us [when] it needs to be tackled on a more widespread level – and certainly not just in school' (SE23). These views perhaps represent polarities: some of the SENCOs simply wanted 'more help to do the job to the best of our ability' (SE11) and 'More say in the whole debate, not just a token gesture here and there' (SE15), indicating a degree of resignation to a situation which requires them to implement 'guidance' irrespective of their ideological or practical engagement with its content.

There was, predictably, even greater circumspection in respect of the inclusion of children whose learning difficulties were associated with EBD. Some SENCOs were adamant that an unconditional commitment to inclusion would mean that they become 'just security staff, keeping kids under control and, in all probability, losing a lot of professional status'

(SE16). In contrast, one primary school SENCO believed that 'You can't be exclusive about inclusion. You either have it or you don't. If you do then you have to deal with all kids on the same terms. If you don't do this then the expression "inclusive school" becomes a complete nonsense' (SE8).

The most striking aspect of these responses, however, was the degree to which virtually all SENCOs in the sample appeared to be recognising that, in order to participate as active agents in the drive towards inclusion, they would need to be removed even more from direct classroom contact with children with learning difficulties. Views supportive of this sentiment are that 'We have never been given the time necessary to fulfil our responsibilities. It's about time now that this was recognised. I can't do justice to a full class of children and deal with the extra impact on SEN organisation of more inclusion' (SE2) and 'I think that, in the end and for better or worse, a SENCO's job will be almost completely non-teaching' (SE19).

SENCOs' views regarding proposed refinements to the Code of Practice

Revision of the Code of Practice is a central feature of *Meeting Special Educational Needs: a programme for action* (DfEE 1998). In this there is an expressed commitment to introduce a revised Code of Practice, to come into effect during the academic year 2000/2001. The sample group of SENCOs were asked to comment on three issues raised in the relevant consultation document (DfEE 1999), each of which have become defining features of the SENCO's day-to-day work in school:

- the function of individual education plans (IEPs);
- SENCO workloads;
- differences between primary and secondary schools.

The function of individual education plans
According to the Office for Standards in Education (OFSTED), 'The preparation and maintenance of IEPs is the greatest area of concern for the majority of the schools' (OFSTED 1997). Each of the SENCOs in this sample believed that there had been a failure, in the Code of Practice, to provide sufficient guidance on the content and layout of an IEP. The Code signals the IEP as a key element of stage 2 provision. Given the importance attached to it several of the SENCOs thought it unhelpful not to have given exemplars: 'I remember that period well because virtually every meeting I went to in the Borough was dominated by us swapping ideas about our IEPs. There was a lot of confusion, and that was mainly because there wasn't really any example to start us off' (SE8). 'When you

came across one which looked good you always tried to get a copy for yourself. There should have been more examples in the Code itself' (SE15). The absence of exemplar IEPs in the Code led to considerable confusion and frustration. For instance, one SENCO stated that 'The original IEPs we had were huge things. When I look back I think it was little wonder that some people in the school refused to fill them in – they were grotesquely complicated. I think it's a good idea that they are simplified' (SE21).

Many of the SENCOs expressed an opinion, quite forcefully, that for the first few years the IEP document itself, rather than the practice it was supposed to represent or promote, had become a paper exercise, a view supported by comments in *Meeting Special Educational Needs: a programme for action* (DfEE 1998). One SENCO provided an illustrative summary of this situation: 'I always remember our first OFSTED [inspection] because there was a rumour going round that the first thing they [the inspectors] would ask to see was your IEPs. It summed up the situation very well for me. We had started to see the SEN pupil as a piece of paper and not as a real person' (SE6). While the SENCOs felt generally satisfied at the current use of IEPs in their schools – one indicated that 'There has to be a record of what we do or are going to do and this is as simple as I can make it' (SE22) – they mostly believed in the merits of the suggestion that 'IEPs are generally most helpful when they are crisply written, focusing on three or four short-term targets for the child' (DfEE 1998, pp.1–16), and in the benefits of providing examples. Some SENCOs, however, argued that a big danger including 'model' IEPs in the revised Code would lead to more prescription: thus, there was a comment that 'in the bad old days the [local education] authority gave us a standardised IEP. It was hopeless and really got everyone's back up. Part of the reason for me was that it was too prescriptive, and I think there is a danger of a similar thing happening again, but this time on a national level' (SE10).

SENCO workloads

Ever since the introduction of the Code of Practice SENCOs have complained of overwork. The first major survey of SENCOs, conducted on behalf of a teacher union, portrayed what was for many the grim reality of post-Code practice (Lewis, Neill and Campbell 1996). OFSTED (1996) indicated that 'Many SENCOs have an over-demanding workload' and that this is exacerbated by the way in which individual schools allocate time and require SENCOs to perform other duties, particularly in primary schools. *Meeting Special Educational Needs: a programme for action* recognises this situation, pointing out that some respondents to the consultation were concerned that SENCOs needed more non-contact time to carry out their jobs effectively' (DfEE 1998, p.17). Given that co-ordination' infers interaction with others, such a statement seems almost tautological.

Responses from this group of SENCOs indicate a perception that little has changed in the imbalance in workload and work patterns between primary and secondary schools. One primary school SENCO said that 'I'm still a class teacher . . . sometimes I feel I'd like more time for my SENCO work because that's really time-consuming' (SE2), while another felt 'a lot of frustration because I have to cram my link visits or EP meetings and things like that into my designated afternoon . . . and it usually ends up that I don't get to see who I want to because they aren't around' (SE4). This position contrasts sharply with the flexibility open to 'full-time' SENCOs: 'Even though we've got over 120 kids on the [special educational needs] register I still find that I'm able to do all the liaison work because my actual contact timetable is very light and I can usually be flexible in the way I do things' (SE20).

Plans to lighten the burden of administrative work were seen by all of the SENCOs as one of the most valuable ways of releasing time in order for them to function effectively. 'I think what most SENCOs would be grateful for is some additional administrative support, coupled with a rationalisation in the number of forms and reports we have to complete. I don't know of anybody from our [local] SENCO forum who would argue against that kind of action' (SE19), was a view supportive of changes in this area, although a primary SENCO felt that 'we are our own worst enemies sometimes because we should prioritise, do the important things and then stop. I don't think there is any point in pretending to cope or just getting by. If you need support you should get it' (SE1).

Differences between primary and secondary schools

The *Consultation Document on the Proposed Revision of the Code of Practice* emphasises that 'it is sometimes suggested that the Code's guidance is more relevant to primary than to secondary schools' (DfEE 1999, p.1) and indicates a commitment to providing more guidance on how secondary schools can meet their statutory responsibilities. Early indications from an on-going study (Digby *et al.* 1999) suggest that such amplification is very necessary. The SENCOs participating in the present study indicate that three factors may have prompted this perception:

- school size;
- early identification and intervention;
- the subject-based nature of secondary school work.

The SENCOs are wholehearted and united in their belief that the task of co-ordination becomes increasingly more complex the bigger the school is: 'I have to liaise with over sixty teachers in this school ... so even without my job of working with support workers and parents I have a pretty full week. One thing that really becomes obvious the more you do this job is that you have to rely on the personality of individuals ... it's the personal contact [really], how you get on with people socially that seems to be just as important. The big thing is that you can't get on with everybody' (SE15). These sentiments are reinforced by a SENCO in a large (450 pupil) primary school, who remarked that 'You have to be very outgoing, flexible and approachable to do this job. I suppose I look on my colleagues as (er) something like a class of children ... not that they're childish or anything but you've got to deal with a lot of different personalities and be considerate of the way that they go about their own job. Sometimes that can be difficult' (SE9).

Some of the primary school SENCOs expressed the sentiment that fulfilling the role in a primary school was more difficult because of the emphasis placed – rightly according to these SENCOs – on early intervention. One of this group noted that '[A SENCO colleague in a nearby secondary school] receives a complete set of records from us, so I think he has a head start on me ... it depends on how good the primary-secondary link is, but I still think secondary SENCOs have more resources for doing less than us' (SE7). Another SENCO added that 'There is not such a big thing made of the Code at secondary schools because a lot of teachers there think that things like reading problems have been tackled already by us' (SE3).

Finally, both primary and secondary SENCOs reported that the subject-based organisation of the secondary school curriculum, and the shift from class to subject teacher in particular, was a major inhibiting factor for SEN and made the SENCO's job more difficult. Two illustrative comments on this theme were as follows: 'I think that some teachers – I'd say more like science or technology teachers – distance themselves from greater involvement, and I have to continually nag them to complete forms' (SE24) and 'I don't think I'd be much good doing a SENCO job at secondary level because I have got used to co-operation with a small group of staff. I can't see that happening when you've got a lot of teachers who are more into their own subject and getting exam passes' (SE6).

'HAVE YOU CURED HIM YET?' SUBJECT TEACHERS, SEN AND THE CODE OF PRACTICE

The opening section of this chapter concluded with some reference to the tensions which appear to manifest themselves in the organisation and provision for special educational needs in secondary schools. The present section looks in greater depth at this issue. Collaboration is central to a SENCO's effectiveness; this places great reliance on co-operation with colleagues who do not hold a specified SEN brief; indeed, there may well be those who are diffident or even hostile to greater involvement with children with learning difficulties, whatever the statutory guidelines specify. Mittler (1993) is categorical about this, observing that while 'the slogan that everyone is a teacher of children with special educational needs is true . . . it is very far from being accepted in practice'. Investigations regarding the views of mainstream subject or class teachers have not been widespread in the period following the inception of the Code. This is rather surprising, given the weight of emphasis placed, at stage 1, on the role of the class teacher. What little that has been forthcoming has related to discrete aspects of SEN provision, rather than to the Code of Practice itself (Bearn and Smith 1998, Allan 1995).

The responses to SEN by subject teachers in secondary schools have important implications for school effectiveness and individual pupil progression. Subject teacher attitudes can impact upon the progress that individual pupils make in a given curriculum area, as well as having an impact on a pupil's choice of subject at Key Stage 4. It is clear, too, that pupil–teacher relationships are likely to influence a child's overall attitude to education, promoting either inclusion or disengagement, with their attendant consequences. Nor can effective whole-school interventions be fostered when there is a prevailing ethos that it is the 'SEN teacher' who is solely responsible for children with learning difficulties – the 'Have you cured him yet?' syndrome.

This section of the chapter draws on work currently in progress (Garner 2000, Digby *et al.* 1999). In this, 600 teachers in primary and secondary schools in England and Wales were surveyed by questionnaire, followed by a series of semi-structured interviews. The data used here are taken from the pilot-study stage of this research, and is restricted to the views of 20 subject teachers in a small group (10) of secondary schools in an outer London borough and a shire county. The group comprises four teachers each in the follow-up subjects: mathematics (coded M1–M4 in the transcript extracts), geography (G1–G4), science (S1–S4), art (A1–A4) and technology (T1–T4). Their views were obtained during a series of follow-up interviews, after the distribution of a pilot questionnaire. Each interview lasted for 30 minutes. The extracts provided centre on three aspects of subject teachers' knowledge and application of the Code:

- its impact on subject teachers' day-to-day teaching;
- the degree to which subject teachers are able to fulfil the Code's expectations;
- their level of contact with the SENCO.

The implementation of the Code of Practice saw the 'head of department' responsible for SEN assume the title of co-ordinator: with this came new responsibilities and patterns of work. But the Code also made important recommendations for the role of the subject teacher; indeed, there is an argument to suggest that the key re-orientation of the Code was to make the subject teacher the focus of *action* on behalf of pupils with learning difficulties.

Reactions of this small group of subject teachers to this situation were mixed; there was certainly little evidence of the underlying principle that emphasised that subject or class teachers were to be in a vanguard position when it came to intervention. 'We have had to make so many changes in the way we teach our own subject that it is wrong to place another burden on us' (S2) was the comment of one science teacher, while a technology teacher maintained that 'Technology is a very different discipline to what it was when I started out as a teacher. It is more complex, scientific and, because of that, I think it has moved away from being the traditional subject for remedial children' (T1).

There was a widespread belief that additional workloads as a result of the Code had resulted in increased stress and, perversely, a general decline in willingness to work proactively with pupils with learning difficulty. Thus, one teacher reported that 'It has been a story of more responsibility for less reward and more stress and aggravations for less in the way of personal fulfilment. I reckon that I did a lot more for low-ability kids without all the bureaucracy' (G3).

But there were some supportive remarks: 'I think that the changes that have taken place in recent years have been to everybody's benefit. I don't feel threatened that SEN is at or near the top of the agenda now' (A2) and 'We got a lot of support, and still do, so that we know what the Code means' (G4) are comments illustrative of this more positive orientation.

The subject teachers in this small survey supported a view that the degree to which they were able to fulfil the Code's expectations was very largely based upon the overall ethos, management and organisation of SEN in their school: 'we have a really supportive set of teachers, led by a senior management which don't duck issues. They are really committed to SEN and support everybody, including our SEN team, to get the best possible deal for these pupils' (S4) is a comment in direct contrast with a more negative interpretation: 'Everybody is so busy making sure that they get their own job done . . . you have to sort your own patch out, because it will be your head on the block at the end of the day. I will be rated by my KS4 exam results, not how sympathetic I am about pupils who have low ability' (T4).

A similar ambivalence was apparent in respect of the level of contact these subject teachers had with their SENCOs. This ranged from high-level and on-going collaboration – as inferred by one art teacher: '[The SENCO] gives us a lot of time, and not when we just ask for it. She ensures we get information on a particular problem pupil well in advance and also is keen to help with . possible solutions to difficulties' (A1) – to minimal interaction, as in the case of one geography teacher who noted that 'we occasionally get a boy who has an IEP, but to be honest I don't take much notice of it because there is so much else to do. Besides, I don't think that our SENCO has enough contact with subject teachers. She has a very romantic view of these kids I think' (G1).

While it is clearly too early to make substantive, generalised comment on the views of subject teachers as a whole it is probably fair to tentatively suggest that teachers of non-core subjects, together with those which are more 'affective' in nature, hold more amenable views regarding the impact of the Code. Considering the recent exposure given to teaching and learning styles in SEN, and the importance of pupil–teacher relationships, further investigations concerning class or subject teachers' beliefs regarding SEN in general would seem to be essential for the successful operation of a revised Code of Practice.

SPECIAL OPERATIONS, OR (RE-)DEFINING DIFFERENCE?

Much has been made, since the days of the Warnock deliberations, of the need to define a new role for special schools. Even in 1978 there was a projection that such schools would become 'resource centres, for all the teachers in the area, for curriculum development and in-service training' (Rogers 1980). Although such anticipation was reinforced within *Meeting Special Educational Needs: a programme for action*, the document gives the continued existence of such schools as separate centres for the education of children with learning difficulties an official sanction, stating that 'There will be a continued role for specialist provision, including special schools. Special schools need to be confident, outward-looking centres of excellence. We want to build on their strengths, and ensure that they are an integral part of an inclusive education system' (DfEE 1998, p.25).

The ideological paradox in this statement is difficult to avoid, and yet it has the benefit of hinting at an underlying unease with polarised views. In the case of the inclusion-segregation debate these are deeply felt, as summarised by Hornby, Atkinson and Howard, who state that:

Some writers have suggested that such inclusion should be regarded as a 'right' of all children with SEN ... Others have warned that widespread adoption of inclusive models will lead to a deterioration in the education provided for many children with SEN, as well as the eventual demise of the field of special education itself.

(Hornby, Atkinson and Howard 1997, p.68)

It is perhaps the case that the concept of clusters remains a point of optimism, certainly in the midst of an ideological battle which shows little sign of abating over time (Dyson and Millward 1997). Thus, if special schools *per se* are to play an integral role in the development towards inclusive practice, it is not simply a case that their function is:

> to give support to regular schools, to develop materials and methods, to gather information and provide it to parents and teachers, to take care of the necessary liaison between educational and non-educational institutions, and to give support when transition from school to work takes place.
>
> (Meijer, Pijl and Hegarty 1997, p.158)

The suggestion is that the mainstream schools function as passive partners in this process. Collaboration via clustering means something rather more than this unequal partnership. An interest in this way of working has been growing during the period following the implementation of the Code (Gains 1994, Lunt, Evans, Norwich and Wedell 1994), although its earlier origins can be traced (Fish 1985, Day 1989). The prospects of partnership between special and mainstream schools have been damaged by the culture of competition and marketisation in education as a whole: league tables, the pressures of external inspection, and increased competition for pupils and resources have all impacted on the willingness of schools to participate in collaborative clusters (Wiltshire 1998).

The present section identifies 'clustering' as one means by which inclusivity can be developed beyond simply a set of concepts on an ideological wish-list. It provides a summary of the views of three 'specialist teachers', all of whom are in the process of completing an award-bearing course in SEN at an institution of higher education. The three teachers (who for the sake of confidentiality are called Hazel, Martin and Wendy) were engaged in a semi-structured conversation regarding their current working relationships with special schools. The extracts presented here are illustrative of three elements of that practice: the nature and extent of partnership, pupil mobility, and teacher development.

[The discussion had been underway for about four minutes.]

Martin: A lot of teachers I speak to feel the same way. You know your local schools, who you can trust and (er) . . .

Hazel: Yes, I'd agree completely with that. One of our schools you can be sure, (um) how shall I say this, will be very rejecting to any request to re-integrate.

Martin: I know, and that is what I was meaning, that you can't do things, no matter how much you might want to, if you don't have the co-operation. I mean (er) it seems wrong (mmm) that (er) if we are judged on rates of re-integration (is that right?) or inclusion then . . . our fate is in the hands of other teachers.

Hazel: Martin, that's exactly right. It is, you know, totally unfair because they could make it a requirement.

Martin: Exactly – can I cut in? It could turn out that you will be paid by rate of re-integration. My union is opposed to performance related pay . . .

Hazel: And if the government is setting its stall out by inclusion then (er) we could find that we could be paid according to how many kids get back into mainstream.

Wendy: That's too far fetched. Hazel . . .

Martin: No, I'd agree with her.

Wendy: But it's basically saying that if a pupil can't go back to mainstream then we will be penalised financially . . . (um) it could not be made to work legally or anything (um) it would be too controversial.

Martin: Maybe that's so. But it still comes back to my point (er) it makes it stronger that unless you are in a school with good relations with local mainstream schools you'll get less money.

Wendy: I'll give you a good example. I work in an EBD school, as you know. I cannot see at least three of our surrounding schools even considering re-integration (er) they'd rule it out without knowing the pupil.

Martin: But that's a special case.

Wendy: Well, there's a lot of EBD schools in a similar position (er) I can think of.

Hazel: (laughs) I think I will have to start being nicer to our mainstream schools . . . (er) . . . (laughs again) . . . I'm being paid by them according to you.

Martin: It's a nightmare . . . (er . . . um) because if they don't want to work with you you've had it. (laughs) What about my mortgage!

[The discussion continues; the next extract is taken six minutes later.]

Wendy: It makes some of what we've said a bit pointless. As an EBD school we know that probably about 95 per cent of the kids we receive will stay with us and . . .

Martin:	But that's a bit defeatist isn't it? I mean, what is your role if . . .
Wendy:	Look, Martin (sighs) (er) we just have to get rid of this political correctness (er) I think it's a con (er) a fraud to say that all kids can go back to mainstream.
Martin:	But if you don't have that aspiration you are going to be seen as (er) a while elephant . . .
Hazel:	But what she's saying is that it's better to be honest. (er) Honesty is the best policy especially where parents are concerned.
Wendy:	Thanks Hazel. (laughs) You can tell you [Martin] don't work with many EBD kids. (laughs) That's not fair.
Martin:	Point taken, but I'm sure you know that I've got a point too.

[The discussion continues: the next extract comes about seven minutes later: the question of professional development, and the role of special schools, had been introduced by the interviewer.]

Hazel:	Again we would have to come back to the level of contact (er) and the relationship with other local schools. My place would love to get subject-related input in some curriculum areas.
Martin:	But would it go the other way?
Hazel:	Like (er) if say we did something on an INSET day for one of the secondary schools?
Martin:	Exactly . . . (er) would they be as open? . . . Because I don't think my school would be considered as a resource centre, (um) as a centre of excellence.
Hazel:	You got to be a bit careful about (er) prejudging this (er) and it's about us too, isn't it? (er) How good we feel about ourselves . . . self-confidence.
Wendy:	And that's a difficult thing now because everybody seems to talk only about inclusion . . . it's the main preoccupation.
Hazel:	Yes. And you know (er) that can't be good because it makes you feel (er) a bit like one of our kids (er) that you're outside looking in . . .
Wendy:	Yes. Yes. Waiting for membership. (laughs)
Martin:	So what you are both saying is that special schools don't stand much of a chance because they are not flavour of the month . . . (er) That's not what it said in the Green Paper.
Hazel:	Correct. But look at what it does say about inclusion! If you don't talk that language you'll be lost.
Martin:	Getting back to the point, I think mainstream teachers could learn quite a bit from some of the stuff we do . . . (er) I don't feel defensive about it.

Wendy: I'm not either, about the actual skills we have. I think what we're both wondering is how much opportunity is there (er) to become the kind of place that will be able to be (er) a resource for mainstream schools.

Martin: Well, yes . . . (er) maybe we need money up to a point to re-equip, but we need a change of values too.

[End of extract; the discussion continued for approximately eight more minutes.]

CONCLUSION

The commentaries contained in this chapter highlight above all the far-reaching impact of SEN legislation, and particularly the guidance enshrined within the Code of Practice. Responsibility for its effective operation cannot simply be the duty of one group of teachers. Thus, while it is the SENCO who has an overt duty, all other teachers are implicated. Nor does this responsibility rest with mainstream teachers alone. And as the movement towards educational inclusion gathers pace in the new century it is apparent that success will be measured just as much in terms of the actions of 'non-specialist' teachers, and those operating outside the mainstream, as it will on the work of SENCOs. Each of these three groups has an integral part to play in developing effective provision: one impression, based on the qualitative data presented above, is that all three groups are inclined to function in isolation, frequently failing to recognise the role tensions that are present. The role of SENCO may, in the future, have to be more responsive to this by assuming a developmental role in relation to all teachers.

ACKNOWLEDGEMENTS

My thanks to Mike Watts, from the Roehampton Institute, London, for bringing the question 'What is the weight of a badger?' to my attention.

REFERENCES

Allan, J. (1995) 'How are we doing? Teachers' views on the effectiveness of co-operative teaching', *Support for Learning* **10**(2), 127–31.

Bearn, A. and Smith, C. (1998) 'How learning support is perceived by mainstream colleagues', *Support for Learning* **13**(1), 14–20.

Davies, J., Garner, P. and Lee, J. (eds) (1998) *Managing Special Educational Needs: the role of SENCO.* London: David Fulton Publishers.

Day, A. (1989) 'Reaching out: the background to outreach', in Baker, D. and Bovair, K. (eds) *Making the Special School Ordinary.* Lewes: Falmer Press.

Department For Education (DFE) (1994) *The Code of Practice on the Identification and Assessment of Special Educational Needs.* London: DFE.

Department for Education and Employment (DfEE) (1997) *Excellence for All Children: meeting special educational needs.* Sudbury: DfEE.

Department for Education and Employment (DfEE) (1998) *Meeting Special Educational Needs: a programme for action.* Sudbury: DfEE.

Department for Education and Employment (DfEE) (1999) *Consultation Document on the Proposed Revision of the Code of Practice.* London: DfEE.

Derrington, C., Evans, C. and Lee, H. (1996) *The Code in Practice: the impact on schools and LEAs.* Slough: NFER.

Digby, B., Lewis, G., Taylor, A. and Yates, G. (1999) *Classroom Teachers' Knowledge and Application of the Code of Practice,* Internal Report, Brunel University School of Education.

Dyson, A. and Millward, A (1997) 'The reform of special education or the transformation of mainstream schools', in Pijls, S., Meijer, C. and Hegarty, S. (eds) *Inclusive Education: a global agenda.* London: Routledge.

Evans, R., Docking, J., Bentley, D. and Evans, K. (1995) *Review of Policy and Practice in Five Authorities.* London: Roehampton Institute Research Centre.

Fish, J. (1985) *The Way Ahead.* Milton Keynes: Open University Press.

Gains, C. (ed.) (1994) 'Cluster models', *Support for Learning* **9**(2), 94–8.

Garner, P. (2000) 'The teacher as the key or the teacher as the padlock? Attitudes of mainstream teachers towards inclusion of children with learning difficulties'. Paper presented at ISEC 2000, International Special Education Congress, University of Manchester.

Hornby, G., Atkinson, M. and Howard, J. (1997) *Controversial Issues in Special Education.* London: David Fulton Publishers.

Lewis, A. (1995) *Special Needs Provision in Mainstream Primary Schools: evidence and policy implications from a national survey.* Stoke-on-Trent: ASPE/Trentham.

Lewis, A., Neill, S. and Campbell, R. (1996) *The Implementation of the Code of Practice in Primary and Secondary Schools: a national survey of perceptions of special needs co-ordinators.* Coventry: University of Warwick, Institute of Education.

Lunt, I., Evans, J., Norwich, B. and Wedell, K. (1994) *Working Together: inter-school collaboration for special needs.* London: David Fulton Publishers.

Meijer, C., Pijl, S. and Hegarty, S. (1997) 'Inclusion: implementation and approaches', in Pijl, S. Meijer, C. and Hegarty, S. (eds) *Inclusive Education: a global agenda.* London: Routledge.

Mittler, P. (1993) 'Special needs at the crossroads', *Support for Learning* **7**(3), 145–51.

Office for Standards in Education (OFSTED) (1996) *Implementation of the Code of Practice*. London: HMSO.

Office for Standards in Education (OFSTED) (1997) *The SEN Code of Practice: two years on, the implementation of the Code of Practice for pupils with special educational needs, a second report covering 1996/7*. London: OFSTED.

Rogers, R. (1980) *Crowther to Warnock: how fourteen reports tried to change children's lives*. London: Heinemann Educational.

Teacher Training Agency (TTA) (1998a) *National Standards for Special Educational Needs Co-ordinators*. London: TTA.

Teacher Training Agency (TTA) (1998b) *National Standards for Special Educational Needs (SEN) Specialist Teachers* (Consultation). London: TTA.

Wiltshire, A. (1998) 'A wider role for special schools?', in Tilstone, C., Florian, L. and Rose, R. (eds) *Promoting Inclusive Practice*. London: Routledge.

7

The special needs co-ordinator in the secondary school

Kate Griffiths

INTRODUCTION

I am a SENCO (Special Educational Needs Co-ordinator) in an 11–18 secondary school in a West Yorkshire town. I work in a Church of England school that is soon to change its status from grant maintained to becoming a voluntary aided school. There are approximately 1,000 pupils on roll. We have a strong Learning Support department comprising one teacher and 11 learning support assistants (LSAs). One of the LSAs is a trained teacher and works in this capacity for 0.4 of the week. Some 26 pupils have statements and there are about 120 pupils on the special needs register.

The school draws pupils from quite a wide catchment area because of its church status, so there is a large sociological spead. The area immediately surrounding the school, however, is fairly deprived, and a significant number of pupils come from this region. The town in which the school is situated has two grammar schools and this does skew the intake. More able pupils tend to opt for the grammar schools and so our school does not have the representative number of these pupils.

LINKS WITH PRIMARY SCHOOLS

The school has a very large number of feeder primary schools. In most years pupils come from 25 to 30 local primary schools. Pupils also travel from neighbouring authorities. We do not have a small number of schools with whom we can develop close ties and pyramidal links.

By December of the year prior to entry we know which statemented pupils have applied to our school and we see a copy of their Statements. At this time I contact both the feeder primary school and the local support service; this service has a teacher working in the school who is able to give me detailed knowledge of the pupil.

After this first contact, if we feel we can meet the pupil's needs, I have further discussions with the feeder school and the parents. I have normally met the parents already at the publicity evening when they discuss their child's needs and find out what provision we have to meet the needs.

Depending on the child's needs I then make further arrangements to assure a smooth transition from primary to secondary school. If it is felt that visits to the school would be beneficial for the child I arrange these. I take the child round the school, familiarise them with such things as the toilets, changing rooms, canteens and classrooms. We look in classrooms, watch the pupils changing lessons and see what equipment they will have to bring to school. I give them a copy of a timetable so that they can discuss this with their teacher or support assistant; sometimes we take photographs and the pupils make a book of the school. If we feel it would help there are opportunities for the pupil to join a Year 7 class.

At the same time I visit the primary school, speak to the class teacher, SENCO and/or LSA. I talk with the pupil and observe them in the classroom. I find out whether the pupil has any particular friend or if there is another pupil who would be supportive. I also find out if there are likely to be any personality clashes or other sources of friction. I attend the child's Annual Review at which the transition is discussed.

At the end of the summer term our school has a transition day when all children moving to Year 7 visit the school. We arrange for the statemented pupil to work with a support assistant so that they are well supported and there is someone in the school that they will recognise on the first day of term.

We not only try to support and include statemented pupils effectively but also any others on the special needs register. The local authority Learning Support Service will be aware of any pupils that are on stage 3 of the Code of Practice (DFE 1994, para. 2:67). A meeting is arranged between the school and the support teachers currently working with these pupils. The needs of these pupils are discussed and the best way to meet the needs is devised.

All feeder schools are contacted by me or the Head of Year in the summer term. Pupils will be discussed and any on the SEN register will be highlighted. I will normally have met and spoken to the parents of pupils that are experiencing difficulties. When the pupils enter the school their records are sent with them and I read and file any records relating to special needs. The Code of Practice has been a great help in formalising and making these records more readily understandable by all.

LIAISON WITH SPECIAL SCHOOLS

The local authority in which the school is situated is committed to inclusion and integration and so there is only a small population of children in special schools. The LEA runs one secondary and two primary special schools. We have never received pupils from the primary special schools but the Learning Support department has developed links with the secondary special school.

The learning support assistants and I have visited the school to obtain advice on teaching various aspects of the curriculum. We have seen how they teach *Macbeth* to Year 9 pupils, we have sought advice on the teaching of Science at Key Stage 4 and we learnt about alternative ways of accrediting pupils' work at Key Stage 4 such as those courses accredited by the Award Scheme and Development Accreditation Network (ASDAN).

We have also shared the education of pupils. We had one pupil with communication difficulties. We felt that she would benefit from the communication classes that the special school runs every morning. The pupil attended the special school for the first hour of the day and returned to us for the rest of the curriculum. This worked very well for a year and the pupil did not appear to become troubled or confused by being part of two schools. It did necessitate, however, very close communication between the two schools. This was achieved by very regular visits from a support assistant, a notebook that the child always carried with her and regular phone calls. During the next year the child spent more time at the special school, also attending college with fellow pupils, although she considered our school to be her 'proper' school. In Year 11 it became more and more difficult to offer a relevant curriculum, and the gap between her and her peers was increasing as they prepared for GCSE and the life of work. She left us at this time and went to the special school full time. The transition from mainstream to special was very smooth as she had already established relationships and was familiar with the surroundings.

The authority has set up a series of half-termly secondary SENCO meetings where new initiatives are discussed and views shared. The SENCO from the special school also attends these meetings so that we have a special and mainstream perspective on the matters being discussed.

What has been disappointing is that there has not been a flow of pupils in the opposite direction. We have offered to give pupils from the special school opportunities to share our facilities and gain experience of a mainstream school. Although the special school has agreed that this would be a good idea they have never taken advantage of this offer. It may be that the school feels threatened and is protective of its clientele for two main reasons. First, the authority is committed to integration so will attempt to place as many pupils in mainstream schools as possible. Secondly, the present government's encouragement towards inclusion may be seen as a further threat to their existence. A new culture needs to be established whereby mainstream and special schools feel able to work closely together in a spirit of co-operation and not mutual suspicion.

LIAISON WITH COLLEGES OF FURTHER EDUCATION

Although there are several further education (FE) colleges that are accessible for pupils at our school we mainly send pupils to only two of them.

The links with FE colleges has developed over the last few years but there is still room for improvement. Around five years ago there was very little communication between the school and the local FE colleges. Pupils would leave us and start a course at the college where the tutors would have no prior knowledge of their needs.

Today we start to prepare for transition in Years 9 and 10. I have a discussion with the careers adviser in school and at transition reviews we also meet the special needs careers adviser for the authority. At these meetings the needs of the pupils are discussed and their preferences for FE courses affirmed.

In Year 11 the careers adviser contacts the college she feels runs the most appropriate course, and arranges an interview and discusses the pupil's needs with the tutor. When the pupil goes for interview, myself or a support assistant and the parents accompany the student so that all questions can be answered and the college is fully aware of the pupil's needs. We also make further visits to the college or have telephone calls to make sure all the information is passed on. With the parents' permission we have also started to send copies of the child's Statement, Annual Reviews and useful notes from their school files. The colleges have welcomed this extra information.

We have a hearing impaired pupil moving from school to college this year and the teacher of the hearing impaired is making sure they are fully aware of her needs.

On occasions we feel that a pupil would benefit from a taster of college to find out which would be the best course for them. Both colleges are very happy to help us with this. Some pupils have spent a week at college during work experience and others have gone for a few days at the end of the Christmas term in Year 11. These visits have been beneficial both for pupils who have made more informed decisions about courses and for the college staff who have developed a better understanding of the pupils' needs.

MANAGEMENT OF IDENTIFICATION AND ASSESSMENT PROCEDURES

As we are a secondary school many of the pupils with difficulties have already been identified in their primary schools and this information is passed on through their records and during visits by staff from our school.

We recognise the limitations of normative assessment. However, on entry every pupil takes a standardised test of reading, spelling and cognitive ability. They also take our own school maths test which is closely linked to the National Curriculum levels 3–5. We also assess any pupil who enters the school after Year 7 and whom we feel could have some difficulty.

We use the information gleaned from these records together with Key Stage 2 Standard Assessment Task (SAT) results, primary school records, parental comments and teacher observation to identify any pupil who appears to have weaknesses. We are looking for weaknesses in a skill area as well as emotional and behavioural difficulties. We are also aware that many pupils with emotional or learning difficulties also have difficulty with social relationships. If we feel that more information would be beneficial I will carry out further tests. I will use a reading test designed to pinpoint particular difficulties, or do a 'miscue analysis' so I can be more accurate about areas of difficulty. If I suspect it is a specific learning difficulty I will again use different tests and have further discussions with the pupil. If I feel there are emotional or social difficulties I will collect further information from their form teacher. If I feel that I need further assessment from an outside agency I will arrange for this. This could be from the psychologist, the learning support teachers, the hearing impaired or visually impaired team, the behaviour support service, the school nurse, the physiotherapist, occupational therapist, speech therapist or the child and family team. The role of these agencies will be discussed at greater length later.

Once it has been recognised that the pupils are experiencing difficulties they are assessed at regular intervals to see if our interventions are successful. These ongoing assessments will continue until we feel that the pupils are able to function without extra support.

PRIORITIES, STRUCTURE AND ORGANISATION OF SUPPORT FOR PUPILS

In some respects I am constrained in the way I offer support by the way the department is financed and by the Code of Practice. Most of the money to finance the department comes from the financial provision made for statemented pupils. The authority puts all statemented pupils into one of five bands according to need and allocates a sum of money according to the band. This money is then totalled and sent to the school in three lump sums. Apart from my salary, most of the salary of one support assistant and half the salary of another, the department is paid from this pot of money. I have to make sure the budget balances.

The first duty of the department is to meet the needs of the statemented pupils according to sections 2 and 3 of their Statements. The Statements written by the authority are not prescriptive and there is a great deal of flexibility for us to provide for pupils in the way we think is best. We have to meet the needs of all other pupils on the backs of the statemented ones.

Most of the resources are used to offer in-class support so I will explain how I organise this first. The first priority when I allocate support is to look at the identified needs on the Statement. If I feel these needs can be met by putting several pupils in the same class or offering similar intervention I will do this. I talk to all departments at the end of the summer term, when they are organising settings for the following year, and encourage them to group pupils so I can offer the most effective support.

During the summer holidays I receive a copy of the master timetable and also have copies of the set lists. I then start to allocate support to areas of need. The support assistants work within departments rather than with pupils. So, as far as possible, I make sure that the one specialising in maths is supporting in that department, the one from the science department supports science, those from the English department support English and so on. This has proved a much more effective way of working as the support assistants know what resources are available, they know what curriculum is being taught and they have many more opportunities for discussion with teachers. I also make sure, again as far as possible, that if a support assistant is supporting a pupil for a subject they cover all the lessons for that subject.

I start to allocate support to pupils with the greatest need or those with specific needs like physiotherapy, support in practical subjects or behavioural support. This goes fairly smoothly for a while and things seem to fall easily into place. Eventually a point is reached when demand exceeds supply and some priorities have to be decided. Priority is given to English and maths, because I feel that if they do not progress in these areas access to many other parts of the curriculum is denied to pupils. Priority is also given to science, both for safety reasons and because this again is a very important subject for their future life. Next, priority is given to subjects such as technology where there is an element of danger for pupils with behavioural needs or poor motor and co-ordination skills. We also try to support pupils with poor co-cordination in PE because there is nothing more frustrating for a pupil than to be standing on the sideline being the last to be picked or being the person who is never able to hit the ball. It does nothing for a pupil's self-esteem. The point comes when compromises have to be made and best-fit solutions used.

This year I have a new tool at my disposal to help with timetabling. It is like a piece of Lego on which I can put blocks. The blocks are colour coded according to faculties. On the block I can write the name of the pupil, the teacher and the room where the lesson is to take place. I am hoping this will make it easier to see all the possible alternatives. The timetable is never set in tablets of stone and is constantly revised throughout the year according to changing needs and priorities. This board makes it easier to alter the timetables and I also have a space to put requests for support so that I can meet them when the opportunity arises.

Apart from in-class support the department also meets the needs of pupils in other ways. Every morning between 9 and 9.30 the pupils have assembly and class registration. We use this time to run various groups. Five support assistants run literacy groups using the Beat Dyslexia scheme (Stone 1997) as a basis. Group size varies from four to eight. These groups are run for pupils who experience the greatest difficulties with literacy in Years 7 to 10. Another support assistant runs a paired reading scheme for Year 7 pupils, using the sixth-formers as volunteers. We have found that this scheme runs best for around 12 weeks and we finish while both partners are still enthusiastic. The support assistant and I train the sixth-formers. In the spring term the same support assistant transfers her skills to running spelling workshops, again for Year 7, using the Spelling Made Easy scheme (Brand 1995). Another support assistant has been trained by the psychologist to run 'friendship groups', broadly based on Circle Time (Mosley 1991). These are run for small groups of pupils who experience difficulties making and establishing friendships or who could become victims of bullying. The same support assistant also runs groups to help those pupils who are experiencing difficulties with French. During this morning time I run a series of groups depending on need.

At lunchtime we open the support room and an adjoining classroom and we are available to offer help with homework or to provide pupils with clarification of lessons. Computers are available for pupils wishing to do research or to word-process their work. The support room also provides a sanctuary for those pupils who find the yard an intimidating experience.

We tend to try to support pupils in the classroom as much as possible but there are some occasions when withdrawal seems a better option. We have a small room that can hold a maximum of eight pupils, and we use this for withdrawal. Pupils are withdrawn for basic skills in literacy and numeracy and for Certificate of Achievement work when it does not dovetail into the GCSE option. One pupil is also withdrawn for speech therapy, to learn sign language and for physiotherapy.

During the lunch hour the support assistant who supports in PE runs the physiotherapy and occupational therapy programmes for the pupils for whom this has been recommended. She works closely with the physiotherapist and the occupational therapist.

We have spent some money this year on simple laptop computers with the aim of trying to increase the pupils' use of ICT. We encouraged those pupils with dyspraxia, specific learning difficulties and poor motor skills to make use of the machines. Unfortunately we have had a great deal of difficulty with the batteries in the machines and this has caused frustration and disappointment. The experiment has not been as successful as we would have liked. We are considering changing to a different machine as it seems the right way foward to have ICT more accessible.

MONITORING AND RECORD KEEPING

The way I monitor pupils and keep records is largely prescribed by the Code of Practice and I have had to modify and fit our system into its restraints. This is not to say that I do not welcome the Code of Practice. It has improved record keeping, encouraged regular monitoring and made me think about effective and manageable targets and the strategies needed to achieve them.

The main concern of our department is how to keep the recording system manageable and not to drown in paper while still making sure that all staff who teach a pupil are aware of his or her needs and of the generic targets set on the Individual Education Plan. When we devised our IEPs, our central concern was that they should be not too arduous for the teacher to fill in and should fit on one side of A4. I feel they cover the main criteria set down by the Code of Practice. The only omission perhaps is that there is no space for parents' comments. Each time I review a pupil's IEP, if the parents are not present at the review I will contact them and explain what progress has been made and what our current concerns are. I inform them of what the school is proposing to do and explain how we feel they could best support their child. I feel this is a better form of communicating rather than sending home a document that is really intended for a different audience. The IEP also does not show the targets that are being set on individual numeracy and literacy programmes because these are usually too specific to be of great use or interest to the subject teacher. The IEP simply indicates the programmes that are in place. We hoped that with this IEP staff would have some input and take ownership.

The system for issuing IEPs works like this:

- I meet with the pupil, assess them and discuss with them perceived areas of difficulty. If it is a review we look at comments of the staff.
- I complete a review sheet with the student present then transfer the agreed targets on to the IEP. On the top of the IEP I indicate which staff should receive a copy.

- I hand the IEP to the senior support assistant who photocopies it and issues a copy to the relevant teachers.
- The teachers indicate what strategies they will use to meet the generic targets then add any targets of their own. They then photocopy the sheet for their own reference and return the original to us. (This makes sure the targets are filled in!)
- When the review is due the support assistant re-issues the IEP for teachers to add their review comments. The sheet is then returned to us.
- I then see the pupil again, fill in a review form and the process starts again.

At the learning support meetings we do look at the IEP and see if it could be more effective. We made minor changes, like putting a tick list for strategies but although we have looked at many different examples the teachers have felt that ours follows the spirit of the Code of Practice, is as streamlined as possible and meets our needs.

Besides IEPs we also keep other records. At the beginning of the school year every teacher is issued with a special needs register. This is more detailed than many registers I have seen. Pupils are listed by form group. The register shows the pupils' names, the stage of the Code that they are on, and the difficulties in learning that they experience. Initially I used to regularly update the register and issue new ones. This became arduous and the cost phenomenal. I now ask the subject representatives to bring their register to the learning support meeting and it is amended hall-termly at the meeting. The representatives are then asked to disseminate this information to their departments.

We do have another record sheet that we use to gain information for statemented pupils prior to their Annual Review. This is a more detailed form and is specifically linked to the needs of the Annual Review.

I have not been able to review IEPs termly – there simply is not enough time during the year. I use the parents' evening as one of the reviews and all the parents of pupils on the register get a personal invitation from me. If there is a big issue I do ask parents to attend at other times in the year, otherwise I will contact them by phone or letter. They are given an opportunity to come in and discuss their child's progress in more detail. Parents generally appear satisfied with this situation.

At present records are largely kept as hard copies in a filing cabinet. I do not have access to the school's computer system yet, although I have requested this. The typing of letters, Annual Reviews and any other correspondence is done on my personal computer at home in the evening. I have a record sheet on which I record dates of reviews and who has returned IEPs. Computers would make a lot of the record keeping easier but I think there are two dangers with them.

- SENCOs with computers tend to print large volumes of information about the child, some largely irrelevant to present needs, because it is sitting on the computer. I have seen some IEPs run to four pages!
- It is very easy to let the computer do the thinking and just pick out targets and strategies from a prepared list rather than thinking about individual needs.

In the filing cabinet I also keep records of any contact I have had, about a child, with parents, outside professionals or school staff.

LIAISON AND PARTNERSHIP WITH PARENTS, OUTSIDE AGENCIES AND OTHER STAFF

I work closely with parents whose children are on stage 3 and above and emphasise that I am always available and ready to speak to them. When we first discuss the needs of their child I tell them I would rather that they contact me about small issues that can easily be resolved rather than wait until they are big issues that are far harder to resolve. During the five years that their children are at school I get to know many of the parents extremely well. If a support assistant works particularly closely with one pupil they very often will also contact the parents regularly and the parents welcome this.

The parents of pupils who are on the special needs register on stage 2 are contacted by me at parents' evenings and at the time of their review. These parents are also told to contact me if they have any issues they wish to discuss and many take advantage of this. I meet the parents of pupils who are on stage 1 at parents' evenings. If a parent rings a Head of Year about a learning difficulty or a request for the intervention of an outside agency, the Head of Year will very often pass the information to me and ask me to contact the parent.

The school has contact with many outside agencies. We have recently started to organise multidisciplinary meetings if there are many agencies involved with one child. These have proved very beneficial and have meant that we can provide much more co-ordinated support.

We have a great deal of contact with the medical services as we have pupils with physiotherapy, occupational therapy and speech therapy programmes. I do have a few discussions with these professionals but most of the liaison is done by the support assistants who deliver the programmes. We are also in regular contact with the local paediatrician, the child psychiatrist and the clinical psychologist. I work closely with social services and the community nurses. Developing personal links with these professionals makes any intervention much more effective.

Once a term I have a planning meeting with the Educational Psychologist for the school, the two teachers from the Local Support Service, the hearing impaired teacher and the Education Welfare Officer. The format of these meetings is clearly laid out. We look at all pupils on stage 3 and above and make sure there are no issues that need to be dealt with. We then discuss school and LEA issues. These meetings seem to be a good idea. They make sure that we prioritise the things that need to be done and that nothing is overlooked. I have further half-termly meetings with the support teachers where these issues are addressed.

Besides these formalised meetings I also have regular discussions with the support teachers and the Educational Psychologist, asking their advice and using them as a sounding board. It is of great benefit to me to have these outside professionals to support me. The co-ordinator's job can be a lonely and isolated one at times, and in these days of league tables we are supporting pupils who are unlikely to bring in the A*s! It is very helpful too to have someone who can act as an intermediary between school and home if things are getting a little sticky!

COMMUNICATION SYSTEMS WITHIN SCHOOL

There are various channels of communication within the school and they all serve a different purpose.

There are regular meetings which are useful forums for sharing information and which also provide opportunities for INSET. Every week I meet with the 11 learning support assistants. At these meetings I can inform them of whole-school issues that affect our department. They can share information from their departments and very importantly we can share information on pupils. If one LSA feels that a child is experiencing difficulties or there seems to be a change in their demeanour or behaviour they can bring their concerns to the meeting. Other LSAs can say if this is a common problem or if it is restricted to one department. They can also share strategies that appear to work with the pupil in other areas of the school. On numerous occasions this has led to early intervention and a swift resolution of a difficulty.

There are half-termly meetings between myself and the nominated representative from every department. These are well attended. These meetings provide me with opportunities to give specific information on pupils and also to update the special needs register, which staff are asked to bring to every meeting. They also provide me with an opportunity for INSET and to give a special needs perspective to school issues. Half-termly meetings are also held with the Head of Pastoral and Heads of Year. We call these 'IEP meetings' and they serve a dual purpose. With the support of the Head of Pastoral and myself, the Heads of Year are responsible for the documentation of those pupils on the SEN register who have behavioural difficulties. These meetings ensure that IEPs are in place, reviews are being held and the register is updated. Pupils whose behaviour has improved are removed from the register and other pupils who are causing concern are added. These meetings also provide a forum for successful intervention strategies to be discussed and information shared about possible targets to put on IEPs.

I feel that our communication system is good because we have LSAs working in every department. The teacher can quickly speak to them and information is shared with everyone through the weekly meetings. The half-termly meetings with departmental staff also means that information can be shared very easily. All staff also know that the department is open to ideas and comments and these are readily given and received.

There is regular communication through the distribution of IEPs, the seeking of comments for reviews and from the information collected for Annual Reviews. These have been discussed earlier.

CONCLUSION

This chapter gives a brief overview of the life of a SENCO in a mainstream secondary school. While talking to colleagues I have found that my experiences are very similar to theirs. We tend to share the same frustrations and areas of difficulty but we are all, almost without exception, supported by an outstanding team of learning support assistants who make the job rewarding and achievable!

REFERENCES

Brand, V. (1995) *Spelling Made Easy.* Cambridge: Egon.
Department For Education (DFE) (1994) *Code of Practice on the Identification and Assessment of Special Educational Needs.* London: DFE.
Mosley, J. (1991) *The Circle Book.* Trowbridge: Positive Press.
Stone, C. (1997) *Beat Dyslexia.* Cambridge: LDA.

8

Teacher support teams for special educational needs in primary schools

Brahm Norwich and Harry Daniels

INTRODUCTION

In this paper, we outline a system of teacher support teams (TSTs) and then report on an ESRC-funded evaluation[1] of this scheme in eight primary schools. TSTs are a system of team support of peers for individual class teachers experiencing teaching difficulties in relation to special educational needs (SENs). Individual teachers request support on a voluntary basis from a small team which usually includes the SENs co-ordinator, a senior teacher and another class teacher. Support is provided through teams of professional peers that respond to the voluntary requests that teachers make for collegial assistance with their own SENs problem-solving processes.

TST research focuses on a significant but neglected area of school development which has the potential to enhance the working conditions of teachers. Many classroom teachers feel that they do not have sufficient training and support to meet many of the challenges presented by children with SENs. TSTs provide a forum for teachers to share teaching knowledge and skill and to express and receive collegial support. In this way TSTs can also enable teachers to learn specific methods and have access to different teaching approaches.

TST development needs to be seen in the context of recent moves towards teaching more children with SENs in ordinary schools and the recognition of whole school approaches to SENs (Visser and Upton 1993). They have particular current relevance to schools with the requirements of the Education Act 1993 that all schools have SENs policies and take account of procedures and practices specified in the SENs Code of Practice. TSTs can be seen to represent a practical embodiment of a school's commitment to SENs and a significant way of implementing a school's policy for SENs.

This research builds on the success of the setting up and the initial

1 ESRC project R-000–34–3859, 'Evaluating Teacher Support Teams: a strategy for special needs in ordinary schools'.

evaluation of TSTs in three primary schools (Daniels and Norwich 1992). The lessons learned in that pilot project were then applied to the ESRC project which is reported in this paper.

RELEVANT LITERATURE

Peer support teams have been discussed in a variety of professional contexts. Quality circles (Karp 1983) are used in industry and have been developed in professional educational psychology (Fox *et al.*, 1990). In the area of mental health consultation, the work of Caplan (1970) has been influential and has been extensively applied, adapted and even mandated in some states of the US (Ritter 1978, Chalfant and Pysh 1989, Graden *et al.* 1985a and b).

There has been much work in this country on support in special needs education in general, and the work of support teachers, SENs co-ordinators and learning support in relation to curriculum development (for example, Hart 1986, Garnett 1988, Dyson 1990, Thomas 1992, Jordan 1994). However, there have only been a few examples of task-oriented peer support groups (Mead 1991, Chisholm 1994). The work of Hanko (1989, 1990) is the best known example of a school consultation and group support approach which has strong connections with the concept and practices of TSTs. Her approach was offered as a way to meet the recommendations for teacher peer support systems which were made in the Elton Report (DES 1989, recommendation 6). The TST approach described in this paper is more similar to the work of the Newcastle Educational Psychology Service, which has been involved in training teachers to act in a support capacity to their colleagues (Stringer *et al.* 1992).

THE WORKING AND NATURE OF TSTS

The operation of a TST can be summarised as follows.

1. Clear specifications of the kinds of teaching problems which could be referred to the teams by the teachers.
2. The responsibility for a request for referral being with the class teachers, not the head teacher or TST teachers.
3. The core team to include appropriately prepared class teachers, whether elected or appointed and not to include head teachers. School-based special needs teachers could be part of the core team or attend on request. Outside support personnel and parents could attend on request.

4. Identifying one teacher to co-ordinate the work of the team.
5. Specifying clear procedures for referral, the conduct of meetings, the analysis of the problems and the design of interventions, implementation, records and follow-up of interventions.

TSTs can be compared with other kinds of school-based and collaborative teacher groups. These include teachers involved in staff and department administrative meetings, in-service training groups, curriculum and general planning groups, statement review groups, outside consultant groups and whole staff case discussions. What distinguishes TSTs is their focus on teacher and teaching concerns, with individual teachers participating on a voluntary basis and there being an analysis of particular teaching concerns with a quick response and follow-up.

THEORETICAL FRAMEWORK

There is much prescription about managing and developing schools to make them more inclusive and effective for SENs (Stoll 1991, Ainscow 1993), but few theories about the conditions which affect the schools' and teachers' tolerance, capability and engagement with SENs. Where an explanatory approach is taken, it is commonly assumed that teachers differ in the extent of their tolerance and this can be related to teacher, pupil and school factors (Ramasut 1989).

Our evaluation uses a theoretical framework built on the concepts of teaching tolerance for children who are difficult to teach (Gerber and Semmel 1985, Gerber 1988). They propose that in the context of limited learning and teaching resources, tolerance is conditioned by teachers balancing the goals of increasing attainments against the goals of reducing the variations between pupils in attainment. Our framework also draws on ideas about a vicious circle in which children with SENs can come to threaten a teacher's professional self-evaluation and so receive inappropriate teaching (Gray and Richer 1988). This social-psychological process may be reconceptualised in terms of teachers coming to perceive some children as beyond their tolerance and capability.

We assume that schools' approaches to pupils with SENs can be understood in terms of *tolerance and active engagement* which operate at the institutional and classroom levels. In actively engaging with SENs, teachers and schools include and provide for the diversity of pupils, while in showing tolerance, schools and teachers cope with the challenges presented by diversity. Active engagement and tolerance are seen as complementary and inter-related processes.

Active engagement involves planned attempts to provide quality learning opportunities for children with SENs and to include them in the general planning and teaching of all children. It is expressed in both the curriculum and behaviour management at a school level, the level and quality of internal and external support for SENs and the differentiation of teaching and class management at the teacher level. Tolerance, by contrast, involves coping with and enduring the challenges and unresponsiveness of pupils with SENs. At a school level, it is expressed through requests for external support, advice or exclusions, a willingness to accept pupils with SENs, satisfaction with the SENs policy and practices and complaints to parents and local education authorities (LEAs). At a teacher level, it is expressed by attitudes to integration and inclusion, by views about the feasibility and desirability of making classroom and teaching adaptations and by personal teaching priorities. It is indicated by teachers' perceptions of how well they can cope with the range of teaching challenges and the teaching demands made by children in their class (see Table 8.1).

We suggest that TSTs may act as a way of increasing teacher tolerance and focus particularly on the individual teacher as TSTs can be understood to influence the tolerance and active engagement of those requesting support. Several assumptions are made in this framework. Firstly, we suggest that teachers come to see pupils as varying in their difficulty to teach and manage and, secondly, that individual teachers have a tolerance range for variations in attainment and social behaviour. Beyond the limits of the tolerance range, teachers come to see pupils as unresponsive to teaching and can come to lower their perception of their teaching competence and professional self-evaluation. This can lead to feelings of insecurity and anxiety which in turn

Table 8.1 Aspects of active engagement and tolerance at the school and teacher levels

	Active engagement	Tolerance
School level	Curriculum management Behaviour management Internal support activity External links	Referral activity Willingness to accept pupils with SENs Support for SENs policy/practice Policy and practice for sanctions
Teacher level	Class organisation/ pedagogy Class management Links with support	Concepts/reasons for support Attitudes to pupils with SENs Personal teaching priorities

can result in less appropriate teaching and even further unresponsiveness from pupils. By this process, teachers can come to confirm their view that certain pupils are beyond their teaching tolerance.

OBJECTIVES AND METHODS

The research had the objectives:

1. To evaluate the processes of setting up and maintaining TSTs.
2. To evaluate the short-term effects and perceived usefulness of TSTs over a period of up to two terms.

Project design

The overall project included two elements: a development part and an evaluation part. Development involved the briefing of schools and training, setting up and supporting TSTs. Training and intervention were introduced in two phases of four schools each with a pre-intervention baseline and monitoring of the processes and effects, as shown in Figure 8.1.

Ideally it would have been desirable to have used a design which permitted the use of a control group. This might have been either control schools not introducing a TST or control teachers requesting support but not receiving TST support. It was not feasible to find or match schools to act as controls, nor to conduct TSTs in schools where some teachers requesting support would not receive TST support. Nor was the alternative design of using a time series design, which required the repeated assessment of variables from pre- to post-intervention, feasible. There were practical difficulties in identifying in advance of starting the TSTs which teachers would request support and about what concerns

School terms	1 Autumn	2 Spring	3 Summer	4 Autumn	5 Spring and to Summer half-term
PHASE 1: 4 schools	Baseline	Training/set up TST	Monitoring	Monitoring	Monitoring
PHASE 2: 4 schools		Baseline	Training/set up TST	Monitoring	Monitoring

Figure 8.1 The TST evaluation design

and, therefore, the fine-grained repeated measures required for this design could not be designed and administered.

The design adopted enabled the collection of quantitative and qualitative data from pre- to post-intervention focusing on school and teacher factors. In departing from an experimental design it meant that any change following intervention could not be simply attributed to the introduction of TSTs. The evaluation was conducted using a 'disciplined eclectic' approach (Shulman 1986) which drew on the systematic use of quantitative and qualitative methods. More specifically, it used the systematic qualitative data collection and analysis methods associated with Huberman and Miles (1984).

The evaluation framework was designed to assess the processes of setting up and running TSTs and to assess the changes following the TST intervention at different levels – the school, class and teacher levels.

Evaluation framework

The evaluation framework covered the main areas, as shown in Figure 8.2.

Data collection procedures. The details of the data collection and analysis for changes in the school and teacher factors (areas 2 and 3 in the evaluation framework) are not reported in this paper. This paper covers the TST setting up and running processes, the case outcome and the perceptions of TST usefulness.

The data on the *processes of setting up the TSTs* were collected by writing up the field notes of the initial meetings with schools, from the documentation of the training programme and from the evaluation questionnaires completed at the end of the training programme.

The data on the *processes of running the TSTs* were collected from logs kept by the TSTs, from observations of the TST meetings, from the questionnaires completed at the end of the monitoring period and from the ratings of the perceived teaching demands before the TSTs were running.

The data on the *case outcomes* were collected from the records of the TST meetings. The data related to the perceptions of the usefulness of TSTs were collected by questionnaires completed at the end of the monitoring period by the head teachers, TST members and referring and non-referring teachers.

Selection of schools

In phase 1 the four primary schools in one outer London borough were invited to participate by the senior adviser for SENs. The pilot study had taken place in this LEA. The phase 2 schools (one from an inner London

(1) BACKGROUND INFORMATION ABOUT THE SCHOOLS
  – number of pupils, numbers entitled to free school meals and with statements, number of teaching staff

(2) SCHOOL FACTORS
  ● *Active engagement in relation to SEN*
    – level of internal SEN support activity, curriculum planning, behaviour management, external links
  ● *Tolerance in relation to SEN*
    – actual and desired referrals for external support, acceptance of children with significant SEN, attitudes to SEN policy and practices, complaints from and to parents and LEAs

(3) TEACHER FACTORS
  ● *Active engagement in relation to SEN*
    – class organisation and pedagogy, class management, links with outside support
  ● *Tolerance in relation to SEN*
    – integration attitudes, desirability and feasibility of SEN class adaptations, teaching self-efficacy, perceived teaching demands, personal teaching priorities

(4) TRAINING FOR AND SETTING UP TSTs
  – initial contact with schools, briefing of schools
  – training days, follow-up support meetings

(5) TST MEETINGS AND THEIR WORKINGS
  – number, duration of meetings
  – details of referred cases
  – roles of TST members, conduct of meetings
  – support for TSTs, encouragement to refer
  – referring and non-referring teachers
    – reasons for non-referring
    – differences in terms of perceived teaching demands

(6) CASE OUTCOMES AND PERCEIVED USEFULNESS OF TSTs
  – kind of support offered, judged outcomes
  – advantages/disadvantages for different parties
  – attitudes to TST continuing

Figure 8.2 Details of the areas covered in the evaluation framework

borough, two from an outer London borough and one from a rural county) were approached directly by LEA personnel and invited to participate. All the schools in both phases were then briefed by project research staff.

RESULTS

This paper only reports on the project results covering the setting up and running of the TSTs, the case outcomes and the perceptions of TST usefulness. For reasons of space it does not include data about the changes in the school and teacher factors included in the evaluation framework above.

The schools

Table 8.2 shows that four of the eight schools were JMI (junior, mixed and infants), three were infants and one was a junior school. The inner London JMI had 59.6% of the pupils entitled to free school meals and nine pupils either with or awaiting statements. The rural JMI, which had the smallest number on the roll, had only 11.6% of its pupils on free school meals and four awaiting or having statements. Most of the outer London schools had between 20 and 30% of its pupils on free school meals.

Objective 1 – the evaluation of the processes of setting up and maintaining TSTs

Setting up and training. The briefing for the phase 1 schools (schools 1–4) was conducted through a general meeting for the head teachers and special needs co-ordinators in October 1992, where the concept of TSTs and the requirements of the project were introduced. The phase 2 school heads and SENs co-ordinators were approached and consulted individually in January 1993. Follow-up meetings for discussion with all the staff were offered to all the schools and taken up by schools 1 and 7.

The three days of training included preparation for consulting with colleagues, setting up a school-based TST and simulations of receiving requests for support and devising appropriate advice. Two TST members were trained for schools 1–3 and three for the remaining five schools. The phase 1 schools were trained during January and February 1993 and the phase 2 schools during May 1993. The teacher evaluations of the training were generally very favourable. Of the 21 teachers rating the training, 16 of the 21 (76%) replied that it was good or very good, with the most valued aspect being the simulation of the TST consultations. At the end of training, 12 of the 21 (57%) respondents felt they had no pressing training needs, whilst six of the 21 (29%) wanted more support in liaising with parents.

All the schools were given at least one individual support visit per term by project staff and one four-way meeting with other schools in their phase. The TST members generally reported that they received sufficient support from the project staff.

TST meetings and working. Some teams took longer to become established and viable than others. The TST team members in some schools, who were despondent initially about referrals, were pleased to see how over time the referrals increased. The referrals also tended to be more frequent in the spring term once the teachers had become more familiar with their classes. TSTs became established and functioned fully in six of the eight schools. In schools 1 and 6 attempts were made to develop teams but without long-term success.

Table 8.2 Background details of participating schools

School profiles	School							
	1	2	3	4	5	6	7	8
Type	JMI outer north London LEA	Infants outer north London LEA	Infants outer north London LEA	Junior outer north London LEA	JMI outer east London LEA	JMI inner London LEA	JMI rural LEA	Infants outer east London LEA
Number of children	444	250	412	346	525	420	172	330
Number of statements								
Current	0	0	0	0	1	4	2	0
Pending	1	6	1	2	0	5	2	1
Number of free meals	±120 27.0%	±87 34.8%	±67 16.2%	±95 27.5%	±150 28.5%	±250 59.6%	±20 11.6%	±80 24.2%
Number of staff	18 full time	10 full time	32 full time	25 full time	16 full time	16 full time	7 full time	8 full time
Average class size	25	30	32	25	31	28	24	25 (reception) 30 (rest)
Number of SENs staff and status allowance	SENCO is deputy head	SENCO on B scale (also class teacher)	SENCO on B scale (also class teacher)	SENCO on B scale (also class teacher)	SENCO is on A scale (also class teacher)	SENCO is deputy head	SENCO 0.4 full time	SENCO is on A scale (also class teacher)

In school 1, despite a majority vote to join the project, a large proportion of the staff, including the head, were very sceptical and, in some cases, hostile to setting up a TST. This was reflected in the small number of questionnaires returned and the comments appended to the baseline questionnaires. A TST did form but did not receive any referrals. This appeared to be related to the way that the TST was presented to the staff by the deputy head teacher in terms of personal stress and counselling. The members of staff did not value this conception of TST.

School 6 experienced difficulty in implementing the TST development process. The planning of meetings and the setting up of administrative arrangements was inhibited by the changes in managerial responsibilities and the general organisational style of the school. Unlike school 1 this was not a matter of the staff rejecting the concept of TST.

TST personnel. The suggestion was made during training that they might include the SENs co-ordinator, a member of senior management and a more junior class teacher. The team composition was then decided by each school. All the TSTs had three members of staff, but with some variations. For example, school 2 set up a staff support team (SST) from the outset, including one non-teaching member of staff (a nursery nurse) alongside the SENs co-ordinator and the nurture group teacher.

Only school 3 changed the membership of the TST during the course of the project. All the other schools planned to change at least one member of the team approximately every year, but had left this longer in the first instance in order to let the new initiative become established.

The TSTs in all the schools met weekly with the typical length of meetings being 30–45 minutes. During that time all the teams usually handled the case of one referring teacher.

The meetings in schools 2 and 3 were held over lunchtime, while the meetings in schools 4 and 7 were held after school (though in school 7 all the teachers involved were released from accompanying their classes to the school buses and the TST meeting was held before a full staff meeting). In schools 5 and 8 the meetings were held during school time, specifically during the last period of the day to reduce pressure on time and so that the teachers were not concerned about their next class. The release of staff was achieved in school 5 by the classes being covered by the head and deputy head and in school 8 by classes doubling up for story time. Only one non-referring teacher (school 5) stated that the meeting time was difficult, though all the schools where the meetings were in the teachers' own time acknowledged the extra burden that this put on staff and that this may have had an impact on the number of referrals. The SENs co-ordinators in both schools where a TST was held in school time (schools 5 and 8) cited this as a very important factor in raising the status of the TST and in school 5 a vital statement of management support for the initiative.

Between six and seven TST meetings were held on average per term over the six schools. In all the schools, the three members of the TST were present for nearly all the meetings. The meetings went ahead with only two members if necessary.

Support for TST. The data from the final questionnaire to all the members of the school teaching staff in the six schools showed support for the TST arrangement. Only three of the 98 teachers from these schools questioned the appropriateness of TSTs. The head teachers were also seen as supportive of TSTs. However, there were comments from some non-referring teachers that their head teacher could have increased her/his support for the TST by making more resources available.

Whilst the majority felt that nothing more could be done to increase support for the TSTs, 38 of the 98 (39%) teachers felt that the opportunity to learn about TST outcomes from teachers who had TST support would have been beneficial. This was also echoed by some SENs co-ordinators and TST team members (three) and also included better briefing about TSTs and more enthusiasm from the head. However, it was believed in all the schools that this would be difficult to achieve without removing the atmosphere of confidentiality and, though some expressed the view that confidentiality was less important than it had been or that it was not vital, none wanted this aspect removed.

Referring to TST. All 41 referring teachers felt fairly or very encouraged about requesting support, while 12 of the 57 (21%) non-referring teachers did not feel encouraged or only slightly encouraged. No problems in arranging times to request support were reported.

Conduct of the meetings. In all the TSTs there were designated roles for the three TST members during the meetings. There was typically one chair, one scribe and one other (e.g. support/tea maker) though the boundaries of responsibility were not rigid. All three were involved in supporting and offering suggestions and the roles generally varied from meeting to meeting. Several observations were made of the TST meetings and these showed that they were conducted efficiently but not formally, with time allocated for putting the referring teacher at ease, analysing the situation, discussing support/strategies, summing up and setting targets to be reviewed. Confidential notes were kept of all the meetings and these were usually held centrally in a locked file to which only the TST had access. Each team also kept details of the meeting arrangements and a weekly log of the requests for support, including information about the pupils involved, age, sex, the kinds of difficulties, the advice provided, the follow-up, others contacted and the outcomes of the TST work.

TST cases. Table 8.3 shows that there were fewer requests for girls than boys. The greater number of requests for children aged 5 and 6 years reflects the larger number of infant and JMI schools rather than a

Table 8.3 Summary of cases dealt with by six TSTs

Pupil age

Age	4	5	6	7	8	9	10	11	N/A
Frequency	1	10	10	8	4	4	4	7	6

Pupil gender

Male	33
Female	14
Both (group)	1
N/A	6

Teacher gender

Male	3
Female	38

Number of cases
49 (some teachers referred more than one case)

Follow ups

Number	0	x 1	x 2	x 3
Frequency	15	26	7	1

Case open or closed

Open	21
Closed	28

Kinds of difficulty referred
(cases can involve more than one difficulty)

Behaviour	24
Learning	19
Social	8
Emotional	4
Child transfer	1
Whole school	2
Whole class	3
Parental request	1
New teacher	1

Behaviour management	12

Forms of support offered
(cases can involve more than one kind of support)

Behaviour management strategies	12
Records of concern	20
External referral	7
Referral within school	7
Special welfare support	4
Involving parents	7
Extra TST time	9
Teaching strategies	11
General support	8
Peer support	2

Table 8.3 (cont'd)

Others consulted	
Head teacher/ senior management	8
Parents	5
Educational psychologist	4
Another teacher	3
Progress centre	2
Nursery staff	2
Social services	2
Educational welfare officer	1
School nurse	1
Family centre	1
Other	2
None	19

N/A, not available.

particularly large number of problems at this age. Most cases had one or more follow-up meetings. Approximately 80% of those recorded as having no follow-up were cases in which the follow-up meeting was pending at the end of term. A total of 28 cases (57%) were considered closed by the teams indicating a sufficient improvement or a change in circumstances.

The majority of the referrals across all the schools were about children's behaviour problems and, to a slightly lesser extent, learning difficulties. In schools 3 and 5, behaviour problems represented the majority of cases, particularly in school 3. In schools 2, 4 and 8 referrals about learning problems outnumbered those for behaviour.

Objective 2 – short-term effects and perceived usefulness

Judged outcomes. The outcome details of the referral meetings were available for schools 2, 4, 5, 7 and 8. The outcomes were generally judged by the TST teams and referring teachers as positive. An analysis of the TST meetings logs showed the following.

1. Ten of the 49 cases (20%) in which specific notes were made about increased teacher confidence and happiness.
2. Sixteen of the 49 cases (33%) in which some degree of child improvement was noted.
3. Fourteen of the 49 (28%) which involved some future action with the consequences as yet unknown.

In only one case was mention made of continuing teacher concern. In no case were there reports of no improvement for the pupils. Data were unavailable for eight cases (16%).

Advantages and disadvantages for different parties. The data was collected from the heads, SENs co-ordinators and referring and non-referring teachers from questionnaires, but also through selected final interviews.

Head teachers. The confidential nature of the TST activities made it difficult for the head teachers to comment on their usefulness. However, the head teachers had no negative comments and where benefits were cited it was felt that the TSTs led to a smoother running school with a happier staff. For example, one initially sceptical head teacher said.

> . . . I've so far been wrong because I didn't want it, I voted against it, I was very sceptical about it for, I thought, very sound reasons, my colleagues on the whole were very much in favour of giving it a go and without doubt they've been proved right.

> The three people who have been to the TST have benefited enormously themselves professionally. Their own status if you like has been enhanced and their own expertise has been developed through this role. So it's been good for them. It's been good for the school because every colleague has had that first port of call for advice. It's been informal and yet there's been a certain formality which itself has heightened its status. So that has been very satisfactory and I think it's certainly, as I said before, influenced individual teachers and individual children and therefore had an effect both on the behaviour policy of the school and the children's learning.

TST members. TST members reported that they had learned the importance of listening to colleagues (18 reports), new strategies for use in classes (six) reports, the similarity of all teachers' difficulties (five) reports and working as part of a team (three) reports. The outcomes for them included feeling useful (seven) reports, learning about colleagues concerns (six) reports and gaining confidence (five) reports.

Referring teachers. All but one of the referring teachers reported that they would be happy to request support again. Almost all (39 out of 41 or 95%) felt that the strategies and approaches offered by the TST were fairly or very workable. All were able to use them and all felt that they had been fairly or very useful. The majority (78%) had also used them with other children. This was true despite the fact that the approaches, strategies or materials suggested were already familiar to the teachers. 'Nothing new but of real value nevertheless' is a quote which summarised a common attitude. The TSTs were seen to help teachers access relevant aspects of their own teaching competence. When asked to define the nature of support they had been offered, the following was reported.

1. Fourteen out of 41 or 34% reported that the TST enabled them to distance themselves from a problem and re-examine their activities.
2. Nine out of 41 or 22% reported that the process enabled problems to be aired.
3. Five out of 41 or 13% reported that the process enabled them to form their own strategies.
4. Five out of 41 or 13% cited the TST as an opportunity to let off steam legitimately and that it was cathartic to talk to sympathetic colleagues with a non-judgemental attitude.
5. Three out of 41 or 7% felt that an approach they were already using was confirmed as appropriate.

Of the 21 randomly interviewed teachers at baseline and follow-up across the schools, only four had made a referral to the TSTs. A typical comment from a referring teacher was as follows:

> It has been very supportive; it's an opportunity to talk and clarify what's going on. It does make you think . . . you can think at home 'Oh, blow it, tomorrow's another day sort of thing', but it does because they then not so much as push you, but they ask you . . . you've got a follow-up date, so something has had to have been done by that follow-up date, so it does help you. Yes, it's good.

Another referring teacher commenting on the special contribution of a TST said that

> there's always been an informal teacher support team anyway and I will still use that – I will go in at the end of the day and say 'Oh what can I do with this child' or 'Have you got ideas?'. So that's still there and I suppose it's still my first port of call because I want something that's immediate. But where I can see it's not just something that's going to go away in five minutes something that I can't do instantly then I will take that to teacher support.

Non-referring teachers. Most of the 57 non-referring teachers (61%) did not consult the TST because they felt that they already received adequate support from colleagues. In addition, 12% felt that they did not have any serious teaching concerns and 2% felt that the timing of meetings was a problem. The majority of non-referring teachers stated that they would refer to a TST in the future if they experienced problems, if they could not solve problems alone (24%) or if they could not talk to colleagues (33%).

If they were to refer, 31% of the teachers stated that they would like to develop strategies for use in class with the children, 21% favoured reassurance that they were coping satisfactorily, 15% wanted withdrawal of the child and 15% wanted in-class support from the SENs co-ordinator.

A typical reason for not needing support from the TST was as follows:

> No I haven't had any contact at all with the teacher support team at all in the time that it's been running. I think because I did feel that I was keeping on top of the class last year, I mean it drained me but I did feel able to cope and because of my network of contacts here I felt I was already receiving a lot of suggestions that I could put into practice.

Not being helped by TST was another reason for not referring:

> I don't see it helping me. That is probably sounding very smug but I've been teaching 36 years . . . there are very few problems that I haven't come across or had to deal with or . . .

In interview, some non-referring teachers expressed doubts about referring to a TST because they were unsure that there would be any practical value. A typical comment of this type came from school 5:

> I don't really mean to imply that it's a paper tiger, but I do think it could be just a sop. If they had hours allocated for support if you went to them or something, then I think it would be much more powerful and I might go along.

The doubts of some teachers about TST were summarised by a TST member in these terms:

> I think that people aren't against it, it's just that some don't feel the need to use it and others perhaps would feel uncomfortable because of losing face, and I think that could be some of it. Also, we have a very supportive staff and that's another reason why I think that it's not being used . . . we think that as long as it's there . . . it can be used whenever it's needed, that's the important thing. It's there as a resource to be used when needed.

Most of the referring teachers (89%) and TST team members (69%) felt that the TST had very or quite positively affected *the work of the SENs co-ordinators*. The positive benefits most commonly included more awareness of special needs across the school, followed by providing a forum for discussion and the sharing of ideas and strategies.

Attitudes to TST continuing. Most of the referring teachers, heads, SENs co-ordinators and TST members expressed the view that the TST had helped the school to a moderate degree to make better provision for special needs. Only two respondents felt that the TSTs had not helped at all, whilst three (two from school 2 and one from school 4) felt that the TSTs had helped significantly.

Most respondents felt that the staff and heads were generally supportive of the TST idea. Difficulties were reported with settling to a pattern of regular meetings in school 8 and a lack of school commitment, the level of EP support and communicating about cover arrangements in school 5.

Most respondents (81%) felt that the head teachers wanted the TSTs to continue. Doubts were only expressed by two teachers in schools 3 and 4 and by one teacher in school 5.

DISCUSSION

The project succeeded in setting up and running TSTs in six of the eight primary schools. The evaluation reported in this paper focuses on the processes of setting up and running TSTs, the perceived case outcomes and the usefulness of the TST arrangements. As such, it is the first reported evaluation of this kind of support arrangement in the UK and is comparable with evaluations of similar schemes in the US (Chalfont and Pysh 1989). However, for funding reasons the longer term outcomes of the TSTs after they had become fully established in the schools were not evaluated.

The evaluation also gave some indicators about the conditions which led to two of the schools not managing to set up TSTs. As discussed in the full project report and elsewhere (Daniels and Norwich 1992, Norwich and Daniels 1996), how schools find out about TSTs is critical for whether they decide to develop and how they set up and run a TST. Schools were briefed about the nature and purposes of TSTs, but still there were some doubts about the significance and implications of the arrangement for particular schools. This stage was important in school 1 which did not receive TST referrals. The person responsible for communicating the TST principle to colleagues did so in terms of personal counselling rather than work-related support. This led to confusion among many staff who did not fully understand the idea of a TST and so questioned the value of a TST for their school. By contrast, the staff in school 6 in phase 2 could see the benefits of a TST, but could not establish and run one. It had difficulties in arranging TST meetings and referrals, which could be attributed to organisational and management factors. This was also the inner London school with the highest number of pupils entitled to free school meals.

Experience in the US indicated that the critical factor in establishing TSTs is the commitment of time and staffing to the arrangement (Chalfant and Pysh 1989). A significant finding in this study was that six schools were able to find time during lunchtime or after school in four and towards the end of the school day in the other two. Schools were also able to widen the membership of the TSTs to include non-teachers and so broaden the support to cover all the members of school staff.

The observation and questionnaire data indicated that the TST meetings were conducted in a professional manner, achieving a good balance between being systematic and sympathetic. The balance of membership between the senior and junior staff and those with specific SENs and other responsibilities worked well. The teams also managed to keep records of their proceedings as required by the evaluation project, but which were necessary for the follow-up meetings.

It is clear that teachers who requested support from the TSTs were focusing mainly on individual pupils about whom they had concerns about their learning and behaviour. These pupils did not have significant difficulties which called for statutory assessment and a statement of SENs. They were pupils with milder difficulties who would be considered to be at SENs Code of Practice stages 1, 2 or 3. However, some requests did not focus on individual pupils, but on whole class or whole school concerns. That teachers were willing to raise such concerns illustrates that TSTs are a teacher-centred strategy for support and, as such, act as a way of linking SENs matters to wider school and class management and development matters. The questionnaire and some interview data indicated that when teachers refer to a TST they are helped to cope with a difficult situation. Their increased confidence can be interpreted as leading to a situation appearing more *tolerable*. This is particularly the case when they find a way of *actively engaging* with a problem which had previously seemed intractable. Referring teachers found that their perceptions of difficulty were validated and enhanced and that the utility of their own intervention strategies was reaffirmed. This was a significant source of encouragement. A structured follow-up which permitted extended systematic discussion was also highly valued. This form of follow-up distinguishes a TST from informal peer support which the TST was seen to complement. Although some of the suggested TST strategies were unfamiliar, most were not. The high level of satisfaction with the advice indicates that the TSTs acted to stimulate teachers to access their pedagogic competence that they had already acquired, but is not available in their particular contexts. Non-referring teachers had distinct attitudes to the TSTs. They either felt that it was not relevant to them or that, although it was not of immediate value, it might be of use in the future.

This study focused on the process factors and the short-term perceived effects for the referring teachers, non-referring teachers, TST members and head teachers. Interviews with selected teachers provided corroborating data to compare with the main questionnaire source of data. However, there was some loss of data as some teachers left the school before the questionnaires could be completed. However, there were also a few teachers, the non-referring ones, who were not interested in completing the forms. There was also some incomplete data about case outcomes from the TST records. Future research into TSTs needs to pay special attention to these practical data collecting matters to finding systematic but non-obtrusive ways of monitoring the TST support process during the TST meetings. As in other studies of school developments, there is a need to find ways of direct monitoring of pupil change following organisational change, in this situation following TST support for their teachers. Further research is also needed into evaluations of the longer term impact of TSTs and the specific nature of the team support process.

These results are revealing and encouraging about the potential of TSTs as a support arrangement in certain primary schools. This has particular relevance to primary schools as the TST is a school arrangement which exemplifies that SENs is a whole school responsibility. TSTs can play an important part in a school's response to the requirements of the SENs Code of Practice.

REFERENCES

Ainscow, M. (1993) *Towards Effective Schools for All.* (Policy Options for Special Educational Needs) Tamworth: NASEN.

Caplan, G. (1970) *Theory and Practice of Mental Health Consultation.* Tamworth: Basic Books.

Chalfant, J. C. and Pysh, M. (1989) 'Teacher assistance teams: five descriptive studies on 96 teams', *Remedial and Special Education* **10**(6), 49–58.

Chisholm, B. (1994) 'Promoting peer support among teachers', in Gray, P., Miller, A. and Noakes, J. (eds) *Challenging Behaviour in Schools.* London: Routledge.

Daniels, H. and Norwich, B. (1992) 'Teacher support teams: an interim evaluation report'. Institute of Education, London University.

DES (1989) *Discipline in schools* (The Elton Report). London: HMSO.

Dyson, A. (1990) 'Effective learning consultancy: a future role for special needs coordinators', *Support for Learning* **5**(3), 116–27.

Fox, M., Pratt, G. and Roberts, S. (1990) 'Developing the educational psychologists' work in the secondary school: a process model for change', *Educational Psychology in Practice* **6**(3), 16–39.

Garnett, J. (1988) 'Support teaching: taking a closer look', *British Journal of Special Education* **15**, 15–18.

Gerber, M. (1988) 'Tolerance and technology of instruction: implications for special education reform', *Exceptional Children* **34**, 309–14.

Gerber, M. M. and Semmel, M. I. (1985) 'The micro-economics of referral and re-integration: a paradigm for evaluation of special education', *Studies in Educational Evaluation* **11**, 13–29.

Graden, J. L., Casey, A. and Christenson, S. L. (1985a) Implementing a pre-referral intervention system. Part I: the model', *Exceptional Children* **51**, 377–84.

Graden, J. L., Casey, A. and Christenson, S. (1985b) Implementing a pre-referral intervention system. Part 2: the data', *Exceptional Children* **51**, 487–96.

Gray, J. and Richer, J. (1988) *Classroom Responses to Disruptive Behaviour.* London: Longmans.

Hanko, G. (1989) 'After Elton – how to manage disruption', *British Journal of Special Education* **16**(4), 140–3.

Hanko, G. (1990) *Special Needs in Ordinary Classrooms, Supporting Teachers.* Oxford: Blackwell.

Hart, S. (1986) 'Evaluating support teaching', *Gnosis* **9**, 26–32.

Huberman, A. M. and Miles, M. (1984) *Innovation up Close: how school improvement works.* New York: Plenum Press.

Jordan, A. (1994) *Skills in Collaborative Classroom Consultation.* London: Routledge.

Karp, H. B. (1983) *A Look at Quality Circles – 1983 annual for facilitators, trainers and consultants.* University Associates.

Mead, C. (1991) *A City-wide Evaluation of PSG Training.* Birmingham: Birmingham LEA.

Norwich, B. and Daniels, H. (1996) 'Teacher support teams in primary schools', ESRC Report (unpublished).

Ramasut, A. (ed.) (1989) *Whole School Approaches to Special Needs.* Lewes: Falmer Press.

Ritter, D.R. (1978) 'Effects of school consultation program on referral patterns of teachers', *Psychology in the Schools* **15**, 239–43.

Shulman, L. S. (1986) 'Paradigms and research programs in the study of teaching', in Wittrock, M. (ed.) *Handbook of Research on Teaching*, 3rd edn, 3–36. New York: Macmillan.

Stoll, L. (1991) 'School effectiveness in action: supporting growth in schools and classrooms', in: Ainscow, M. (Ed.) *Effective Schools for All.* London: David Fulton Publishers.

Stringer, P., Stow, L., Hibbert, K., Powell, J. and Louw, E. (1992) 'Establishing staff consultation groups in schools', *Educational Psychology in Practice* **8**(2), 87–96.

Thomas, G. (1992) *Effective Classroom Teamwork.* London: Routledge.

Visser, J. and Upton, G. (1993) *Special Education in Britain after Warnock.* London: David Fulton Publishers.

9

Working with outside agencies

Caroline Roaf

INTRODUCTION

In the UK, the 1990s have seen a gradually increasing development of the Special Educational Needs Co-ordinator (SENCO) role in relation to the different professional circles in which they work. First, in the inner circle of their colleagues in school, the classroom teachers and the different curriculum and year teams each have their own distinctive style and make their own distinctive demands on their pupils. SENCOs will be familiar with these differences and their effects. Their overview enables them to develop whole-school approaches to ensure that curriculum access becomes a reality. Secondly, for the educational agencies outside the school such as Special Educational Needs Support Services (SENSS), Educational Welfare Service (EWS), youth services, careers service and the local education authority (LEA) officers and advisers, the SENCO is a key intermediary. Thirdly, for the agencies beyond education, health and social services, police and the voluntary sector (itself an increasingly diverse sector making a significant impact in school), the SENCO represents the interface between school and community. The slow movement since the 1981 Education Act towards the inclusion of all children in mainstream settings has pushed SENCOs closer to all these boundaries and has made the cultivation of effective intra- and inter-agency relationships a priority. For many SENCOs the co-ordination role, in which, according to dictionary definition, 'parts are brought into proper relation', is now outstripping what was until relatively recently predominantly a teaching role.

In this situation, SENCOs need the assistance of a mental map and command of the metaphorical language which inter- and intra-agency work seems to generate. The use of the word 'outside' is itself metaphorical, suggesting the existence of a box or a room or possibly a house or garden. It is worth playing around with this idea to find metaphors which suit the different types of agency interaction with which SENCOs are now familiar. For me, a helpful metaphor is the playing field.

Put the playing field in a leisure park with a pavilion or two and we achieve a picture with some resemblance to the mix of profession, agency and institution in which the SENCO operates. In my park are a number of playing fields for different ball games separated by large stretches of rough ground. Each game is played according to its own rules and etiquette, and the players rarely stray out of their allotted space. The balls, however, are less easily controlled and some, for whatever reason, are to be found in the rough ground between. This chapter is about who goes into the rough ground to look for them, who else they meet out there, how they can best interact and what they decide to do with the balls they find.

This is by no means an easy task given the other roles held by many SENCOs, especially in primary schools. Finding time to develop the role with agencies beyond the school is difficult and those agencies are themselves under pressure. Matters are further complicated because of each agency member's unfamiliarity with the hierarchy, status, codes of practice and legislation governing the others. Agency members also vary in terms of their practical experience, understanding and interpersonal skills. In this situation much can be gained from an approach which, while recognising these difficulties, develops existing systems to structure inter- and intra-agency relationships slowly and formally within schools and local communities. Too often:

> Practitioners continue to feel threatened by, and anxious about, inter-agency collaboration. Where conflicts arise these are often attributed to personalities and individual agency difficulties rather than to the lack of a structure which would support and validate collaboration. There is little perception that effective joint working might alleviate the problems of the agencies as well as those of the young people.
> (Roaf and Lloyd 1995, p.1)

This chapter looks first at the legislative and historical background to the role of the SENCO in the UK in relation to outside agencies. It then considers the factors which seem to have been associated with successful inter-agency co-operation in the past. Finally it applies this understanding to the work of the SENCO and offers suggestions for successful strategies and practice.

RECENT LEGISLATION

The 1994 Code of Practice

Of the seven areas the Code suggests the SENCO or 'designated teacher' should be responsible for, only one specifically mentions external agencies (DFE 1994, para. 2:14). Later sections state that effective implementation of policy will only be possible:

> if schools create positive working relationships with parents, pupils, the health services and the local authority social services departments (SSD), as well as with LEAs and any other providers of support services. Many children with special educational needs have a range of difficulties and the achievement of educational objectives is likely to be delayed without partnership of all concerned.
>   (DFE 1994, para. 2:27)

However, while para. 2:38 sets out the duties placed by the 1989 Children Act and the 1993 Education Act on schools, LEAs, the health services and the social services to co-operate, it does so with the let-out clauses reminiscent of the 1981 Education Act: 'so long as the request is compatible with their duties and does not unduly prejudice the discharge of any of their functions' (Children Act 1989, Section 27), or 'subject to the reasonableness of the request in the light of available resources' (Education Act 1993, Section 166). These clauses may be a necessary caution for inter-agency enthusiasts but also stifle them. Thus while guidance is provided on the kind of relationship and reciprocity workers in education can expect from those in health and social services in relation to children with physical, mental health or social needs, the language is couched in terms of 'should' and 'may', and the arrangements as to how this should come about are not specified.

Agency co-operation is also required to maintain a balance between universal and targeted provision. In its 1994 report the Audit Commission stresses that:

> In areas such as education and primary preventative health care, the main task is to ensure worthwhile and well-organised universal provision and encourage universal uptake. In others, such as child protection, the task is to identify and provide services on a selective basis. In the latter case, failure to target means not only a waste of resources but also a failure to ensure the well-being of those children who slip through the net of universal services, or for whom universal provision is insufficient.
>   (Audit Commission 1994, para. 10)

One of the key themes identified by the Commission 'To fulfil the expectations of the Children Act and the NHS and Community Care Act, and provide the most cost-effective support to children in need' (para. 10) was that the provision of services must be jointly co-ordinated and based on partnership between agencies and parents.

1997 Green Paper and 1998 Action Programme

In spite of this encouragement, it was still unclear to most practitioners how this degree of co-operation was to be achieved in practice. In the political and economic climate of the last Conservative government, practitioner attempts at collaboration depended on local initiative, often between committed individuals working in isolation. By contrast, the Labour government in 1997 was notable for its public reaffirmation of the need for collaborative working. The 1997 Green Paper declares 'The Government, LEAs, other local agencies and business need to work together in supporting the education of children with SEN' (DfEE 1997, p.69). Nonetheless, the paper poses questions rather than answers: 'What are the barriers to improved collaboration . . . ? How can these be overcome?' (DfEE 1997, p.72). Thus the 1998 Action Programme to meet special educational needs, while committing the government to 'promote "joined up thinking" between central Government Departments in the development of policy [and] . . . improvements locally, both in relation to strategic planning and effective delivery of services' (DfEE 1998, p.33), does not specify how joined-up thinking will translate into joined-up practice.

PAST HISTORY

At this point, it is worth looking back to some earlier thinking on inter-agency cooperation to identify factors associated with successful inter-agency working in the past. Most writers on the subject agree that it is necessary but difficult to achieve.

> It is easy to argue the value of inter-agency liaison and collaboration: the interrelatedness of personal, social, educational and health needs, issues of effectiveness and 'value for money' and so on are all reasons for working together. But working together is not easy, and exhortation is not enough.
> (University of Leicester Manual for Managers on Part III of the Children Act 1989, p.14)

> There can be no inquiry or report published in the last twenty or so years on major problems affecting children's welfare that has not strongly underlined the need for multi-professional collaboration in services.
> (Wilson 1993, p.10)

Furthermore, according to Hornby (1993), children are at the centre of different domains and different discourses and have, on this account, more professionals involved with them than any other group. They are also more exposed than others to 'wicked issues'. This concept, developed originally in the USA, was introduced to the UK relatively recently. Hodgkin and Newell (1996) use the term to describe policy problems which are 'intractably complex issues where the nature of the problem and the solution are not fully understood, and which involve more than one department and [are] not dealt with satisfactorily by any' (Hodgkin and Newell 1996, pp.32–3). According to Clarke and Stewart they include:

- environmental issues and an aspiration to sustainable development
- problems of crime and an aspiration to safe communities
- problems of discrimination and an aspiration to an equitable society
- problems of poverty and an aspiration to more meaningful life.
  (Clarke and Stewart 1997, p.1)

These require harmony between government, agency and professional purpose of the kind attempted in, for example, Norway or Canada, in relation to children and families in the context of the development of a good and just society (Adler 1994). Without this, attempts to overcome 'wicked issues' can only be remedial or, at best, of local significance. This has added importance for two reasons. First, all four 'wicked issues' have a bearing on children's lives and children are consequently more adversely affected by the failure of agencies to co-operate than any other group. Secondly, the problems generated by these issues require agency responses which target provision flexibly without jeopardising universal provision. In the school context this dilemma is one with which SENCOs are only too familiar.

In the UK, the history of attempts to resolve this conflict through joined-up thinking and action can be traced back to World War I and the arrival of the Child Guidance movement in this country from America. In a wider context, in relation to public services, the Beveridge Report's survey of the national schemes of social insurance and allied services (HMSO 1942) introduced the concept of a seamless web of services to a post World War II generation keen to tackle class division, inequality and deprivation. The holistic approach to public services encouraged by Beveridge was picked up by other thinkers of the time. The Kilbrandon Committee, for example, reporting in Scotland in 1964, was set up in response to concern over increased juvenile offending in the 1950s and 1960s, 'to consider the provision of the law of Scotland relating to the treatment of juvenile delinquents and juveniles in need of care or protection or beyond parental control' (Kilbrandon Report 1964, para. 1). The report recommended altering the mechanisms of juvenile justice in Scotland to establish juvenile panels and 'matching field organisation' (para. 232). This led to the establishment of the Scottish Children's Hearing system, a system unique to Scotland. For Kilbrandon:

> Delinquency is predominantly an activity of the young . . . emphasis ought to be given to preventative and remedial measures at the earliest possible stage . . . . This implies . . . a procedure which from the outset seeks to establish the individual child's needs in the light of the fullest possible information as to his circumstances, personal and environmental.
>
> (Kilbrandon Report 1964, p.39, para. 78)

The system depended on resources provided by health, social services and social work agencies and was therefore interested in the development of policies relating to the provision of these resources. For some, the emphasis on preventative work in the development of the Scottish juvenile justice system led to a system which was intrinsically inter-agency:

> It may be that the Scottish system of large regional authorities, child-centred practices and the consensus framework of the children's hearings, have all contributed uniquely to a climate which is conducive to such [inter-agency] initiatives.
>
> (Gill and Pickles 1989, p.vi)

Subsequently in England and Wales, a succession of government reports such as Plowden (CACE 1967), Seebohm (HMSO 1968) and Warnock (DES 1978) and others from organisations such as the Audit Commission, the National Children's Bureau and other charitable foundations have for many years recommended holistic, inter-agency approaches to children and families. Intermediate Treatment, an initiative springing from the more inclusive and preventative approaches to the treatment of young offenders expressed in the 1969 Children and Young Person's Act, was likewise characteristic of the late 1960s and 1970s.

Inter-agency co-operation has therefore a long history in relation to the primary care agencies involved with children and young people. This is mirrored by an equally long history of co-operation in the business world. The combined effect is that there is now an extensive literature, going back to at least the 1960s and 1970s, on the subject of co-operation and no shortage of material through which to analyse factors contributing to success. Some of these factors are summarised here and are then examined for their effect on local practice among SENCOs.

FACTORS CONTRIBUTING TO SUCCESSFUL INTER-AGENCY WORKING

Legislation

Legislation has notably advanced the cause of minority groups in this country, starting with the 1970 Education (Handicapped Children) Act, followed by the Sex Discrimination Act (1975) and the Race Relations Act (1976), the 1981 Education Act, the 1989 Children Act, and the more recent 1997 Green Paper on SEN, 1998 Action Programme for SEN and the development of the Social Exclusion Unit. These have provided an enabling framework affirming advocacy, rights and equal opportunities, the prerequisites of inclusion.

Values and principles

Over the same period, society's values and principles and government's expression of these developed from the assimilation, equal but different, social welfare models of the 1960s towards the 1970s' emphasis on social justice and positive action. The 1990s have seen the gradual shift in thinking under successive Conservative administrations from needs-based to rights-based approaches to public services, alongside the development of the free market economy. It remains to be seen how these will be synthesised into New Labour's 'Third Way'. How, for example, will the debate develop between those who see eradicating poverty as the main weapon against social exclusion and those who see education in this role? For many SENCOs the interaction is close and provides the rationale for their involvement with other agencies. This perspective may not, however, be shared or understood by those with whom they work.

Commitment of public figures and organisations

In the past, great public figures have lent their names to the movement for social justice. The names of these figures ring in our ears: Barnado, for example, succeeded in the twentieth century by leaders such as Beveridge, Kilbrandon, Seebohm, Plowden and Warnock. Latterly, the collective conscience seems to be held by pressure group and charitable foundation. Examples are Rowntree, Gulbenkian, the National Children's Bureau, the Children's Legal Centre and Young Minds which together produce a steady stream of reports and journals promoting research, the exchange of information and participative approaches to the development of a just society for young people. A common feature is the encouragement of inter-agency practice, reinforced since 1997 by government policy.

Clarity over concepts, definitions and the client group

A major change in relation to young people has been the gradual shift from segregation and categorisation, the perception of children as objects and of disability as deficit, to the concept of children as citizens with rights and responsibilities commensurate with their age and experience. There are many semantic and philosophical issues still to be resolved in this area. Writers such as Swadener and Lubeck (1991) and Moss and Petrie (1997) caution against the indiscriminate use of expressions such as 'in need', 'at risk' because they reinforce society's negative image of children and the tendency to compartmentalise and objectify them still further. For Swadener and Lubeck a preferred term is 'at promise'. Recent SEN literature likewise, and for the same reasons, stresses diversity and inclusion. The tendency, however, as expressed in the Audit Commission passage quoted earlier, is to compartmentalise young people into categories and target them for action without any accompanying improvements in universal provision.

Inter-agency structures

Legislators have made notably few attempts to design the structures that would make inter-agency work a reality. Yet when such a structure has been devised, it has generally been effective. Among the very few examples are the Scottish Children's Hearing, the Multi-Professional Assessment (MPA) for children with special educational needs and the Working Together protocols (DoH 1998) for abused children. Of these, the MPA is interesting since it is, in effect, a paper exercise, albeit an inter-agency one. It can only, therefore, have limited success as an inter-agency structure since it does not necessitate round-table meetings of practitioners. One other potential candidate, the Joint Consultative Committee, was advocated by the 1973 National Health Service Act to promote a joint community approach. Although regarded by Warnock as vital for the co-ordination and development of services for children and young people with disabilities or significant difficulties' (DES 1978, para. 15.49), the report also recognised that these local committees vary considerably in effectiveness and some lack the status and prestige necessary to exert a major influence' (para. 16.30). Thus it seems that effective long-term inter-agency work relies on structures that command respect and that agencies are required to use.

Inter-agency strategies

While it can be argued that the most effective strategy is a structure, other movements, notably Child Guidance and Intermediate Treatment, have been influential in the professional lives of a generation of practitioners such as social workers, probation officers, child psychiatrists, educational psychologists, GPs, youth workers and teachers. In spite of the movements' gradual demise during the 1970s and 1980s, practitioners trained in these fields have survived professionally to influence the development of the youth strategies and children's services plans of the 1990s. In these, Scotland, with its very early development of coherent youth strategy, led the way. Children's services plans have been mandatory throughout the United Kingdom since 1997. However, while they have encouraged fresh approaches to the development of inter-agency perspectives among senior policy makers, SENCOs may well be unaware of their existence in practice.

Terminology used to promote co-operation

The vocabulary used to describe various forms of co-operation has increased significantly in recent years and has shifted away from terms such as multi- and inter-professional work, to terms such as inter-agency and inter-organisational work. Other phrases such as partnership, networking, collaborative advantage and meta-strategy indicate a trend towards larger units and the recognition that professionals and para-professionals are now employed in a range of private and public sector agencies. These trends are also a measure of the influence business organisations now have on public sector agencies.

Agency strategies and structures to promote co-operation

Meanwhile, agencies themselves have had to develop intra-agency values, strategies, structures and terminology to reflect their own growing complexity. These mirror those developing between agencies and pre-date them. An example is the development of the multi-disciplinary team supported by senior management and policy makers. Within these teams, multi-disciplinary, intra-agency training has been a feature. Although Seebohm and Plowden long ago advocated training in social work for doctors and health visitors, the inter-agency element in professional training has been slow to develop and is still a weak element in most initial professional qualifications. Nonetheless, opportunities for inter-agency experience have opened up in other ways. The financial constraint on all public services, leading to severe cutbacks in public services, has led to the involvement of local authority agencies in a number of inter-agency projects supported by funding from national government or charitable sources. Much of this has been experimental and developmental, and inter-agency co-operation has been a strong feature with an emphasis on staff development and practitioner research (Gill and Pickles 1989). Funding bodies have tended, however, to set up short-term pilots so that agencies' statutory responsibilities are not undermined.

Resources

Lack of agency resources seems, until very recently, to have been almost invariably presented as a reason not to co-operate rather than as a reason for doing so. The gradual accumulation of experience gained in inter-agency projects and the breaking down of professional barriers in the more fluid, mixed economy of the 1990s, seems to be reducing professional sensitivities somewhat. Agency practitioners such as health visitors, teachers, doctors, social workers and police officers are more willing than before to identify the inter-agency component in their ordinary agency job description. Moving outside an agency boundary is therefore less threatening and practitioners are less vulnerable than before to complaints from senior managers that they are acting beyond their remit. Examples of joint or shared funding have been few, however. As we have seen, the Scottish Children's Hearing system depended on resources provided by health, social services and social work agencies, as indeed has the provision for children with complex and multiple special educational needs. More recently, inter-agency support for children with emotional and behavioural difficulties, for truants, young homeless people and young offenders has come about as the result of specific government and charitable funding. Traditionally, however, agencies have been reluctant to jeopardise existing agency work to fund inter-agency projects and have relied instead on independent funding. Agencies have found it hard to re-prioritise rapidly enough to meet the volatility of some young people's needs. Consequently, monitoring organisations such as the Audit Commission report evidence of misuse of resources, delays and lack of accountability (1992, 1994).

Quantitative data

Quantitative data is an important factor underpinning successful inter-agency work. It provides the evidence on which to make a case for innovation and co-operation. Practitioners are often unwilling to leave the safety of their agencies, nor risk current services for the majority, for the sake of a tiny minority. Thus justification for inter-agency work depends on the justification for it numerically. Early attempts at inter-agency work arose from concerns about juvenile offending, for which some data was readily available. Special needs legislation was based on health service and other surveys carried out in the 1960s and 1970s. Latterly the publication of school attendance and exclusion figures has raised awareness of these problems and of the need for a collaborative response from agencies and the need to share data. Exposure of issues such as child abuse, young homelessness or permanent exclusion among primary school children has combined powerfully with the statistical evidence to bring inter-agency work in from the margins of agency activity to its core. Within schools, we see this reflected in the trend to move SENCOs into school senior management teams or to combine the role with that of the head teacher.

FACTORS IDENTIFIED BY AGENCIES AND YOUNG PEOPLE

The factors already identified have interacted in different ways over time and under different political regimes. Taken together, however, they constitute a formidable weight of evidence. Significantly, when practitioners and young people themselves are asked what they see as the main barriers to co-operation, their comments depict a range of issues which broadly confirm the factors identified in the literature. A study in the early 1990s (Roaf and Lloyd 1995, p.2) found that despite the wealth of provision for young people, parents and young people are often bewildered about how to access specialist support. They are often unaware of their rights and responsibilities, and conflicting legislation can confuse the situation. Problems are compounded for older children as different agencies have different responsibilities for people at 16. In addition, delays in assessment can be critical and sometimes young people get 'lost' in the system.

For agencies, the same study found that problems of working collaboratively are often put down to problems with individuals or a particular agency. For example:

A whole agency may be made a scapegoat for the failure of an inter-agency project . . .

Each discipline . . . has problems defining what they offer in relation to each other.

Agencies can spend too much time working on their own with [a client] and too little time in co-operation with other agencies to make effective joint plans . . .

Agencies also find it difficult to agree joint procedures for action . . .

Each agency has its own culture, language, aims and priorities. This makes its difficult for practitioners working together to see the young person as a whole and to offer a 'seamless service' . . .

There is limited understanding of what inter-agency work means in terms of skills and practice and of its potential to alleviate the problems of the agencies as distinct from those of the young people.
(Roaf and Lloyd 1995, pp.2–3)

This and other studies confirm these same difficulties and offer solutions suggesting, as did the literature, that the existence of an inter-agency structure was the single most important factor underpinning all the others. Success for an inter-agency project was associated with a well-defined management structure in which a multi-agency, multi-disciplinary team was supported on the one hand by an inter-agency senior management policy and planning group, and on the other by an effective networking system to provide feedback about gaps in provision, to identify needs and resources, and to facilitate the free flow of information among a wide range of practitioners. In general, effective structures of this kind:

- are solution focused;
- provide opportunities for creative thinking;
- challenge professionals to overcome inter-agency boundaries/ professional jealousies/vested interests;
- invite professionals to consider, and support them towards, more collaborative ways of working;
- maintain progress in the face of political change or vacuum.

The study found that examples of good inter-agency practice have a number of characteristics in common. These are:

- Formal commitment and support from senior management and from political to practitioner level.
- Formal and regular inter-agency meetings to discuss ethical issues, changes in legislation and practice, gaps in provision and information sharing at all levels to develop short- and long-term strategies.
- Common work practices in relation to legislation, referral/assessment, joint vocabulary, agreed definitions, procedures and outcomes.
- Common agreement of client group and collective 'ownership' of the problems, leading to early intervention.
- Mechanisms for exchange of confidential information.
- Frameworks for collating data and statistical information across the agencies that can inform all practice including ethnic monitoring.
- Monitoring and evaluation of services in relation to inter-agency work.
- Joint training in order to understand each other's professional role.
(Roaf and Lloyd 1995, p.4)

THE ROLE OF THE SENCO IN RELATION TO OUTSIDE AGENCIES

Turning to the role of the SENCO, we see the same patterns at work. A comparison between the factors contributing to success gleaned from the literature, and the problems experienced on the ground by practitioners and young people suggests that both factors and problems can be sorted into four generic areas. In the context of the school, these concern:

- policy,
- organisational structures,
- professional practice,
- financial arrangements.

Successful work with 'outside' agencies requires SENCOs to have developed a clear picture of how their own school functions in relation to these areas and a basic understanding of how other agencies function. In terms of policy, for example, the three primary care agencies have different values with Education being in a somewhat anomalous position. Social Services and Health are primarily concerned with risks to life, whereas Education is concerned with life chances. This contrast governs some of the disparity between these three agencies in terms of their priorities, and explains the frustration experienced by, for example, the teacher who cannot understand why Social Services has closed the case of a child regarded as educationally at risk for lack of adequate care at home. However, Education's objectives, intensified in schools, have traditionally tended to be based on concepts of excellence and norms which depend on abstractions, ideas of what can be achieved by some, and of what behaviours are to count as 'normal' and manageable. Until relatively recently, the school system as a whole was designed to select out those who did not conform and whose life chances were then, by definition, most at risk. It is then the turn of the social worker to feel frustrated with the school. A key question, therefore, is how agencies and their practitioners can be encouraged to co-operate effectively when their fundamental tenets are in opposition. A further factor is the interplay which exists within each agency between universal, preventative work and individual case (and crisis) management. The tension between these two dimensions can be extreme, particularly at times of financial constraint and political disapproval. Ideally a balance is held by all three agencies, but if under duress this balance cannot be maintained, then children and young people end up in the rough ground between agency boundaries. Once there, they become difficult to find and, when found, individual agency workers have difficulty accepting responsibility for them. It is then the turn for the parents to feel frustrated. They sometimes use graphic metaphors to describe their feelings:

> He was offending while truanting from school. A mixture of the two. In the end we felt like tennis balls because education said it was a social problem and social services said it was an education problem, and we were just going backwards and forwards from one to another. (Parent of 14-year-old boy)
>   (Roaf and Lloyd 1995, p.2)

The problem is that the *organisational structures* which would enable the work involved in the care and education of this young person to be shared equitably between the relevant agencies frequently do not exist. Without them, boundary disputes are almost inevitable regardless of what funding might or might not be available. Boundary disputes over who does what will be further exacerbated by differences in *professional practice.* Only recently (since the mid-1990s) has literature considered the question of interprofessional competencies, acknowledging that interpersonal skills are a core skill and can be taught. A recent guide for the development of partnership in the public, private, voluntary and community sectors, considers that 'Interpersonal skills are the secret weapon of a successful partnership management process' (Wilson and Charlton 1997, p.49).

> One cannot ignore the importance of interpersonal skills in any management process. These are skills which can be taught and can be acquired . . . . But skills cannot be bolted on where there is no willingness to be open about one's own position or to the different views of others.
>   (Wilson and Charlton, 1997, p.50)

Finally, the *financial arrangements* required to enable agencies to co-operate successfully over time have proved extremely difficult to make. Joint funding mechanisms of the kind which Warnock envisaged being facilitated by Joint Consultative Committees have either been underfunded themselves or ineffective. The result is over-dependence on independent sources which have been unwilling to support long-term work which in their view was the responsibility of government. Short-term grants for pilot projects have therefore been the norm.

Nonetheless, in spite of these potential difficulties, there is much the SENCO can do to overcome them. Indeed in some respects SENCOs are in an enviable position compared with their colleagues in other agencies. They see their charges every day, the school is a microcosm of society complete with a range of 'agencies' in the form of subject departments and year teams. They can, and do, with relatively little interference from others, set up the organisational structure needed to ensure effective policy making, case management and networking. They develop the interpersonal skills required for effective co-ordination. Since the introduction of local financial management in the early 1990s, there is also a significant budget 'indicated' for special educational needs since, under the terms of the 1994 Code of Practice, the school's governing body should, in relation to children with special educational needs, 'establish the appropriate staffing and funding arrangements and maintain a general oversight of the school's work' (para. 2:7). Effective special needs departments in the larger primary schools and most secondary schools in fact operate within a structure which bears all the hallmarks of the strategy proposed for effective work between agencies. Similarly, effective SENCOs will recognise in themselves and their schools the features of good practice characteristic of successful inter-agency projects.

A comparison of the inter-agency model with the secondary school special needs department shows a number of parallels, for example:

- A strong expression, in the SEN policy, of commitment to equal opportunities and a school ethos valuing diversity.
- Commitment from governors, head teacher and senior management to uphold and monitor the policy. A group representative of the school community appointed to oversee policy making in relation to SEN and equal opportunities, to review priorities and ensure these are entered in the school development plan will enhance this further.
- A multi-disciplinary team of practitioners (i.e. with a range of teaching skills and experience of diversity) including, for example, learning support assistants, counsellor, youth workers and volunteers, to whom teachers, parents and children themselves may refer for advice, support and active intervention in the form of specialist teaching, counselling or referral to outside agencies. The work of this team becomes more effective if it is jointly funded by a partnership of schools (Cade and Caffyn 1994).
- SENCOs provide the LEA, governing body and head teacher with a detailed analysis of student and school needs on which to fuse the allocation of delegated funds to promote the objectives of the SEN policy. The management of resources and funding is transparent and SENCOs and governors responsible for SEN play a full part in their allocation.
- A meetings structure enabling external agencies to meet regularly with heads of year, SENCO and other relevant staff.

Current practice in relation to this last point varies. In some LEAs, special educational needs support services (SENSS) arrange termly meetings for each of their schools, or families of schools, at which policy is reviewed, trends noted, training needs identified and referrals recommended for individual cases requiring attention from services such as educational psychology, E2L, EBD and other SEN outreach services. These regular round-table consultation meetings ensure a co-operative approach to a school and a more holistic response to young people's needs. Educational social workers tend to require more frequent, weekly meetings in school but benefit similarly if they can meet Heads of Year in the company of the SENCO and where, they exist, the school counsellor. Traditionally, the educational social worker came into school to meet with each Head of Year separately. Schools bringing Heads of Year together for this purpose with the SENCO have found that the combined experience and different viewpoints in the group has many benefits. Heads of Year, ESW and the SENCO can agree support packages, can take prompt action which can be followed up in the next weekly meeting. Challenges to school ethos, policy and accepted practice can be tackled in a safe environment and mutual support offered to colleagues, including those from outside agencies, undertaking difficult casework. Although the cost in staff time may seem high, it is repaid in effective case management, the maintenance of staff morale, school ethos and efficient working relationships with outside agencies. These meetings encourage the development of creative solutions and ensure a range of opinion is heard. The decisions then made are more likely to ensure a fair outcome since the SENCO, as advocate for the young person and holder of additional resources is present and can relieve a Head of Year who may well be under pressure from classroom teachers to exclude a child from a particular class or even from the school.

Finally, SENCOs should appreciate that they are already considerably skilled as inter-agency workers, as indeed are their colleagues in other agencies. SENCOs who have developed a secure structure within their own institutions will be in the best position first to co-ordinate universal and targeted provision in their own institution and with other education agencies, and secondly, to join with others to design the inter-agency structures each community needs to maintain the young people belonging to it within their local support networks.

REFERENCES

Adler, L. (1994) 'Introduction and overview', in *The Politics of Linking Schools and Social Services: the 1993 Yearbook of the Politics of Education Association*, 1–16. London: Falmer Press.

Audit Commission (1992) *Getting in on the Act. Provision for pupils with special needs: the national picture.* London: HMSO.

Audit Commission (1994) *Seen but not Heard: co-ordinating community child health and social services for children in need.* London: HMSO.

Beveridge Report, *see* HMSO (1942).

Cade, L. and Caffyn, R. (1994) 'The King Edward VI family: an example of clustering in Nottinghamshire', *Support for Learning* **9**(2), 83–8.

Central Advisory Council for Education (England) (CACE) (1967) *Children and their Primary Schools* (The Plowden Report) London: HMSO.

Clarke, M. and Stewart, J. (1997) *Handling the Wicked Issues: a challenge for government.* Birmingham: University of Birmingham Institute of Local Government Studies.

Department For Education (DFE) (1994) *Code of Practice on the Identification and Assessment of Special Educational Needs.* London: DFE.

Department for Education and Employment (DfEE) (1997) *Excellence for All Children: meeting special educational needs.* London: HMSO.

Department for Education and Employment (DfEE) (1998) *Meeting Special Educational Needs: a programme of action.* London: DfEE.

Department of Education and Science (DES) (1978) *Special Educational Needs. Report of the Committee of Enquiry into the Education of Handicapped Children and Young People* (Warnock Report), London: HMSO.

Department of Health (DoH) (1998) *Working Together to Safeguard Children: new government proposals for inter-agency co-operation.* Wetherby: DoH.

Gill, K. and Pickles, T. (eds) (1989) *Active Collaboration: joint practice and youth strategies.* Glasgow: Intermediate Treatment Resource Centre.

Hodgkin, R. and Newell, P. (1996) *Effective Government Structures for Children: report of a Gulbenkian Foundation inquiry.* London: Calouste Gulbenkian Foundation.

Hornby, S. (1993) *Collaborative Care: interprofessional, inter-agency, interpersonal.* Oxford: Blackwell.

HMSO (1942) *Social Insurance and Allied Services* (The Beveridge Report). London: HMSO.

HMSO (1968) *Report of the Committee on Local Authority and Allied Personal Social Services* (Seebohm Report). London: HMSO.

Kilbrandon Report, *see* Scottish Home and Health Department/Scottish Education Department (1964).

Moss, P. and Petrie, F. (1997) *Children's Services: time for a new approach.* London: Institute of Education, University of London.

Plowden Report, *see* Central Advisory Council for Education (England) (CACE) (1967).

Roaf, C. and Lloyd, C. (1995) 'Multi-agency work with young people in difficulty', *Social Care Research Findings* **68**. York: Joseph Rowntree Foundation.

Scottish Home and Health Department/Scottish Education Department (1964) *Children and Young Persons Scotland* (The Kilbrandon Report) Edinburgh: HMSO.

Seebohm Report, *see* HMSO (1968).

Swadener, B. B. and Lubeck, S. (eds) (1991) *Children and Families 'at Promise'.* Albany: State University of New York.

University of Leicester (1991) *Children in Need and their Families: a new approach. A manual for managers on Part III of the Children Act 1989.* Leicester: University of Leicester School of Social Work and Faculty of Law and the Department of Health.

Warnock Report, *see* DES (1978).

Wilson, P. (1993) 'Child and adolescent mental health. Planning, funding and management of multiprofessional services: a discussion paper', *Young Minds Newsletter*, 14 June.

Wilson, A. and Charlton, K. (1997) *Making Partnerships Work: a practical guide for the public, private, voluntary and community sectors.* York: Joseph Rowntree Foundation.

10

Talking and working together

Neil Mercer

INTRODUCTION

This chapter will address how knowledge and understanding can develop when learners talk and work together without a teacher. 'Collaborative learning', as it is usually called, is important in our everyday lives. Think back through your own life: you will probably find, as I do, that a lot of knowledge and many valuable skills have been acquired through talking and working with people who were not, in any formal sense, your teachers. And this may not simply be a matter of being helped to learn by a more able friend: I know that on some occasions my own understanding has improved through having to explain something to a friend who understood it *less* well and asked for help. One good test of whether or not you really understand something is having to explain it to someone else. And an excellent method for evaluating and revising your understanding is arguing, in a reasonable manner, with someone whom you can treat as a social and intellectual equal.

However, the history of educational practice shows that talk amongst students has rarely been incorporated into the process of classroom education. Traditionally, talk between learners in the classroom has been discouraged and treated as disruptive and subversive. Although ideas may have changed to some extent in recent years, pupil–pupil talk is still regarded suspiciously by many teachers. As any teacher will confirm, one way that they feel that their competence is judged by senior staff, pupils, parents, and the rest of the world is: can they keep their classes quiet?[1] Of course, the reasonable explanation for the traditional discouragement of pupil–pupil talk is that, as an incidental accompaniment to whole-class, chalk-and-talk teaching, it is disruptive and subversive. Even in less formal regimes, teachers have an understandable concern with limiting the amount of 'off-task' talk that goes on. So while the experience of everyday

---

1 On the subject of 'keeping 'em quiet', see Denscombe, M. (1985) *Classroom Control: A Sociological Perspective.* London: Allen & Unwin.

life supports the value of collaborative learning, educational practice has implicitly argued against it. Is there evidence from research which can tell us more about the value of collaborative talk and activity?

RESEARCH ON COLLABORATION IN LEARNING

Communication between learners has not figured prominently in theories of the development of knowledge and understanding. Piaget, in his early work, sketched out a role for the significance of interaction between peers – it helped children to 'decentre', to become sensitive to other perspectives on the world than their own.[2] In his later work, with its focus on the activities of individuals, he did not give the topic much attention. But there have been some interesting recent developments in the Piagetian tradition. Followers of Piaget such as Willem Doise, Anne-Nelly Perret-Clermont and Gabriel Mugny have used the concept of *socio-cognitive conflict* to take account of how a child's understanding may be shifted by interacting with another child who has a rather different understanding of events.[3] The basic idea is that when two contrasting world-views are brought into contact, and the resulting conflict has to be resolved to solve a problem, this is likely to stimulate some 'cognitive restructuring' – some learning and improved understanding. The concept of socio-cognitive conflict has some interesting potential for the study of joint activity in the classroom. But neo-Piagetians have not studied the actual talk involved in such conflicts of ideas – perhaps because, (as I have suggested elsewhere, language still occupies a relatively marginal role in their theory). The main aim in most of their research has also been to determine whether interaction improved later *individual* performance (rather than being interested in the construction of knowledge as a shared entity).

Vygotsky's theory, on the other hand, is essentially concerned with teaching-and-learning, rather than joint learning. Some of his neo-Vygotskian followers have researched learners' joint activity, but unlike the Piagetians they have tended to stress co-operation rather than conflict.[4]

2 For a discussion of this aspect of Piaget's work and its relation to other research on collaborative learning, see Light, P. and Littleton, K. (1994) Cognitive approaches to group work. In P. Kutnick and C. Rogers (eds) *Groups in Schools.* London: Cassell.

3 See for example Bell, N., Grossen, M. and Perret-Clermont, A-N. (1985) Socio-cognitive conflict and intellectual growth. In M.W. Berkowitz (ed.) *Peer Conflict and Psychological Growth (New Directions in Child Development no.29).* San Francisco: Jossey-Bass. Also Doise, W. and Mugny, G. (1984) *The Social Development of Intellect.* Oxford: Pergamon Press.

4 See, for example, Wells, G. (1992) The centrality of talk in education. In K. Norman (ed.) *Thinking Voices: The Work of the National Oracy Project.* London: Hodder & Stoughton.

Most of this research involves adapting ideas from the study of 'asymmetrical' (i.e. teacher–learner) relationships to the study of more symmetrical ones (i.e. learner–learner). Thus Bruner[5] talks of how a 'more competent peer' can provide the scaffolding support for a learner, but this leaves an interesting question unanswered: what if peers are not more competent? Others have since suggested that having to explain your own ideas to someone you are learning with, whatever their relative ability, is useful because it encourages the development of a more explicit, organised, 'distanced' kind of understanding.[6] But we still lack suitable concepts for dealing with this process.

Although theory may not have kept pace, there has been a great deal of research interest in collaborative learning in recent years. Collaborative activity has been researched in various ways – through large-scale surveys of life in many classrooms, experiments in which pairs or groups carry out specially-designed problem-solving tasks, and detailed analyses of the talk of pairs or groups of children working together on curriculum-based tasks in school. One of the strengths of recent research on talk and learning, in fact, is that it has been so multidisciplinary and diverse in its methods. I will briefly review each of these lines of enquiry, and try to draw out the main points which are relevant here.

Surveys of classroom activity

Although it is certainly true that talk amongst pupils has tended to be discouraged in schools, at some times and in some places communication and interaction between children in the classroom has been officially sanctioned. Since the 1960s, a 'progressive' philosophy of education has encouraged 'group work' in British primary schools, in which children sit together around tables and are allowed to talk (at least to a limited extent) as they work. It is surprising, then, that little was known about the quality of most of this group work until the 1980s, when a large-scale research project called ORACLE[7] observed and evaluated practice in a large number of British primary schools. Did this provide evidence of the value of talk

5 Bruner, J. (1985) Vygotsky: A historical and conceptual perspective. In J. Wertsch (ed.) *Culture, Communication and Cognition: Vygotskian Perspectives* (p.24). Cambridge: Cambridge University Press.

6 See for example Fletcher, B. (1985) Group and individual learning of junior school children on a microcomputer-based task. *Educational Review* 37, 251–61; and Hoyles, C., Sutherland, R. and Healy, I. (1990) Children talking in computer environments: New insights on the role of discussion in mathematics learning. In K. Durkin and B. Shine (eds) *Language and Mathematics Education*. Milton Keynes: Open University Press.

7 Galton, M., Simon, B. and Croll, P. (1980) *Inside the Primary Classroom (the ORACLE Project)*. London: Routledge & Kegan Paul.

and joint activity for children's educational progress? The brief answer is 'no'. To be more precise, ORACLE did not show that collaborative activity was not valuable, it showed that it rarely happened. In most of the primary classrooms the researchers observed, the fact that children were sitting together at a table did not mean that they were collaborating. Usually, children at any table would simply be working, in parallel, on individual tasks. While they might well talk as they worked, and while they might possibly talk to each other about their work, the activities they were engaged in did not encourage or require them to collaborate or to talk about their work. ORACLE's surprising conclusion, then, was that most British primary classrooms were not good testing grounds for the value of collaborative learning and talk.

Since then, further research by members of the ORACLE team and others has provided mixed support for the value of group-based learning activities in classrooms. One clear implication of these findings is that we should not assume that group-based learning is inevitably valuable – it depends on what purpose it has, and how it is organised by the teacher. In their review of studies of group work in primary classrooms (and some experimental studies) Galton and Williamson conclude: 'For successful collaboration to take place, pupils need to be taught how to collaborate so that they have a clear idea of what is expected of them'.[8] This is very relevant to our interests here, so far as it goes. However, little of the research reviewed by Galton and Williamson included any close analysis of pupils' talk.

In the late 1980s, the National Oracy Project provided a wealth of information about talk in British schools, including such under-researched topics as children's own conceptions of how talk helps learning. It also succeeded in demonstrating the relevance of understanding the role of talk in learning for teachers of all curriculum subjects (not just English).[9] This was not done through surveys, but rather through the gathering of 'case studies' of classroom observations and practice, usually written by teachers themselves. In its early stages it provided some revealing information about what children think their teachers think about the value of talk in the classroom – that 'talk stops you working', 'talking is not work' and 'if you are allowed to talk, the work is not important'. I was closely involved with the National Oracy Project, and it seems to me that

---

8 Galton, M. and Williamson, J. (1992) *Group work in the Primary Classroom* (p. 43). London: Routledge.

9 See Open University (1991) *Talk and Learning 5–16: An In-service Pack on Oracy for Teachers*. Milton Keynes: The Open University, which contains many case studies and also an audiocassette of children engaged in a wide range of talk activities; also K. Norman (ed.) *Thinking Voices: The Work of the National Oracy Project*. London: Hodder & Stoughton.

one of its main achievements was to raise teachers' awareness of the potential value of talk, and so improve the status of classroom talk amongst both teachers and pupils.

Experimental research

In Europe and the USA in recent years there have been many experimental comparisons of children working in pairs or groups. Typically this research has focused on outcomes – for example, do children achieve better results when working competitively or co-operatively? – and also usually on individual learning outcomes (rather than the process of learning together). Some of the findings of this research support the value of collaborative learning: but others have shown how under some conditions working with a partner is *less* effective than working on your own. Some experiments have been designed to determine what makes the crucial difference. One factor that does seem important is whether or not the experimental conditions are such that the children *have* to communicate and collaborate to solve a problem (rather than simply being allowed to do so).[10] On the basis of studying children working in pairs (without teacher support) on computer-based problems, the psychologist Paul Light suggests that having to use language to make plans explicit, to make decisions and to interpret feedback seems to facilitate problem-solving and promote understanding. One of the tasks used by Light and his fellow researchers was a kind of adventure game, in which the quest was to find and rescue a king's crown, hidden on an island (shown on a map on the computer screen). Choosing from a range of possible strategies, the children could manipulate several characters and means of transport to avoid the pirates who blocked their way. The analysis of children's talk showed that those pairs who did most verbal planning, negotiation and discussion of feedback were the most successful in solving the problems.[11] Using talk to reconcile conflicting suggestions for action seemed particularly important, and successful pairs also seemed to be those in which decision-making was most evenly

---

10 See for example Light and Glachan's studies of children doing the 'Tower of Hanoi' problem. Light, P. and Glachan, M. (1985) Facilitation of problem-solving through peer interaction. *Educational Psychology* 5, 217–25.

11 See Barbieri, M. and Light, P. (1992) Interaction, gender and performance on a computer-based task. *Learning and Instruction* 2, 199–213. Also Light (1991) Peers, problem-solving and computers. *Golem* 3(1), 2–6; Blaye, A., Light, P., Joiner, R. and Sheldon, S. (1991) Collaboration as facilitator of planning and problem-solving on a computer-based task. *British Journal of Developmental Psychology* 9, 471–83; Light, P. (1993) Collaboration learning with computers. In P. Scrimshaw (ed.) *Language, Classrooms and Computers.* London: Routledge; and Light and Littleton (1994, see note 2).

shared between partners. Under such conditions, both children of a pair often learned better than when working alone. On the other hand, this research does not support the idea that working with 'a more competent peer' (as Jerome Bruner put it) is necessarily helpful for learning, as children who were considered to be of similar ability seemed to learn better than those in more asymmetrical pairs. Working with a more knowledgeable and capable partner who dominates decision-making and insists on the use of their own problem-solving strategies may hinder rather than help the less able.[12]

There has also been some recent interest in how collaborative activity affects the quality of thinking. For example, some experimental research has considered whether discussion helps children to generalise what they have learned (by 'generalise', I mean the extent to which they are able to use what they have learned in one situation, through solving one specific kind of problem, to deal with other related situations and problems). This interest arose because previous research had shown that, as a rule, children do not find it easy to generalise their understanding from one kind of problem or one area of the curriculum to another.[13] To some extent, this seems to be because their understanding is often 'procedural' rather than 'principled' – they learn to follow some practical procedures (e.g. learning a particular method for doing long divisions, or for doing science experiments and writing them up) without ever coming to understand the underlying principles involved.[14] There is now support for the idea that through sharing ideas, children can achieve more generalisable kinds of understanding if they are actively helped and encouraged to do so. For example, George Hatano and Kayoko Inagaki investigated how well some Japanese six-year-olds could use their experience of raising one kind of pet animal (e.g. a goldfish) to make sense of the life processes and care needs of other living things. One of their conclusions, which is particularly relevant here, is that when children had to share ideas about caring for animals – to explain, discuss and

12 Light, P., Littleton, K., Messer, D. and Joiner, R. (1994) Social and communicative processes in computer-based problem-solving. *European Journal of Psychology of Education* 9(2), 93–110; and Messer, D., Joiner, R., Light, P. and Littleton, K. (1993) Influences on the effectiveness of peer interaction: Children's level of cognitive development and the relative ability of partners. *Social Development* 2(3), 279–94. See also Hoyles, C., Healy, L. and Pozzi, S. (1992). Interdependence and autonomy: Aspects of groupwork with computers. *Learning and Instruction* 2, 239–57.

13 See for example Lave, J. (1992) Word problems: A microcosm of theories of learning. In P. Light and G. Butterworth (eds) *Context and Cognition: Ways of Learning and Knowing.* Hemel Hempstead: Harvester-Wheatsheaf.

14 For a discussion of 'procedural/principled' understanding, see chapter 6 of Edwards, D. and Mercer, N. (1987) *Common Knowledge.* London: Methuen/Routledge.

sometimes justify the opinions they held – this led to a better, more generalisable and 'principled' understanding.'[15]

Research on talk between pupils in the classroom

Experiments can be useful for identifying which factors in the complex reality of joint learning and problem-solving seem more important for success than others. But it is difficult to draw implications for educational practice from experiments which were carried out under controlled conditions away from the normal life of classrooms and on tasks which are unrelated to the content of school curricula. Moreover, the great majority of experiments have been concerned with the outcomes of joint activity, and not the process itself. It is therefore interesting to look at the findings of a different style of research altogether, one which has concentrated on the process of discussion in classrooms rather than on its outcomes, and see whether it leads to similar or different conclusions. Two pioneers of this kind of research were Douglas Barnes and Frankie Todd, whose research in the 1970s is described in their classic book *Communication and Learning in Small Groups*.[16] They showed how knowledge can be treated by pupils or students as a *negotiable commodity* when they are enthusiastically engaged in joint tasks. They suggest that pupils are more likely to engage in open, extended discussion and argument when they are talking with peers outside the visible control of their teacher, and that this kind of talk enables them to take a more active and independent 'ownership' of knowledge. As Barnes and Todd put it:

> Our point is that to place the responsibility in the learners' hands changes the nature of that learning by requiring them to negotiate their own criteria of relevance and truth. If schooling is to prepare young people for responsible adult life, such learning has an important place in the repertoire of social relationships which teachers have at their disposal.[17]

Barnes and Todd provide some examples of talk being used to good effect to construct knowledge and understanding, and in ways that are educationally appropriate. A good example is where, after a discussion of a topic, one of the group summarises what has emerged from the various

---

15 Hatano, G. and Inagaki, K. (1992) Desituating cognition through the construction of conceptual knowledge. In P. Light and G. Butterworth (eds) *Context and Cognition: Ways of Learning and Knowing.* Hemel Hempstead: Harvester-Wheatsheaf.

16 Barnes, D. and Todd, F. (1977) *Communication and Learning in Small Groups.* London: Routledge & Kegan Paul. (A new edition of this book is expected in 1995.)

17 Barnes and Todd (1977, note 16) p.127.

contributions speakers have made. The next sequence is from their book. A group of 13-year-olds were discussing Steinbeck's novel *The Pearl*, and various members had commented on episodes in the book which they found unconvincing. After one such comment (the one by Barbara, below), Marianne offered a summary as follows:

Barbara: (*Returning to previous sub-topic*) I think he should describe more, you know. It's supposed to be about diving and pearls.

Marianne: (*Summarising consensus already attained*) Yeah we don't think we don't think there's adequate description.[18]

In this kind of summary recap and *reformulation* is often made by teachers who are leading a class discussion. It is not a common feature of 'everyday discourse', but it is an important feature of both 'educational' and 'educated discourse'. Perhaps Marianne was taking as her model for educated discourse her teachers' past contributions to educational discourse. Barnes and Todd also show how some group discussions seemed to achieve nothing at all, in educational terms. In the following example, a group of girls are discussing 'Gang violence' and using their own experience to explain why boys fight each other. (Note: brackets show simultaneous speech.)

Elizabeth: It wasn't an argument, he din't even er, anyhow, why do you think boys fight in gangs like this? . . . Yes, Shirley.

Shirley: I wasn't saying nothing.

Elizabeth: [My mother says that . . .

Catherine: [It's, it's, it's like a match in't it?

Shirley: Yeah.

Elizabeth: Yeah it is . . .

Catherine: Mind you it's impossible to change now, isn't it?

Shirley: Yeah.

Elizabeth: Chains

Catherine: [Mind you

Elizabeth: [Chains

Catherine: If them people didn't watch the programmes that they put on, some of 'em wouldn't do it.

Elizabeth: Yeah that's it they get most of the violence off the telly.[19]

And so the girls continued, say Barnes and Todd, at great length. They comment: 'What we see going on here is not the use of talk to construct

---

18 Barnes and Todd (1977, note 16) p.67.

19 Barnes and Todd (1977, note 16) p.75.

new meanings but a set of unexamined platitudes which are never made quite explicit. If they had been made more explicitly, they would have been more available to criticism and modification. The girls do not advance their understanding in this extract; they merely reiterate half-understandings which they already possess'.[20]

Barnes and Todd are suggesting that classroom discussion has to meet certain requirements for explicitness which would not normally be required in 'everyday' discourse. Relevant information should be shared effectively, opinions should be clearly explained and explanations examined critically: that knowledge should, be made publicly *accountable*. Whatever value the talk might have had for consolidating the girls' friendship, or commiserating about the failings of their male companions, there is no reason to believe that this discussion was helping them to advance their analytical understanding of issues in a way that was *educationally* appropriate. Barnes and Todd argue that the successful pursuit of educational activity through group work depends on learners (a) sharing the same ideas about what is relevant to the discussion; and (b) having a joint conception of what is trying to be achieved by it. These points have been supported by other subsequent research.[21]

Social relationships

Education never takes place in a social or cultural vacuum. Although schools are places with their own special kinds of knowledge and their own ways of using language, and their own power relationships, they do not stand outside the wider society. And learners have social identities which affect how they act, and how other people act, in the classroom. At one level, this point may be glaringly obvious to teachers, who are every day made aware of the diversity of their students. It is more easily forgotten by researchers whose tunnel vision locks them into the study of certain aspects of intellectual development and learning (I speak here from my experience as both a teacher and a researcher). However, many researchers are now realising that social and cultural factors must be given more attention;[22] and as research by Biggs and Edwards illustrated, even teachers may be unaware of quite how such factors affect what goes on in their classrooms. There has not yet been a great deal of research on the effects of social and cultural factors on collaboration in the classroom, but there are some findings which are very relevant to both research and practice.

20 Barnes and Todd (1977, note 16) p.73.

21 See Galton and Williamson's (1992, note 8) review of research.

22 See Light and Littleton (1994, note 2); also Pozzi, S., Healy, L. and Hoyles, C. (1993) Learning and interaction in groups with computers: Who do ability and gender matter? *Social Development* 3(3), pp. 233–41.

Gender relations is one topic that has, in recent years, been studied by both experimental and observational researchers. For instance, Joan Swann has shown very clearly how the different interactive styles of boys and girls can influence the ways knowledge is constructed, and so affect the quality of the learning experience for those involved.[23] Although there is a lot of individual variation amongst males and females, male students of all ages tend to dominate discussions, to make more direct and directive comments to their partners, and generally tend to adopt more 'executive' roles in joint problem-solving. These kinds of differences are perhaps now well appreciated, at least in general terms, by teachers and researchers; the problem is, as Swann says, knowing what to do about them.[24] However, she also highlights some 'blind spots' in the ways collaborative talk is evaluated, and her argument carries clear messages for researchers and teachers. A good illustration is her analysis of some video-taped examples of collaborative activity produced by a local education authority for the training of teachers, which compared children working in different girl–boy pairs.[25] On the video, 'successful' and 'unsuccessful' collaborations were illustrated by pairs building model cranes together from Lego, with 'success' apparently being measured by the design quality and sturdiness of the crane they made. But Swann points out that the 'success' of one pair was only achieved by a girl submitting to her male partner's verbal bossiness and accepting the role of his 'assistant'. In this role she had little influence on the design, her views were not taken seriously and a lot of the talk consisted of him giving her instructions. Swann points out that the collaboration and interaction were only being evaluated in terms of outcome (i.e. how well the crane was constructed), not *process*, with the result that some important aspects of the quality of educational experience for the children involved were being ignored.

Research has shown that while boys often dominate mixed-sex pair and group activity, sometimes the 'more able' students (of either sex) seem to be those who tend to take control.[26] All such findings draw our attention to the need for teachers and researchers to be clear about what criteria they are using to evaluate collaborative activity. The basic question is: 'what are the students expected to get from it?' If one reason for encouraging joint activity is so that all students get the opportunity to use

23 Swann, J. (1992) *Girls, Boys and Language*. London: Blackwell.

24 Swann, J. (1994) What do we do about gender? In B. Stierer and J. Maybin (eds) *Language, Literacy and Learning in Educational Practice*. Clevedon: Multilingual Matters.

25 See Swann, J. (1992) as in note 23.

26 See Pozzi, S., Healy, L. and Hoyles, C. (1993) Learning and interaction in group with computers: When do ability and gender matter? *Social Development* 2(3), 222–41.

language actively to solve problems, and another is to free them from the constraints of teacher-led discourse, it is hardly satisfactory if some students are often still trapped in reactive roles and have to contend with a different form of dominance.

A rather different aspect of social relations is the effect of friendship on the quality of discussion. Research in this fairly new field is well illustrated by an experiment by Margarita Azmitia and Ryan Montgomery, who set pairs of 11-year-olds some problems that required logical, scientific reasoning (one was a Sherlock Holmes type of mystery, involving death from a poisoned pizza). They found that when children were paired with friends rather than mere acquaintances, they did more explicit, 'scientific' reasoning through language and so solved the problems more successfully.[27]

What kind of talk should be encouraged, and how?

The research I have reviewed does not provide a neat set of findings which can easily be integrated or reconciled. But my review leads me to the conlcusion that talk between learners has been shown to be valuable for the construction of knowledge. Joint activity provides opportunities for practising and developing ways of *reasoning with language*, and the same kinds of opportunities do not arise in teacher-led discourse. This conclusion can be used to justify 'group work' and other forms of collaborative activity in the classroom. But the research also shows that while encouraging talk between learners may help the development of understanding, not all kinds of talk and collaboration are of equal educational value.

It is possible to distil from the findings of research a description of a kind of talk which is good for solving intellectual problems and advancing understanding. First, it is talk in which partners present ideas as clearly and as explicitly as necessary for them to become shared and jointly evaluated. Second, it is talk in which partners reason together – problems are jointly analysed, possible explanations are compared, joint decisions are reached. From an observer's point of view, their reasoning is *visible* in the talk.

The research also helps us describe some favourable *conditions* for the emergence of this kind of talk. First, partners must *have* to talk to do the task, so their conversation is not merely an incidental accompaniment. Second, the activity should be designed to encourage co-operation, rather than competition, between partners. Third, participants must have a good,

---

27 Azmitia, M. and Montgomery, R. (1993) Friendship, transactive dialogues, and the development of scientific reasoning. *Social Development* 2(3), 202–21.

shared understanding of the point and purpose of the activity. And fourth, the 'ground rules' for the activity should encourage a free exchange of relevant ideas and the active participation of all involved. It also helps, as one might expect, if partners have an established, friendly relationship. There are some messages for both teachers and researchers in this list, which I will take up later in the chapter.

BACK TO THE CLASSROOM

I want now to look at some examples of children talking together in classrooms. The three sequences which follow were all recorded in a school in which I was researching as part of the SLANT (Spoken Language and New Technology) project.[28] Overall, we recorded approximately 50 hours of classroom talk in ten English primary schools. Our main interests in the project were to see how computer-based activities stimulated talk amongst children, and to understand the role of the teacher in organising and supporting joint activity at the computer. Other publications by the SLANT team deal with computer-related matters; but here I want to use the SLANT recordings to illustrate some general features of the quality of talk of children working together and the teacher's role in supporting it. The three sequences I have selected come from sessions which varied in length from about 35 to 90 minutes, reflecting differences in the kinds of activities that the children were engaged in. The sessions that provided these sequences were recorded over a period of 14 months in the same school – a modern primary with a mixed catchment on a city housing estate. The children in them were all aged 9–10 years, and came from the same locality. Each of the pairs or groups involved were recorded working in sets of related sessions, spread over days or weeks, and researchers also spent some time talking to both the teachers and the children. In all three sequences, the children can be observed to be solving some kind of problem and talking as they do so. And in all of them, the children can be seen to be well 'on task', in that they are dealing enthusiastically with legitimate aspects of the work they have been set by their teacher.

I have much more information about each of these sequences than I

---

28 SLANT was a joint venture of the University of East Anglia and the Open University, funded by the Economic and Social Research Council. It involved schools in Buckinghamshire, Cambridgeshire, Northamptonshire and Norfolk. For a brief account of the project, see Mercer, N. (1994b) The quality of talk in children's joint activity at the computer. *Journal of Computer Assisted Learning* 10, 24–32. See also note 33 below. For a more general socio-cultural perspective on computers and learning, see Scrmshaw, P. (1993) (ed.) *Language, Classrooms and Computers*. London: Routledge.

can easily share with you here. But on the basis of the limited information I can provide, I would like you, the reader, to do the following activity. First of all read through all three sequences. Look at the background information that I give before each one, but ignore for now the comments that I make later, after the final sequence. Drawing on what I have said earlier in this chapter, consider the following questions for each sequence in turn:

1. Do the children disagree at all?
2. Do they ask each other questions?
3. Do they share knowledge which is relevant to the task?
4. Do they seem to have a common understanding of what the task is about?
5. How well does the discussion seem to embody the kind of 'ground rules' for reasoning and problem-solving that are important for educational success?

After doing this, read the later comments I make and compare your analysis with mine.

In the first sequence, two ten-year-old boys, Sean and Lester, are using the program Smile,[29] which provides a series of mathematics-related puzzles. The puzzle that they are doing involves finding an elephant lost in New York (its streets being represented by a grid on the screen) by keying in co-ordinates and reacting to computer feedback on how close they get to their hidden target. Following their teacher's instructions, they take consecutive turns to key in pairs of co-ordinates. They have been doing the puzzle for about five minutes.

Sequence 6.1: Finding the elephant

Lester:	1, 2, 3, 4, 5 (*counting grid squares on the screen with his finger, before he takes his turn*).
Sean:	1. It's there.
Lester:	So it has got to be . . .
Sean:	5, 4 (*suggesting co-ordinates*).
Lester:	(*ignoring Sean*).
	4, 3. No, we have had 4, 3.
Sean:	4, 5. No, 4, 4.
Lester:	4, 3 (*presses keys for his turn*) What! (*he fails to find the elephant*)

29 The 'Smile' software was produced by the Inner London Education Authority in 1984.

	That's easy, I know where it is, opposite. (*both sit silently for a while, looking at the screen*)
Lester:	I can do it.
Sean:	(*still staring at the screen*) No, not up, down.
Lester:	It can't be.
Sean:	It can.
Lester:	I know where it is. (*Sean eventually takes his turn, but fails to find the elephant*)
Lester:	I told you it weren't over there. (*He then takes his turn, without success*)
Sean:	Eh, heh heh heh (*laughing gleefully*).
Lester:	Which one just went on? I don't know (*says something unintelligible*).
Sean:	1, 2, 3, 4, 5, 6 (*counting squares*).
Lester:	I know where it is.
Sean:	I got the nearest.
Lester:	(*counting squares*) 1, 2, 3, 4, 5, 6, 7, 8.
Sean:	I got the nearest, 5.
Lester:	So it has got to be 1, 8.
Lester:	2, 8.
Sean:	Oh, suit yourself.

The second sequence is from a session in which two 10-year-old girls, Katie and Anne, were working on the production of their own class newspaper, using some desktop publishing software for schools called Front Page Extra.[30] They were friends, who had successfully worked together before. Their teacher had helped them load the program and set up the screen for their immediate task, which was to design and write their front page. At the point the sequence begins, they have been engaged in the task for about an hour and a quarter and are trying to compose some text for the front page.

Sequence 6.2: Fantabuloso

Katie:	Okay, so right then. What shall we write?
Anne:	We can have something like those autograph columns and things like that and items, messages.
Katie:	Inside these covers. (*pause*) Our fun-filled . . .
Anne:	That's it!
Katie:	Something . . .

---

30 'Front Page Extra' was produced by R. Keeling, Newman College, in 1988 and distributed by Buckinghamshire County Council.

Anne: Something like that!

Katie: Yeah.

Anne: Inside this fabulous fun-filled covers are – how can we have a fun-filled cover? Let me try.

Katie: Inside these (*long pause*) . . .

Anne: Hah huh (*laughs*).

Anne: You sound happy on this. Fantabuloso (*laughs*).

Katie: Inside these, inside these fant, inside these fun-filled, no inside these covers these fantastic these brilliant . . .

Anne: Brilliant . . .

Katie: Is it brilliant?

Anne: No.

Katie: No. Fantast fantabuloso, shall we put that?

Anne: Yeah (*says something inaudible*) fantabuloso.

Katie: Fan-tab-u-lo-so.

Anne: Loso. Fantabuloso.

Katie: Fantabuloso oso.

Anne: Fantabuloso ho!

The third sequence shows a group of three children aged 9–10 (two boys and a girl) using a program called Viking England, a kind of historical simulation package which allows children to take on the active roles of Viking raiders planning an invasion of the English coast.[31] They had all recently been working in different groups, but two of them had worked together before. In response to events and to questions which appeared on the screen, members of the 'raiding party' had to decide what resources were required for the raid, how to overcome the opposition through strategy, and so on. In this sequence they are trying to decide which of four possible sites they should raid (a monastery, a village of huts, a castle or a harbour).

Sequence 6.3: Planning a raid

Diana: Let's discuss it. Which one shall we go for?

All: (*inaudible – reading from instructions*)

Peter: 1, 2, 3 or 4 (*reading out the number of options available*). Well we've got no other chance of getting more money because . . .

Adrian: And there's a monastery.

Diana: And if we take number 2 there's that (*inaudible*) . . .

Peter: Yeh but because the huts will be guarded.

---

31 'Viking England' was produced by Fernleaf Educational Software Ltd., Gravesend.

All:	Yeh.
Adrian:	And that will probably be guarded.
Diana:	It's surrounded by trees.
Peter:	Yeh.
Adrian:	And there's a rock guarding us there.
Peter:	Yes there's some rocks there. So I think, I think it should be 1.
Adrian:	Because the monastery might be unguarded.
Diana:	Yes 1.
Adrian:	1 yeh.
Peter:	Yeh but what about 2? That, it might be not guarded. Just because there's huts there it doesn't mean it's not guarded, does it? What do you think?
Diana:	Yes, it doesn't mean it's not. It doesn't mean to say its not guarded does it. It may well be guarded. I think we should go for number 1 because I'm pretty sure it's not guarded.
Adrian:	Yeh.
Peter:	Ok, yes, number 1 (*he keys in 1 on keyboard*). No (*computer responds inappropriately*).
Adrian:	You have to use them numbers (*he points to the number keys on right of board, and Peter uses them to obtain the right result. Adrian begins to read from screen display*). 'You have chosen to raid area 1.'

I will now comment on each of the three sequences.

Comments on Sequence 6.1

In this sequence, we see two boys actively and enthusiastically engaged in their task. They argue about who knows best, sometimes trying to justify their claims by recourse to the evidence on the screen. They offer suggestions, comments and advice on each other's actions, and ask each other a few questions. In the session as a whole, there was a lot of talk, and it was all 'on task'. But consider the sequence as a piece of joint constructive problem-solving, and especially as one which would help the boys develop their ability to deal with problems in an 'educated' way, and its quality is doubtful. The talk nearly all consists of short assertions, rebuttals or comments which are not constructive. They ignore each other's remarks, and when one asks for information the other does not provide it. Superior knowledge is often claimed, but not offered helpfully. Sequence 6.1 was typical of most of the talk in this session. The amount of real collaboration – in the sense of sharing of ideas, joint evaluation of information, hypothesising and decision-making, or even taking any advice offered – was minimal. The boys effectively redefined this supposedly collaborative activity as a *competitive* one. They took alternate turns: but then so do opponents in tennis. In the session as a whole, each time they did the puzzle, whoever happened to key in the last pair of co-ordinates before the elephant was found, claimed this vociferously as a personal victory. It was difficult to see what either boy was learning about 'learning through talk', or about maths, from doing this activity. They both seemed to understand the concept of co-ordinates already, and their strategies did not seem to change or develop as they played.

Comments on Sequence 6.2

In this sequence, we see Katie and Anne talking through their text. They ask each other questions (though Anne's question 'how can we have a fun-filled cover?' seems more the expression of a problem rather than a request for information from her partner), they make suggestions and offer some reasons for the decisions they take. They confirm and validate each other's statements, explicitly ('That's it!') or implicitly by repeating them ('Inside these . . .'). They are not only constructing their text together, they are constructing a joint understanding of what the text should be like. They clearly enjoy working together, perhaps reflecting a shared history of successful collaboration. There is only one real disagreement: they do not challenge each other's suggestions, and do not seem to feel the need to justify opinions or explain their reasons.

Comments on Sequence 6.3

In Sequence 6.3 we again see some children on task, asking each other questions, commenting and making suggestions. They discuss the various options, and also remind each other of relevant information. They are using talk to share information and plan together. They discuss and evaluate possible courses of action and make joint decisions. There is a lot of explicit reasoning in the talk. What is more, this reasoning is essentially *interactive* – not really reducible to the form and content of individual statements, but more to do with how the discourse as a whole represents a social, shared thought process. There was a lot of this kind of talk in the Viking England activity, in which the children seemed to be reasoning together and building up shared knowledge and understanding to a new level through their talk.

THREE WAYS OF TALKING AND THINKING

I will now use the analysis of sequences 6.1–6.3 to typify three ways of talking and thinking.

1. The first way of talking is **Disputational talk**, which is characterised by disagreement and individualised decision-making. There are few attempts to pool resources, or to offer constructive criticism of suggestions. This is how Sean and Lester talk in Sequence 6.1. Disputational talk also has some characteristic discourse features – short exchanges consisting of assertions and challenges or counter-assertions.
2. Next there is **Cumulative talk**, in which speakers build positively but uncritically on what the other has said. Partners use talk to construct a 'common knowledge' by accumulation. Cumulative discourse is characterised by repetitions, confirmations and elaborations. We can see Katie and Anne talking like this in Sequence 6.2.
3. Last is **Exploratory talk**, in which partners engage critically but constructively with each other's ideas. Diana, Peter and Adrian talk like this in Sequence 6.3. Statements and suggestions are offered for joint consideration. These may be challenged and counter-challenged, but challenges are justified and alternative hypotheses are offered. Compared with the other two types, in exploratory talk *knowledge is made more publicly accountable* and *reasoning is more visible in the talk*. Progress then emerges from the eventual joint agreement reached.

'Disputational', 'cumulative' and 'exploratory' are not meant to be descriptive categories into which all observed speech can be neatly and separately coded. They are analytic categories, typifications of ways in which children in the SLANT project talked together. What I am attempting to do here is elaborate the concepts of disputational talk, cumulative talk and exploratory talk into models of three *distinctive social modes of thinking*, models which help us understand how actual talk (which is inevitably resistant to neat categorisation) is used by people to 'think together'.

Three levels of analysis

To describe and evaluate the actual talk which goes on in any collaborative educational activity, we need to incorporate the models of talk into an analysis which operates at three levels (I am using 'level' here to mean something like 'depth of focus'). The first level is *linguistic*: we examine the talk as spoken text. What kinds of 'speech acts' do the students perform? (Do they assert, challenge, explain, request?) What kinds of exchanges take place? (That is, how do speakers build their conversations, how do they respond and react to each other's talk?) What topics are discussed? It is at this level that we can see that 'disputational talk' typifies talk dominated by assertions and counter-assertions, with few of the repetitions and elaborations which characterise 'cumulative talk'. 'Exploratory talk', in comparison, typifies talk which combines challenges and requests for clarification with responses which provide explanations and justifications.[32]

The second level is *psychological*: an analysis of the talk as thought and action. What kinds of 'ground rules' do the speakers seem to be following? How do the ways the speakers interact, the topics they discuss and the issues they raise, reflect their interests and concerns?[33] To what extent is reasoning visibly being pursued through the talk? We may be able to use the models of talk to typify the kind of communicative relationship that the speakers are acting out, and the ground rules that they use to do so. So, for example, in disputational talk the relationship is competitive; information is flaunted rather than shared, differences of opinion are stressed rather than resolved, and the general orientation is defensive. Cumulative talk seems to operate more on implicit concerns with solidarity and trust, and the ground rules seem to require the constant repetition and confirmation of partners' ideas and opinions. Exploratory talk foregrounds reasoning. Its ground rules require that the views of all participants are sought and considered, that proposals are explicitly stated and evaluated, and that explicit agreement precedes decisions and actions. Both cumulative and exploratory talk seem to be aimed at the achievement of consensus while disputational talk does not. In disputational talk, although a lot of interaction may be going on, the reasoning involved is very individualised and tacit. In cumulative talk, by comparison, ideas and information are certainly shared and joint decisions may be reached; but there is little in the way of challenge or constructive conflict in the process of constructing knowledge. Exploratory talk, by incorporating both conflict and the open sharing of ideas represents the more 'visible' pursuit of rational consensus through conversation. More than the other two types, it is like the kind of talk which has been found to be most effective for solving problems through collaborative activity.

If we want to make some judgements about the educational value of any observed talk, an additional level of analysis is needed. This could be called the cultural level, because it inevitably involves some consideration of the nature of 'educated' discourse and of the kinds of reasoning that are

---

32 Terry Phillips uses the term 'exploratory talk' to describe only the preliminary stages of examining and sharing information, and uses 'argumentative talk' for the process of debate itself (Phillips, T., 1990, Structuring talk for exploratory talk. In D. Wray (ed.) *Talking and Listening*. London: Scholastic. However, I feel that the term 'argumentative' has negative, disputational connotations. I believe that I am using the term 'exploratory' in a similar way to Douglas Barnes, in Barnes, D. (1992) The role of talk in learning. In K. Norman (ed.) *Thinking Voices*. London: Hodder & Stoughton.

33 See Edwards, D. (in press) Towards a discursive psychology of classroom education. In C. Coll (ed.) *Classroom Discourse*. Madrid: Infancia y Aprendizaje.

valued and encouraged in the *cultural* institutions of formal education. And here, it seems to me, the analytic category of exploratory talk deserves special attention. It typifies language which embodies certain principles – of accountability, of clarity, of constructive criticism and receptiveness to well-argued proposals – which are valued highly in many societies. In many of our key social institutions – for example, the law, government administration, research in the sciences and arts, and the negotiation of business – people have to use language to interrogate the quality of the claims, hypotheses and proposals made by other people, to express clearly their own understandings, to reach consensual agreement and make joint decisions.[34]

Some psychologists and language researchers have suggested that educated discourse is unlike much everyday discourse because it is 'disembedded' or 'decontextualised', so that words are dealt with free of context, in terms of abstract meanings. For example, Margaret Donaldson suggests that the essence of the most advanced kinds of intellectual thought and language is 'the ability to attend to the meanings of words themselves'.[35] However, 'decontextualisation' seems an unsuitable term for describing the essence of educated discourse. Look, for example, at one kind of educated discourse, the language of a country's legal system. Donaldson gives this as an example of a detached, decontextualised mode of language use. But legal language stands upon a vast foundation of history, and making sense of it as a professional takes years of training in the conventions of courts and legal documents and a knowledge of events (e.g. important court cases) which have gone before. The language of the professionals in any court room, or in any legal document, is a heavily contextualised form of discourse. Lawyers are expected to make their statements accountable to canons of law and to justify assertions by presenting evidence. The language that Donaldson and others call 'decontextualised' or 'disembedded' has, I would say, two quite different characteristics: it is language in which *reasoning is made visible* and in which *knowledge is made accountable* – not in any absolute terms, but in accord with the 'ground rules' of the relevant discourse community.

I would, however, like to retain one central and important element of

---

34 This scheme of analysis emerged from work with Rupert Wegerif, but also draws heavily on the work of Eunice Fisher, Terry Phillips, Peter Scrimshaw and all involved in the SLANT project (though they are not responsible for any inadequacies). See in particular Fisher, E. (1993) Distinctive features of pupil–pupil classroom talk and their relationship to learning. *Language and Education* 7(4), 239–58; and Wegerif, R. (1994) Educational software and the quality of children's talk, *Centre for Language and Communications Occasional Papers No. 40.* Milton Keynes: The Open University.

35 Donaldson, M. (1992) *Human Minds.* London: Allen Lane. See also Donaldson, M. (1978) *Children's Minds.* London: Fontana; and Wells, G. (1986) *The Meaning Makers* (Chapter 8). London: Hodder & Stoughton.

the arguments made by Donaldson and others. This is that if we encourage and enable children to use language in certain ways – to ask certain kinds of questions, to clearly describe events, to account for outcomes and consolidate what they have learned in words – we are helping them understand and gain access to educated discourse. Of course, there is much more involved in taking active part in any 'educated discourse' than using talk in an 'exploratory' way. There is the accumulated knowledge, the specialised vocabulary and other conventions of any particular discourse community to take account of. But exploratory talk represents qualities that are a vital, basic part of many educated discourses. Encouraging it may help learners develop intellectual habits that will serve them well across a range of different situations.

It might seem that I am suggesting that children – students – should have yet another alien set of 'ground rules' imposed on them, but that is not so. The following sequence comes from a discussion between Eunice Fisher (one of the SLANT researchers) and a group of four six-year-olds in one of the project schools. She was trying to discover their views on the value of 'discussion'. The children have already said that they sometimes discuss things when they work together.

Sequence 6.4: What do you do with discussion?

Researcher:	And then what would you hope to do by discussing it, what do you think that you would get in the end?
Peter:	It would help you by telling you what – making people agree with you, so we've got, um, well – making people agree with you, letting people agree, um, so we got, so we've got two people who want the same thing.
	(*and later, talking about activity outside the classroom*)
Researcher:	Angela, what about you? Do you discuss things outside too?
Angela:	Well, when we don't think something's, um, when I don't think, when we don't think something's right in the game, we just actually have to stop it and discuss what is, what is happening, what's the wrong thing.
Researcher:	Suppose you disagree, what happens then?
Angela:	Pardon (other children are talking)?
Researcher:	Supposing, supposing you say something and your friend that you're discussing it with says the opposite, what do you do next, what do you do then?
Angela:	You have to discuss something which is like, half what the other person says and half (*gestures two 'portions' with her hands*) which is what you said.
Researcher:	Right.

Angela: Yes, you just put it together so that it's . . . (*as her speech tails off, she brings her hands together*).

In this extract, some very young schoolchildren try to explain an important function of language which is difficult to put into words. You can see the thinking process in the unfinished phrases, the false starts and the 'ums'. But they are talking about real experience, and that experience is the basis of exploratory talk. There is no evidence from research to show that anyone is incapable of exploratory talk. What is more, there is no reason to assume that the basic principles of exploratory talk are alien to children. The ideal of a speech situation in which everyone is free to express their views, and in which the most reasonable views gain general acceptance, is implicit in many areas of social life. Even if people often violate the principles involved, they are still invoked as ideals.

ENCOURAGING EXPLORATORY TALK

I now want to consider the role of a teacher in encouraging the use of certain ways of talking. By the time that the SLANT project had been running for about a year, it had become clear that for many of the recorded sessions both teachers and researchers (who had reviewed the recordings) were disappointed with the quality of talk which had taken place. The kind of talk which we came to typify as 'exploratory' occurred sporadically and only occasionally throughout the sessions. In most sessions, the children rarely seemed to spend much time considering and evaluating information, ideas were often only partially expressed and, in some pairs and groups, partners seemed to ignore each other's views, or the talk and decision-making was dominated by a few of the group members. Also, the children involved seemed to be operating disparate sets of ground rules for doing collaborative activities at the computer. For example, while some seemed to feel that the views of all partners should influence decisions, others seemed to assume that decision-making lay with the person operating the keyboard. Yet others seemed to define the keyboard operator as merely a clerk, with most contributions of ideas and instructions coming from others in the group acting in an 'executive' capacity. Some partners insisted on passing the keyboard between them after each 'go', while others used longer-term divisions of labour. These matters were discussed at length by teachers and researchers, and in accord with the 'action research' philosophy which informed the project, this led to some of the teachers designing new, different kinds of activities.

In the school in which sequences 6.1–6.3 were recorded, this discussion resulted in the following plan for action. First, researchers and the teacher selected one educational computer program (from those in use in the school) which seemed to provide a good basis for a collaborative activity which would *require* the children to share information and make joint decisions. This was Viking England, as described at the beginning of Sequence 6.3. Teacher and researchers then discussed what ground rules the children might be encouraged to follow, though the final decision about what these would be and how they would be presented was left with the teacher. She eventually decided that she would stress the importance of:

- sharing all relevant information and suggestions;
- having to provide reasons to back up assertions and opinions and suggestions;
- asking for reasons when appropriate;
- reaching agreement about what action to take, if at all possible;
- accepting that the group (rather than any individual member) was responsible for decisions and actions and for any successes and failures which ensued.[36]

The teacher then planned for her class some awareness-raising activities on talk and collaborative activity, away from the computer. Eight three-person groups were set up by the teacher. Each group included at least one child with special needs in literacy, another who was an able and fluent reader, and consideration was taken of how children's personal styles and relationships in the class might affect who would work best together. In their groups, the children then did some activities intended to raise their awareness of the nature and quality of classroom discussion. These were taken and adapted from some published material on 'oracy' for teachers,[37] and included such activities as:

(a) Listening to a tape of sound effects. The group had to try to decide together what they thought each was, nominate a 'writer' to record their ideas and then report back to the class.
(b) Each child had to describe to their group an event that had happened to them during their Christmas holiday. One of the listeners then re-told the story to the class.

---

36 For fuller accounts of this activity by the teacher and researchers involved, see Dawes, L., Mercer, N. and Fisher, E. (1992) The quality of talk at the computer. *Language and Learning*, October 1992; and Dawes, L. (1993) Special report: Talking points. *Junior Education*, February 1993.

37 Brooks, G., Latham, J. and Rex, A. (1986) *Developing Oral Skills*. London: Heinemann. Also Open University (1991) *Talk and Learning 5–16: An In-Service Pack on Oracy for Teachers*. Milton Keynes: The Open University.

(c) Two of the group sat back-to-back and one of them had a minute to draw a shape or pattern. That person then described the shape and the other had to draw it from this description (with other group members as an attentive audience).

The teacher also led some group and class discussions about 'arguments', 'taking turns' and other topics related to taking part in conversations. Through picking up ideas and opinions offered by the children, the teacher was able to gain some insights into the children's current understanding of how discussions should be conducted. She was also able to make clear some of her own ideas on how groups should operate, to which the children seemed quite receptive. She continued to stress the need for all relevant views to be heard, for agreement to be sought if possible, and for groups rather than individuals to feel responsible for decisions reached and actions pursued.

The children then went on to do collaborative activities at the computer, in pairs or groups of three. But before each group began this activity, the teacher reminded them of the earlier activities and encouraged each of these new sets of children to explicitly rehearse the 'ground rules' for discussion that they would follow. The result was a dramatic increase in the amount of 'exploratory' talk in these groups, in comparison with earlier recorded activities. It also seemed that the enthusiasm and involvement of the children were improved. It is worth stressing that this particular school is not one with a 'privileged' catchment area: the housing estate surrounding it has more than its share of social problems and the effects of unemployment, and the children involved in the project included some with recognised social and psychological problems. One of the children in Sequence 6.3 was in fact facing possible exclusion from the school for persistent bad behaviour.

I have concentrated here on the apparent effects of the teacher's preparatory work (the talk awareness activities and the ways she set up the groups) rather than the contribution made by the Viking England computer software. The choice of that software, or at least that kind of software, was probably very important for the success of the initial activity.[38] But the ground rules that were established in this way were not just used for Viking England, and were successfully applied by the children in other, non-computer-based activities. The next sequence was recorded some months later, when the same teacher was rehearsing the ground rules with a group of 10-year-olds who were about to begin an activity (not computer-based) in which they had to identify various

---

38 For a discussion of possible effects of software on talk, see publications listed in note 28, p.198.

animals of the Brazilian rain forest. She has just established that they have all the pictures of animals that they require (I have marked words she stresses in bold type).

Sequence 6.5: Rehearsing the ground rules

Teacher: The next thing you've got to do is to decide **between** you which is which. So if you have a reason for thinking that's (*holding up a picture of a manatee*) a scarlet macaw you say 'I think it is because it has flippers' (*children laugh*). So you then would have to accept someone else's opinion if it was different from yours, so you would say something like 'Do you agree?' (*one boy says 'no'*) or 'I think that's wrong' (*boy says 'yes'*). And the person who was going to disagree with you wouldn't just say 'no', you would have to have a reason for disagreeing. What (*addressing Paul, the boy who spoke last*) would be your reason for disagreeing with that (*she shows him the picture*) being a scarlet macaw?

Paul: Because macaws don't have flippers.

Oliver: Because the macaw is a parrot! (*laughing*)

Teacher: Right. Whatever point of view you want to put over, you will have to try to think of your reason for giving it.

The children then went on to do the activity, and the next sequence is an extract from a later stage when they were trying to classify all the animals as either 'herbivores' or 'carnivores'.

Sequence 6.6: Classifying animals

Emmeline: Now we've got a fish – uh – the . . .

Oliver: What sort, the piranha?

Emmeline: No, the little, not the scaly one.

Maddy: Lun, lungf . . . (*hesitating*)

Oliver: Lungfish.

Maddy: It probably feeds on things in the river, because it's not going to go out and catch a monkey or something, is it? (*all laugh*)

Emmeline: Yeah. Could bri . . .

Oliver: (*interrupting*) There is of course river plants, some of them do feed on river plants, and leaves that fall in the river.

Maddy: Yeah, it's probably a herbivore.

Ben: We haven't got anything to tell.

Emmeline: What do you think it should be?

Oliver: No, actually I think we should put it in 'carnivore', most fish are.

Emmeline: No, because, ma . . .

Oliver: (*interrupting*) It's our best, and most fish are, isn't it?

Emmeline: (*interrupting*) Yeah, but we've got this one here, and this one here (*she indicates some fish cards in both 'carnivore' and 'herbivore' piles on the table*).

[*The discussion continues, unresolved, until Ben says . . .*]

Ben: Let's have a vote, have a vote.

Emmeline: Yeah, let's have a vote.

Ben: (*to Oliver*) What do you think?

Oliver: I think 'carnivore'.

Ben: (*to Maddy*) What do you reckon?

Maddy: I think 'herbivore'.

Ben: (*to Emmeline*) What do you reckon?

Emmeline: 'Herbivore'.

Oliver: What do you reckon? (*to Ben*)

Ben: (*laughing, looking sheepish and uncertain, doesn't answer*)

Oliver: Come on, this isn't worth it, it's a lungf. . .

Ben: Carnivore.

Oliver: Carnivore, that's two each.

Ben: Let's, OK (*he prepares to toss a coin*).

Oliver: No, don't bother flipping a coin, it's meant to be . . .

Ben: (*interrupts, tosses coin*) Flip.

Oliver: . . . thinking!

Ben: Heads or tails?

Oliver: Lung, no, shush!

Emmeline: It's heads. Well, you win.

Oliver: (*picks up the 'lungfish' card and reads*) 'The lungfish has a pair or lungs and small gills and burrows in the mud and breathes air.' It can't be a herbivore because what would it eat when it's on its own in the sand? There's nothing to eat.

The children then resumed their debate about the lungfish, and eventually decided that they had insufficient information and would leave the card separate and return to it 'at the end' when the teacher returned. The session which provided Sequence 6.6 was not a perfect model of equitable, rational discussion: in their excitement the children sometimes interrupted each other, the boys sometimes tried to dominate proceedings, and the reasons given for making decisions were not always valid. But there was certainly a lot of exploratory talk, as illustrated in the sequence. We can see that the children ask each other questions, they appeal for everyone's views, they try to justify their views rationally and by recourse to evidence. They try to reach agreement through the democratic process of a vote. When that fails, Ben does propose (with Emmeline's support) that they resolve the dilemma through the non-rational process of tossing a coin. But notice then what Oliver does – he objects, reminds the group of the ground rules agreed for the activity ('it's meant to be *thinking*!') and pulls in some additional relevant information for the group's consideration. Faced with this appeal, the children resume their rational debate.

I have given just one example, from one school, of how talk of an 'exploratory' type was encouraged amongst learners. My purpose is simply to illustrate a possibility made real, achieved through the sharing of knowledge between researchers, teachers and learners. But evidence for the importance of helping learners acquire, understand, use and appreciate the value of ground rules for conducting discussions which are rational, equitable and productive is emerging from sociocultural research elsewhere. Baker-Sennett, Matusov and Rogoff give the following example of an American teacher rehearsing some similar ground rules for a group of girls aged 7–9 who are going to perform their own version of the story of Snow White:

Teacher:	You'll vote as a group and you'll say, 'OK, do we want to do it the old way or the modern way?' and everyone will have to discuss it and say the pros and the cons. When having a little group there are certain things that make it hard. One guy has an idea and says, 'MODERN, MODERN! I want it modern'. Does that help the group?
Kids:	(*in unison*): No!
Teacher:	Or if some kids just sit there and don't say anything, does that help the group?
Kids:	(*in unison*): No!
Teacher:	OK, so you have to figure out a way to make the group work. What if I said, 'I have seen groups that have too many chiefs and no indians?' What do I mean? Leslie . . .
Leslie:	That means that too many people are taking over the group.
Teacher:	Everybody want to be the boss and nobody listens. So that might be a problem that you might have to solve with your group. Because you might always need some workers and some listeners. Part of this will be figuring out how to make your group work . . . There will be some adults in the room to help but a lot of the time it will just be up to you to say 'wait a minute, we need to compromise' or 'we need to vote on it', rather than just one guy taking over.[39]

---

39 Baker-Sennett, J., Matusov, E. and Rogoff, B. (1992) Sociocultural processes of creative planning in children's playcrafting. In P. Light and G. Butterworth (eds) *Context and Cognition: Ways of Learning and Knowing*. Hemel Hempstead: Harvester-Wheatsheaf. See also Lyle, S. (1993) An investigation into ways in which children 'talk themselves into meaning'. *Language and Education* 7(3), 181–97; and Berrill, D. (1991) Exploring underlying assumptions: Small group work of university undergraduates. *Educational Review* 43(2), 143–57.

Notice that, in both this example and in Sequence 6.5: *Rehearsing the ground rules*, the teachers use some well-established techniques for guidance. Both sequences are attempts by teachers to draw out from the children some salient information from their past shared experience. Both teachers try to *elicit* aspects of the ground rules from the children, and in so doing are asking 'closed' questions to which they know the answers. The first teacher explicity *confirms* the correctness of Paul and Oliver's responses with the comment 'Right'. The second teacher *reformulates* Leslie's response, so as to make her (the teacher's) intended point more clearly. Some people might see both sequences as unfortunate examples of teachers doing most of the talking, constraining children's responses and imposing the teacher's own interpretation of ground rules on children's activities. I see them as examples of teachers doing the job they are expected to do, of guiding the construction of knowledge.

SUMMARY AND CONCLUSIONS

Although talk amongst learners has tended to have low status in formal education, recent research provides some good reasons for encouraging learners to talk and work together in educational activities. However, research does not support the idea that talk and collaboration are inevitably useful, or that learners left to their own devices necessarily know how to make best use of their opportunities. A sociocultural perspective on classroom education supports the use of collaborative activity, but it also highlights the need for a rationale, in terms of both procedures and principles, for the activities learners are expected to do as part of their education. What is more, learners themselves need access to that rationale; and it has to be rationale that they find convincing. Of course, learners, even those young ones entering infant school, are never 'blank slates' on which their teachers must inscribe all educationally relevant skills. Children over 9 or 10 may have learned all the language strategies they need to engage in exploratory talk (and so in educated discourse) without having been taught them. They may well already use them to good effect on occasion (research like Janet Maybin's suggests that children have more opportunity for explaining and justifying in their informal conversations than they normally do when they are 'on task' in class).[40] But they need guidance on how to use talk. There are good reasons to believe that pupils and students are often unsure or unaware of

---

40 Maybin, J. (1994) Children's voices: Talk, knowledge and identity. In. D. Graddol, J. Maybin and B. Stierer (eds) *Researching Language and Literacy in Social Context.* Clevedon: Multilingual Matters.

what they are expected to be doing and achieving in educational
activities, and that teachers often provide little useful information about
such things to them. It cannot be assumed that learners already possess a
good understanding and awareness of how best to go about 'learning
together' in the classroom.

I know that I have not given much space here to such matters as
children's social identities and personal histories, which are important for
the organisation and evaluation of any collaborative activity. But there are
communicative and intellectual dimensions to the organisation of
collaborative activities which are also important if the activities are
intended to contribute to children's educational progress. Simply sitting
them down with a shared task may stimulate talk, but of what kind and
quality? It may be that too often the organiser of collaborative activities
does not have a clear notion of what kind of talk they are trying to
encourage and for what reason. As Terry Phillips[41] points out, 'Why?' is a
neglected question in planning collaborative activity. Teachers may take
the ground rules for granted or, perhaps under the influence of a
'progressive' educational ideology, they may think that is wrong to guide
students' activity so precisely. Too often learners have to try to make sense
of the activity as best they can, being given little help in understanding
and appreciating the ground rules they are expected to follow. How can
we expect them then to make the rules their own?

I have suggested that it is possible to identify particular ways of talking
that represent different social modes of thinking, and I have argued that it
is both desirable and possible to encourage learners to use some of those
ways of talking to construct knowledge together. It is also necessary for
teachers and learners to establish some agreement about what 'talk' in the
classroom is for and how it should be conducted. There is evidence from
other research as well as my own to support this view. But there is no
evidence to suggest that such preparation for collaborative activity is a
normal part of life in most schools or other educational institutions,
anywhere in the world.

---

41 Phillips, T. (1992) Why? The neglected question in planning for small group work.
In K. Norman (ed.) *Thinking Voices*. London: Hodder & Stoughton. See also Sheeran,
Y. and Barnes, D. (1991) *School Writing: Discovering the Ground Rules*. Milton Keynes:
Open University Press. Also Westgate, D. and Corden, R. (1993) What we thought
about things: Expectations, context and small group talk. *Language in Education* 7(2),
115–26; Barnes, D. and Sheeran, Y. (1992) Oracy and genre. In K. Norman (ed.)
Thinking Voices. London: Hodder & Stoughton.

Helping readers who have fallen behind

Frank Merrett

Some 10 years ago an article was published describing an approach called Pause, Prompt and Praise (Wheldall, Merrett and Colmar 1987) for those who were making slow progress in reading. This involves using well-structured procedures in one-to-one tutoring, using peers, teachers, parents or other adults as tutors. More recently, there has been a recognition that many pupils fail to reach expected standards in reading at Key Stage 2. Likewise, there are many students entering secondary schools who, although they can read simple texts, are not capable of reading reasonably quickly and with enough understanding to profit fully from the books with which they are asked to work at this stage. It seemed opportune at this time to remind teachers of these well-researched and very successful remedial techniques and to describe some of the more recent practical studies and findings from research.

The point was well made some time ago in the Bullock Report (DES 1975) that failure to make even a modest start in reading by the age of seven puts a child at educational risk, not merely because a good deal of learning depends on the ability to read, but because poor readers are less likely to receive skilled attention as they get older. Standards of reading in British schools have come under further scrutiny recently and there is no doubt that many children are reading at levels well below their potential (Davies, Brember and Pumfrey 1995, DfEE 1996, Macmillan 1997). One of the most serious problems facing secondary education in Britain today is the large number of pupils who start their secondary courses without being able to read well enough to profit from the texts given them by their specialist teachers. Some of the evidence for this comes from discussions with a number of secondary teachers, especially Special Educational Needs Co-ordinators, in the West Midlands. In one school, a recent investigation disclosed that 37 per cent of entrants had reading ages two years below their chronological ages.

Children who get off to a good start with their reading are likely to find pleasure and enjoyment in it. Pleasurable reading provides a great deal of practice and reading skill burgeons. As Clay (1979) pointed out, skilled readers become very adept at self-correcting their own mistakes so that their ability to cope with harder texts increases rapidly without much help from teachers or other adults, although encouragement is always helpful. On the other hand, pupils who are slow at learning to read and who fall behind their peers are likely to get much less practice. Reading for them is a chore, not a pleasure and, thus, they fail to get as much practice as the rest. They do not learn to cope with more difficult texts on their own as their fellows do and, accordingly, they fall further and further behind. What they need is one-to-one attention from a more skilled reader to help them along and provide support and encouragement. Constraints of time and opportunity make it difficult for teachers to provide this help, especially in secondary schools.

Most secondary teachers are highly skilled in their specialisms, believe them to be of supreme importance and are keen and able to do a really good job at teaching them. However, they assume that the job of teaching reading has already been done at the primary stage. Thus, many are quite unaware of the difficulty that some of their pupils have in coping with the set texts. Even those who become aware have neither the skill nor, above all, the time to do anything to remedy the situation. The most common solution to the problem, that of taking children out of their regular classes to teach them to read, has obvious problems of its own.

A SUGGESTED SOLUTION TO THE PROBLEM: PERSONAL TUTORING

One method of providing the necessary help which can be effective, if properly organised, and which has a long pedigree, is personal tutoring. After all, the best way of learning some new skill is in a face-to-face situation with one who is already skilled, and that is just what tutoring provides. Such tutoring has been shown to be very effective not only for improving reading but for other subjects as well (Wheldall and Beaman 1996). It should be stressed at this point that the 'Pause, Prompt and Praise' procedures are not meant for youngsters who are just beginning to read but rather with those who have made a start, but then failed to make normal progress. It is very important that tutoring takes place on a regular daily basis, little and often being the rule. The role of the teacher is of prime importance in the whole enterprise, for making all the arrangements and generally keeping tabs on progress. Peer or parent tutoring in no way reduces the function of the teacher but rather enhances it.

One of the major objections to peer tutoring, as a process, is that the parents of the tutors employed may object to their children teaching others rather than being taught themselves. However, in the words of the seventeenth-century Czech scholar and teacher, Comenius, 'He who teaches learns'. There is no doubt that in the process of teaching someone else, tutors improve their own skill in the subject. Indeed, one of the best ways of becoming master of a subject is to teach it to another person because, in explaining it to someone else, you learn to understand the subject matter thoroughly. Several studies involving tutoring have shown this to be the case – for example, Topping (1987), Wheldall and Mettem (1985) and Winter and Low (1984). Other, more recent, studies are described later in this article.

THE BIRTH OF 'PAUSE, PROMPT AND PRAISE'

The set of remedial reading strategies now known as 'Pause, Prompt and Praise' was developed within a research project carried out by T. Glynn, S. McNaughton and V. Robinson whilst they were working at the Education Department of the University of Auckland in New Zealand. It was supported by a research grant from the New Zealand Child Health Research Foundation. The procedures were first described in their book, *Parents as Remedial Reading Tutors: Issues for school and home*, which was subsequently published in England under a new title, *Pause, Prompt and Praise: Effective tutoring for remedial reading* (McNaughton, Glynn and Robinson 1985). This later edition included a monograph by Glynn and McNaughton, first published in 1985, reporting a number of successful replications of the original study. The book reported details of the project which was carried out in a suburb (Mangere) of Auckland, New Zealand where housing was state financed.

This project was strongly linked to the earlier reading research of Professor Marie Clay reported in her book *Reading: The patterning of complex behaviour* (Clay 1979). Basically, Clay argues that in learning to read, children develop a number of quite complex strategies for predicting and working out unknown vocabulary. Learning to read is seen as a process of making mistakes (often referred to as reading errors or miscues) and gradually developing more efficient strategies using contextual cues, which relate to meaning and syntax, and graphical cues, which relate to the visual pattern of letters and words. As individuals learn to read, they gradually learn to cope with reading material which is increasingly more difficult, and so they become independent readers.

Glynn, McNaughton and Robinson had already concluded that making mistakes is very important and is to be expected in the learning process.

Children, like the rest of us, learn through making mistakes. Those learning to read quickly and successfully do this by themselves, because they soon become aware when what they have read does not make sense, but others, making slower progress, need help. Clay had already established that skill in self-correction is a characteristic of good, fluent reading. McNaughton and Glynn (1981) examined the timing of feedback when children were reading aloud and found that if teachers or tutors delayed their attention to errors instead of interrupting immediately, thus allowing readers the chance to correct themselves, then they produced more self-corrections and reading accuracy improved.

The Mangere Home and School Project, having considered fourteen families at the outset, was finally carried out with eight tutors (seven mothers and one aunt) working with eight boys, all of whom were several years behind in reading, for various reasons. A full account of how this research project was carried out and its results may be found in Merrett (1994), as the original books are now out of print.

THE 'PAUSE, PROMPT AND PRAISE' PROCEDURES

Although these procedures are now generally referred to as 'Pause, Prompt and Praise,' there is more to it than just pausing, prompting and praising. It is an approach which stresses that children learn to read by reading, not by learning a large number of separate words or sub-skills. As already mentioned, the procedures were designed to help pupils who have begun to read but who are making slow progress or none at all. It is essential for success that three important elements are supplied by the organiser of a reading project using pause, prompt and praise.

The importance of reading level

The first of these is the provision of reading material at an appropriate level. Here, the 5 per cent rule is very helpful. If a child makes fewer than four mistakes when reading a passage of fifty words, then that text is appropriate for reading for pleasure. The success rate is such that the reading will be reasonably fast, meaning will be clear and interest maintained. If the pupil makes more than ten errors in reading a passage of similar length, then it is far too hard and this is often referred to as 'frustration level' for the reader. The child will be struggling to gain any meaning from the passage and will probably give up trying. Harrison (1980) refers to the fact that many children, even among those making satisfactory progress, find reading rather boring. He quotes one girl's comment as follows: 'If I start reading a book and come to a word that I can't read I think, "Oh, that book's too hard", and I just put it down.' The size of the print and the general appearance of the text can also be off-putting for the unskilful reader.

In order to ensure success, we must provide reading material such that the child is encountering some unfamiliar words but knows enough words to be able to make good predictions, even if some of these are errors. The right level of reading material can be broadly assessed by checking the child's rate of reading accuracy. If this rate is below 80 per cent, the text is too difficult, whereas if the child is reading at over 95 per cent accuracy, it is clearly too easy. At a rate between 90 and 95 per cent accuracy, promotion to the next level should be seriously considered. An ideal level for children learning to read, with all the advantages of making mistakes, is between 80 and 90 per cent accuracy.

There is a simple and straightforward rule of thumb for ensuring that the text being read is at the most suitable level of difficulty. Listen to the child reading the first 100 words in the piece and count the number of errors. From this, the percentage accuracy may easily be calculated. If time is short, the same calculation may be obtained from counting the errors from the first fifty words read and a decision can then be reached as to the suitability of the text. This is very similar to the 5 per cent rule mentioned above. Another way of assessing the relative difficulty of a piece of prose is to ask the child to place a finger on every word he cannot read and understand. If all five fingers have been placed on one page the text is too hard for that child.

Monitoring progress

The second element is that the child's progress should be carefully monitored with respect to the text, using running records and simple miscue analysis in order to identify particular difficulties so that they can be addressed and techniques improved. The reader may be found to have special weaknesses or display gaps in the skills necessary for decoding text. When peer tutors are being employed, the task of recording errors cannot be expected of them. Detection and remediation of weaknesses in reading skill must remain with the teacher, who will be able to gain knowledge of progress with errors and error correction from listening in or, better still, from audiorecordings made of the tutoring sessions. It may be possible, however, for tutors to note common errors made by their tutees to guide the teacher.

Giving feedback

The third important requirement is that reading tutors should provide appropriate feedback as they listen to the child read. It is important to stress that mistakes (errors or miscues) are to be expected. Anyone learning to read will make mistakes. It is an important, indeed an essential, part of the process. As already mentioned, in any skill-learning process, such as learning to ride a bicycle, making mistakes is a good thing. By carefully monitoring the children's responses to text the teacher can readily work out if they are making average, or even better than average progress and if they are using efficient predictive strategies. It is in the tutor's response to the reader that pausing, prompting and praising are involved. These procedures are detailed in Wheldall, Merrett and Colmar (1987) and in Merrett (1994) and are summarised in Figure 11.1.

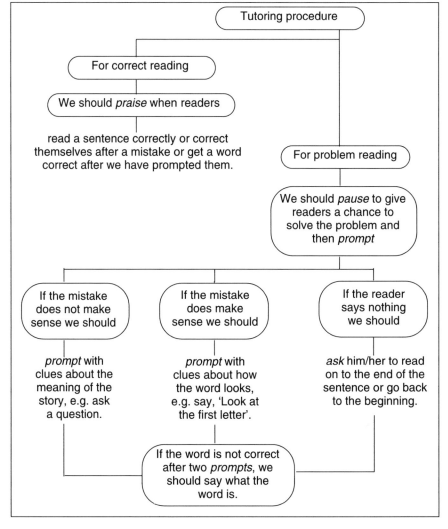

Figure 11.1: The pause, prompt and praise procedures

Tutor and learner should sit comfortably side by side so that both can easily see the text. Before beginning to read, it is good if they look through the book together so that the tutor can try to pick out any especially long or difficult words and anticipate unusual or unfamiliar situations. It is much easier to do this if the book is already familiar to the tutor or if the tutor has a chance to see the book beforehand. However, quite a lot of information about the content may be gained from looking at the title and the pictures contained within the book and discussing them together.

Remembering and learning to carry out these procedures appears, at first sight, to be a complex business but it has been shown that with careful training and practice, both adults and children are able to do so very competently. Training takes some time, however, and must not be skimped. Careful preparation of tutors will pay off in the long run. A sheet with the tutoring procedures on it, as in Figure 11.1, can be used as a prompt for the tutors to begin with but, with practice, they can soon be expected to carry out the procedures without it. Finding appropriate and effective prompts can be a challenge for tutors, except for the brighter ones. Praising can also present problems for some. It is a good plan for tutors to be encouraged to compile lists of praise statements which they find effective so as to have a variety at their disposal. Part of the training should involve role-playing in which tutors practise by tutoring each other before working with slower readers.

EARLY STUDIES SHOWING SUCCESS OF THE STRATEGY

In the years immediately following the Mangere study, Glynn and McNaughton carried out a number of other studies using the same procedures. However, one of the most thorough studies using pause, prompt and praise within a cross-age peer tutoring framework was that carried out by Wheldall and Mettem (1985), which has also been described in some detail elsewhere (Merrett 1994, Wheldall, Merrett and Colmar 1987).

Following a conference held at the Centre for Child Study in the University of Birmingham, a course was run for teachers interested to learn more about the 'Pause, Prompt and Praise' procedures. Thirty-three teachers enrolled for the course, which ran for ten weeks. The objectives were to teach teachers of older children (10–13 years) how to use the procedures themselves and then to help them set up programmes of their own using either peers or parents as tutors (Merrett, Wheldall and Colmar 1987).

As a direct result of the course, fourteen projects were set up for individual pupils, several teachers organising more than one. Most of the tutoring periods lasted for 10–15 minutes and typically took place three times per week. Some of these projects were tutored by the teachers themselves, some by parents and some by older siblings. In all cases, teachers were entirely responsible for initiating and monitoring the projects, which lasted from 4 to 23 weeks. In addition to the individual projects, some teachers were also able to organise programmes for groups of children with reading problems.

The children taking part in these projects were mainly between 9 and 12 years old. They were two, three or even four years behind in their reading skills despite a great deal of effort and energy having been spent by teachers over the preceding years. With almost all of them, worthwhile gains in reading age or in book levels were made in the space of a few weeks of tutoring using the pause, prompt and praise procedures.

For the very first time, most of them began to make progress at a rate fast enough to begin to catch up in their reading skills. The main objective was to encourage pupils' independent reading skills, and it is believed that this holds out some hope for low-progress readers through peer and parent tutoring. Nevertheless, as with paired reading schemes, reports of long-term follow-up studies are rare.

LATER STUDIES INVOLVING PERSONAL TUTORING

Wheldall, Colmar and Freeman (1991) successfully trained community volunteers to use the pause, prompt and praise procedures with one group of six low-progress readers and compared them with another (control) group who were tutored by untrained community volunteers, who did little more than listen to the children reading. The pupils were from a metropolitan residential school which offers short-term intensive remedial programmes for pupils with learning difficulties. Generally, in studies like this one, arrangements are made for tutees to have the same tutor throughout so that a relationship may be developed between them, and this is believed to enhance the effectiveness of tutoring. However, because of the way the community volunteers were employed, these students had a different tutor each day of the week, but this did not prevent the tutoring strategy from being very effective.

In 1993 Houghton and Bain worked with 14-year-old 'below average' readers who were trained to tutor eight students of similar age for whom English was a second language. Of the eight tutees, three were Yugoslavian and two were Vietnamese whilst the others were Indonesian, Rumanian and Malay/Chinese. The tutors were generally about 4 years behind with their reading and each was paired with a student of the same sex and roughly the same reading level. The tutors gained an average of

8.2 months and the tutees a mean of 9.6 months in reading accuracy. For comprehension, the average gains were 14.4 months and 13.7 months respectively and all these gains were significant statistically.

The pause, prompt and praise procedures might be thought by some teachers to be rather too complex for some pupils to learn although this has not been found to be so in practice. Houghton and Glynn (1993) sought to show that the three feedback procedures could be taught separately and successively instead of all together. The participants in this study were all ten members of a class of below average readers (mean age, 13.10 years) withdrawn because of their problems in reading. Each student was matched with a same-sex peer of approximately the same age and reading ability and the better reader in each pair was designated as tutor. Once again, both tutors and tutees made substantial gains.

Several researchers have made attempts to compare peer tutoring using different strategies, such as paired reading, in order to see which is the more effective. These include Cusack (1993), Leach and Siddall (1990), Osborne (1991) and Patch (1993). This is a difficult exercise because learning a skill and then putting it into effect is a very personal affair and the difficulties which people encounter are likely to be very varied. In addition, it is quite difficult to determine the stage which a person has reached in their skill at reading, and even more difficult, with the instruments that are available, to gauge any improvement. It is worth noting here that while 'Pause, Prompt and Praise' is very effective with pupils who are seriously behind with their reading, some of the less structured techniques, like paired reading, work well with pupils who have less severe problems.

PAIRING STUDIES

Other researchers have carried out studies into pairing (for example, Topping and Whiteley 1993). They drew attention to the fact that in the majority of studies relating to peer tutoring, pairings were of same sex on the basic assumption that this would make for the best results. There is very little empirical evidence to show whether this is the case or not. A wide review of studies by Sharpley and Sharpley (1981), whilst reporting some studies which showed advantages for same-sex pairings and others which did not, concluded that 'there is little support for the view that same-sex pairings are superior to opposite-sex dyads. There is also no support for the opposite contention' (pp.58–9).

Mottram set up an experimental study in order to examine the effects of sex pairing for pause, prompt and praise tutoring (Merrett and Mottram 1997). The tutees were all from Year 7 in a large mixed-sex comprehensive school in the West Midlands of England. The tutors were Year 10 pupils of the same school. Mottram had four sets of dyads in which the tutees were matched for reading ability, as measured using the New Macmillan Reading Analysis (Vincent and Mare 1985), allocated randomly to male–male, male–female, female–female and female–male pairing. All tutors were taught to use the pause, prompt and praise techniques and through recordings made of each tutoring session it was ensured that the strategies were, in fact, carried out. This was a further demonstration that peers can be taught to use the pause, prompt and praise procedures effectively.

Pre- and post-project reading scores were compared and showed no significant differences between the groups. Same-sex and opposite-sex pairings had no observable effect and there was little evidence to indicate that single-sex pairings were any more beneficial to tutees than mixed-sex pairings. Whilst the sex of the tutor appeared to have no effect on the tutoring outcome, some of the boys expressed the opinion that they would prefer to be tutored by a girl. Analysis of preferences arrived at through the completion of a questionnaire showed that tutees who had been allocated to a tutor of the sex they would have chosen, given the chance, did better than those whose choice was not fulfilled. Thus, it is possible that being able to choose one's tutor may be an important factor in the success of a peer-tutoring project.

CONCLUDING COMMENTS

Many of the research projects which have been described so far have drawn attention to the fact that not only has peer tutoring brought about changes in the academic skill of reading but has improved some aspects of the social context as well. Attention has been drawn to improvements in pupils' ability to co-operate with each other and to appreciate the problems of others. Several of the schoolwide studies have stressed this aspect of tutoring programmes. These include Franca (1983), Limbrick, McNaughton and Glynn (1985) and Houghton and Glynn (1993).

Since the original Mangere study, little has been done to find out why the techniques work so well and which of the elements are most essential. Merrett and Thorpe (1996) set up three tutoring groups, of which one used the normal pause, prompt and praise procedures, one used pausing and prompting but no praising and the third was a comparison group. Both experimental groups had far better results than the comparison group but those that had all three elements did best of all, showing that praise is a very important element in the procedures.

It has been clearly demonstrated that the pause, prompt and praise procedures work and more recent studies have shown that they may be used to help children with varying degrees of need. We now know more about why they work and understand better the optimum conditions under which they may be applied. It is to be hoped that these facts will encourage their greater use in schools.

REFERENCES

Clay, M. (1979) *Reading: The patterning of complex behaviour.* Auckland, New Zealand: Heinemann Educational Books.

Cusack, H. M. (1993) 'A comparative study of the efficiency of paired reading and relaxed reading using peers as tutors'. M.Ed. dissertation, University of Birmingham.

Davies, J., Brember, I. and Pumfrey, P. (1995) 'The first and second reading Standard Assessment Tasks at Key Stage 1: A comparison based on a five-school study', *Journal of Research in Reading* **18**, 1–9.

Department of Education and Science (DES) (1975) *A Language for Life* (The Bullock Report). London: HMSO.

Department for Education and Employment (DfEE) (1996) *Results of the 1995 National Curriculum Assessment of 11 year-olds in England.* London: DfEE.

Franca, V. M. (1983) 'Same age peer tutoring among behaviourally disordered middle school students: academic and social benefits to tutor and tutee', *Dissertation Abstracts International* **44**, 459.

Glynn, T. and McNaughton, S. (1985) 'The Mangere Home and School Remedial Reading Procedures: continuing research on their effectiveness', *New Zealand Journal of Psychology* **14**, 66–77.

Harrison, C. (1980) *Readability in the Classroom.* Cambridge: Cambridge University Press.

Houghton, S. and Bain, A. (1993) 'Peer tutoring with E.S.L. and below average readers', *Journal of Behavioural Education* **3**, 125–42.

Houghton, S. and Glynn, T. (1993) 'Peer tutoring of below average secondary school readers using pause, prompt and praise: The successive introduction of tutoring components', *Behaviour Change* **10**, 75–85.

Leach, D. J. and Siddall, S. W. (1990) Parental involvement in the teaching of reading: A comparison of hearing reading, paired reading, pause, prompt and praise and Direct Instruction methods', *British Journal of Educational Psychology* **60**, 349–55.

Limbrick, E., McNaughton, S. and Glynn, T. (1985) 'Readings gains for underachieving tutors and tutees in a cross-age tutoring programme', *Journal of Child Psychology and Psychiatry* **26**, 939–53.

Macmillan, B. (1997) *Why Children Can't Read.* London: Institute of Economic Affairs.

McNaughton, S. and Glynn, T. (1981) 'Delayed versus immediate attention to oral reading errors: effects on accuracy and self-correction', *Educational Psychology* **1**, 57–65.

McNaughton, S., Glynn, T. and Robinson, V. (1985) *Pause, Prompt and Praise: Effective tutoring for remedial reading.* Birmingham: Positive Products.

Merrett, F. (1994) *Improving Reading: A teacher's guide to peer-tutoring.* London: David Fulton Publishers.

Merrett, F. and Mottram, S. (1997) 'Do boys or girls make better reading tutors? An empirical study to examine children's effectiveness as tutors using the pause, prompt and praise procedures', *Educational Psychology* **17**, 419–32.

Merrett, F. and Thorpe, S. (1996) 'How important is the praise element in the pause, prompt and praise tutoring procedures for older low-progress readers', *Educational Psychology* **17**, 419–32.

Merrett, F., Wheldall, K. and Colmar. S. (1987) 'A "pause, prompt and praise" course: New procedures for teachers concerned with pupils making slow progress in reading', *Behavioural Approaches with Children* **11**, 102–9.

Osborne, M. P. (1991) 'Teaching parents to use pause, prompt and praise and paired reading strategies at home: a study comparing the effectiveness of the two methods'. University of Birmingham.

Patch, S. (1993) 'A comparison of paired reading and pause, prompt and praise: two programmes designed to improve reading and comprehension levels of pupils protected by statements of special educational need, using parents as tutors'. M.Ed. dissertation, University of Birmingham.

Sharpley, A. M. and Sharpley, C. F. (1981) 'Peer tutoring: review of the literature', *Collected Original Resources in Education* **5**(3), 7–C11.

Topping, K. (1987) 'Peer tutoring paired reading: outcome data from ten projects', *Educational Psychology* **7**, 133–5.

Topping, K. and Whiteley, M. (1993) 'Sex differences in the effective use of peer tutoring', *School Psychology International* **14**, 57–67.

Vincent, D. and Mare, M. (1985) *The New Macmillan Reading Analysis.* London: Macmillan.

Wheldall, K. and Beaman, R. (1996) *And gladly teche: Increasing individual instruction using peer tutors* (videocassette). Sydney: Macquarie University Special Education Centre.

Wheldall, K. and Mettem, P. (1985) 'Behavioural peer tutoring: training 16 year-old tutors to employ the "pause, prompt and praise" method with 12 year-old remedial readers', *Educational Psychology* **5**, 27–44.

Wheldall, K., Colmar, S. and Freeman, L. (1991) 'Employing community volunteers to tutor low-progress readers using the pause, prompt and praise tutoring procedures', *Positive Teaching* **2**, 93–9.

Wheldall, K., Merrett, F. and Colmar, S. (1987) '"Pause, Prompt and Praise" for parents and peers: effective tutoring of low-progress readers', *Support for Learning* **2**, 5–12.

Winter, S. and Low, A. (1984) 'The Rossmere peer tutor project', *Behavioural Approaches with Children* **8**, 62–5.

12

Listening to children

Irvine S. Gersch

The initiative described in this chapter started around 1981 and aimed to extend and increase the active involvement of children in their assessment. This period has seen many changes in education, including ones affecting children with special educational needs: changes in attitudes about the desirability of children living in care settings, changes to the management of schools, and most importantly changes in attitudes about children's rights.

However, it has to be said that although there has been some progress in including children more actively, such progress has been patchy, unsystematic and slow. Indeed, there remains a wealth of untapped resource for teachers, schools and other professionals, in listening to what children say about their schools, their education and their needs; there is a gold mine of ideas, views, feedback, information and motivational energy awaiting discovery.

As an educational psychologist, I have been fortunate in working at several levels, within schools, within an LEA context, with parents, with professional colleagues, with trainee educational psychologists often wanting to undertake action research in the area of pupil involvement, and with teachers. At an LEA level, as principal educational psychologist opportunities were afforded to me to review LEA procedures for children with SEN and to contribute to council policy on SEN, such that pupil involvement could be included. In short, over the past 15+ years, it has been possible to develop a pupil involvement project in one locality, an area of east London, and to take several opportunities to influence research and practice and to develop new tools.

In this chapter, I outline the historical triggers to the project, and then review briefly some specific projects which have been carried out. This is followed by a description of a general model for developing new tools for eliciting pupils' views, and a discussion of some of the issues and dilemmas raised for professionals. Finally, a checklist for SENCOs is suggested and some concluding comments offered.

All of the projects have in fact been published elsewhere, and a full reference list is included for those interested in examining any of these projects in more detail, or seeing the actual student report forms described.

I have argued elsewhere (Gersch 1987, 1992) that there are at least three key reasons for increasing the active involvement of pupils in their education. These are pragmatic, moral and legally supported. From a practical point of view it is obvious that children hold a wealth of information about their own learning, progress and attitudes, and about school generally. Such data is of immense practical utility to teachers and others in devising plans and work. It is also argued that, morally, if one is going to alter another person – for example, through a behaviour programme or Individual Education Plan (IEP) – then it is only right that they are fully involved, understand what is happening and give their informed consent. The legally supported reasons are within the United Nations Convention on the Rights of the Child (1989) Articles 12 and 13, and the 1989 Children Act as supporting the notion of child self-advocacy.

The projects described here are:

1. The child's report
2. The pupil report
3. The student report
4. The excluded student report
5. A motivational checklist for the classroom
6. Student involvement in a whole-school systems change
7. An LEA assessment procedure
8. Council policy
9. Some research surveys.

It should be stressed that these projects are simply opportunistic and pragmatic examples of *ways* of increasing the active involvement of children in their education. What matters is the principle of seeking ways of doing this. For example, the student report, while proving to be a most positive, concrete and practical device for engaging children in a discussion of their views and attitudes about school, is still dependant upon the ethos and climate of the interaction. In short, there needs to be a true *listening ethos* where pupils' views are respected and encouraged if the exercise is going to have any meaning. The alternative is that the child's views are collected in a sterile, automatic and ultimately meaningless way.

It will be for each professional to develop their own techniques, ways and means of eliciting pupils' views and engaging children in a meaningful discussion, probably more dependant upon an open, trusting and encouraging relationship than forms or reports alone.

Finally, I have found it useful to conceptualise the idea of increasing the active involvement of children as a *continuum* rather than an 'all or nothing' state (Gersch 1992). There is no doubt that all teachers, psychologists, LEAs and relevant professionals do actually involve children in their assessments, educational plans and possibly feedback. However, the question raised might be about the *degree* of active child involvement on a continuum:

Not at all	To some degree	Moderate	To a high degree	To a very high degree

The challenging questions to be raised for SENCOs might be, therefore:

(a) Where would you currently assess your position on the continuum?
(b) What could you do to increase your position along the continuum?

HOW IT ALL BEGAN

In the 1980s I was the specialist educational psychologist at a social services observation and assessment centre. When children experienced a breakdown in their home circumstances and, in addition, were deemed not to be able to attend their previous school, arrangements were made for them to be transferred to the centre. Admission was usually for a period of about ten weeks so that an assessment of their needs and future plans could be carried out. Thus, children found themselves in a strange institution, with unknown adults, often bewildered and unsure about what was happening to them and why. They were also concerned about their future.

The assessment would conclude with a case conference, which considered reports from a child psychiatrist, social worker, teacher and educational psychologist.

At that time, I attended a conference for educational psychologists in which a seminar called 'Barbara's case conference' revolved around a play written by a number of youngsters in care. The psychologists were invited to play different parts. The play simply depicted a social services case conference through the eyes of the child. In short, the child's views were ignored, rationalised, missed out or worse contradicted.

The moral was most powerful: how could you leave out the child? At the end, we all felt moved by this simple truth and omission. I probably learned more from that dramatic experience than all the other lectures and seminars put together.

I returned to the observation and assessment centre, and introduced a child's report to be added to the conference papers. Staff had to be won over, and subsequently more care was taken over things said about children. We also found that guidelines for adults were needed to empower children. I recall overhearing one child telling her adult helper that she didn't like certain foods. The adult helper replied saying that the child was absolutely wrong and since the helper was writing down the child's responses, she simply wrote down her own views. Clearly, staff training was required!

Ultimately, we produced a child's report with several headings, including their views about school, home, the centre, hobbies and pastimes, and the future. The form was evaluated after two years and found to be an important part of the assessment and valued by children and staff. Most significantly, it appeared that the report had encouraged constructive dialogue between children and care staff, and helped some children think positively about their future.

THE PROJECTS

The child's report (Gersch and Cutting 1985)

This has already been discussed and was the basis of other tools and techniques developed. Some of the key points worth highlighting are that the report was formatted so that children could have the chance of answering questions in a manageable way. It focused their responses on their recent history, current views and future wishes and it included them in the whole process of assessment more directly than hitherto. The questionnaire was evaluated by inviting the feedback of children themselves about the form, and changes were made in line with their suggestions. The child's report remained a permanent element of the assessment procedure until the centre eventually closed some years later.

The pupil report (Gersch 1986, 1987, 1990)

Having appreciated the utility of the child's report in a social services care setting, it seemed a logical next step to transfer the ideas to an education one. In the early part of the 1980s we had a number of students in a special class in a secondary school. These young people had previously attended a special school for children with learning difficulties. As part of their statutory assessment, it was suggested that we pilot a pupil report, to act as the child's advice under the 1981 Education Act. The aim would be to elicit their views about their school, teachers, subjects, special education needs and future plans.

The categories in this report were:

- School background
- Present school
- Special needs
- Friends
- Hobbies and interests and out of school activities
- The future
- Additional comments.

Given the support of the LEA, school and parents as well as capturing the interest of the children, the forms were duly completed and added to the child's statement. It is fair to comment that many of the children reported that they enjoyed giving their views, some (sadly) saying this was the first time anyone had taken a real interest in their feedback about their education. As with the earlier report, guidance was required for adult helpers. An evaluation revealed that more space was needed for the students to elaborate their feelings, that the format needed overhauling to make it attractive and that the word 'student' was preferable to 'child' or 'pupil'.

The 1994 student report (Gersch 1995, 1996)

Under the 1931 and 1996 Education Acts, advices are sought from a number of professionals to inform the LEA whether the child should be subject to a statement of special educational needs. Further, if a statement is to be drawn up, these reports are used to determine the nature of that statement.

We now sought to extend the student report to provide advice to the LEA for those children having a statutory assessment.

The original report was developed by adding graphics, new headings, pictures and student-friendly language.

The headings include:

- School
- Special needs
- Friends
- Life out of school
- Feelings
- The future
- Anything else.

Several key points are worth highlighting:

(a) The report provided an opportunity for constructive dialogue between school staff and student in a unique way.
(b) The tool itself was exposed to student review and improvements were made systematically, year on year.
(c) The end result itself is best regarded as a practical device which can and should be altered over time to fit specific needs and requirements.
(d) Children's views should he included and afforded status in their own right. Some professionals have said that they summarise the student's views in their own report. While this can be helpful, there can be little objection to students' reports being afforded the same space in documentation as those of others.

This document has proved helpful but we are currently developing a more specific student advice form which is more abbreviated, more directly related to the statement headings and which is translated into different community languages. This should be ready during 1999 and will be modified to fit the new Code of Practice due in 2001.

The excluded student report: 'Where do I go from here?' (Gersch and Nolan 1994)

Following a research project into the attitudes and difficulties perceived by students excluded from school (Gersch and Nolan 1994) there was evidence that many students experienced the exclusion as both traumatic as well as puzzling, and indeed many did not really direct their thoughts towards their future plans.

Such students needed support to manage their behaviour, emotional support, counselling, clear guidelines, and clearer communication with parents and others. They also needed an advocate, a small group to work with for a period of time after the exclusion, a positive relationship with at least one teacher, and help to re-integrate into a new school on a phased and gradual basis.

As a result, two educational psychologists in the team (Nolan and Sigston 1993, reported in Gersch and Nolan 1994) compiled and piloted a special report format for the use of excluded students.

The aim was to increase the active participation of excluded students in the decision making and planning process. It was developed to encourage parents and professionals to seek the views of excluded students in a structured way, and to help such students reflect upon their experience and plan for the future. It provided the basis for a structured interview and could be used by educational psychologists, education welfare officers, social workers or specialist teachers.

The headings in this report, entitled 'Where do I go from here?', were:

1 My work
2 The teachers
3 The other kids
4 Leading up to the exclusion
5 The exclusion itself
6 Why I did what I did
7 What I am looking for in another school.

A motivational self-grading checklist for the classroom (Gersch and Brown 1985)

On a visit to a junior school, my advice was sought about a particular ten-year-old child. The teacher wished to explore ways of motivating him to complete work, stay on-task and, of course, make faster progress with his schoolwork. We began considering ways of enhancing this child's motivation. During our deliberations, however, it became clear that there would be major benefits in planning a whole-class system rather than just for one child.

A system was devised which involved every child being given a list of 15 tasks to complete on a 'to do list' for the day. Other columns were 'work completed' (which the child had to tick when the task was done), and self-graded score (which the child had to rate from A to D, from excellent effort, to good effort, to satisfactory effort, to not very good effort).

Finally there appeared a column for the teacher to add in his or her grades of the child's efforts. The teacher's grade was then converted to points (A = 3 points, B = 2 points and C = 1 point) and the points totalled weekly. Points were exchanged for rewards such as free time, choice of work on a Friday, going to help in another younger class, on the basis of one point for one minute earned.

The sheet was signed at the end of each week by the child, the teacher and the head teacher, and sent home for the parents to see and sign.

The sheet was eventually evaluated at the end of the year, with feedback being sought from the children, the parents, the teacher and the head teacher. The key findings were that the system had been enjoyed by more than 90 per cent of the pupils in the class, and that 56 per cent of the children said they were working harder. All of the children enjoyed receiving rewards, listing their preferred options as playing, watching TV or video, drawing, chalking on the board chatting and, interestingly, helping out in another class with younger children.

Only a few parents responded to the evaluation questionnaire, but those who replied did so in favour of the system. Other responses, together with those from the children, suggested a finer grading scale to a five-point one, which was subsequently developed (see Figure 12.1).

The teacher felt that the system was useful, albeit tiring for pupils, and drew attention to important discussion between herself and children regarding the gradings. Pupils often under-estimated their performance and effort. She reported that children seemed to develop greater self-discipline, their effort had improved, and she certainly wished to continue with the system.

Several features of the system are worth highlighting (Gersch 1987):

(a) It encourages children to develop organisational and study skills.
(b) It encourages children to assess their own efforts.
(c) It encourages frequent and specific feedback from teacher to pupil.
(d) It encourages greater responsibility in children about their work.
(e) Work tasks are broken down into small, manageable chunks.
(f) The process encourages two-way understanding between teacher and learner; children begin to predict their teacher's views and the teacher may learn much about the child's self-image.

As adults, do we not find the 'to do list' motivating when faced with large projects?

Student involvement in a secondary whole-school systems project (Gersch and Noble 1991)

One secondary school approached the educational psychology service expressing concern about disaffection and poor attendance in a group of Year 11 students. A steering group was set up and ways explored of organising a whole-school systems project.

The particular school already had in place relatively elaborate decision-making machinery, including departmental and full staff meetings at which vital decisions were debated, proposed and decided upon. It was therefore agreed that we would set up five small groups to investigate the causes of disaffection and to make recommendations to the staff meeting.

The innovative element of the working parties was the involvement of students, and indeed those who were particularly disaffected or not attending school. Interestingly, these young people were very happy to attend school regularly for this purpose, which itself shows how much students want to talk about their school and education.

WORK RECORD SHEET   SHEET NO . . . .

Name . . . .   Week beginning . . . .
Date . . . .   Class . . . .
Teacher . . . .

	TASKS TO BE DONE	TICK WHEN DONE	PUPIL'S GRADE	TEACHER'S GRADE	POINTS
1					
2					
3					
4					
5					
6					
7					
8					
9					
10					
11					
12					
13					
14					
15					
				Total points	

A = Excellent effort (4 points)   Comment . . . .
B = Very good effort (3 points)   Signed . . . .(Pupil)
C = Good effort (2 points)   Comment . . . .
D = Satisfactory (1 point)   Signed . . . . (Teacher)
E = Not very good (0 points)   Comment . . . .
REWARD MENU   Signed . . . . (Head teacher)
1 point = 1 min of free time   Comment . . . .
Maximum 60 minutes   Signed . . . .(Parent)

Suitable free time activities: indoor games, art, reading, hobbies etc.

© London Borough of Waltham Forest

This form may be reproduced for non-commercial use within your own organisation, subject to the acknowledgement of the source being made. The use of this material for all other purposes is subject to the written consent of the copyright holder, being the London Borough of Waltham Forest.

School Psychological Service, Summerfield Centre, Leyton Green Road, LEYTON, London E10 6DB

Figure 12.1 A motivational self-grading checklist for the classroom

Each of the five working groups comprised two teachers, two students and an external consultant. The consultant came from outside the school and was either an educational psychologist or a specialist teacher engaged in a local project to combat truancy in the area. The consultants met regularly to discuss progress and to receive support from the principal educational psychologist.

Each working group met weekly for about an hour and a half, over the course of a term, and was given three main issues to address:

1. What do you think are the causes of the disaffection and truancy in the school?
2. What could the school do to improve the situation?
3. Prioritise three main proposals to take to the full staff meeting for decision.

It was very evident that the groups worked hard in a focused way to produce many positive, constructive and intelligent ideas. Students reported that they enjoyed the meetings, which were conducted in an informal and relaxed way, and of course implicitly acknowledged the importance of student views.

The end result was the production of a number of creative proposals ranging from improved work areas, feedback about work, staff–student communication, assessment, a pupil council, a newsletter and use of school for activities beyond the school day.

Many of these ideas were implemented and in a subsequent evaluation a year later there was evidence of some (slight) improvement in attendance but a reported improvement in the communication and relationships between staff and students.

This project highlights the point that there is merit in involving students actively in whole-school developments as well as in respect of individual programmes. Such initiatives are likely to create a shared feeling of ownership among young people, enhance their feelings of responsibility and moreover elicit some creative and productive ideas in respect of school improvement.

An LEA assessment procedure (London Borough of Waltham Forest 1994)

At around the time of the publication of the Code of Practice, Waltham Forest decided to develop local guidance for SENCOs and schools. A folder entitled 'AAA' (Assessment, Achievement, Action) was produced. This folder contained blank record sheets that could be used with children with special educational needs as well as formats for reviews, record keeping and progress monitoring.

The objectives of this project were:

- to produce guidelines for schools on the early stages of assessment and intervention for children with SEN;
- to publish documentation for record keeping about action taken and reviews;
- to provide advice to the LEA regarding appropriate publicity and training to implement the new procedures.

The contents of the files were drawn up by SENCOs and educational psychologists working in small groups, and then referred to an LEA steering group for consideration. The steering group comprised head teachers and LEA officers, union representatives and other interested parties. On completion, the new AAA system received the full support of the local council in commending its use in schools.

At every stage of development, consideration was given to involving the pupil as actively as possible, both in completing specific forms and in giving their views about their special educational needs.

Pupil questionnaires were drawn up entitled 'Me and my work' which were amended for children of different ages. This questionnaire asked the children about their own view on their work, situations faced at school, and the type of help and support needed. Children were also to be very actively involved in the preparation and review of their Individual Education Plan (IEPs).

The end result was a handbook for schools entitled *Assessment, Achievement, Action: a handbook for special educational needs co-ordinators: procedures for planning and reviewing the progress of children and students with SEN* (London Borough of Waltham Forest 1994). The file provides guidance on the Code of Practice, definitions, policies for bilingual children, and supporting information. It holds diary sheets, action summaries, examples of the pupil's work. Most importantly, it contains forms which can be used to elicit the child's views, attitudes and feelings which are so critical to the success or otherwise of the SEN assessment process.

Council policy

As said earlier, one of the aims of the pupil involvement initiative was to seek opportunities to extend the concept of increasing the participation of children in their education. Consequently, when the education department decided to consult widely with a view to developing and updating its SEN policy, the opportunity was taken to incorporate the learner's perspective into such policy. Ultimately, an SEN policy was adopted by the council which stated that the views of learners should be included wherever possible and students actively involved in their education. Such a policy is of help in the development of projects and gives a clear indication of the views of council members. It gives general support to more detailed initiatives.

This particular development completed the picture for providing projects at various levels:

- the individual child level;
- the classroom level;
- the school level;
- the education department (SEN panel) level;
- council level.

SOME RESEARCH PROJECTS

During the course of the above initiatives some small-scale research was carried out to ascertain the views of teachers, other professionals and indeed pupils about their school leaders (Gersch 1992, Gersch and Gersch 1995).

A school survey of attitudes towards pupil involvement (Gersch 1996, Gersch, Pratt, Nolan and Hooper 1996)

In May 1994 a survey was carried out with schools in one London borough. The aim of the study was to survey the views of schools and colleges about pupil involvement and to ascertain any trends. Of the 87 organisations contacted, some 40 per cent returned completed questionnaires. Although limited, as a snapshot the findings are of interest and revealed the following:

- The concept was important and welcomed in their school or college.
- There had been an increase in such involvement over the past ten years.
- Children had greater involvement in the assessment process.
- Children were occasionally involved in the decision-making processes of the school.
- There was a growing use of pupil councils.
- Some students were involved in victim/bullying support groups, pupil run newspapers, and selecting rewards and participating in school development plans.

The attitudes of allied professionals on pupil involvement (Gersch and Gersch 1995)

A similar research study on pupils' views examined the perspectives of different professionals: a community paediatrician, a physiotherapist, a speech therapist, a child psychiatrist, a social worker, an educational welfare officer, an educational psychologist and a specialist teacher. Although the sample was small, the views appeared to be generalisable. All these professionals thought that the child's view was important. However, there were distinct differences between professional groups, with medical specialists giving greater weight to family views. Some felt that children under the age of 21 were not sufficiently mature to understand the consequences of their decisions. Others said that the child's view had to be interpreted in the context of other points of view, for example those of teachers and parents.

It is fair to comment that while advocating the importance of listening to children, one should bear in mind the fact that children are still growing, changing, developing and learning. Thus, professionals and other adults retain a duty of care to ensure the child's welfare and best interests rather than their immediate preference.

Pupils' views of their head teachers (Gersch 1992)

Finally, as part of my doctoral research into what makes an effective secondary school leader, pupils were asked for their views about headship. Pupils felt it important for head teachers to be available to them, to be fair, visible and to set an example. In order of priority they listed the following functions as important to them, and thought that head teachers should:

- help individual children when they have problems;
- meet parents when pupil standards fall;
- meet parents to discuss progress;
- encourage a pleasant atmosphere in school;
- allow children to talk to him or her privately;
- get to know the children well;
- remind the pupils of the rules;
- stick up for the children when teachers have been unfair;
- inform pupils what is happening in school;
- stress kindness and good manners, through personal example.

SOME ISSUES AND DILEMMAS ENCOUNTERED

There is little space here for elaborating in depth some of the issues encountered during the evolution of the initiative and projects, but it is felt important to identify some of these for consideration. More detailed discussion can be found in Gersch and Gersch (1995) which examined the issue of professional advocacy on behalf of children and Gersch (1996) which considered potential role conflicts of those working with children with SEN.

Some of the key issues might be:

- How does one deal with other colleagues who might feel that children should be seen and not heard?
- Are some children not mature or capable enough to participate? (In my experience even very young children and students with severe learning difficulties can make some choices about their educational programmes.)
- How does one deal with parent–child dislike?
- What about scope needed for children to negotiate, try things and change their minds?
- How do adults distinguish what a child needs from what he or she prefers or wants?
- What if the SENCO comes into conflict with their head teacher over ways of meeting a child's needs? What then happens to the child's views?

A CHECKLIST FOR SENCOs

Whatever dilemmas exist in schools that attempt to take seriously the notion of pupil self-advocacy, the fact remains that there is an expectation of engagement with pupils' views in the Code of Practice (DFE 1994). The Code (para. 2:37) advises schools to consider how they:

- involve pupils in decision-making processes;
- determine the pupil's level of participation, taking into account suitability for age and experience;
- record the pupil's views;
- involve pupils in implementing individual education plans (IEPs).

It is therefore very important for SENCOs to consider the extent to which pupils' rights to be heard are embedded into the school curriculum. SENCOs might specifically question the following:

- Are children taught study skills to become independent learners?
- How is the self-esteem and confidence of pupils being developed?
- How do children view the culture of the school? Is success valued or is there a subculture that detracts from achievement?
- How far do children understand the assessment process? Is it explained to them? Who does this? Is their understanding checked?
- To what degree are students actively involved in identifying their educational needs, planning targets and support, implementing IEPs, monitoring their progress, developing the school's SEN policy?
- How are students involved in the preparations for their transfer to new schools, colleges or school leaving?

Finally, at a whole-school level, the SENCO might wish to:

- ask all the children how far they feel actively involved in the school;
- trawl ideas from other schools, colleagues and the literature;
- share ideas with the whole staff, including the head teacher and senior staff, given the critical role of the school leadership and school culture;
- consult with children, parents, governors, educational psychologists, specialist teachers and LEA officers, and others who might be able to offer ideas.

CONCLUSION

This chapter has outlined some practical projects and tools for increasing the active involvement of pupils in their education, and posed some particular questions to SENCOs in respect of their practice. Experience over time has shown that, particularly in respect of the development of tools such as the student report, several steps are required:

1. Clarify the aim of the assessment or data-gathering exercise.
2. Examine what methods are currently available and used.
3. Consider ways of increasing the active engagement of pupils.
4. Draft a format or response sheet for children to use.
5. Pilot your device with a small number of children and seek their views about it.
6. Provide guidance for those adults needed to help children complete the form.
7. Evaluate the form or response sheet over time, e.g. in a year.
8. Modify the form and ensure that it is kept up to date.

However well presented or indeed positively evaluated any of these pragmatic devices, one cannot substitute the importance of a trusting, listening, open, non-judgemental relationship between SENCO and pupil. Such skills are complex and may require training and supervised practice, on the part of staff as well as children.

ACKNOWLEDGEMENTS

The author would like to thank the following for their kind permission to use some of the ideas previously published elsewhere: International Thomson Publishing Services Ltd, Falmer Press, David Fulton Publishers, Macmillan Press Ltd, Professor Tony Clive: University of Luton, Tony Bowers: Cambridge University Institute of Education.

The views expressed in this article remain those of the author and not those of the authority in which he was employed.

REFERENCES

Gersch, I. S. (1986) 'Increasing the involvement of children in assessment', *Newsletter of the BPS Division of Educational and Child Psychology* **23**, 20–2.

Gersch, I. S. (1987) 'Involving pupils in their own assessment', in Bowers, T. (ed.) *Special Educational Needs and Human Resource Management*, Chapter 10. London: Croom Helm.

Gersch, I. S. (1990) 'The pupil's view', in Scherer, M., Gersch, I. S. and Fry, L. (eds) *Meeting Disruptive Behaviour: assessment, intervention and partnership*, Chapter 7. London: Macmillan Education.

Gersch, I. S. (1992) 'Pupil involvement in assessment', in Cline, T. (ed.) *The Assessment of Special Educational Needs: international perspective*, Chapter 2. London: NFER Nelson.

Gersch, I. S. (1995) 'The pupil's view'. Paper in briefing pack for schools on the Code of Practice, published by the National Children's Bureau in association with the DFE.

Gersch, I. S. (1996) 'Involving children in assessment: creating and listening ethos', *DECP Educational and Child Psychology* **13**(2), 31–40.

Gersch, I. S. and Brown, K. (1985) *Pupil Self-graded Work Record Sheet*. London Borough of Waltham Forest.

Gersch, L S. and Cutting, M. C. (1985) 'The child's report', *Educational Psychology in Practice* **1**(2), 63–9.

Gersch, I. S. and Gersch. B. (1995) 'Supporting advocacy and self-advocacy: the role of allied professions', in Garner, P. and Sandow, S. (eds) *Advocacy, Self-advocacy and Special Needs*, 126–53. London: David Fulton Publishers.

Gersch, I. S. and Holgate, A. (1991) *The Student Report.* London Borough of Waltham Forest.

Gersch, I. S. and Noble, J. (1991) 'A systems project involving students and staff in a secondary school', *Educational Psychology in Practice* **7**(3),140–7.

Gersch, I. S. and Nolan, A. (1994) 'Exclusions: what the children think', *Educational Psychology in Practice* **10**(1), 35–45.

Gersch, I. S., Holgate, A. and Sigston, A. (1993) 'Valuing the child's perspective: a revised student report and other practical initiatives', *Educational Psychology in Practice* **9**(1), 36–45.

Gersch, I. S., Pratt, G., Nolan, A. and Hooper, S. (1996) 'Listening to children: the educational context', in Davie, R., Upton, G. and Varma, V. (eds) *The Voice of the Child: a handbook for professionals*, Chapter 2. London: Falmer Press.

London Borough of Waltham Forest (1994) *Assessment, Achievement and Action: a handbook for special educational needs co-ordinators; procedures for planning and reviewing the progress of children and students with SEN.* London: Waltham Forest LEA.

13

Pupil participation in the social and education processes of a primary school

Jacquie Coulby and David Coulby

INTRODUCTION

This chapter is concerned with three themes: self-advocacy, pupil behaviour, and the management of a primary school. At the primary phase, 'pupil participation' might provide a less jargonised equivalent for self-advocacy. The bulk of the chapter is concerned with strategies to encourage the participation of young children in the running of their own school lives. The reference to children with special educational needs here is direct rather than tangential. The school which we describe has its fair share of children formally and informally perceived to have such needs, and they form part of this chapter. But the real relevance of what we describe to the schooling of children perceived to have special educational needs lies in our assumption that such needs are actually generated within classrooms and schools. Pupil behaviour and the management of the primary school are themes which we have previously attempted to connect (Coulby and Coulby 1990). The vast majority of children perceived to have special needs are those who have engaged in behaviour in school which teachers and head teachers have found unacceptable. The bureaucratic and pseudo-scientific procedures and belief systems whereby this lack of acceptance of behaviour is formalised into the various categories of 'need' in order to legitimate exclusion have been thoroughly described elsewhere (Tomlinson 1981, 1982). In seeking to reduce the number of children subjected to these procedures we have sought ways of reducing the amount of pupil behaviour likely to be considered unacceptable, and encouraging teachers to consider critically the boundaries of what they are prepared to accept. It is a truism that the majority of special needs work takes place in mainstream schools; it should be equally obvious that the majority of this work is concerned with prevention.

Self-advocacy, then, is a third theme which might be seen to sit uneasily with the first two. If the theory and practice is that by generating appropriate managerial, pedagogical and curricular systems then the incidence of both learning and behaviour difficulties can be dramatically reduced, then what space does this give to student individuality in any form? The question is all the sterner when it concerns children of primary school age. Self-advocacy with young adults could itself be seen as part of a management system designed just as much to control as to liberate. Few primary school age children lack individuality. Indeed, the systems approach to learning and behaviour difficulties which we have repeatedly advocated might be seen as an organised way of constraining – to use no harsher word – such individualism in the interests of social control and intellectual conformity. Self-advocacy or pupil participation is a necessary third category for two important reasons. First, the systems we describe are not designed to engender either academic or behavioural conformity. On the contrary, they are designed to allow all pupils to fulfil their potential and to prevent them being exposed to the processes and institutions of segregation. Secondly, if these systems were imposed by teachers on young pupils they would not work anyway. It is the harsh imposition of arbitrary systems – admittedly somewhat different from those we advocate – which in the past has encouraged pupil resistance and nonconformity with the associated negative educational results for all concerned. If pupils are placed at the centre of the social and educational processes of the primary school then the resulting systems will not be something imposed upon them but rather the institutionalisation of their own self-development. If the children are involved in the formulation and modification of the maximum number of aspects of these systems then they will have a much greater potential to be liberating as well as successful.

Self-advocacy or pupil participation is an essential part of a primary education which seeks to minimise the number of pupils whose needs are formally found to be 'special'. More portentously, pupil participation is an essential element of a primary education in a democratic society.

The remainder of this chapter is divided into four sections:

- behaviour policy and ethos;
- democracy and individualism;
- involvement of pupils and parents in the school curriculum;
- special needs.

Batheaston Church of England Voluntary Controlled (CEVC) Primary School is a medium-sized school serving a socially mixed locality on the fringe of the city of Bath. The children are aged from four to eleven. There is a playgroup closely connected to the school and located in one of its rooms but there is no nursery. The policies and practices which we describe below are by no means unique to this school, but they form part of a unified approach to learning and behaviour which is widely supported by teachers, non-teaching staff and parents.

BEHAVIOUR POLICY AND ETHOS

These two items are treated together since they are inseparable and central elements of school policy. The school has an explicit 'behaviour policy', a document designed to share strategies with those such as students or supply teachers who are temporarily attached to the school. The children know that all the staff care about them and their behaviour. All staff therefore make it their responsibility to know all the children and to have a response to anything they come across. Similarly all staff are equally valued, teaching and non-teaching staff alike, and all are committed to the educational and social life of the school. All staff are used to reward good achievement – children frequently go and show other teachers, the cook, the secretary, etc., a good piece of work. Other children are also told about things of which a particular class feels proud, such as a wall display, and are invited in to see it. Once a week, children's work is shared with the whole school in a special assembly. A check is kept that all children's good work is shown regularly, and the other children are invited to come to classes to see displays and presentations. When a child has made a significant improvement or produced a really special piece of work then this may feature in a badge assembly (see the next section) and/or result in a letter acknowledging the achievement being sent home to parents . . .

Social mixing across age groups is encouraged. When the four year olds start school, each is matched with a special friend. These are generally the nine and ten year olds. They collect the younger children and take them out to play; they usually organise games for them; help them to mix; help them with coats, etc. They also go to lunch with them when they first stay and help them to get their food; they collect them and take them to assemblies, where they sit with them, explaining things and helping them to listen quietly. This experience provides responsibility for the older children as well as assistance, friendship and a role model for the younger ones.

Children are encouraged to be involved in the process of behaviour management. The children are encouraged to observe and identify appropriate 'good' behaviour and to praise each other. They are involved in developing the school and class rules . . . Their ideas are sought in particular problem-solving sessions. The difficulties of individual children in terms of learning and/or behaviour are talked about openly, seen as temporary, and children who help with these are specifically praised and thanked. Children are treated respectfully and spoken to politely. If ever something goes wrong, the inappropriate responses/behaviour are identified through individual/group discussion, alternative strategies identified, solutions/apologies worked out and, if necessary, sanctions enforced. If the misdeed is significant the parents are contacted and involved in the discussions or sanctions.

A variety of opportunities, such as role play and assemblies, are used to help children develop strategies for difficult group situations such as how to say 'no' when the rest of a group say 'yes' (to a cigarette, for instance) or how to respond as a group to unfriendly or unsporting playground behaviour. Assemblies are frequently used in this way; they provide the children with a training in self-presentation, debate and self-articulation. High expectations of behaviour and the commitment to learning for all children are linked to a differentiated curriculum and specific attention to learning difficulties. Central to the school's approach is the identification, appreciation and reward of good work and behaviour. This focuses on effort and attitude as well as on achievement.

Responsibility is a necessary part of advocacy/involvement. The pupils are clearly responsible for many aspects of the running of the school. This involvement is itself a training in shared responsibility as well as an indication that everyone is involved in ensuring the smooth running of the institution. Some examples may help. Every day the children in the oldest class work through a rota of whole-school responsibilities for about a quarter of an hour: litter collection in the playground, tidying cloakrooms and library, delivering messages for the head teacher and secretary, helping to prepare the hall for lunches, watering plants. In this way the older children are motivated to encourage other pupils to take responsibility for the fabric and processes of their environment. Other pupils run the tuck shop and generate orders according to the popularity of items. Pupils of all ages regularly act as guides to the school for visitors.

DEMOCRACY AND INDIVIDUALISM

Bringing up children either as a parent or as a teacher is a task which operates between a series of tensions. Perhaps the most important of these is that between encouraging and developing individuality on the one hand and inculcating a wide range of social norms on the other. The emerging skills, interests, characteristics and idiosyncrasies of the child need to be nurtured and channelled while at the same time childish egocentrism and selfishness need to be constrained to take account of the rights and needs of peers, of adults, of institutions and occasions (traffic, mealtimes), and of wider society. Put in different terms, this is the tension between individualism and self-direction, each with its potential for competition and conflict on the one hand and co-operation on the other. To err on one side is to encourage solipsistic individualism; to err on the other is to insist on institutional and social conformity. Elsewhere (Bash, Coulby and Jones 1985) we have made a distinction between socialisation and social control to attempt to elaborate this tension.

However, it is obviously always a matter of balance which each parent or school must attempt to maintain with each child.

For a primary school even to have a behavioural policy is for it to stress one side of this balance. But without such a policy a school is likely to encourage behaviours which will ultimately limit the learning possibilities and indeed the opportunities for individual development of all pupils. The paradox is that without some support for social and individual norms it is impossible to create an atmosphere and an environment in which individual learning and growth can occur. Character is not disarticulated from society and its institutions: rather it is shaped within them. It is the extent of this shaping which is the delicate matter of professional balance. The section above dealt with institutional behaviour policy. Within that policy for control it is clear that there are stresses on equality and individuality. This section outlines those aspects of the school's policy which also seek to maintain that side of the balance. It is within this section that policies which most closely connect with those associated with involvement/self-advocacy are likely to be found. In the terms of this chapter, these policies are concerned with the involvement of individual children in the school and that of the school in individual children. These policies are only possible against a background of clear expectations for equality and opportunities for daily group discussion and constant modelling by adults of responsibility and participation.

The school operates to a firm policy of equality. This applies to the familiar categories of race, gender and class, but also to those perceived or categorised as having special educational needs (see p.261).

Issues of status – as between teaching and non-teaching staff, staff and parents, and indeed staff and pupils – are minimised wherever this is possible. Parents and ancillaries work independently alongside teachers in both classrooms and playground. Children refer to all staff by their first names. (This policy has not been controversial with parents or the community though at one point it generated considerable hysterical copy in the local newspaper.)

The products of the children are seen to permeate in the management and presentation of the school. The school logo was chosen from a competition of the designs of children at the school. As well as being a statement of co-operation and equality, it is clearly the product of a child. It features prominently on the school's official notepaper, on school uniform and on official documents such as the prospectus. It semiotically asserts the primacy of the children in the structures and identity of the school.

In more formal democratic terms there is a School Council (for a recent, national account of how these can work see Haigh 1994). This consists of two elected representatives from each class who meet with the head teacher once a term. Obviously the council in no sense controls the school. However, the following account of one meeting is an indication of the extent to which children can participate in the formation of decisions which influence their everyday lives. We quote these minutes in full since they also give an insight into the way in which behaviour policies are arbitrated and implemented in order to ensure the maximum consensus and support. They also indicate that even the youngest children can participate actively at this level, bringing items to the agenda as well as participating in the discussion.

Minutes of Councillors' Meeting
Tuesday, 19th April

1. Uniform

Everyone felt they did want a uniform and some felt it should be obligatory. We discussed how we could not actually insist on it. The Councillors felt that we should encourage it.

Wearing denim was discussed and it was to be OK if SMART (not old), and new and dark. We all agreed there was a problem with Y6, whose parents were saving to get a new school uniform for Secondary School. We decided we should encourage everyone to wear it, and if they couldn't manage all of it, at least to get a navy or red top.

2. Football

The young children felt it was not fair that they could only play in the big playground. There had been lots of complaints. So, after much discussion, it was agreed that: if damp, Class 5 and 6 mixed would play football in the top playground, with the rest of the school in the big playground; if dry, Class 5 and 6 would play football on the bottom grass. The rest of the school would have the top playground and top grass, and Classes 1, 2, 3 and 4 would have football in the big playground. PLEASE NOTE: Everyone felt that GIRLS CAN PLAY FOOTBALL (even if they are not too good at it), and anyone in Class 5 or 6 can play. If anyone says 'you can't play football' they get banned for the rest of that day and the next day.

3. New arrangements

Alternative weeks table duty and eating list. So, eat first and do tables. Gemma, Luke, Anthony and Katie are to do the new rotas.

4. School Fund Friday Collection

A suggestion was made and taken up to get more playground equipment. Cake money and the Friday silver collection will go towards this.

5. Monitors for playground

Cathy would work out some monitors for all the playground equipment. Ideas of some things to get out to play with: cones, tunnels, hoola hoops, basketball ring and ball, high jump stands to use for goal posts, jacks. Ideas for designs/drawings on the playground: shadow clock, long jump, marked racing area on bottom playground or outside Class 6. We decided to ask children for donations of equipment – things for outside, cars, Lego, etc. It was requested that we put up mirrors in both loos. Everyone thought this an excellent idea.

6. Class 5

Class 5 had made lots of complaints about always being last for dinners. A solution was found: Class 5 and 6 will take it in turns, alternate weeks to eat first/last. On the week that they eat first, they will also clear away the hall. Everyone thought that this was a good idea and the Class 5 and 6 Councillors agreed to draw up the rotas. Jacquie said she would explain it to the lunchtime supervisors.

7. Playground behaviour

Councillors felt that Class 6 sometimes taught the little ones rude words. Jacquie will speak to the children about this in assembly. Councillors said that karate and play fighting was seen by many as a nuisance and also some people felt left out. After discussion, the following was decided and Jacquie agreed to inform everyone at the next assembly (and to tell the lunchtime supervisors):

1. Karate and play fighting: From now on, this is totally banned. If people want to play in this way they should do so out of school. Anyone playing karate/fighting would be taken by the lunchtime supervisor to Jacquie and kept inside for a lunchtime as a reminder.

2. There will now be a ban on saying 'you can't play': From now on, if someone tells you can't play, we'd like you to tell the lunchtime supervisor who will talk it over with you and take the child who has said 'you can't play' to Jacquie, who will make them stay inside for a lunchtime. This includes the footballers and everyone else.

The meeting was then closed and councillors agreed to feed back all these agreements to the rest of the school in assembly.

The discussion and decisions here go a long way beyond tokenism. A further decision, which is linked to the uniform issue at the beginning of these minutes, may be used to reinforce this. When a noticeable number of children started to come to school wearing denim – which actually met the uniform requirement of being either red or navy – the issue was referred to the Parents' Voice group to ascertain their views. After much discussion this group could not reach a clear decision so they in turn referred it to the School Council as the most appropriate point where advice could be offered. Further, the school recognises that pupils have their own priorities when it comes to the allocation of resources collected through fundraising. The School Council provides the forum in which these priorities can be itemised.

All but the oldest class operate a system of appointing a Special Person each day. This is mainly done by rota, but can be managed to match birthdays or difficulties such as an anxious child going to the dentist. The Special Person has certain enjoyable responsibilities – taking the register to the secretary, choosing children to line up and so on. In several classes, the Special Person is responsible for monitoring the noise level and reminding children if it is meant to be a particularly quiet time (the aim being for them all to gain experience of focusing on appropriate/ convenient levels of noise as well as fulfilling the function of maintaining a quiet working atmosphere). At the end of their special day, the Special Person has to identify one or two people who have behaved in a friendly way: they are encouraged to describe *how*. They then award these children a sticker for friendly behaviour. The older children tend to discuss friendly behaviour slightly differently. They have a Child of the Week system. Each child in turn is the focus of class observation and discussion. The children are invited through the week to write on a wall chart the ways in which the Child of the Week has performed well, in terms of friendly, co-operative behaviour, work or attitude. The child in question also expresses any difficulties they have with behaviour at the beginning of the week, and their classmates offer suggestions and support. At the end of the week, they take their wall chart home to keep.

Another policy which balances between the development of individuality and the control of behaviour is that involving whole-school badges. In this case the repertoire of desirable behaviours was evolved through staff discussion. Having agreed these, appropriate badges were made. Each class has three regular badges: 'I have done some beautiful work'; 'I have behaved very well'; 'I have done some excellent work'. Every week, the class teachers nominate children for these badges; the children can make nominations to the teachers. Each class teacher also chooses a few of the following general badges: 'I have tried extremely hard'; 'I have been very polite and cheerful'; 'I have completed all my work this week'; 'I have been extremely friendly and co-operative'; 'I have worked well with other children'; 'I have done some brilliant work'; 'I have made a big step forward'; 'I have done something very special'; 'I have made a tremendous achievement'; 'I have been really helpful'; 'I am good at homework'; 'I have been a star'; 'I have had some great ideas'; 'I have been really good at lunchtimes'. There is a weekly badge assembly. The aim is to keep a regular discussion going about what sorts of actions make up 'good' behaviour. The teachers write a covering sentence saying what the child has specifically done, for instance, *how* a child was co-operative to another child. The children value the badges and take them very seriously: parents, teachers and other children tend to praise the children wearing the badges for the week. Once again, teachers would ensure that *all* children received a badge sometimes.

School and class rules are also developed democratically. This process is described elsewhere (Coulby 1986). The key elements at school level are: behaviour is an important topic of general discussion in all classes; children work out what rules are necessary to the safe and effective conduct of the school. The overarching framework is that there should be as few rules as possible and that they should all be phrased in a positive way. Children work in small groups in class to evolve the appropriate rules; this process is then repeated at school level. When the list is finalised it is ratified by all the classes; the final formal list is signed by all the children and staff.

INVOLVEMENT OF PUPILS AND PARENTS IN THE SCHOOL CURRICULUM

Participation by both teachers and pupils in the formation of the school curriculum has been severely reduced by the introduction of the National Curriculum in the wake of the 1988 Education Act. The subjects to be studied and even the smallest details of topics and themes have, since then, been prescribed by the central government for England and Wales.

However, in the light of the government's acceptance of the Dearing proposals for radically slimming down the curriculum (Dearing 1993a and b, DFE 1993), there will soon be space in the primary school to teach knowledge beyond and different from that prescribed in the National Curriculum. Potentially this returns a great deal of autonomy to primary teachers and greatly increases the scope for pupils' involvement in their own education. While it may not be possible for very young children to map out the knowledge and skills they wish to acquire at school, if pupils have no say whatsoever in the curriculum, then they are likely to see knowledge as something inflicted on them without their choice or participation. Similarly parents often wish to have some say in what their child learns at school. This is very rarely a matter of attempting to constrain the curriculum, but stems from their knowledge of the strengths, weaknesses and progress of their particular child. Certainly if pupils and parents have no say in the actual business of the school or the curriculum, then it will be all the easier for them to become alienated and remote from the institution as a whole. This section explores some of the strategies whereby, within the confines of the National Curriculum, the primary school might seek to involve parents and pupils in curriculum planning.

In some ways to ask to what extent pupils can define their own curriculum is to miss the details of autonomy within the school day. Even within the constraints of the National Curriculum it is possible for pupils to be independent learners. From reception age, children at Batheaston, as at many other primary schools, learn to choose their own media and materials for the task in hand. They locate the appropriate learning materials within the classroom and school and select and collect them themselves. In this way they develop the skills of independent learners and self-directed resource managers. They take some control over the way in which their time is spent in school. By bringing books and items into school from home to show and share with others, they make their contribution to the direction in which themes and topics are developed. Periodically display areas in the school are designated for the exclusive use of the pupils. This allows them to determine which achievements in which areas are worthy of publicity and acclaim. A paired reading scheme allows older children to assist in the learning of younger ones and as well as enhancing co-operation gives them the opportunity to take some responsibility for the curricular work of the school.

Perhaps the most important formal process with regard to participation in curriculum planning is that which involves the annual questionnaires and parental interviews. Once a year, usually in February, pupils and parents take part in an annual review of how curriculum work is progressing and what the school can do to support it further. This is done through three questionnaires. Parents fill out their questionnaire (Figure

13.1) at home, the teachers complete a parallel questionnaire (Figure 13.2), while the children fill out a detailed self-assessment form (Figure 13.3).

The children's contributions show an ability and enthusiasm, even at an early age, to perceive their own progress and their needs. They look at issues such as: the pace at which they work; with whom; in which area of the curriculum they need help; their friendship skills; their ability to select and organise equipment.

When all three questionnaires have been completed, the parents and the teacher meet to talk about them. At this parent interview, they use the three questionnaires to identify the child's current areas of achievement and ways of developing those further. They also organise together specific support for any difficulties. They concentrate on working out which particular skills and activities need to be the focus for the next year. This is sometimes in terms of subject areas like science, but more frequently it involves a detailed scrutiny of the pupil's development potential: specific targets such as concentration on reading non-fictional books or working on hand–eye co-ordination in both drawing and writing are then agreed. These targets are then summarised in a home–school contract (Figure 13.4), which entails curricular aims for the child during the following year, both at home and at school.

When the contract is finalised, it is signed by the teacher and the parent and each retains a copy. The contract is then discussed with the child both at home and at school and the targets remain as a focus for the ensuing year. They are often used as the framework for the more refined individual termly learning targets which again involve the participation of the parents and pupils.

As well as the statutory assessment and reporting required by the National Curriculum, the school has developed profiling (Records of Achievement) as an appropriate way of monitoring and recording each child's progress. Particular attention is paid to recording both the subject material covered and the level of achievement attained by each child. In this way, profiles are compiled for all the children containing evidence and examples of their learning, copies of reports written for them, teacher-, parent- and self-assessment sheets, specimens of outstanding work, etc. These profiles belong to the children, and access to them is always open: they are sometimes shared together during quiet reading time. They form a cumulative record and history of each child's development in the school. The children take them on to secondary school where they can be continued. The profiles document one way in which the children retain ownership of the curriculum.

Questionnaire for parents

Name of child: ....

1   Do you think your child is happy at school?   Yes ☐   No ☐

2   How would you describe your child? (Please tick or cross.) Add details if
    necessary.

☐ Confident	☐ Creative
☐ Anxious	☐ Imaginative
☐ Co-operative	☐ Able to choose own activities
☐ Able to share	☐ Well organised
☐ Caring	☐ Good at concentrating
☐ Able to take turns	☐ Able to complete activities
☐ Moody	☐ Able to listen well
☐ Cheerful	☐ Able to follow instructions
☐ Tolerant	☐ Good at making decisions
☐ Thoughtful	☐ Clearly **understands** parents' expectations for
☐ Lively	behaviour
☐ Lively	☐ **Co-operates** with parents' expectations for
☐ Persevering	behaviour

3   Is there anything that happens at home which might affect your child's
    performance at school, and that you think we should take into account?
    e.g. poor sleep pattern; parent shift work demands; parents' separation, etc.

4   Do you think your child mixes happily with other children?   In school ☐
    Out of school ☐

5   Are there interests, achievements we should record that we might not know
    about, e.g. cubs, swimming, gym, hobbies, etc.?

6   Are there any activities which your child loves or is particularly interested in at
    school?

7   In school, what do you think your child is really good at, at the moment?

8   What do you think your child needs more help with?

9   What are the most important things you wish your child to develop during the
    next year?

10 Do you think it is best left to the teacher or yourself? Or would you like us to
    show you ways to help your child with this?

11 If you are able to spend time doing things with your child (e.g. playing, hobbies,
    outings) is this   frequent ☐   regular ☐   occasional ☐?
    What type of activities do you do?

    Do you need ideas?   Yes ☐   No ☐

12 We do already ask you to fit in listening to your child reading, sharing books, etc.
    as part of the PACT scheme. Are you confident to do this? Would you like some
    help, e.g. with children who are difficult to motivate?
    Yes ☐   No ☐

Figure 13.1 Questionnaire for parents (© Batheaston Primary School 1991)

13 Did you find the curriculum/planning evening helpful?
   Yes ☐   No ☐   Unable to attend ☐

14 In response to your comments last year, we have acknowledged the need for a similar scheme to support maths activities at home, e.g. sharing simple puzzles and practical activities, once a month. How do you feel about this?

15 We feel that your children will succeed better if they feel that you think that school and learning are important. Please comment.

16 Is there anyone else you feel would have some useful information which would help us in teaching your child, e.g. childminder; separated parent; other family member; parent's partner with whom child lives.
   Please note: Because of the 1989 Children Act, we are now required to provide separated parents with copies of all reports. Please ensure that we have appropriate details.

17 What do you think are the most important things your children should learn at school to prepare them for the situations they will meet in the future?

18 Apart from making school more stimulating and interesting, do you think having parents in to join the children with their activities has helped your child to learn? Please comment.

19 If you were given support, would you be interest to help at school in any of the following ways?
   Around the school generally   ☐
   (e.g. library, bookshop, making equipment, sharing skills with staff or pupils)
   In your child's class   ☐
   In a different class   ☐
   Fundraising   ☐
   Would this be on regular basis   ☐   or occasionally ☐?

20 There have been a lot of negative discussions about education in the media recently. Has this affected your view about our school?

21 Did you feel that the aims identified in the contract last year were easy to fulfil?
   For us ☐   For you ☐

22 Please use the back of this sheet if there is anything else you would like to tell us about your child.

23 Please indicate the time which would be most convenient for you and your partner to meet with your child's teacher for half an hour.
   Between 8.45–12.00 ☐   1.00–3.00 ☐   3.00–5.00 ☐

Please return this questionnaire by .... Thank you.
© Batheaston Primary School 1991

Figure 13.1 (cont'd)

Teachers' assessment questionnaire

Name of child: ....

1 Is the child happy at school?   Yes ☐   No ☐
   Comments:

2 Would you describe the child as:
   ☐ Confident   ☐ Creative
   ☐ Anxious   ☐ Imaginative
   ☐ Co-operative   ☐ Able to choose own activities
   ☐ Able to share   ☐ Well organised
   ☐ Caring   ☐ Good at concentrating
   ☐ Able to take turns   ☐ Able to complete activities
   ☐ Moody   ☐ Able to listen well
   ☐ Cheerful   ☐ Able to follow instructions
   ☐ Tolerant   ☐ Good at making decisions
   ☐ Thoughtful   ☐ Clearly understands teachers' expectations
   ☐ Lively   ☐ Co-operates with teachers' expectations for behaviour
   ☐ Persevering

3 Are there any indications that the child's performance at school is affected by external circumstances, e.g. late arrival, tiredness, enthusiastic parents, etc.?

4 Does the child mix happily with other children?   Yes ☐   No ☐

5 What evidence do we see of activities at home, e.g. reading?

6 What activities do we think the child loves and is particularly interested in?

7 What do we think the child is really good at, at the moment?

8 We think the child needs a little extra help at the moment with:

9 In the next year, the child might need specific help with: School ☐ Home ☐

10 How do you perceive parent interest in helping the child with educational difficulties?

11 Are you happy about the way the PACT scheme is working with this child?

12 Does the child share with you activities done at home?   Yes ☐   No ☐

13 Re: Last year's contract:

14 Does either parent get involved with class activities? Please comment.

15 How does the child respond to other adult helpers in school?

16 Any further comments?

Signature:..   Date:..............................

Figure 13.2 Questionnaire for teachers (© Batheaston Primary School 1991)

Children's self-assessment form

My name is ....
I am .... years and .... months old in ....

1 (Please tick)

	I enjoy	I'm good at	I'd like help with
Story-writing	☐	☐	☐
Handwriting	☐	☐	☐
Computer	☐	☐	☐
Spelling words	☐	☐	☐
Reading	☐	☐	☐
Construction kits	☐	☐	☐
Painting and drawing	☐	☐	☐
Maths activities	☐	☐	☐
Science	☐	☐	☐
Technology	☐	☐	☐
Geography	☐	☐	☐
PE	☐	☐	☐
Making music	☐	☐	☐
Singing	☐	☐	☐
Dance	☐	☐	☐
Drama	☐	☐	☐
History	☐	☐	☐
Assemblies	☐	☐	☐
Listening to stories	☐	☐	☐
Talking to the class	☐	☐	☐
Working with children from other classes	☐	☐	☐

2 Do you have enough time to finish your work?   Yes ☐ No ☐
   If not, which subject is hardest to finish?

3 Do you like the room: Quiet ☐ A bit noisy ☐   Noisy ☐

4 Who is it best for you to sit with to work well? Why?
   Do you like it when there are other grown-ups to help you with your work?
   Yes ☐   No ☐

5 Where in the room do you like to work best?

6 What is the most important thing you learn here?

7 What do your parents think is the most important?

8 What are you best at?

9 What would you like to get better at?

10 Do you like being at school?   Yes ☐ No ☐ Sometimes ☐

11 What do you like about playtimes?

12 What do you NOT like about playtimes?

Figure 13.3 Children's self-assessment form (© Batheaston Primary School 1991)

13 How could we make lunchtimes better?

14 Do you tell your mum or dad about the activities you've been doing?

Yes ☐   No ☐

15 Are they pleased with you, or do they think you could do better?

16 Do you think you could be better?

17 If you could change something about your class what would it be?

18 Do you find it easy to stay friends with people?

19 Do you think it is important to make your work attractive?   Yes ☐   No ☐

20 Do you like your work to be displayed on the wall?   Yes ☐   No ☐

21 Do you like your name on it?   Yes ☐   No ☐

22 Who do you like to see your work?

23 Do you know where to find everything you need?   Yes ☐   No ☐

24 How do you like to work?   On your own ☐   In a group ☐   With a partner ☐

25 Do you have lots of nice work which shows exactly how clever you are,
   or haven't you shown us yet?   I have ☐   I haven't ☐

26 What is your favourite thing about school?
   What is your favourite thing to do at home?

Signature of child:..   Date:...............................
Signature of adult:..   Date:...............................

© Batheaston Primary School 1991

Figure 13.3 (cont'd)

Two small final examples may further demonstrate the varieties of this ownership. The school is committed to evaluation of its policies and ensuring that this evaluation is used, where appropriate, to modify practice. The first non-competitive sports day gave rise to considerable discussion among both pupils and parents. It became clear that nearly all the pupils preferred the non-competitive approach but that a number of parents still liked the competitive day. A compromise of having a non-competitive sports day every alternate year was arrived at. A similar conflict occurred over the annual leavers' assembly. The ceremony whereby each leaver came to the front of the hall accompanied by music and then sat facing the audience was recognised as being very emotional. Parents concerned at the tears requested that the leavers should sit facing the front like the other children. This was tried for one year. However, it

Home–school contract

Name of child: .... Class: ....
Agreed areas of achievement/strengths:

Suggestions for further development
(a) At school:
(b) At home:

Areas in which the child could make substantial improvement (including behaviour, in specific terms):

Suggestions for action, both at school at at home:

Please use the reverse for specific request/other information.
Parent(s):
Teacher:
Head teacher:

Figure 13.4 Home–school contract

transpired that the leavers themselves thought the emotion was appropriate to the occasion and so, after a deputation by the pupils to the Year 6 teacher and the head teacher, the original format of the assembly was restored. The ability of the pupils to determine the curriculum in these small but symbolic matters emphasises the school's attempts to give them responsibility for and ownership of their own learning.

SPECIAL NEEDS

The ethos of the school is that its learning and behaviour policies will mean that it will be able to educate children perceived to have special needs provided there is adequate support. Special needs are talked about openly, and it is commonly understood that all children might well have such a need at some point of their school career and that therefore many of them will be working on individually designed special tasks. Careful continuous assessment is carried out to try to identify such needs at an early stage. Whenever necessary, additional support is organised, and the general approach is to acknowledge that all children are individual and work at different levels and paces in separate areas of the curriculum.

A special needs teacher works one afternoon each week to support the work of the co-ordinator. As part of this time, the special needs teacher plans appropriate activities in conjunction with the class teacher and provides guidance and training for the teaching assistants. Every day all the teaching assistants devote from half to one hour of individual support for children with special needs. Class teachers use the specific information about a child with special needs to inform their daily plans and accordingly to differentiate learning activities. When events and outings are planned it is acknowledged by the whole group from the outset that these will present a challenge to the behaviour of some pupils. Part of the preparation then is to make suggestions as to activities that children can do on a bus journey or who they should sit next to, how to handle meetings with new children or adults, ideas for groupings, etc. In this way any children with potential behaviour difficulties are motivated not to disappoint the support and commitment of the group.

A final example may illustrate the general awareness and sympathy for particular educational needs. The footballers wanted a new set of school kit and decided to raise the money themselves. The whole of the class discussed what would be the most effective sponsorship approach to parents. When they settled on the idea of a – subsequently popular – sponsored spell, the difficulties of two children within the group were recognised. The children developed the solution of having highly differentiated spelling lists. The awareness of differential achievement was handled openly but respectfully and a joint solution was found for a commonly owned difficulty.

This chapter has focused on policy and practice in a particular primary school. These policies are not at all in themselves unique. Many other schools are pursuing at least equally progressive policies with regard to children's involvement and special educational needs. Rather the example has allowed us to focus on the way in which a school attempts to walk the tightrope between the need for social control and conformity and the development of the full potential of each individual. This balance operates between the fearful polar opposites of our society: repression and growth, indoctrination and education, conformity and individuality, totalitarianism and democracy. Between these appalling alternatives every teacher and every head teacher must walk. Policies which seek to ensure the involvement and participation of young children in their primary schools are a way of ensuring that, when we fall, it is in a particular direction.

REFERENCES

Bash, L., Coulby, D. and Jones, C. (1985) *Urban Schooling: theory and practice.* London: Cassell.

Coulby, J. (1986) 'A practical approach to behaviour in the primary school', *Primary Teaching Studies* **1**(3), 91–7.

Coulby, J. and Coulby, D. (1990) 'Interviewing in junior classrooms', in Docking, J. (ed.) *Education and Alienation in the Junior School*. London: Falmer Press.

Dearing, R. (1993a) *The National Curriculum and its Assessment: interim report*. York/London: NCC/SEAC.

Dearing, R. (1993b) *The National Curriculum and its Assessment: final report*. London: SCAA.

Department For Education (DFE) (1993) *Interim Report on the National Curriculum and its Assessment: the government's response*. London: DFE.

Haigh, G. (1994) 'Voices of reason', *TES*, section 2, 27 May, 1–2.

Tomlinson, S. (1981) *Educational Subnormality: a study in decision making*. London: Routledge and Kegal Paul.

Tomlinson, S. (1982) *A Sociology of Special Education*. London: Routledge and Kegan Paul.

Classroom strategies for teacher and pupil support

Rena Harris-Cooksley and Robert Catt

In this chapter we adopt a case-study approach to the role adopted by a teacher-researcher who, as a member of a Behaviour Support Team, intervened to overcome the specified classroom management difficulties of an experienced but struggling teacher. The teacher-researcher acted as advocate for both the harassed classroom teacher herself and a group of pupils who had, seemingly, opted out of learning and who had become extremely disruptive. The support offered took the form of mediation between and the reconciliation of some conflicting purposes and oppositional approaches, together with the initiation of a series of classroom management strategies.

Much of our chapter will be descriptive, even anecdotal, and will draw upon:

– the teacher-researcher's field notes;
– discussion with the class teacher involved;
– comments and illustrative drawings from pupils;
– evaluation and observation notes from a teaching colleague.

Of more than peripheral interest, too, is the collaborative approach which informs this chapter and, working within an essentially naturalistic paradigm, we aim to weave together a number of different voices to form a pattern illustrating the importance of self-esteem in learning and to emphasise the need for pupils as well as their teachers to be able to operate with some sense of dignity and self-worth. Ethical issues have been carefully weighed; the anonymity of all those involved, other than the teacher-researcher herself, has been ensured; we are particularly grateful to the classroom teacher who has participated in and encouraged this retrospective portrayal of the difficulties with which she was at that time confronted.

Our chapter ends with some reflective points drawn from a discussion between the two authors.

CLASSROOMS, TEACHERS, TALKING AND LEARNING

If speech in childhood lays the foundation for a lifetime's thinking, then how can we prize a silent classroom? (Britton 1987)

The role of language in learning, and talk in particular, is an acknowledged and well-established feature of current practice. The rise of 'oracy' within the past thirty years has been thoroughly explored and documented (cf Maclure *et al.*, 1988) and once seemingly esoteric theories emphasising the relationship between language and the development of thought have been presented in accessible forms (cf Wood 1990). A welcome feature of recent classroom research is an examination of discourse detail drawing attention to the mechanisms, strategies and complexities which characterise classroom dialogue. On a more practical note and particularly useful for busy teachers are those organisational suggestions which are so coherently expressed in the NCC's Teaching, Talking and Learning Key series (NCC 1991) built largely upon the very successful work of the National Oracy Project.

Our concern in this chapter, however, is that despite the acknowledged value of talk in classrooms, its management can be so problematic – and is particularly so in the case we shall be exploring.

Non-participant Field Notes (First Visit)
Teacher reluctant to go into class.
At desk – involved with nearest pupils.
Requested quiet for register.
Six pupils arrive late.
Some still noisy – moving around room ignoring request to sit down for quiet reading.
X refused to co-operate with instruction to move on to carpet. Teacher didn't argue – said 'OK'. Other pupils: 'That's not fair' . . . 'He always gets what he wants'.
Pupils on carpet – very restless: shoving, poking each other, continuing conversations.
Teacher interacting with nearest pupils.
No positive feedback to pupils.
Pupils return to places very noisy, pushing: 'He's got my . . .' 'Can't find my . . .'.
Pupils not organised for task. Calling out: 'This is boring' . . . 'You're copying me' . . . 'Miss!'
Six pupils very loud, calling out, two sulking, out of seats.
Some refusing to work: 'I'm not doing this. This is rubbish'.
M shouting. Teacher tells him to work on carpet.

Teacher interacting with two pupils. No feedback to class.
Girls mainly on-task – no contact with teacher.
Many pupils off-task but not re-directed.
Playtime – pupils leave room without tidying up: rush out.
Chairs, bags everywhere.

Context

The ten-week programme of support took place in a co-educational mainstream middle-school in an outer London Borough. The school had a mixed catchment area and strong links with parents.

The Year 6 mixed-ability group comprised 17 boys and 9 girls from a variety of social and ethnic backgrounds. Although the gender imbalance was acknowledged the school's senior managers felt it was not possible to organise the class in any other way. The class teacher, however, felt that the gender imbalance contributed to the difficulties which pupils experienced in their interpersonal relationships within the classroom.

There were further concerns about the special needs of several children within the class. Two pupils had statements of special educational need and both pupils had difficulties in establishing and maintaining friendships amongst the peer group. The class teacher felt this was largely the result of the effects that their often angry aggressive outbursts had on the flow of lessons. Their behaviour often interrupted lessons when the class teacher's attention was taken up with refereeing disagreements or disciplining inappropriate behaviour such as calling out, name calling and refusal to co-operate with instructions. The other pupils in the group seemed unable to cope with this behaviour and were reluctant to work in groups which included either of the statemented pupils. The class teacher reported that many of her planned lessons were either abandoned or that learning outcomes were unsatisfactory from her point of view. She neither felt that the classroom environment was one which was 'calm and purposeful' (DES 1989) nor that the pupils had the social skills which would enable them to build relationships and handle the unreasonable behaviour of others.

Concern amongst parents, other staff, pupils and the class teacher herself was such that an urgent request for help was made to the Borough's Behavioural Support Team.

The class teacher was experienced in working across the middle-school age-range and felt confident in her ability as a teacher. She described her role as that of 'a facilitator for learning' and had always structured her classes in order to foster 'a child-centred and collaborative' approach heavily dependent upon group work. Although she used a teaching style which she had always found to be successful, she reported almost immediately that there were difficulties in managing the class. During the first half of the Autumn term there were increasing difficulties initially attributed to individual pupils but then ascribed to the class as a whole. She began to feel that she was failing and, uncharacteristically, began to lose confidence in her abilities. She sought the help and advice of her head teacher and it was at this point – within the first half-term – that the school made a request for help.

'Now the bell's gone!'

Extracts from Working Notes Following an Initial Interview with the Class Teacher

The class teacher spoke about specific behavioural difficulties saying that the worst things seemed to be: '. . . calling out . . . name calling . . . never listening to each other or me . . . fighting in the classroom . . . spending more time sorting out their arguments than working . . . have to abandon most "fun" activities like practical group task or PE games . . . they can't or won't follow instructions . . . very noisy all the time . . . I end up shouting at them then they get moody . . . Now the bell's gone and I'll have to go back in there . . . It's only Monday morning . . . There's the whole week to get through yet!'

Strategies

'They just don't listen!'

> It is particularly important when setting up a teacher-outsider partnership to discuss problems, their probable causes and possible solutions. (Bowers 1989)

Following initial observation of the class at work a discussion immediately took place in an informal and non-threatening setting, between the head teacher, class teacher and the teacher-researcher. A variety of strategies, including work with individual pupils, was considered before an 'advocate' approach was agreed whereby the teacher-researcher would work collaboratively for and with the class teacher and the class as a whole. A shared understanding of the problem was established, together with desired outcomes against which teaching roles could be negotiated and a programme of support could be planned.

Information and observations were pooled allowing the class teacher and teacher-researcher to establish broad aims:

- to encourage pupils to develop skills and knowledge which would help them build and sustain positive relationships thereby enabling them to work co-operatively in groups;
- to use a collaborative teaching approach which would support the class teacher in acquiring and taking ownership of some techniques for effective classroom management so that she could encourage the generalisation and maintenance of skills taught to pupils;

and immediate goals:

- that pupils should respond positively towards one another and towards adults;
- that pupils should be able to use the skills taught to achieve a group task.

The programme was planned to cover a ten-week period with the teacher-researcher team-teaching with the class teacher during two regular mornings each week in either the classroom or main hall as appropriate. Protected timetable time was also set aside for half an hour during each Monday morning for planning and reflection.

Pressure from the class teacher influenced the decision to begin the programme of support immediately. It was also immediately clear that it would be necessary to agree a set of well-defined boundaries for behaviour within the classroom setting. Although the programme was planned using a structured approach suggested by Spence (1980) flexibility was retained so that the sessions could be tailored to meet the emerging needs of the group. This is a factor identified by Curtis (1983) as important for the success of a social skills training with primary school pupils. A three-point plan was agreed whereby pupils could be encouraged to generalise and maintain the skills they had learned:

(i) skills should be related to the settings in which the behaviour was expected to occur – e.g. listening to each other and the class teacher especially in the classroom environment – but should also be reinforced in other settings – e.g. the main hall;
(ii) collaboration between the class teacher and the teacher-researcher would enable the identification and reinforcement of target behaviours on a daily basis;
(iii) all pupils should be given opportunities to work in groups which included positive role models so that peer pressure could be effectively harnessed.

Pupils' perceptions

Selected Extracts from the Teacher-Researcher's Field Notes
'Your mother lives in a wheelie bin!'

Before starting on the programme I knew it would be necessary to establish a relationship with the class. I visited the school with the intention of introducing myself to the group. I was very nervous. I'd never met a class quite like this. They took no notice of me whatsoever. I think, quite genuinely, they had no interest in yet another adult who'd just walked into their classroom. After a while I said, quietly, 'Raise your hand if you can hear me.' Slowly – thankfully – some did, then others noticed and yelled 'Shutup!'. The noise level dropped until there was quiet and their attention was focused on me.

I grabbed this first opportunity to acknowledge those who had responded immediately. I said how pleased I was that everyone was now quiet and how I had been particularly impressed with the way in which some members of the class had been ready very quickly: they were sitting up, looking towards me, having stopped their conversations.

My agenda at this point was to set out some ground rules and establish expectations – mine of them and, perhaps more importantly, to find out what they expected from me! What had I let myself in for, I wondered?

I introduced myself to the class telling them some of the kinds of activities we would be doing. I began by telling them something about my job and how I worked and was quickly told 'We know why you're here. It's because we're naughty!'. As I got to know them better they said things like: 'Teachers don't like us. Nobody wants to teach us.' I asked them what they felt 'the problem' was and they quickly identified some familiar difficulties. They said there was far too much noise. People were always shouting out and calling across the room. There was a lot of name calling. Some told me how upsetting the name calling could be, particularly when it was aimed at their mothers. A favourite taunt was 'Your mother lives in a wheelie-bin!' and this would usually be enough to start a fight. They claimed that school was boring; that the teacher was always shouting at them because some people in the class were always getting out of their seats, walking round the class and banging rulers on the desk. During this initial discussion I took every opportunity to reinforce and clarify the behaviour I wanted to see happening. For example, I ignored shouted out answers/contributions, turning to someone with their hand up saying 'I'm going to ask you because you have your hand up' or 'good, you waited for your turn to speak'.

Three rules

I used a good many prompts to establish three ground rules which I wrote up on the board. In a way I was trying to establish with the class the basic conditions they would need if teachers were not to shout at them and if they were going to do interesting work. It was heavy going but I used a lot of questions: 'Why do teachers get angry with you?' and 'What makes it difficult to be heard by other people?' and I re-worked the answers, 'So it's better if only one person speaks at a time', etc. (ignoring the shouters) so that they had some sense of owning the rules:

(i)   everyone has the right to speak and be heard;
(ii) everyone has the right to opt out of an activity (but they would be helped to do it at the end of the session so no cop outs!);
(iii) all four legs of the chair should remain on the floor all the time. (This was an essential ground rule because swinging around on the chair legs often resulted in someone crashing to the floor or over-balancing and pulling the desks apart in an effort to retain balance.)

The programme

The ten-week programme was designed to provide opportunities for pupils and their teachers to work together in an acceptable classroom environment. Many of the activities introduced pupils to effective grouping procedures and helped them to focus upon how decisions and choices within the classroom are made.

There is insufficient space here to provide a detailed description of the activities with which many colleauges will be thoroughly familiar. Rather, we have indicated the outline structure of the programme together with source material for those who may wish to pursue ideas. The activities, in general, are drawn and developed from the excellent resource material provided in *Ways and Means* (Kingston Friends Workshop Group 1989).

The initial preparation for the work to be carried out with this class involved meeting with the class teacher to establish a shared understanding of what we wanted to achieve with the group, the kinds of activities that would be used, any materials that would be needed, and reaching agreement on roles and responsibilities. My agreed role was to plan the programme, prepare any materials that would be necessary, lead the sessions and to take responsibility for classroom management during the sessions.

The first session was used to establish the ground rules which would be in place and to make clear to the pupils my expectations as far as behaviour and participation were concerned. As this class had been formed from two other classes and I had not taught them before, I felt it was important that they should begin by getting to know each other and by establishing rules which would allow everyone to feel comfortable within the group.

Once the rules had been established, the class teacher agreed to use some time during the week to allow the pupils to record them and make a poster which could then be put up at the front of the room. In this way anyone who came into the room would be able to see what the rules were during the sessions. It also meant that the rules could be referred to and reinforced when necessary.

This process of establishing ground rules was in itself an opportunity for me to begin to highlight any positive points that emerged. For example, I was able to draw attention to 'good' behaviour that was already happening – examples of attentive listening, turn-taking and following instructions. I was able to give the pupils some feedback about what they were able to do. This was important for both them and their teacher as both parties had been focusing on what was happening, e.g. '*They* never listen; *they* can't get on' – '*She's* always shouting; *she* doesn't listen to us; teachers don't like us because we're naughty and noisy . . .'.

The next step was to use this feedback as a way of beginning to look at how positive qualities can be represented as symbols. They came up with various suggestions such as an ear to represent attentive listening, a smiley face or joined hands to represent friendship. I led the discussion so that it began to focus on pupils themselves and things they were good at or enjoyed doing. The aim at this point was to provide an opportunity for them to exchange information about each other in a safe way, i.e. they would be able to disclose information without feeling awkward or being embarrassed by the negative comments of others.

Week One

I used affirmation activities from *Ways and Means* (Kingston Friends, *op. cit.*, p.34) as introductory 'warm ups'. These provided opportunities for the pupils not only to get to know one another, but to focus on themselves too. We began by making name badges. This was an activity which combined Labels and Likes with Labels and Goods. The task was to begin a name badge which gives three positive messages about the wearer:

(i) something I like to do (e.g. read, listen to music, play sport);
(ii) something I am good at (e.g. football, computer games, swimming);
(iii) something good about me (e.g. friendly, helpful, sharing).

The badges were made on circles of card and were worn for every session.

Week Two

The badges were central to a follow-up activity: Interviews and Introductions. This encouraged the pupils to speak and listen to one another and then, taking turns, they shared one piece of information about each other with the whole class. The discussion which followed the activity highlighted the point that it is much easier to talk about someone else's positive attributes than one's own. We were then able to look at the difference between being able to acknowledge one's strengths and boasting and the feelings involved in this self-disclosure. Many of the pupil's said that they would have felt embarrassed to speak to the group about themselves and were worried that people would make fun of them. Others expressed surprise about some of the things they found out about each other.

Week Three

I wanted the pupils to begin to see each other in a more positive light and to begin to explore the feelings they experienced when receiving positive feedback. I began to introduce further affirmation and listening activities drawn, again, from *Ways and Means* (Kingston Friends, *op. cit.*, pp.39, 42, 47, 48).

'Lifemaps', an activity from *Global Teacher, Global Learner* (Pike and Selby 1990, pp.109, 110) was used to provide further opportunities for information sharing and finding out what sorts of life experiences they had in common. Some of these experiences included the death of a pet or a grandparent, separation from parents because of hospitalisation, significant changes in pupils' lives such as moving school or class, moving house or friends moving away.

Again, my aim was to enable the pupils to practise speaking and listening to one another, and to support them in valuing one another by modelling emphatetic responses.

Reflection at the end of each session was an important part of the work. We looked at a number of aspects of the sessions – these included looking at the feelings experienced by individuals during the activities and then attempting to relate these to other life experiences. So, for example, when individuals spoke of their feelings of frustration or anger when not being listened to, they were encouraged to try and imagine what other people feel like in the same situation (parents, teachers, peers). In this way, it was possible to draw out general principles and to relate these to interpersonal relationships.

At the end of each session the pupils were also asked to reflect upon their behaviour and to assess how well they thought they had managed as individuals on a scale of 1–5. In later sessions when they had been involved in group tasks, they were asked to assess how well they had managed both as individuals and as a group. They were encouraged to consider how they had contributed to the achievement of the group task. I was hoping that in this way they would begin to see how as individuals they had a responsibility to the group and to be able to identify behaviour which was both helpful and unhelpful.

Week Four

To reinforce these principles we used the hall for what we called grouping activities. These started as very simple games which were intended to provide opportunities for the pupils to be in groups with others for very short periods of time.

Getting into groups was a major area of conflict with the pupils in this class. They usually refused to co-operate unless they were in friendship groups. In view of this I was anxious to present the grouping activities in as non-threatening a way as possible.

The first session here involved the pupils in simply walking around the hall on their own, not having any contact with one another and following any instructions given by me:

(i) walk around the hall slowly;
(ii) when I call 'Stop', touch the floor and change direction.

After three or four circuits I changed the instructions slightly:

(i) walk around the hall on your own;
(ii) when I call out a number (e.g. 'Three') make a group of that size with the nearest people to you;
(iii) as soon as you are in a group sit down on the floor.

Positive feedback was given to reinforce success – e.g., 'Good . . . Well done. . . . This group was ready first: they got together quickly and sat down.'

The next step was to form mixed gender groups which I knew would not be easy. Again it was necessary to make this 'safe' so, using the same numbers activity, I changed the instructions slightly by breaking down the number called out, e.g. 'Five: that's a three and a two' which meant three boys and two girls, or vice versa. Again, groups were asked to sit on the floor as soon as they were formed. Praise and positive feedback were used to reinforce success.

Inevitably some groups had difficulty in forming quickly but, rather than focusing on individuals, subsequent discussion was directed towards the procedures that had been helpful in enabling groups to get together easily and fluently.

As they became more relaxed about getting into groups in this setting, I began to introduce simple tasks so that instructions became more demanding:

(i) when I call out a number get into a group of that size;
(ii) sit down when you as a group are ready;
(iii) now make a shape of, e.g. letter A; a number 4, a house, etc.

These activities were great fun and the pupils enjoyed their sessions very much. The discussion at the end of each session looked at how the groups had functioned, how tasks had been achieved, at individual contributions and participation and decision-making processes. In some groups leaders and organisers emerged whilst in other groups this was not so apparent. Where one group was consistently less successful we looked together at what might be going wrong for them. To help in this process we reflected on what had contributed to achievement in the successful groups. Sometimes I reorganised the groups to enable some pupils to work with others who were good role models so that they could have the experience of working with a successful group.

Another strategy I used to help groups was to allow those who were successful to be observed carrying out a task, then using discussion to identify the things that helped the group work together.

When discussing ideas about what people did that was helpful in enabling the group to achieve the task, pupils were able to identify certain behaviours as important:

– sharing ideas;
– listening to each other;
– everyone having something to do which they felt they were able to do;
– being able to stay cheerful even if you don't get your own way;
– helping each other.

Week Five

The classroom sessions used activities which focused on the component skills for successful group work. *Global Teacher, Global Learner* (Pike and Selby, *op. cit.*, Chapters 7 and 8) and *Ways and Means* (Kingston Friends, *op. cit.*, pp.49–59) provided a more substantial basis for the development of listening skills, enabling us to establish a set of classroom rules through negotiation. These activities involved going through the process of reaching agreement and exploring feelings experienced along the way.

This was an important part of the whole programme as we were dealing with the very issues these pupils found the most difficult to embrace. The 'Steps to Solutions' activity (Kingston Friends, *op. cit.*, p.103) provided a most useful framework for looking at areas of real disagreement. It helped the pupils and their teacher to distance themselves from the problem and see it as *a problem* rather than *their problem* or *my problem.* It was a technique which both pupils and teacher continued to use even after the end of the programme.

Week Six

We then moved on to establish a set of classroom rules using the principles of the negotiation activities, 'Picture Ranking' and 'Agreeing to Disagree' (Kingston Friends, *op. cit.,* p.95). A list of possible classroom rules was generated by both pupils and adults. The rules were then written on separate cards and displayed around the room. The next step was to agree a set of between three and five positively framed rules. I felt it was important that the pupils were clear about how they should behave rather than how they should not behave. This would provide an effective scaffold for both them and their teacher in that they would know when they were behaving appropriately and, by implication, when they were not. The teacher would be able to reinforce this by offering feedback and praise appropriately. This involved going through the process of reaching agreement and exploring the feelings experienced along the way.

At this point in the programme parents were involved when we asked them to support the system of rules, rewards and sanctions put together and agreed by the pupils. It was important to have parental support as it reinforced the feeling of ownership for the pupils and gave status to the work they had been involved in. It was also a means of sharing the work with parents.

Week Seven

The focus was now on group tasks with opportunities to practise skills in 'real' settings. This was important as it enabled pupils to have experience of how these skills could help them in two important ways:

- they would be able to form positive relationships with one another;
- they would be able to work together more effectively and therefore increase their opportunities to learn.

We used the co-operative squares activity (Kingston Friends, *op. cit.,* p.63 and Pike and Selby, *op. cit.,* p.166) as a means of raising awareness of the issues or demands of group co-operation and to look at the feelings associated with group task achievement.

An activity used at this stage was a non-verbal task which we called tower building: the numbers grouping strategy was used from Week 2 to arrange pupils in groups of four. Each group was given six sheets of paper and six strips of sellotape. The task was to see which group could build the highest, most attractive, most stable tower. 'Cheating', i.e.

talking, resulted in the group forfeiting one sheet of paper. The activity was then repeated using discussion as a means of communication.

Weeks Eight and Nine

These two weeks were used for a group task: 'Desert Island Classroom' (Kingston Friends, *op. cit.*, p.117). This was a means of practising all the skills and techniques we had been working to develop and relating them to curriculum-based activities. Pupils were encouraged to take responsibility for both individual and group achievement. They were required to discuss, plan and negotiate, report back and listen in both small and large group settings. It was necessary to agree rules, follow instructions and reflect on individual and group performance. In order for them to acheive this they had to use sequences of behaviour involving problem-solving, perspective-taking and self-evaluation. These are the complex process skills which Curtis (1983) and Davies (1983) attribute to social competence. The level of adult help required by the class for this activity was minimal. Observation notes from these sessions confirm that there was a high level of co-operation between group members during these activities.

Week Ten

The final session was used for an evaluation of the whole programme. This was an opportunity for pupils and teachers to reflect upon what had been achieved and to look at 'what next'.

DID THE PROGRAMME SUCCEED?

No inflated claims for the success of the programme are being made. However, observable change in classroom behaviour and evidence of the improved esteem of both the class teacher and pupils at the end of the ten-week period can be drawn from these sources:

Independent observation

The observations of an advisory teacher were invited and, as these selected notes indicate, there was some clear contrast with observations made at the beginning of the programme:

- Session: Finishing off work – variety of tasks: Maths, Science and Language work.
- Pupils working in pairs or threes.
- Noise level low – talking quietly; mainly girl-girl, boy-boy interactions.

- Request for help – boys to adjacent girl who gave help then returned to her task.
- X refused to work initially; teacher-pupil negotiation successful – on-task now.
- Two pupils doing science experiment – negotiated roles – who does what, what to do first discussed then started.
- Teacher moving around room from group to group.
- Sudden loud outburst – M shouting. Teacher ignores at first then gives 'look' – quiet now.
- Most pupils seem on-task – writing, drawing, reading.
- M calling out. Teacher gives verbal request not to do it again.
- Feedback to pupils is positive – 'That's good!' 'Yes', etc.

Staff feedback

A number of the class teacher's colleagues were interested in the programme and its activities; they were a source of encouragement and positive commentary upon the improved progress of the class.

Reflections from the class teacher

Comments upon the programme from the class teacher indicate both that change is possible but that progress is neither smooth nor unproblematic:

> I'm much more relaxed. I accept things I wouldn't have done before – for example, if 90 per cent of the class is working, I'm happy.
> The class is now beginning to gel. They were very rude to one another, took no responsibility for their actions, did no work unless it was formal. They could do no group work at all even when choosing their own groups.
> The class is now beginning to behave – but some days it's like going back to square one! They work well in groups that they chose: book making, model making present no problems now. They still have real problems listening to instructions – if we could remedy this. They still fight amongst each other and this must be improved if possible.
> I begin to feel it possible to make the class one real unit – that they can feel a sense of belonging; that they can work independently and take responsibility for their own actions so that they can take pride in their work and their classroom.

Pupil evaluation

Throughout the programme and usually at the end of each Monday session, pupils were encouraged to reflect upon their behaviour and progress. Towards the end of the programme a more direct evaluation was conducted and, in addition to some detailed discussion, pupils were asked to draw themselves as they were behaving before the programme began and as they were behaving currently . . . although the crudity of the evaluation tool is acknowledged there is . . . evidence of pride in the progress made and of increased esteem. Here, however, we would be cautious in that some drawings and pupil comments indicated a certain amount of realistic doubt that gains made might not last beyond the support programme.

However, as we indicated in our introduction, our purpose here is not to recommend a specific and unproblematic package of strategies. Rather, we have tried to describe something of what can be achieved through carefully-planned intervention and advocacy: working, that is, on behalf of others to achieve orderly and dignified conditions within which learning can best take place. Different classroom environments and different contexts will require different approaches and, rather than working towards a seemingly neat closure, we feel it more in keeping with the dialogical construction of our chapter to conclude with some selected reflections drawn from a discussion between the two authors.

DISCUSSION

RC: What I take from your programme of – let's call it intervention and support – is that optimistic belief that things can be changed. So many of us have probably been in that 'The bell's gone!' situation but what's needed is that belief that this isn't inevitable. Things can be done. Change is possible.

RHC: My experience is that classroom factors like those I met at the beginning of the programme just result in negative outcomes for everybody. Self-esteem falls; feelings of helplessness and hopelessness are expressed. Pupils and teacher respond angrily or apathetically towards one another. They all come to view themselves as non-achievers and label themselves as people who can't manage. Labels are then applied by other staff, pupils and parents. The class becomes the difficult class. The teacher is seen as ineffective. The negative cycle perpetuates itself and the learning environment deteriorates. And that can't go on. The role of the teacher in my view, is to find a way of allowing herself and her pupils to speak and be heard in an environment where mutual respect is encouraged, acknowledged and practised.

RC: Do you mean giving dignity to each other?

RHC: Yes, dignity and status. Giving status by identifying good role models and amplifying success. And this can be acquired without shouting loudly. It can be done – but teachers know this – with a look, a comment, a nod or a smile. By showing approval and giving feedback and reassurance.

RC: And I've noticed in all our discussions that you never point the finger at anyone. You never say it's the pupils' fault or it's bad teaching or bad organisation.

RHC: That's right. I wasn't there to make value judgements, but then it was easier for me – I was detached, I didn't get worn down by it. But I could sympathise wholeheartedly with the class teacher's situation. I'd been there myself. With this particular group it was hard work. I had to use all my own tried and tested strategies to keep them with me for an hour. It was easy to see how she could be worn down by the end of the day.

RC: Isn't there a danger, though, of ignoring the bigger picture? I mean the class teacher clearly felt there were organisational problems – the gender split within the group, for example – and shouldn't they be tackled at a management level rather than putting the emphasis on what might be called coping strategies?

RHC: I'm not saying that poor organisation shouldn't be criticised or should be ignored. But in this case that was the situation and, although senior management were aware of the difficulties, the class teacher just had to get on with it. Like most teachers she was working in a situation which was far from ideal and she had to cope. But I wasn't just helping her to cope and that's the advocacy thing. My role was to be an advocate for the teacher and the pupils . . . That meant mediating between them and engaging them all in activities where they could see things from another's perspective – like setting the classroom rules and taking turns in speaking, for example. Both parties were able to exchange views, reach agreement and disclose how it felt not to be listened to; to have to give up something you wanted.

RC: A good deal has been written about classroom environments – that need for a kind of psychological safety which is so important but which was clearly lacking in this case.

RHC: We certainly gave a lot of attention to the physical layout of the classroom and the way in which pupils were grouped. In addition the class teacher was introduced to a number of techniques and strategies. There's nothing particularly original about them: they're ideas I've developed from various sources, as we all do. But these weren't just about coping; they were about constructing a worthwhile learning environment. Underpinning everything we did was the attention and feedback given to listening and following instructions and lots of opportunities to practise were provided. When we were team-teaching I was always consciously trying to highlight the opportunities which presented themselves for acknowledging and praising appropriate pupil responses.

RC: You often talk about 'appropriate response' and 'behaviour' and 'reinforcement' and a lot of what you describe seems to derive from behaviourist psychology. As you know I feel uneasy about that because I think there's a tendency to overlook the deeper structures of teaching and learning and those processes which are less obviously observable. But then when I look over your programme in detail I don't think you're being merely 'behaviourist' in your approach: I think that you and the class teacher – like all good teachers – are quite rightly eclectic; you're drawing upon a range of useful theory. A crucial feature which, I think, takes the whole thing a stage further beyond the mere management of behaviour is your attention to reflection. This is particularly evident when you ask the pupils to give attention to what they've been doing in each session. I think you're getting close to what is called 'metacognition' – the idea of the mind turning back on itself. You did that repeatedly with the children and with the class teacher too when you went through that regular process of joint deliberation which involved far more than just planning things together.

RHC: Yes, I tried to do that but it needs a very explicit framework – a scaffold is the buzz word. The class teacher and I were able to agree about a framework in our weekly meetings and evaluation sessions. Then, when I was teaching the class, I'd ask pupils to reflect upon their achievements as individuals. I might do that through discussion by getting them to do it more formally on a one (could be better) to five (brilliant) scale. Then as we went on they were able to progress from self to group assessment so they were thinking about achievement on two levels – as individuals and as a group as a whole resulting from individual contributions to the group task. We talked about this a lot together – the pupils, the class teacher and I – at the end of every session where we'd always have a discussion. We looked at what we'd managed to do, what we felt we'd gained, if anything, and the needs emerging from the session. It was also a real social session in which to practise skills like listening to points of view responding with relevant comments, valuing the comments of others and waiting for a turn to speak. And it helped us to generalise, to look at real problems in other social settings – things like friendship issues came up a lot for discussion. And what emerged strongly from that was what you might call the 'modelling' of appropriate ways of expressing feelings or making criticisms in a non-threatening way.

RC: We're back to dignity again.

RHC: Yes, it's all to do with self-perception, self-esteem and feeling that it's 'okay' to expect to be heard and to expect to be part of shaping what happens to you and around you in a classroom or school setting. That's what I mean when I talk about self-advocacy. Young people do have these social skills but sometimes they need to learn to use them appropriately if they're to conduct themselves with dignity. Our role as adults is to provide opportunities for and to enhance and accelerate developing skills like those we concentrated on here so that they can cope with the demands of the school and classroom setting and increase their learning opportunities.

RC: But don't we already know that?

RHC: Theoretically, yes. However, it seems to me that many adults seem to pay lip-service to the idea but don't follow it up in practical terms. You see, I'm talking about appropriate behaviour in classrooms which, for some teachers, might mean submissive behaviour. We're getting here into the debate on individual values and expectations.

RC: This is where your programme connects with my interest in speaking and listening. I absolutely agree that we need to structure opportunities to develop speaking and listening skills, and that means establishing orderly conditions. But that has to be done in the interests of genuine learning not just for ritual knowledge and control. I think that takes great skill, particularly in developing a purposeful dialogue with pupils, and it's something we don't always give enough attention to. But then when you're talking about advocacy it sometimes seems to me that you're talking about collaboration, about exchanging ideas. And that collaborative environment in education is certainly desirable but it's not something many colleagues enjoy. To them especially, your supportive programme might seem a bit of a luxury.

RHC: Well, it wasn't that because it was a pretty desperate situation. But I still feel that teachers can become advocates for each other through discussing their practice and problems and by adopting strategies of self-advocacy. But the trouble is, teachers don't get enough positive feedback themselves. Nobody tells them they're doing well and they need more of that.

RC: And more attention to research of this kind.

REFERENCES

Bowers, T. (ed.) (1989) *Special Educational Needs and Human Resource Management.* Beckenham: Croom Helm.

Britton, J. (1987) 'Vygotsky's contribution to pedagogical theory', *English in Education* **21**(2), 1–8.

Curtis, M. (1983) 'Social skills training in the classroom', *Behavioural Approaches With Children* **7**, 3–17.

Davies, G. (1983) 'An introduction to life and social skills training', *Journal of Maladjustment and therapeutic Education* **1**, 13–21.

Department of Education and Science (DES) (1989) *Discipline in Schools* (The Elton Report). London: HMSO.

Kingston Friends (1989) *Ways and Means.* Kingston: Kingston Friends Workshop Group.

Maclure, M., Phillips, T. and Wilkinson, A. (eds) (1988) *Oracy Matters.* Buckingham: Open University Press.

National Curriculum Council (NCC) and National Oracy Project (1991) *Teaching, Talking and Learning at Key Stages 1–4.* London: NCC.

Pike, G. and Selby, D. (eds) (1990) *Global Teacher, Global Learner.* London: Hodder and Stoughton.

Spence, S. (1980) *Social Skills Training with Children and Adolescents: a counsellor's manual.* Windsor: NFER-Nelson.

Wood, D. (1990) *How Children Think and Learn.* Oxford: Blackwell.

15

Pygmalion lives on

Janice Wearmouth

Why do teachers not differentiate more in class to meet pupils' needs? One reason, of course, is that it is both time-consuming and costly in resources. However, there may also be another reason. It may also be because differentiation to meet individual and group needs may encourage so-called less-able pupils to achieve more than they are expected. Any overachievement of 'low' achievers challenges the stratified and hierarchical model of pupils' abilities, which itself is still the prevailing paradigm for many teachers and schools, reflecting not just the belief system of individual teachers, but also the institutional view of the school as a whole. Many institutions expect, maintain and approve the anticipated hierarchy of pupil achievement. If this was not the case, differentiation would be accorded a higher priority in all schools, time and resources would be found, and it would become the norm.

Teacher discomfort resulting from unexpected pupil acheivement is no new phenomenon, of course:

> The more the upper track (top ability set) children of the experimental group gained in IQ, the more favourably they were rated by their teachers. The more the lower track children of the control group gained in IQ, the more unfavourably they were viewed by their teachers. No special expectation had been created about these chidlren, and their slow track status made it unlikely in their teachers' eyes that they would behave in an intellectually competent manner. The more intellectually competent these children became, the more negatively they were viewed by their teachers.
> (Rosenthal and Jacobson 1968)

There are lots of pressures in a school system to keep things the same. The need to maintain equilibrium in that system challenges the assumption that differentiation of curriculum, teaching approaches and materials will be just a matter of time and training, as the following example illustrates.

ONE TEACHER'S EXPERIENCE

'Shirley White' was appointed to the position of Special Needs Co-ordinator (SENCO) at 'Greenways Upper School' on the retirement of the previous incumbent. Greenways Upper is situated in a still-prosperous town in a shire county. In the days of the 11+ exam, it used to be a grammar school, and still maintains its very strong academic traditions. In some departments, there remained the old stereotype of straight didactic teaching in mixed-ability groups with one level of text for all, high-level achievement of the 'brightest', the less-able labelled 'dim' by some, and teachers' expectations of a hierarchy of achievement. For years after the school became comprehensive, the special needs department had been run as the equivalent of a dyslexia department. Most 'special needs' pupils were tested through the Bangor Dyslexia Test. There were good reasons for this, historically. To be thought dyslexic in a predominantly middle-class school where a lot of parents have the money to go to one of the dyslexia associations is perhaps a lot less threatening to academically low-achieving pupils in an academically high-acheiveing school than to be thought 'thick'. One can, with credibility to one's mates (who also may well not be ashamed to go on being 'a mate', as long as one is not considered 'thick'), claim that one fails badly in tests and exams because one is 'dyslexic'. In a sense, this is all right as long as the special needs teacher actually does attempt to make provision for all kinds of need, and goes along with the dyslexic label for all, purely for the sake of the pupils' self-respect. However, in this particular case, that did not happen. The work of the department was confined to a very small number of pupils. In this school, 'behavioural difficulties', for example, were largely ignored by the Head of Special Needs, or deemed to be somebody else's responsibility.

In a recent interview, Shirley recounted how, on her appointment, she had realised in advance what some of the implications of the history of the school would be, but had not understood how strong would be the pressure in some areas to make sure that things stayed the same and that pupils' academic performances conformed to teachers' expectations. She recollected how, shortly after her arrival at the school, the members of one particular department expressed a wish for her to become involved with helping in the differentiation of GCSE coursework for pupils who experienced difficulties with literacy. Shirley already knew some of these pupils because she taught them as a discrete group in a special option designed to support the development of their literacy. She agreed to work with the members of the department and discussed with them the first piece of work to be differentiated. It was decided that all pupils would be expected to complete the same task but that some would receive much more structured support than others through simplified follow-up worksheets, additional staff supports in class, and the use of laptop word processors.

In the beginning, Shirley went into the lessons, helping pupils *in situ*. Some asked for the use of laptop word processors, to which they had been introduced in the extra option lessons they had with her. Follow-up work was done in her lessons, with the full consent and agreement of the staff in the department concerned. The work expected of these pupils was broken down into short steps, and typed up on the laptops by the pupils themselves.

The particular pupils reacted not, apparently, by feeling stigmatised by the extra support, but by pushing Shirley into giving up more and more of her time, all her non-contact periods and lunchtimes for six weeks, until they had finished the work. Because it took them longer than most other pupils, extra time for completion was negotiated between her and the mainstream teachers. None of those who experienced difficulties with literacy skills left their study incomplete.

The net effect of all this on departmental staff was the complete opposite to that on the pupils concerned. The effect on Shirley was also both full of contradictions and highly stressful. Out of seven full-time teachers, four were distinctly unhappy, and Shirley suddenly became aware that she was the object of a considerable amount of criticism from the department generally. It was stated that the differentiated approach to the less literate pupils was 'unfair' because they had produced work of a higher standard than some of the other pupils. How would differentiation by outcome operate if the expected hierarchy of achievement was disrupted? And, of course, it was true that these pupils had been given a different, more structured, approach to their work. Other comments in like vein came out then, and later: 'Did you know that R (on Statement for moderate learning difficulties) is doing better now than quite a lot of the others? That's not right. The help he gets should be available to everyone.' This kind of comment begs the question about whether the others could be achieving more with a different kind of teaching anyway.

The pupils, on the other hand, were very pleased with themselves, one in particular:

L. C.:	Please can you run me off another copy?
Shirley:	Why, L.?
L. C.:	Because I want to take it home to show my Mum. [*Never been known before!*]
One of the lads, S.:	Look at how much I've done. I've never written ten pages before.

What happened next in that particular department? The following year, Shirley was asked to confine her activities solely to in-class support on a rota basis. There was now no possibility of working with any one teacher, pupil or group of pupils because her time was spread so thinly. Shirley felt that she was effectively marginalised. It also seemed to her that the work given to some pupils was even less appropriate than before.

WHOSE TRUTH?

Is there anything to be learned from recollections such as Shirley's? Hers is, after all, not the only 'truth' that might be told about this episode. It may simply be an exaggerated, biased, subjective account, unrecognisable to anyone except herself. Perhaps she lacked the interpersonal skills that would enable her to relate positively with the other staff concerned and it was for this reason that they did not wish to work closely with her any more. Perhaps she lacked the insight needed to promote a change in teaching styles in the school. Or perhaps there were a whole range of other factors that she had not considered. On the other hand, this account does raise some issues that are worth exploring:

- the concepts underlying how teachers categorise children;
- the worth to schools of children who experience difficulties in learning when schools, themselves are constrained to vie for position on the league tables;
- the role of the SENCO in promoting curriculum change when change would threaten the existing system.

ISSUES ARISING

What are the concepts underlying where teachers draw lines between children? Assessment in schools, traditionally, is all about putting pupils in rank order of achievement. The comment 'It's not fair. R is on statement so he gets extra help and does better now than some other pupils' has little to do with the notion of helping each child to reach her or his potential, or of assessment in relation to some criterion, but much more to do with the rank ordering of pupils. Comments such as 'Why should J be given 25 per cent extra time on his GCSE exams? It's not fair to the other pupils who are not given the extra time' are, in Shirley's view, very revealing. J is not being viewed as an individual with needs special to him that must be met if he is to achieve anything of his potential. Nor is his extra help viewed as a tool to help him reach the next target. Teaching styles reflect a profound, personal belief in a particular model of the human being, and are adapted to conform to this belief. 'Differentiation by outcome' can be construed as the ultimate justification of 'Leave well alone. Natural ability will out'. Dearing's 20 per cent of pupils who will not achieve four or more A–C grades at GCSE by 1997 certainly supports this stratified-by-design model of pupil outcome.

This particular school was already doing very well indeed in the academic league table. What possible payoff could there be to worry about the lack of achievement of the non-achieving 10 per cent at the bottom and spend valuable time differentiating work for them? They would never contribute in any positive way to the school's position in the league table. Add to this the potential threat to the system that is known and understood, if pupils begin to change place in achievement rankings, and we have an interesting scenario: 'Teachers may require a certain amount of preparation to be able to accept the unexpected classroom behaviour of the intellectually mobile child' (Rosenthal and Jacobsen 1968, p.179)

Where, though, does all this leave the SENCO in the ordinary school? Certainly, working first with the staff who are already committed to the ideal of giving pupils an equal opportunity to reach his or her potential through access to a broad, balanced curriculum. But the SENCO offering help in whatever form – in-class support, withdrawal, one-to-one – is in essence discriminating positively in favour of some children. It seems to me that when some children, unexpectedly, start to achieve more than others, there is a fundamental challenge to the personal belief system which the individual teacher will do his or her very best to overcome and fight. If the belief system of the whole school depends on a stratified view of pupils, the situation presenting to the SENCO is much more difficult, of course. For how is it possible to change a whole belief system without threatening or undermining the whole organisation? The SENCO who fails to recognise this is bound to make matters much worse for pupils who experience difficulties in learning. Insecure systems will clamp down to protect themselves. Insecure teachers may well tighten their grip around teaching techniques and styles which are tried and tested. Children who do not achieve in the conventional sense in school are always a challenge to a teacher's sense of self-worth, anyway. One measure of a teacher's success is how far he or she can facilitate pupil achievement. It is possible to cope with the notion that some pupils will not achieve in one's lessons but one is still a 'good teacher' in one's own eyes, provided that these same pupils are judged by everyone else as 'unteachable', and 'unable to achieve'. Once that stereotype is challenged, the SENCO is in for a hard time.

LESSONS TO BE LEARNED

What are the lessons to be learned in all this? Firstly, I suppose, simply to recognise that the Learning Support Department must play the long game if differentiating for the individual child is not the current norm in the school. Change will not happen quickly when it involves fundamental differences in teachers' models of the child and the institution. One person's positive discrimination towards the disadvantaged is another person's discrimination against the majority: 'Organisational change that is to be permanent is a lengthy business, and results cannot be achieved hastily. Currently it is estimated that 3–5 years are needed for a fundamental organisational change in commercial or industrial organisations. There is no reason to believe that hospitals or schools would be any more amenable to change' (Georgiades and Phillimore, quoted in Easen 1985).

To the SENCO struggling with a system where the predominant pressure is to stay the same, it is a constant source of frustration to know that one of the important features of the *ideal* adaptive schools' system is where 'Internal demand for change is constantly stimulated and considered legitimate. Needs are asserted and problems identified on an ongoing basis' (McLaughlin 1976).

There are, of course, various possible solutions. The requirement to differentiate for pupils who experience difficulties in learning must come from the top in school, i.e. from the head, by diktat if necessary. SENCOs walking into schools and collecting around themselves little groups of interested staff, while with the best of intentions, is not enough. Apart from availability of the necessary monies, there is nothing to stop a head teacher deciding to reward staff financially for putting in the necessary time to differentiate materials adequately.

But there will be no real, lasting change in institutions unless there is a critical mass of individuals within it who want that change. To hide from the fact that teachers hold, and will continue to hold, irreconcilable models of the child and the teaching process in their heads does not help. One head I interviewed a few years ago kept repeating: 'The trouble with my staff is that they need to be re-educated' – as if he knew best. He was not a popular man. The critical mass of staff in his school, in his perception, did not sympathise with his view of education.

One effective way of exposing the debate to discussion is by requesting that particular concepts related in specific ways to equal opportunities issues are written into the School Development Plan, and then clearly operationalised through its working. The aim, for example, of 'improving the quality of learning for all pupils in the classroom' can be seen to meet the triple targets of differentiation *per se*, meeting the needs of the most able, and meeting the individual special needs.

Issues such as pupils being made to fulfil teachers' prophecies, and school systems being threatened by the unexpected, need to be brought right out into the open during school in-service education and training days. Pupils' life chances are too important for us not to do this. Common understandings, if not agreement, can be reached through overt, deliberate discussion, if those responsible for staff training are quite clear about the issues themselves. As a group, I believe that teachers designated as having responsibility for the special needs area in schools have also to be very clear in their own minds what equal opportunities are all about for pupils. For me, 'equal opportunities' means an equal opportunity for a pupil to reach his or her potential. The purpose of the school curriculum is to facilitate each child reaching his or her potential. That is why it must be broad and balanced. For most children, the broad, balanced curriculum is already accessible. For some, there is no access unless there is appropriate differentiation. Differentiation, therefore, stands squarely in the centre of the equal opportunities arena. If there is no differentiation for some, there is no possibility of an equal opportunity to reach potential.

CAUSE FOR OPTIMISM

Fortunately, despite our best endeavours to keep the 'less-able' down, some pupils manage to achieve anyway. There is an apocryphal story about a lad who knew himself to be intelligent, but had not shown much promise in the early years at school – to the extent that the principal advised him not to opt for the academic stream of the high school he was about to enter. He, however, ignored the advice. In later years, just before he was to receive his PhD degree, he decided to write to the principal:

> Mr Wilson,
> My name is Fenwick F. Fenwick. I was one of your pupils, and, before I graduated (left junior high school) in 1956, you told me it would be a 'bloody wonder' if I made it past sophomore (second) year in the academic stream at high school.
> This is to inform you that on June 15, shortly after 2.30 pm, I shall be receiving my PhD in Astrophysics from Ivy University.
> Yours sincerely,
>
> Fenwick F. Fenwick

Shortly before the degree ceremony, a reply arrived from the principal: 'It is a bloody wonder!'
Yours sincerely,

Wilson W. Wilson
(Kohn 1973)

REFERENCES

Dearing, R. (1994) *The National Curriculum and its Assessment.* London: SCAA.

Kohn, P. M. (1973) 'Relationship between expectations of teachers and performance of students', *Journal of School Health* **43**.

McLaughlin, M. W. (1976) 'Implementation as mutual adaptation change in classroom organisation', *Teachers' College Record* **77**(3), 339–51.

Easen, P. (1985) *Making School-centred INSET Work.* Milton Keynes: Open University.

Rosenthal, R. and Jacobson, L. (1968) *Pygmalion in the Classroom.* New York: Holt, Rinehart and Winston.

16

Therapeutic provision in mainstream curricula for pupils with severe motor difficulties

Pilla Pickles

INTRODUCTION

In recent years an increasing number of pupils with severe motor difficulties have been placed in mainstream schools. Severe motor difficulties may affect some or all limbs, may limit hand function, cause problems with fine and gross motor movement and, sometimes, with speech and language also. Most, though not all, pupils with such difficulties will have a medical diagnosis. A diagnosis may have been given at birth, at about the age of two or a later date, though, deteriorating conditions such as muscular dystrophy may not be diagnosed until the child attends school. Some children may have physical difficulties as a result of an accident or illness, which can happen at any age. It must be remembered that, in the same way as other children, they may also have learning difficulties, dyslexia, dyspraxia, asthma, epilepsy, vision and hearing difficulties or hidden handicaps affecting their visual–auditory perception or eye–hand co-ordination.

Every child is an individual – a child with severe motor difficulties is even more of an individual. Disability affects people in different ways; it is dangerous and impossible to predict the intellectual abilities, emotional needs, outcome of different physical disabilities and the level of independence a child may attain. The therapeutic and medical needs of pupils with severe motor difficulties are likely to change and develop over time. It is important that teaching and support staff understand and are able to respond to these changing needs. This requires on-going liaison with therapists, doctors, the wider support team and parents to ensure that equipment, positioning, medical needs and access to the curriculum remains appropriate and to plan for life skills.

Enabling pupils with severe motor difficulties to engage fully with the broad, balanced curriculum of a mainstream school requires careful thought and planning. Those responsible for overseeing provision for these pupils in school must take account of a number of factors which include:

- issues related to the support team which has been designated to work with the child: its nature and function, ways of working which incorporate a holistic view of the child, the role of the SENCO in liaising with support and school staff and disseminating information, use of the individual education plan as a tool for communciation and collaboration;
- target setting, to include: long- and short-term goals, the importance of establishing a baseline, ways of embedding therapy into classroom activities which include the use of real objects and games;
- time considerations.

The discussion of these issues below is of relevance particularly in the primary sector, although its principles apply at any level.

THE SUPPORT TEAM: NATURE, ROLE AND FUNCTION

Children with severe motor difficulties and their families are likely to have support from a very large team or network of supporters in health, social services and education. Successful inclusion of these pupils depends on teamwork between school, parents and all members of the wider support team. As well as school-based staff, the team might include physiotherapists, occupational therapists, speech and language therapists, nurses, doctors and conultants in the health service, advisory and support teachers including vision, hearing and physical and educational psychologists based in educational central services, and professionals in social services. Parent/carers are also key members of the support team, knowing the child best of all. Partnership and planning for the future with parent/carers is very important. The needs of the parents and the child within the family should be seen as a whole.

A lot more than access

Physical access and suitable facilities are vital components for the inclusion of pupils with severe motor difficulties into mainstream schools, to ensure access to the school environment and to enable pupils to be as independent as possible. Dignity and emotional needs should always be considered, especially in positioning, toileting and transfers. Money must pay for ramps, lifts and toileting facilities, but successful inclusion is dependent on much more than money. The philosophy, commitment, support and liaison between school staff and the wider support team is crucial.

Integration is sometimes incorrectly used synonymously with inclusion. Functional integration allows the possibility of inclusion, but does not itself achieve it. Inclusion is a process which recognises that impairment and disability are common to all, and which values the individual as a person, enabling access, equality and achievement. It is about a whole-school policy, where the community accepts and values diversity. Valuing diversity also means valuing a variety of teaching methods needed to meet individual needs. Acknowledging that children may sometimes need a quiet environment, one-to-one or small-group teaching and recognising that teaching methods may need to vary as needs change, are all part of inclusion. It is vital that the school, parent/carers and the wider support team have the same understanding of inclusion, to avoid misunderstandings.

Working with the whole child

Historically, finding a cure and 'normalising' the child with severe motor difficulties was seen as the priority for medics and therapists, and the educational, emotional and social needs of the individual were secondary. Working with the whole child and planning to meet changing needs is now seen as the priority. Each member of the multi-disciplinary team has their own expertise and training and together they provide a picture of individual needs. It is the school's job to liaise with the wider team of professionals and plan access to the curriculum. Every area of need is important, including medical and physical needs, for without appropriate planning for the whole child, pupils are likely to have difficulties. Planning for life skills is also crucial to enable pupils to be as independent as possible in the present and the future. Planning to meet the needs of the whole child requires commitment, on-going training, good planning and an understanding of all the issues.

The role of the SENCO

With such a large support team it is essential to establish a key worker in school and the most likely person is the SENCO (special educational needs co-ordinator), though it could be another member of the school-based team. The key worker's role is to orchestrate the team, ensuring good liaison between team members, so that teachers can plan how best to meet a pupil's individual needs, including educational, social, emotional, medical and therapeutic needs. The key worker holds information from all members of the support team and it is their responsibility to make sure this information is recorded and passed on to other members.

The school will need the support, advice and backing of the support team to feel confident in meeting the needs of individual pupils. Most teachers have had no specialist training in teaching children with severe motor difficulties and success is likely to depend on how well this team is able to support the teacher. Although the head teacher has the ultimate responsibility for the organisation and running of the school, most of the SEN work is often delegated to the SENCO, including management of support staff and liaison with the multi-disciplinary team. Schools develop their own staff and liaison with the multi-disciplinary team. Schools develop their own policies and their own ways of managing SEN. The SENCO, however, must not be thought of as the only support in school. All class teachers are responsible for meeting the needs of the pupils in their class. Every teacher in the school must take a share in the responsibility for pupils with SEN by establishing good links with the wider team, probably through the SENCO.

Liaison forms and files

It is important that every member of the team is aware of the input of others. Information recorded by the support team needs to be easily accessible. One simple way is for every member of the team to record their visits on the same liaison form, which can then be copied for filing and sent home to parents. These can be filed in an A4 ring binder for each child with up-to-date information and liaison forms, reports, individual therapy advice, the Individual Education Plan (IEP), information on specialist equipment, medication and feeding etc. Older pupils might use a ring binder the size of a small Filofax or passport.

It should be remembered that this is an open file and should not contain anything which cannot be shared.

Parents, pupils and members of the support team and school staff should agree the presentation and use of the file. It should then be the responsibility of each team member to communicate with the rest of the team via the file, meetings and phone calls.

Use of the Individual Education Plan

Most pupils with severe motor difficulties will have a statement of special educational needs setting out long-term targets. These targets need to be refined into short-term, achievable targets, which are regularly reviewed and monitored. The IEP is the structure for this to happen and includes the specialist teaching arrangements made to meet those needs and collaboration and effective working relationships with social services, health services and local education authorities. The IEP 'should be developed with the help of outside specialists, but should usually be implemented, at least part, in the normal classroom setting. The plan should ensure a co-ordinated cross-curricular and interdisciplinary approach which takes due account of the child's previous difficulties' (DFE 1994, paras 2:108, 2:109).

The IEP is the tool for communication and collaboration between all services. It is neither sensible nor practical for pupils to have a number of individual, separate programmes. One well-written IEP can cover a variety of targets including education, physical, therapeutic, medical, social, behavioural, independence and self-care targets. Prioritising targets within the wider support team is important, as it is not possible to cover all the targets all of the time. Regular reviews of the IEP will ensure that targets remain appropriate and achievable.

TARGET SETTING

Long- and short-term targets

Life-skill and long-term targets need to be broken down into small achievable targets and it is important that parents and professionals understand how short-term targets move towards long-term goals. Targets need to be clearly and precisely written and achievable in the short term. A life-skill, long-term physical target might be for the pupil to stand and walk with a walker. The long-term target might be for the pupil to stand and bear weight. The short-term target might be for the pupil to use a prone stander in a low angle position, twice daily for 20-minute sessions, in class, taking some weight on the body and raising the angle of the stander by a few degrees with success. Including parent/carers and pupils in planning for life-skill goals ensures their understanding, commitment and motivation.

When including motor-skill targets, specific equipment should be detailed with how, when and where it would be used. Handling and positioning the pupil is also important to record as it may require use of a hoist or two people to position and this needs to be incorporated in the planning. A risk assessment should be carried out for pupils requiring positioning in specialist equipment, ensuring that staff are advised on appropriate and safe ways of handling.

Establishing a baseline

With the support of the wider team, it is important to establish a baseline for each pupil with complex needs to ensure that the activity is achievable cognitively, physically and therapeutically. Therapists will provide a therapeutic baseline, doctors a medical baseline, while teachers need to establish a baseline for the pupil's cognitive abilities. This will produce a clear picture of what the pupil can achieve and should form the basis of the IEP, enabling teachers to plan appropriate activities covering specific areas of the curriculum and therapy targets linked to the curriculum.

Many pupils with complex needs will have additional adult support in class who will be able to record the pupil's achievements. Whenever possible pupils who are unable to write should be taught to 'mark' with a pen or pencil. Using multiple-choice answers, a simple record sheet can be devised for activities and games, to consolidate learning and to increase the pupil's independence. This is also an important part of assessment, highlighting the need for any additional teaching. Naming and using objects functionally in curriculum activities establishes a picture of the pupil's concepts in all areas. Some pupils may have quite large gaps in their understanding. It is sometimes easy to presume pupils have concepts, which in fact they do not have.

Common targets for therapy

Although therapy targets are specific to individuals, there are common targets which are appropriate to many:

- Voluntary movement – using hands and fists together.
- Grasp, hold and release.
- Using two hands – bilateral activities.
- Keeping the body central – midline and crossing the midline.
- Involuntary movements – fixing positions.
- Use of an open, flat hand.
- Isolating the fingers for fine manipulation.
- Strengthening the index finger and fingers.
- Pincer grasp – thumb and finger together.
- Eye–hand co-ordination – visual motor ability.
- Perception – making sense of information.
- Proprioception – where we are in space.
- Visual and auditory perception – making sense of what is seen and heard.
- Perceptual motor skills – planning motor skills to address clumsiness.
- Sensory defensiveness.
- Mobility – inside and outside.
- Self-care skills – toileting, dressing, washing, eating, etc.
- Weight bearing on flat hands to aid sitting, crawling and kneeling.
- Building upper arm strength.
- Turn-taking.

- Giving and following directions – barrier games.
- Use of rhymes, particular sounds, consonants and vowel digraphs.
- Directional words and prepositions.
- Word finding, recalling, naming and categorising objects.

Embedding therapeutic targets into the curriculum

Therapy should be seen as part of everyday living and the responsibility of the whole team. Teachers, parents and assistants require a full understanding of therapy and therapeutic aims, combined with good liaison and training, otherwise the danger is that therapy will always be seen as something to be 'done' to the child by therapists 'to make things better'. It is clearly not possible for any therapist, whether speech and language, physiotherapist or occupational therapist, to achieve all therapy goals in one treatment session a week. On-going therapy within the curriculum and in daily living is possible by training teachers, assistants and parents.

Therapy is not only an activity carried out by a therapist at 2 o'clock on a Thursday afternoon. It is about daily living skills, such as how the child sits, stands, walks, reaches, graps, talks, eats, drinks, speaks, sings, plays, how they hang up their coat and a lot more besides. Therapy should be included as part of the curriculum and functional mobility around school, wherever possible, leaving few if any out-of-class therapy sessions for specific timed sessions. However, individual sessions with therapists remain vital to monitor and extend treatment and give further advice and support, based on continual assessment. Other specific therapy sessions may continue to be required, best carried out at home or school in a quiet, private environment.

When planning the curriculum, teachers need to ask themselves 'How can I introduce speech and language therapy, physiotherapy and/or occupational therapy into this task?' School staff need to understand the importance of good seating and positioning, matching positioning to different activities and that, for example, pupils should not be expected to sit without support, while learning crucial educational concepts. It is not expected that teachers and assistants should take on the role of therapists, but work in partnership with them as part of the wider support team. In this way they will gain further skills and an understanding of therapy issues and be able to include therapy in the curriculum.

Specialist equipment and seating

Individual pupils may be assessed for specialist equipment by therapists. It is important that these assessments are carried out in partnership with the school and parents and that school staff understand the reason for using specific equipment at specific times. Different positioning aids blood flow, promotes bone development, avoids long-term damage to the skin, avoids muscle contractures and is more comfortable. There is a huge variety of specialist equipment often used in schools, including specialist chairs, floor sitters, standers, walkers and tricycles.

The aim in seating is to achieve good sitting and hand function and to avoid positions which encourage involuntary movements and contractures. It is particularly important to position a child well for independent recording, activities using pencil and paper, feeding, use of communication aids and access via technology. Pupils need to be able to concentrate on the task rather than on standing or sitting and may require different positioning for different tasks.

Consolidation

Children with severe motor difficulties may not have been able to internalise concepts such as direction, shape, size, height and weight, because of their inability to explore the environment and objects. They often require adult facilitation, making them more likely to be passive learners, lacking independence and unable to consolidate learning in the same way as the majority of pupils. Pupils in this situation are likely to switch off.

It is vital for teachers to devise activities to enable consolidation and repetition, using a multi-sensory approach, utilising the pupil's auditory, visual, tactile and sensory skills. These activities will also enable the pupil to internalise a wide range of general concepts such as perception, distance, depth, weight, etc. Thinking laterally to plan activities to meet the greatest needs, as well as majority needs, is cost effective in time and energy. Activities or games with learning and therapeutic targets using real objects and utensils ensure that therapeutic targets are used functionally, included into everyday learning and are accessible to all.

Although some games may have therapy targets for specific pupils they remain extremely good to teach all pupils, because the learning targets remain the same. It is how the games are played, which enables different therapeutic targets to be incorporated. Multi-sensory games are particularly useful to teach children with any kind of special need as learning is positively reinforced through the senses.

Use of real objects

The use of real objects in curriculum activities immediately introduces a multi-sensory approach. The objects are felt and touched, having different colours, textures, weights, sizes, etc. Use of objects enables occupational therapy targets to be practised, such as grasp and release, use of flat hand, isolating and strengthening the index finger, pincer grasp, hand–eye co-ordination, bilateral activities, crossing midline, perception, body awareness, sensory–tactile defensiveness and others. They also allow speech and language therapy targets to be introduced through turn-taking, giving and following directions, listening skills, use of rhymes, initial, medial and end consonants and vowels and diagraphs, directional and descriptive words, word order and recall of words and many other targets.

Objects can be used to teach and consolidate concepts in all areas of the curriculum, for example:

- Put objects starting with 'f' in the silver box.
- Put three red cubes in the round box.
- Put things that float in the box with diagonal stripes.
- Put Victorian objects on the pentagon.
- Put minims on the treble clef.
- Put things that rhyme with 'bell' on the pyramid.

Choice of objects and containers

Choice of objects is very important if specific individual therapy targets are to be met. Consider size, weight and texture, linking the objects to the curriculum wherever possible, to consolidate and teach. Objects should be appropriate to the pupil's cognitive level and interest and to the pupil's level of comprehension, use of language and communication targets. Use larger objects for bilateral activites using two hands and for pupils with poor fine motor skills, gradually reducing objects in size over time. Use tiny objects (not too small to swallow) for pupils needing to practise pincer grip, and objects with different textures for those with tactile defensiveness.

Parents and children are often happy to help build a collection of objects, and charity shops and jumble sales are a good source.

- Good quality plastic farm, zoo and wild animals.
- Real and toy household objects.
- Dolls' house furniture.
- Natural objects such as pebbles, sticks, conkers, acorns and leaves.
- Plastic and real fruit and food.
- Food packets and washed, safe cans and containers.
- Cubes and bricks of different colours, shape and sizes.
- Dolls' and real clothes.
- Artifacts linked to history.

- Play and real money, cheque books, stamps, envelopes.
- Balls of different sizes, colour and texture with sounds.
- Photographs or pictures of objects more difficult to find can be attached to foam.

Objects can be stored in alphabetical order, by topic or category.

Objects can be placed in and taken out of containers – bags, boxes, baskets, tins, bowls – therefore choice of containers is crucial to teach and consolidate learning and therapy targets in a functional way. Choice of containers by shape, colour, size, material, texture, etc., introduces further learning elements and language to activities. Match the container to the pupil's learning needs, for example use a rectangular box if the pupil can only recognise a square and a circle. By referring to the shape of the box functionally in the game, the pupil will learn the concept. Consider and plan the exact terminology used to describe the shape of the container for individuals, for example:

- round – circle, circular, cylindrical, sphere, spherical
- triangle – isosceles, equilateral, scalene, triangular.

Containers can also teach and consolidate:

- Colours – gold and silver.
- Stripes – horizontal, vertical, diagonal, etc.
- Shapes – square, circle, rectangle, pentagon, hexagon, etc.
- Materials – wood, plastic, metal, cane, cardboard, paper.
- Texture – rough, smooth, hard, soft, furry, etc.
- Size – big, little, small, long, middle sized, bigger, smaller than, etc.
- Everyday items – cornflake box, biscuit, tissues, cake tin, washing-up bowl.

Objects can be placed on pictures instead of in containers allowing more complex mathematical shapes and curriculum pictures to be used. An older pupil might be asked to 'Put a mammal starting with W on the Roman soldier'. A younger pupil might be asked to 'Put a cat on the tree'.

The position of the containers/pictures is vital to ensure that occupational, speech and language therapy targets are met. They might be placed centrally, directly in front of the player for bilateral targets using both hands, or placed at one or both sides so the pupil has to reach out or cross the midline, or placed at different heights. Pupils can be directed to put specific objects in, on, under, by left, right, in front, behind, etc., the container or picture as part of the activity.

Game instructions

Planning how the players will be instructed in a game is crucial and must be appropriate for individuals. Cards are a simple way to give instructions using pictures, photographs, words, symbols, Braille or any combination. Pupils may also be given directions using Makaton, BSL or sign-supported English. Bilingual pupils may read their own script with or without additional English and some pupils might read instructions and direct the other player in a language they are studying, e.g. French, or might read in one language and direct the other player in English. Pupils playing the same game/activity may be given their instructions in different ways; for example, one may read symbols or pictures and the other words. They must, however, be able to communicate the instructions to another player.

Adapting cards for access

Ordinary cards can be adapted by attaching them to foam of different thicknesses using rubber bands; this makes them easier to grasp.

Alternatively, a piece of laminated card can be stuck to one side of the foam and ordinary cards fixed to the laminate with self-adhesive Velcro, Blu-tac or strong magnetic tape. Cards can also be attached to wooden blocks or toy bricks, using rubber bands, Velcro, Blu-tac or magnetic tape and can then be pushed or lifted. Building upper arm strength can also be achieved by attaching cards to long boxes, filled with different amounts of sand, etc., and firmly secured. Gradually increasing the weight in the boxes will help build upper arm strength. Pupils are likely to be motivated if they understand the benefits, for example greater strength in using manual wheelchairs. Care must be taken to ensure that any picture, symbol or writing is clearly printed and is of the right size, printed on the background to meet the needs of individual pupils.

Using tongs, tweezers and pegs

Objects can also be picked up with tongs or tweezers. There are many different types and sizes of tongs, tweezers and squeezers, and use of them helps to strengthen and isolate the index finger and thumb, aiding pen/pencil grasp. Use of them also increases finger dexterity and fine manipulation, develops hand–eye co-ordination and replicates regular and spring-loaded scissor action. Tongs can be used in any activity involving the use of objects or cards on foam. Small tongs can be used to pick up objects with one hand while larger tongs can be used with two (bilateral).

Spring-loaded pegs and clips have the same action as tongs and tweezers and therefore use and strengthen the same muscles with the same therapeutic benefits. Different pegs and tongs require different muscle strength to be squeezed and this could be considered when planning for individuals. Muscle strength can be gradually built up over time in hands, wrists and fingers. There is no reason why two pupils playing the same game cannot use different pegs or tongs.

Pegs can be used to clip together cards with the same colours, textures, words, letters, numbers, symbols, pictures; for example, 'Peg together a picture of a Viking soldier and matching words'. Different numbers and colours of pegs can be pegged on to a whole variety of boxes, clothes, cards and objects. Pegs with cards attached can be pegged on to objects, matching a picture, photograph, word, initial letter, colour or shape to the object.

Spoons

Spoons can also be used to pick up and move objects in a game; this can aid feeding and self-help skills, encourage and develop fine motor control, hand–eye co-ordination and dexterity. An occupational therapist should always be involved in assessing pupils with more complex needs when introducing the use of tools, as there may be neurological reasons for using one tool rather than another. Care must be taken to match the spoon to the pupil and to think carefully about the container. Containers with straight sides are often easier to use than those with rounded sides. Spoons have different depths, affecting their ease of use. Spoons can also be used in sand or water play, e.g. 'Put the biggest/heaviest piece of play-dough in the square box' or 'Put three spoons of sand into the orange bucket'.

Tubes and guttering

Use of guttering and flexible tubes such as tumble-drier extractor tubes (bought in DIY shops) can extend a simple tabletop activity to include gross motor skills. The activity may have the same learning targets, but different therapeutic targets. Fine motor control, dexterity, grasp and release, hand–eye co-ordination and the other therapy targets in the tabletop activity remain the same, but the addition of a long, flexible tube means that at least one player stands and moves. One pupil holds the end of the tube, 'reads' a card and drops the appropriate object into the tube. Another pupil, holds the other end of the tube, and is directed where to place the object, replicating the containers. This might be into hoops of different colours, large boxes or bins of different shapes, large pictures or a map, etc. As well as extending tabletop activities, new games can be devised using the tube and various balls or beanbags and incorporated into PE and games lessons.

Lightweight barriers

A simple, lightweight barrier erected between two pupils also enables speech and language therapy targets to be included in curriculum activities.

One pupil 'reads' the instruction cards. The pupil on the other side of the barrier, with the objects and containers, follows the instructions, for example 'Put the house in the square box'. The barrier is then removed to check if the instructions were carried out correctly. Pupils may have different instruction cards, using words, pictures, symbols, etc. The emphasis is placed on the ability to give instructions via speech, signing or use of communication aids, though the learning targets might be to read specific words.

TIME CONSIDERATIONS

Time is the enemy for pupils with severe motor difficulties. They are likely to take longer moving around the school, going to the toilet, eating, drinking, washing hands, changing position in class, writing, reading and sometimes communicating and thinking. They are also likely to have to carry out more activities than other pupils (e.g. physiotherapy, occupational therapy and/or speech and language therapy exercises) and may also require adminsitration of medicine, drinks and tube feeding during the day. It is hardly surprising that they may also become more tired and need to rest at times! One of the main difficulties for teachers is the time taken out of class to carry out therapy programmes resulting in pupils missing out on important lessons.

CONCLUSION

Successful inclusion of pupils with severe motor difficulties requires a whole-school, inclusive approach to education with on-going training and a real understanding of therapy issues. It is important that there is a partnership with parents, an understanding that the child is part of the family and that independence and life skills are crucial for pupils to be as independent as possible in the future. Including therapy functionally in the curriculum will enable pupils to gain greater skills, which in turn will give them greater access to the curriculum and to life.

Curriculum activities using objects and utensils can be devised as a resource to teach all pupils. By adding different containers in a variety of positions, using different utensils, barriers and appropriate instruction cards, the same activities/games can include therapy targets and meet the individual needs of many pupils. The curriculum learning targets, general instruction cards and objects for the game can be devised for the majority of pupils and stored in a zipper wallet. Additional instructions and utensils can be added, as and when required, to meet the needs of individual pupils. Using the same sized instruction cards, filed in an index cards box and collecting boxes, utensils and objects, filed alphabetically or by category, means that customising games for individual needs is very simple.

Consolidation is required for therapy in the same way as for learning, but care must be taken to ensure that the therapy targets are not too hard for individuals and they do not dominate what is essentially a learning game.

Adding different instruction cards can also give the activities/games a new dimension. Instructions for simple literacy and numeracy activities can be written in French or German for use in language lessons. Instructions written using Braille, symbols or signs are also an invaluable resource to introduce alternative communication to mainstream pupils as part of disability awareness, equal opportunities and inclusion. Mainstream pupils may also use these instructions to learn an alternative means of communicating to enable them to communicate with pupils who may attend their school. Learning in this way is cost effective in time, effort and money. Initial planning and collecting the objects and utensils is probably the most difficult stage, but once set up, is an inclusive way of teaching.

REFERENCES

Department For Education (DFE) (1994) *The Code of Practice on the Identification and Assessment of Special Educational Needs.* London: HMSO.
Pickles, P. (1998) *Managing the Curriculum for Children with Severe Motor Difficulties: a practical approach.* London: David Fulton Publishers.

17

Teachers and differentiation

Philip Garner, Viv Hinchcliffe and Sarah Sandow

The National Curriculum (NC) provoked much anxiety among teachers of children with special needs, both in ordinary and in special schools. Although at first it was widely assumed that there would be much disapplication of the NC, especially in special schools, that has not been the case. Certainly among some teachers of pupils experiencing severe learning difficulties (SLD) it has been argued that the NC is largely an irrelevance (Hinchcliffe 1994), being incompatible with the mainly developmental curriculum being followed in such schools. A group of teachers following an in-service course in the SLD curriculum identified a number of serious anxieties when reviewing Curriculum Guidance 9 The National Curriculum and Pupils with Severe Learning Difficulties (Hinchcliffe *et al.* 1992):

> It is precisely this principle of entitlement and the relevance of Programmes of Study [POS] to children with profound learning difficulties that are critically discussed here. This group has questioned both the way that the principle of 'entitlement' has been taken on board by SLD schools and how this principle has almost been treated with reverence in the wealth of literature published in the wake of the 1988 Education Reform Act [ERA]. Members of this group, all teaching children with profound and multiple difficulties, have been grappling with the initiatives of the ERA in the classroom and are becoming increasingly sceptical as to whose interests the National Curriculum Attainment Targets [ATs] and POS are serving. It is maintained that whatever the arguments of a centrally imposed curriculum for raising standards in mainstream schools, the relevance of all of this to children with profound and multiple learning difficulties is highly debatable. It seems that only a few people, in print anyway, are prepared to challenge and debate its relevance.

> The National Curriculum Council [NCC] states that when the NC was being formulated, 'it was impossible to legislate for the enormous diversity of special educational needs'. We believe this statement to be both a simplification and a retrospective 'cop out'. Few, if any, members of the

National Curriculum Working Party can have had experience of teaching children with severe learning difficulties . . .

Why should teachers of children with profound and multiple learning difficulties [PMLD] have to mould existing good practice to POS which, in the main were not written for, and are arguably, not relevant to this client group? Some tenuous links of common practice to National Curriculum POS are seen in this NCC document. In the section on suggested methods of doing a curriculum audit, a 'clap hands' singing activity is described in which a child in a group is seen to fall off his chair. The NCC's National Curriculum POS references to these events are 'responding to aural stimuli', 'exploring how to make and experience sounds', and 'receiving explanations' (presumably, why the student fell off his chair). Is this type of referencing really necessary? It rather suggests milking NC Programmes of Study for a relevance that is not really there, and this ignorance is reflected in the token references to the needs and interests of these children.

So as far as children with SLD are concerned, it appears that these teachers believe that differentiation of a common curriculum leaves too many needs unaddressed in the scramble for entitlement. S. J. (1992) also argued against the relevance of the NC, and cited parents' as well as teachers' anxieties. Teachers made the following points:

It's too rigid, it doesn't take into account the students' individual needs. The curriculum may become too structured. When teaching children with SLD, a teacher should be able to continue and develop a lesson provided that there is positive interest and stimulation for the pupils. It is inhibiting to have to change a lesson in order to cover the whole of the NC. The NC subject divisions do not take into account the way children with SLD need to be taught (real situations with cross curricular input) or what they really need to be learning (life skills). It does not start at an early enough stage of development. Some children will be working towards level one for the whole of their school career, for them it does not provide a framework for progression in learning, they just fail.

However, others take the view that children with SLD can and should be given access to the NC as a matter or right. They should, according to T. P.:

be treated as active learners. To be able to get the most out of education they must be able to interact with people and their environment. Fagg *et al.* (1990) stress the importance of interaction and communication in giving pupils with SLD access to the NC. 'The NC documents currently available all assume within their content, a level of growth of interpersonal and communicative skills which are central to the achievement of the programmes of study and attainment targets.' For pupils with SLD this cannot be assumed. Pupils must be helped to develop the skills. Teachers should create the opportunities, through chosen activities, for pupils to learn and practise interactive skills.

D. D. also stresses the importance of interactive skills in work with autistic children, noting that hierarchical learning (such as in the NC) causes problems where development is not simply delayed but is also distorted or uneven. Considering the needs of Katie, an autistic child, she writes:

It is important not to disapply children like Katie from the National Curriculum. One concern if this comes about is that they may be deemed ineducable. The other concern is that the child's entitlement to the National Curriculum is denied. Jordan and Powell (1990) described autistic children as having a 'distorted rather than merely delayed pattern of development. This (they said) causes difficulties whenever learning is organised into hierarchies as in the National Curriculum'. Obviously the National Curriculum has completely changed the structure of the learning environment in schools such as this one. However, for the children who do not fit the hierarchy there needs to be opportunity to provide them with strategies to develop.

There is a need for functional contexts to ensure learned skills are generalised. This is especially relevant in role play and other language orientated situations, e.g. setting a context for language. In a teasing/jokes situation, Katie needs to know what response is required at home or at school, so that she avoids moments of confusion that generally lead to confrontation.

Specific training is quite often required. This is illustrated in the role play, ability to reason and dealing with teasing and jokes. In these instances Katie is given a set way of responding and as this is established opportunites to generalise these skills are developed.

It is also essential to create a thinking environment for a child like Katie. The sequencing objective is to assist in establishing this. Katie's major difficulty is in organising her thoughts and she is inclined to lean heavily on adults or other children for prompts in difficulties. This is the most important element of Katie's learning programme. Because she is so fragmented it would be easy to concentrate on the negative elements and use these as an excuse for little progress. It is far more honest and positive to recognise that Katie's learning might be slow and inconsistent at the moment but as she matures and becomes more organised her learning may become quicker.

Clearly, such attention to detail and recognition of differently paced learning is hard to reconcile with the need to cover a wide range of subjects and activities as required by the NC.

However, some teachers are more sanguine about the possibilities of working within the NC. Even children with PMLD are considered by O. J. (1993) to be able to learn within this framework. O. J. describes work at KS1 in Science carried out with a group of non-ambulant preverbal children with PMLD. She regards 'entitlement' as a positive thing, but recognises that 'it is not always appropriate for all of these children to be restricted to the topics and content directed by the Science NC'. O. J. continues to describe her work by looking at the principles of the NC in the light of learning theorists. Here O. J. shows the advantages of theorising out of practice, rather than in advance of it: it is obvious that she has observed and explored the child's learning and then related it to theory:

> It is interesting that the majority of those special schools that have been stated by OFSTED to have failed inspection, have done so primarily for not adhering to the National Curriculum.
>
> Are the sentiments behind Curriculum Guidance 9 based on empty statements? The worst scenario is that the NCC have no understanding of the needs of children with PMLD, and are going to recommend schools to teach inappropriate material, to the detriment of our pupils' education. I can justify my KS1 unit in terms of the National Curriculum but more importantly, it has been devised after assessing the needs of the pupils. I would not advocate teaching all of Level 1 science to this class, nor will I be restricted by specific learning outcomes. The unit is child-centred, based on relevant aims and objectives.
>
> The children in this class are functioning at very early levels of development, five of them corresponding developmentally to Piaget's sensory-motor period (relating to the first two years of life in a normally developing child). Mike is fairly typical, developmentally, of the children in this class. He is functioning in stages two, three and the lower portion of 4 according to the Uzgiris and Hunt scales of infant psychological development. Mike can be very vocal but scored low on vocal imitation, as he did on gestural imitation – his development is particularly behind in this area. He does not interact with people. Mike does not seem to make the distinction between people and objects. Mike's assessment has been included to give a clearer indication of the developmental level of the children in this class. The sixth child in the class is more advanced than the sensory-motor stage but as she started school for the first time this year (she is almost 11 years old) she has a lot to learn. We are not clear at this stage how much the absence of education and limited exposure to some language is affecting her responses.

If we accept Bruner's assertion that 'any subject can be taught effectively in some intellectually honest form to any child at any stage in development' (Bruner 1963), the problem is not whether or not to teach science (a hypothetical question as the National Curriculum does not allow us this choice – unless the child has been disapplied) but how to teach it. The first principle drawn from Piaget's theory is the view that learning has to be an active process because knowledge is a construction from within (Schwebel and Raph 1974, p.99). Both Bruner and Vygotsky agreed that action is important in cognitive development but unlike Piaget, they did not adhere to the view that educators should wait for the children to be ready to learn (Smith 1988). A teaching programme for this class must be active and involve the children in intervention from, and interaction with other people. The children's chronological ages bear little relation to their psychological development – as educators we must intervene and try to facilitate development. I think it is important to consider Vygotsky's theory of the Zone of Proximal Development (ZPD). The ZPD 'focuses on the phase in development in which the child has only partially mastered a task but can participate in its execution with the assistance and supervision of an adult or more capable peer' (Rogoff and Wertsch 1984, p.1). It is the 'distance between the level of performance that a child can reach unaided and the level of participation that she or he can accomplish when guided by another more knowledgeable individual' (Rogoff and Wertsch 1984, p.77). The ZPD is concerned with a child's potential developmental levels. Bruner expressed a similar idea with his metaphor 'scaffolding', in which not only a child's existing level is taken into account, but how far they can progress with help (Smith 1988). ZPD and scaffolding bring to the fore the notion of 'potential' development and the importance of intervention to achieve this. A teaching programme must attempt to move the children forward. It is also relevant to keep in mind Bruner's Spiral Curriculum, i.e. that knowledge arises out of a process of deepening understanding. He implied that even quite young children could grasp ideas in an intuitive way which they could return to later and move progressively towards more complex levels of difficulty (Smith 1988). Therefore what we teach the children can be built on later. There may not be any immediate, visible outcomes, but, according to the Spiral Curriculum, the pupils can build on their experiences in the future.

The pupils in this particular class will be working within Key Stage 1 of the Science Curriculum. There are four Attainment Targets – I have chosen to teach a unit from Life and Living Processes, Attainment Target 2. This unit will focus on the children's own bodies and their senses. This area of learning is important for the children in addition to meeting the requirements of the National Curriculum. 'Sensory input initiates perception' (Brown 1977, p.48). The unit will be on 'Our bodies' but will focus on what our bodies can do, i.e. the senses.

The Science Curriculum states that 'To communicate, to relate science to everyday life and to explore are essential elements of an initial experience of science' *Science in the National Curriculum* (DFE 1995). This unit will use materials from the immediate environment (as far as possible) and explore those materials using all the senses. To avoid sensory confusion the lessons will attempt to focus on one sense at a time. The School Physiotherapist, Nurse, and Speech Therapist will be asked to assist and give advice in three of the sessions. It is important to consult other professionals when planning any programme.

Children's skills and concepts in science are developed best through an active rather than passive approach and especially through exploration and interaction with their environment (Benson 1991 in Smith 1988, p.48). This teaching unit is based entirely around activities (also in accordance with Piaget, Vygotsky and Bruner's views about active learning). Although this unit was primarily written for the science curriculum it has cross-curricular links. This is important as subjects should not be seen as separate entities taught in isolation – education should be round/whole. For a subject to be relevant it must have links with other curriculum areas. This unit will incorporate aspects of Physical Education, Drama, PSHE, IT, Art, Communication and Language. 'An important feature of an interactive approach is the acquisition and development of language skills. By using relevant and varied contexts within which to set activities, the understanding and acquisition of language concepts should be enchanced' (Benson 1991 in Smith 1988, p.48). Language used with the children must of course be relevant. All of the children are preverbal so while it will be important to explain what is going on and ensure the pupils are familiar with the parts of their bodies and object labels (names of objects) these instructions must be kept simple and to the point. It will be as important for staff to be sensitive to and respond to the children's own vocalisations or other forms of response, to encourage the development of intentional communication.

Following this introduction, O. J. describes a comprehensive programme which moves from whole body awareness to specific exploration of hands and feet, always differentiating the experiences to take account of children's likes and dislikes. Finally the focus moves to exploring the other senses: vision, hearing, taste and smell. The detailed programme is included here to illustrate the high level of detail with which teachers of children with PMLD plan and carry out their curricula:

Our Bodies:
A Science Unit, working in Key Stage 1, Attainment Target 2, specifically designed for students with PMLD.

The Unit is divided into 11 lessons, however some may need repeating to reinforce ideas or to capitalise on positive experiences.

Aims:
For the pupils:
– to find out about themselves
– to be aware of their whole body
– to recognise names of body parts
– to develop ideas of what their bodies can do
– to enjoy stimulation of the senses.

Objectives:
For the pupils:
● to focus on own body.
● to become familiar with the names of body parts.
● to respond to stimulation of the senses.
● to have positive experiences.

Before the Unit:
– Collect/take photos of each child in the class.
– Tape the voices of the children in the class.
– Sew on tinsel, bells, bright pompoms, fur; glue on glitter to gloves and socks.
– Consult with Physiotherapists, Nurse and Speech Therapist.
– Make feely bags.
– Discuss Aims and Objectives of the Unit with Support Staff.

Activities:
1. Focus – Whole body.
Use 'TacPac' – this lesson will take about an hour to complete. Begin by singing 'Hallo'.

Follow the instructions in the pack. Make sure that the room is warm and that all the equipment is ready before the lesson.

2. Focus – Body/try to recognise self and others.
Use 'Good Morning' session – look at photos of self and others. Pupils try to select own photo from choice of two (R's photo has fur on it; T's has bells as they are visually impaired).

This activity will be used every morning.

Outline of bodies – Children lie on a large piece of paper (individually) and outline is made of their bodies. Go around bodies several times with a big paintbrush or broom (not with paint!) so that they feel their outline. Show pupils the outlines (these could be painted in an Art session).

Have Physiotherapist go through simple stretching exercises – sing songs, e.g. 'I've got a body'.

3. Focus – Movement: kinaesthetic and vestibular.
Concentrate on the words: swing, backwards, forwards, round, up, down, slide.

Begin with the 'Roller Coaster' game (instructions in the 'Fun Fair' pack) – to bring children together as a group and introduce movement. Put soft play equipment around hall to make the game more exciting.

Swing the children (individually!) in a blanket – sing: 'What shall we do with . . .'.

Slide along floor in a sack or on a blanket.

Slide down playground slides – using both the metal and roller ones.

Spin on a rotating chair.

It would be preferable to begin with all the children watching each other but if they are not focused or lose interest, the group can split and go ahead with activities (all children will need two staff for lifting, etc).

4. Focus – Hands.
Begin by massaging hands.

Put prepared gloves on children's hands – take time to try and put all fingers in. If necessary use Velcro to keep gloves on – do not do this if the child shows any signs of distress.

Take gloves off and look at hands through magnifying glasses.

Turn lights off and focus on hands with torch beams.

Put paint on hands – encourage children to do this themselves – make hand prints.

5. Focus – Hands.
Begin by massaging hands. Use gloves as in previous lesson.

Have children put their hands into feely bags – encourage them to explore themselves.

Verbal then physical prompts – do not force.

Put paint on hands – encourage children to do this themselves – make hand prints.

6. Focus – Feet.
Begin by massaging feet. Use socks as in previous lesson.

Put prepared socks on children's feet. Encourage them to look.

Take socks off. Put paint on feet – encourage children to do as much as they can on their own. Make feet prints.

Encourage the children to put their feet into the feely bags – use verbal then physical prompts, but do not force.

7. Focus – Feet.

Begin by massaging feet. Use socks as in previous lesson.

Encourage the children to put their feet into the feely bags – use verbal then physical prompts, do not force.

8. Focus – Eyes.

Begin by putting hats on and looking in the mirror – sing 'R's got a black hat . . .'.

Put glasses on the children, use bright rimmed glasses/ sunglasses/glasses made in Art session – look in the mirror – sing 'My eyes are dim, I cannot see . . .'.

In a dark room use torches and ultra-violet light to focus on themselves/objects.

9. Focus – Hearing.

Begin as in previous lesson with hats and song etc.

Use the mirror to look at ears – use false ears/ear-muffs.

Listening activities – 'Walkmans' (tapes of own voices + music, songs), musical bumps, stethoscope, large shells, etc. Use the Resonance Board for the visually impaired.

10. Focus – Taste and Smell.

Begin again with hats, etc.

Put coloured sunblock on noses – put on children's fingers and encourage them to put it on themselves – use the mirror.

Speech Therapist to lead tasting session.

11. Focus – Taste and Smell.

Begin with hats, etc. Put on sunblock as in previous lesson.

School Nurse to lead teeth cleaning session.

Throughout, O. J. stresses the importance of evaluating both the teaching and the learning that is going on. The whole unit is designed so that the children will be aware of their bodies and are able to discriminate between their senses: it fits easily into the National Curriculum.

These detailed programmes demonstrate that the curriculum, including the National Curriculum, can be used to give a framework for teaching 'in an intellectually honest way' at any level. This is not simply a matter of differentiation in the conventional sense, but of identifying the starting points and learning programmes for a number of children working together, and producing programmes which are individual but also highly social, true child-centred learning, in fact. Where teachers are faced with learning difficulties in the mainstream, these programmes may seem the height of luxury. It is, however, possible to draw lessons from the examples about how IEPs are constructed, from the inside out – at any level. For example, another teacher (A. B.) views differentiation as part of her task as a support teacher in secondary history classes. She sees differentation as part of the process of improving teaching and learning for all pupils, but rejects the use of the term to segregate children within an overtly inclusive system. To me an emphasis on meeting individual needs does not have to be packaged up with efforts to 'sort and separate' children. Differentiation is perceived as 'giving an opportunity for children with different strengths and weaknesses to participate in the same learning activity, in different ways'.

A. B. applied this principle to a session on the abolition of slavery, one of a series in which children at KS3 had already considered the slave resistance movement. Working with a 'bottom set' it is notable that she recognised that individual differences required different options for children with different abilities and communication skills:

> This lesson aimed to develop pupils' awareness that there can be number of different reasons or causes for events and that these can be interconnected.
>
> More specifically, it was intended to help pupils to develop or further their understanding of certain concepts/terminology with which they may not yet be very familiar, such as 'economic', 'politician', 'humanitarian' and 'religious' motives for actions. It also aimed to develop some knowledge about the ideas and beliefs which drove the sequence of events which led to the abolition of the slave trade and emancipation of the slaves in British colonies and, later, in the USA.
>
> The children are all in a bottom set, but they still obviously differ with regard to many factors such as literacy, ability to communicate ideas orally, general grasp of concepts, relevant background knowledge and vocabulary, interest and commitment to the subject, ability to work co-operatively with other children, etc. In this lesson, I wanted to enable those who have very low levels of literacy to learn and demonstrate their knowledge and understanding, and to minimise the burden of reading and writing. I wanted to provide the opportunity for those who have particular strengths in oral work to make a contribution that might not be made so well through their written work. I chose to incorporate a few quick and easy informal brief 'tests' with minimal literacy demands to obtain some evidence to indicate which children may still not understand some of the key concepts. This information can be used to guide their next lesson. I also made assessments of other factors such as level of engagement and degree of success with various tasks, so that I could hopefully tailor future lessons more closely to individual needs.

Main differentiation methods

I wished to enable children with very low levels of literacy to participate in the same intellectual task as all the other pupils, so I tried to create a few different kinds of opportunities to obtain information and to demonstrate understanding within a whole class activity.

'Considerate' text – conversation scripts

For listening or reading I used a conversation format to cover main points mentioned through four or five chapters of the textbook used in the school (Heinemann History: Black Peoples of the Americas, 1992). The main strategies I tried to use in making the scripts included: avoiding unrealistic assumptions about background knowledge; making connections between motives and actions more explicit; deletion of excess detail; inclusion of familiar images to aid mental representation of more abstract ideas; use of familiar language and references as much as possible; replacing unfamiliar vocabulary items and words that moderately poor readers might find difficult to decode or listeners to understand.

The scripts could be 'accessed' either by reading or listening, depending on the abilities of the individual children. The task connected with the scripts was a categorisation one which minimised literacy demands while focusing attention on important terms that will be later encountered frequently in history. These terms were also taught explicitly beforehand.

Speech preparation and delivery, using pupils' strengths for collaborative small group work

The task of preparing a speech in a small group could enable each group member to contribute an idea or suggestion and interact with the ideas of others even though only one scribe was needed. It could also allow group members who did not really grasp the concepts or information at the presentation stage of the lesson to clarify their understanding through small group interaction with peers.

The actual delivery of the speech provided an opportunity for any group member who had the confidence to give a speech in front of the class to do so, even if they couldn't read the speech and had to rely on memory. I knew that several of the statemented pupils do not have this oral confidence. They should be able to draw on all the new concepts and information encoutered in the lesson.

Repetition of key points in different ways. The summary gap fill sheet gave a more straightforward, text book-like account of events and the reasons for them. This was planned to come after the explicit teaching of terminology and after the illustrative conversation scripts. I wanted to explicitly teach meanings of words 'economic', 'political', 'humanitarian' and 'religious', so that the children could supply the definition and, later, correctly apply these words to a situation. (I expected that all the children would know what 'religious' means but that many would have, at best, only a vague awareness of the other terms, particular 'economic'.) I wanted to repeat these four terms quite frequently so that the children would understand them and feel less threatened when they encountered them in their reading. One way to do this was to get them to categorise each speech as illustrating one or more of these motives for wanting to end slavery. This involved listening and thinking but hardly any writing (they only had to choose the correct word and copy it into a chart).

Pupil grouping. I had intended to choose group members in order to achieve a balance of abilities for the task of preparing the speech. (Although the pupils ended up choosing their own groups, they chose quite well and a balance of abilities, especially to do with literacy, was present in all groupings.)

Varied assessment and recording methods planned
- Chart filled in by pupils with the instruction 'treat this like a test and do your own'.
- Pupil speeches (photocopies provided later by teacher to put in exercise books).
- Gap-fill for revision summary without need for time consuming copying.
- True/false (minimal written response).
- Teacher ratings of involvement, behaviour and quality of pupil talk.

Activity one Whole class – questions by teacher, eliciting background knowledge the children already have.

Introduce theme: 'Why did some white people want to end slavery?' Explicitly teach simple definitions of 'economic', 'political', 'humanitarian' and 'religious' reasons.

Activity two Pupils listen to definitions and/or read them on sheet. Alert pupils to need to listen to conversation scripts to work out what reasons were being put forward in each one. State that in some cases there might be more than one reason.

Tell pupils they will later be preparing their own speeches in groups so they should listen carefully to the conversations because they will be making similar points in their speeches.

Activity three Conversation scripts – get the better readers (volunteers) to read them. Some pupils read scripts aloud, others listen.

Activity four All pupils choose and write/copy correct word(s). Tell pupils to fill in the chart using one or more of the given words, after they hear each conversation, as a kind of test.

Activity five Small group task – some to make oral contribution of ideas, one to be scribe for group production of anti-slavery speech.

Give instructions for a group task on making a speech against slavery, using all four categories of reasons, using any information they have been given this lesson or in previous lessons. One person to write, all to contribute.

Make groups of three, ensuring that each contains one child with adequate ability to be a scribe. Aim for a mix of ability to grasp concepts. Both teachers go ground to monitor group work, remind them about goal of including all four categories of reason in their speech, check understanding, ensuring that all members have a role.

Activity six Whole class listen to all the speeches. Pupils can decide which group member will deliver the speech, but the teachers should encourage someone who has difficulty reading to do it from memory (in other words, not the scribe).

All speech makers to be listened to carefully and applauded. Pupils to be given a photocopy of all group speeches later (supplied by teacher).

Activity seven Whole class reading or listening to summary of events read out by teacher, then completing gap-fill together.

Give out gap-fill summary sheet (Activity three) 'British opposition to slavery in the Americas'. Do as whole class exercise, reading text aloud, filling gaps as we go, on the sheet. This can be used as a timeline exercise if time is available at end of lesson.

Note: The purpose of this gap-fill was mainly to avoid time spent copying the summary which is needed in the exercise book for possible exam revision later. Providing it this way was intended to focus their attention more than if there were no gaps, and to allow for further checking of comprehension and consolidation of main points by teacher.

Activity eight Whole class reading or listening to check understanding through minimal writing response.

Give out 'True or false' sheet (Similar purpose to gap-fill). Pupils listen or read the sentence pairs and write down the letter (a) or (b).

If time, they can then either copy out the true ones into their exercise books or paraphrase the correct sentences in their own words or slower writers could cross out the false ones and stick the sheet in their book so that only the correct ones remain for later revision.

CONCLUSION

The range of activities described in this chapter illustrates the way in which teachers have taken on board differentiation by input, process and outcome, in ways which make a great number of curricular topics accessible for pupils of all levels of ability. The modifications contained in the 'Dearing version' of the NC will hopefully free teachers to develop the sorts of innovations described here. Some teachers of pupils with severe learning difficulties may still fret at what they see as an unnatural alignment of some aspects of the SLD curriculum to fit the NC, but some developments, such as the science topic elaborated here, show how the framework can give structure to existing content and stimulate powers of invention. In the ordinary school, the detailed description of a differentiated history curriculum is surely infinitely preferable to yet more 'basics' delivered by despairing teachers to bored pupils denied the more interesting activities in which their classmates participate.

REFERENCES

Benson, C. (ed.) (1991) 'The science curriculum: an interactive approach', in Smith, B. (ed.) *Interactive Approaches to Teaching the Core Subjects.* Bristol: Lame Duck Publishing.

Brown, G. (1977) *Child Development.* London: Open Books.

Bruner, J. S. (1963) *The Process of Education.* New York: Vintage Books.

'Dearing' Version, *see* SCAA (1993)

Department For Education (DFE) (1995) *Science in the National Curriculum.* London: HMSO.

Fagg, S., Aherne, P., Skelton, S. and Thornber, A. (1990) *Entitlement for All in Practice.* London: David Fulton Publishers.

Hinchcliffe, V. (1994) 'A special special need: self advocacy, curriculum and the needs of children with severe learning difficulties', in Sandow, S. (ed.) *Whose Special Need?* London: Paul Chapman.

Hinchcliffe, V. and SLD Course Team (1992) 'Review of NCC Curriculum Guidance 9', *Quest* **1**(2), 18–19.

Jordan, R. and Powell, S. (1990) *The Special Curricular Needs of Autistic Children: learning and thinking skills.* Ealing: Association of Head Teachers of Autistic Children and Adults.

Rogoff, B. and Wertsch, J. (1984) *Learning in the Zone of Proximal Development.* London: Jossey-Bass.

Schools Curriculum and Assessment Authority (SCAA) (1993) *The National Curriculum and its Assessment: final report* (The Dearing Report). London: SCAA.

Schwebel, M. and Raph, J. (1974) *Piaget in the Classroom.* London: Routledge.

Smith, B. (1988) 'Which approach: the education of children with severe learning difficulties', *Mental Handicap* **17**(3), 111–115.

Index